D0990888

NOT BY
REASON
ALONE

NOT BY REASON ALONE

Religion, History, and Identity in Early Modern Political Thought

Joshua Mitchell

THE UNIVERSITY OF CHICAGO PRESS
Chicago & London

JOSHUA MITCHELL is assistant professor of government at Georgetown University.

The University of Chicago Press, Chicago 60637
The University of Chicago Press, Ltd., London
© 1993 by The University of Chicago
All rights reserved. Published 1993
Printed in the United States of America
02 01 00 99 98 97 96 95 94 93   1 2 3 4 5

ISBN: 0-226-53221-6 (cloth)

Library of Congress Cataloging-in-Publication Data

Mitchell, Joshua.
    Not by reason alone : religion, history, and identity in early
modern political thought / Joshua Mitchell.
          p.   cm.
    Includes bibliographical references and index.
    1. Political science—History.   2. Luther, Martin, 1483–1546—
Contributions in political science.   3. Hobbes, Thomas, 1588–1679—
Contributions in political science.   4. Locke, John, 1632–1704—
Contributions in political science.   5. Rousseau, Jean-Jacques,
1712–1778—Contributions in political science.   6. History
(Theology)—History of doctrines.   7. Christianity and politics—
History.   8. Identification (Religion)—History of doctrines.
I. Title.
JA81.M54   1993
320'.01—dc20   93-3048

The paper used in this publication meets the minimum requirements of the American National
Standard for Information Sciences—Permanence of Paper for Printed Library Materials,
ANSI Z39.48-1984.

Verily thou art a God that hidest thyself,
O God of Israel, the Savior.

Isaiah 45:15

. . . your iniquities have separated you from your God;
and your sins have hidden His face from you,
so that He will not hear.

Isaiah 59:1–2.

CONTENTS

I HAVE HERE SEVERAL IDEAS: that the historical horizon of early modern political thought is for the contemporary mind a stumbling block; that thinking about the historical dialectic begins with biblical interpretation; that this kind of thinking is at the heart of the political thought of Luther, Hobbes, and Locke; that no profound thinking about politics in the early modern period has been without a theory of history, biblical or otherwise (as in the case of Rousseau); that supplementarity, concealment, identity and difference, and trace are theological thoughts long before they emerge as post-modern ones; and that efforts to dissever the political truth from the profoundly interwoven thinking about the soul, politics, and history in early modern texts condemn scholars of the history of political thought to numbing debates whose terms are wholly contemporary and, consequently, historically provincial.

The procrustean reflex is unavoidable at the outset; that it persists, that some measure of fluency in the theological discourse of the authors we study does not supplant a reflex that ventures only far enough to wonder whether Hobbes, Locke, and Rousseau were believers (whatever this might mean!), is less tolerable. The task of the historian of political thought is to understand how the past was *not* like the present, how it became what it is, rather than how it always was what it is; we betray our charge if we find in, say, Hobbes and Locke, first instances of an "individualism" that would deny the preeminence of "community." This, regrettable enough, is our discourse, not theirs. The only service Hobbes and Locke provide should we treat them in this way is to offer passage through a tenure system that requires a low enough level of debate that many may join in, yet one complex enough so that erudition and sparring are possible. The liberal-antiliberal debate, for example, which revolves around the question of the primacy of the "individual" or the "community," has become both pedestrian and pedantic; it mocks the profundity of thought there to be grasped in early modern texts, and tempts scholarship to become a pretext for inbred debates that grow old because they are merely contemporary. The charge of latent solipsism, often leveled against the early moderns, may more accurately apply to current scholarship than to the object of its study.

The liberal-antiliberal debate, it seems to me, is wrongly put. The real question is what kind of individual and community emerge from one or another reading of the history that is deemed politically authoritative. Neither the "individual" nor the "community" is the point of departure for thinking in early modern thought; the content of both derives from a history which situates and specifies their character. The spuriousness problem affects political theory more pervasively, I am tempted to say, than it does the more quantitatively oriented subfields of political science. The terms of the contemporary debate preempt the prospect of escaping from a vicious polarization, a self-enclosed discourse the content of which, finally, is as ephemeral as ether.

Primary misunderstandings foster secondary errors. The most prevalent, perhaps, pertains to whether a vision of politics based on the solitary individual is enough; whether we can live with a politics which in no way purports to nourish. The retort is often that early modern politics never purported to nourish; its great contribution was to insist that politics could not nourish. Sustenance could not be found within its domain. Politics is neither the arena of noble action and supreme human happiness, nor an enchanted world in which moral rectitude may reign; modern politics for the Greeks would be foolishness, and for Christians a stumbling block. It is, as Weber claimed, an arena in which one must bear much.

This compound error is, however, based upon a half-truth; for the idea of bearing much is not the wholly secular doctrine it appears at first glance to be. It is quite consonant with a tradition of Christian thinking, and, in fact, my argument here is that early modern thought is the political arm of that religious tradition. To bear much; to live in accordance with God's absence from history, or rather His hiddenness, while awaiting Eternity; to live in history while awaiting the End: this was required of those for whom biblical history revealed the present standing and obligation of human beings toward each other and toward God.

For human beings so situated in *this* kind of history, God is neither wholly absent nor present; politically, life is neither wholly enchanted nor utterly disenchanted; politics is neither the most noble realm of human activity and happiness nor a morally empty realm where interest—abetted, of course, by that child of light, reason—reigns supreme. There is, it seems to me, a certain genius in early modern thought. Understanding human existence in the way that it did provided a justification for a form of association that stands between the now unachievable politics of ancient virtue (following Tocqueville) and the unthinkable—though in another sense, *only* thinkable—politics of interest. Early modern thought gives us neither an enriched and enriching germ of the grain, nor chaff; rather it offers the remaining portion from which comes our daily bread. While we may wish for more, this substance sustains human life. To demand more is hubris; to accept less, inhuman.

For Rousseau, of course, biblical history is not authoritative. The search for a politically authoritative history does not, however, end with Rousseau's arrival. Indeed Rousseau, Hegel, Marx, Mill, Nietzsche, and Heidegger, to name only the most prominent, can be seen as continuing in the belief, as much biblical interpretation would have it, that the identity of the soul and narrative of history are linked. They, however, recur to different histories in order to make this linkage. Just where we stand, in this age where biblical history and all other histories that narrate the unfolding or veiling of the soul have been repudiated or, in Nietzsche's words, "have conscience against them," and in which the very notion of history is problematic, is not at all clear. Equally unclear is how a politics that would steer its way between the too-much of the ancients and the too-little of many contemporary commentators may be defended without such a history. However one reads the extraordinary events of history that mark the close of the twentieth century (whether they are portentous or signify nothing new), I do not think I am alone in intuiting that at best we are only waiting with a cautious optimism that falls all too frequently into either trepidation for the future or into boredom and dissatisfaction with an existence without a meaning that is just over the horizon, just beyond the grasp of reason alone. From the early modern vantage, I submit, this dim longing is both encouraging and foreboding.

Many of these thoughts had their origin in classes taught by Ron Puhek, Guenther Roth, David Greenstone, Robin Lovin, Stephen Holmes, Nathan Tarcov, Joseph Cropsey, and Langdon Gilkey, largely at the University of Chicago from 1984 to 1989. The patience and provocations of my teachers were as invaluable as was the depth of their knowledge about early modern political thought and its relationship to Christianity. Additionally, correspondence with Eldon Eisenach at various stages of this project gently prompted me to rethink certain crucial issues. Beyond these immediate guides stands my father, the late Richard Mitchell, whose work and thoughts on religion and politics in the Muslim world inspired me in ways I only now begin to understand; and my mother, Alita Mitchell, whose stalwart disposition steered me imperceptibly toward Reformation thought and the topic I have investigated here.

Finally, generous support from the John M. Olin Program in the History of Political Culture, the Lynde and Harry Bradley Foundation (both at the University of Chicago), and a Dilthey Faculty Fellowship for Interdisciplinary Research from George Washington University made it possible to complete this manuscript in a timely manner. Certain arguments and contrasts between authors were drawn out of the work as a whole before publication here as a book, and for permission to include them in the entire work I would like to thank *The Review of Politics, The Journal of Politics, The Journal of Religion, Political Theory,* and *The American Political Science Review.*

IDENTITY AND ORIGIN

I DENTITY AND ORIGIN tend inexorably to be linked. This is no less true of persons than of a people. For both, "who" is often considered inseparable from "whence." Origin—the founding, broadly conceived—either constitutes identity (the ontological claim)[1] or *should* constitute it (the normative claim)[2] long after it has receded into memory.

The contemporary debate about the identity of early modern political thought is no less immune to this linkage of identity and origin. Here, too, the effort to establish identity involves an inquiry into the thought of the *original* progenitors of the modern political vision—usually Hobbes and Locke—in order to specify what it *really* is. In a double sense this linkage of identity and origin is relevant to my work. First, my investigation and treatment of Hobbes and Locke are efforts to establish something of the identity of modern political thought. This procedure is uncontroversial, though perhaps overworked.

Second, and more controversial, my search presupposes that the identity of early modern thought was established (by Hobbes and Locke; Luther and Rousseau I will disregard for the moment) through an inquiry into origins as well. The linkage of "who" and "whence," in other words, was no less compelling for Hobbes and Locke than it is for us. While there is a massive difference with respect to the "whence" of which they speak and the "whence" to which we recur, the *manner* of inquiry is nevertheless the same. The content, and not the procedure, is different.[3]

I am concerned, then, with two questions at once: What is the identity of early modern thought? And what was Hobbes and Locke's understanding of the implications that the preeminent account of origin available to them (biblical history) had for political identity? My effort to establish the identity of early modern thought by going back to *its* historical origin presupposes that at that point (of origin) a similar project was undertaken; only there, what was gone back to was biblical history. The theoretical difference between them and us is in respect to *what* is taken to be the proper horizon of history within which origin, and hence identity, can be known. Hobbes and Locke (as well as Luther and Rousseau) do not look back several centuries, as contemporary theorists do, to discover and argue about their own political identity; that they don't is pregnant with meaning. It suggests that contemporary theory, even when it would wish to *defend* Hobbes and Locke, completely misconstrues the historical horizon of modern political thought, and, hence, the basis of its defensibility. Their thinking cannot be defended, I suggest, on the field of the history of ideas! Rousseau aside, for Luther, Hobbes, and Locke, the historical horizon was not established by the *tradition,* but rather by Christ.

> Forasmuch as ye know that ye were not redeemed with corruptible things, as silver and gold, from your vain conversation received by tradition from your fathers; but with the precious blood of Christ, as of a lamb without blemish and without spot.[4]

With respect to the general question of history (I will come to a more refined treatment shortly) my thesis is that the thought of Luther, Hobbes, Locke, and Rousseau provides an answer to the question: Where does humankind stand with respect to the significant events that constitute what I will be calling *politically authoritative history?* And what, as a consequence, can be said about human identity? Fully understood, my claim is that the political thought of Luther, Hobbes, Locke, and Rousseau is inexorably bound to the history they invoke, and that through the history they invoke they are attempting to reconcile human beings to who they veritably are, yet often only dimly intimate. Early modern thought, in a word, is an attempt to grasp the implications of a politically authoritative history, the horizon of which is, for us, *strange,* and whose pertinent events establish the standing and identity of humankind as well as the political task at hand.

WHAT POLITICALLY AUTHORITATIVE HISTORY IS NOT

By politically authoritative history I mean that history invoked, the implications of which authorize or legitimate a particular political order, extant or envisioned, which simultaneously *situates* psyche or the soul in a narrative it *knows* to be true yet might wish to evade. It is important to understand, in the case of the four authors considered here, that politically authoritative history is not history of the sort found in, say, Hume's work,[5] where cultural attributes that impose themselves upon the manifold articulations of history simultaneously specify the origin and identity of a people and distinguish one people from another, or history of the sort found in, say, Voltaire's attempted subversion of the biblical and superstitious accounts—his conjunction—that predominated in his day.[6] For purposes here, politically authoritative history corresponds neither to cultural constancy (and the atavisms that presumably would obtain were cultural life to be apocalyptically transformed) nor to that history knowledge of the purpose of which is grasped *wholly* by the human mind rather than only nominally revealed to it. The kind of history I will explore here is quite different. For Luther, Hobbes, Locke, and Rousseau politically authoritative history exists for the faculty of reason as a *trace,* which is binding even though it is, in the final analysis, only nominally revealed.[7]

It would be a mistake to think that the distinction being made here is between biblical and secular histories; were it so, suspicion would rightly be raised about Rousseau's place in this study. The "secularization thesis" only partially overlaps the distinction made here. The notion that the "philosophy of history [which] originates with the Hebrew and Christian faith . . . ends with the secularization of its eschatological pattern"[8] fails to capture the subtleties involved. Rousseau, unlike the others, does not recur to the Bible, yet his history is surely not a secularized eschatology. Voltaire he is not. While bold, Rousseau is not audacious with respect to reason's powers.

The more helpful distinction is between histories which are apprehended by reason alone and those that find reason powerful yet ultimately insufficient. The presecular-secular distinction confuses this important matter and would force Rousseau to confirm the enlightened sentiment which would insist that "our eyes are now opened,"[9] that we have lost our original innocence—without for a moment wondering what such a thought might mean about how far we have *really* come! Rousseau notes that "melancholy is the friend of delight."[10] The often melancholy tone of the secularization thesis may be thought of, in this regard, as the friend of Hegel's delight (the transposed Good News of the Word made flesh!); melancholy follows in the path of (reason's) delight. To go back before Hegel: might this require that we dispose of trajectories of thought which restrain us to remorsefully following Hegel's lead?[11]

What is significant about these four authors is that the Source out of which the psyche or the soul originates and the foundation for political authority is at present obscured from full view—hence my use of the term "trace." This is no less true of Rousseau than of Luther, Hobbes, and Locke. The state of nature is, for Rousseau, the functional equivalent of the *Deus Absconditus* of Luther, Hobbes, and Locke: the preeminently real for all four is *not here now.*[12]

Because of this *absence of epiphany,* the search for origin, identity, and the foundation of political authority can only amount to a recollection, an anamnetic recovery, of a truth that bears decisively on human life, but which has only been partially revealed thus far in history—or, in Rousseau's (and Nietzsche's) case, increasingly concealed or obliterated as history recedes from the constitutive events. What is recollected and recovered are not the "actual events" of history in any conventional sense, to be sure, but this makes it no less *binding.*

The bearing this recovery has on the psyche, and for political action, is not diminished because of this partially revealed character. To the contrary, the residual trace forever points toward the ineffable that is hidden yet politically binding. That which is binding for all four authors is disclosed to the soul either *beneath* reason in faith (Luther), *to* reason from Revelation (Hobbes and Locke), or *before* reason through the heart (Rousseau). In any event, for all four, the faculty of reason, and the "actual events" of history which can be ostensibly known by it, are not sufficient to the task of comprehending *politically authoritative* history. It must be known in some other way. The implication this has is perilous, of course, for historiographic efforts that aspire to convey purely neutral facts that are acquired by sober reason alone in order that zealotry and injustice be unmasked. These may (and must) be unmasked; yet the method, fully applied, is no more hospitable to political forms which aspire to genuine equanimity than to those that do not. The reasoning of the philosophers, Rousseau says, "turns out to be good only at destructive criticism."[13] Especially in times of crisis, but not only then, the authorization for a politics of justice cannot stand on the faculty of reason alone.

CONVENTIONAL VIEWS OF EARLY MODERN THOUGHT

That early modern thought can be best understood as an investigation of biblical history—or, at any rate, *another* horizon of history which reason alone cannot grasp—is, of course, a view not widely held. A variety of other interpretations of early modern thought, some defending it, others detracting from it, still possess currency, due in no small part to intellectual inheritance and disciplinary pressure. Arguments recurring to the relative ontological status of "the individual" and "the social,"[14] to the influx of a Republican ethos into a political world evacuated by the Reformation,[15] to the eclipse of "the political" in modern political thought,[16] to the distinction between the ancients and the moderns,[17] to Marxian categories,[18] to rational politics and moral autonomy,[19] to the emergence of separate value spheres,[20] to Aristotelian Catholicism,[21] to an ahistorical social contract theory,[22] to representative government,[23] and to sentiments from the Scottish Enlightenment[24] have been devised to interpret early modern thought—and for the most part still hold sway. In certain respects, these arguments diverge wildly from one another. As I have said, however, in all this a common denominator obtains: the scant interest in Luther's, Hobbes's, Locke's, and, to a lesser extent, Rousseau's writings on history is vastly disproportionate to the extent and importance of their speculations on this subject.

It is no secret, of course, that Luther, Hobbes, Locke, and Rousseau *do* recur to history of one form or another when they attempt to provide a foundation for political authority, but the meaning of their effort and its theoretical relevance have not, I think, been adequately grasped. The prevailing tendency has been to see the theology of Hobbes and Locke, for example, as a recapitulation of prevailing dogma rather than as an exposition of a truth that is somehow binding. This view is unsatisfactory.

Equally important, no theoretical framework has yet been devised that is able to comprehend the overarching pattern unifying the work of these authors as a whole.[25] That these authors did invoke history to authorize one view and reject another is clear. Too often, however, their views of history have been dismissed *prima facie,* as irrelevant to their purportedly expressly political thought, without due consideration to the internal coherence of their views of history, to how these views relate—not to mention undergird—their authors' political conclusions, and without regard to the recurrent pattern found in the work of these authors taken together. This tendency to disregard biblical history has been particularly evident, for example, in many contemporary discussions of Hobbes and Locke for whom, it is often argued, the nonhistorical social contract is their seminal contribution to the history of political thought.

Two Forms of Politically Authoritative History

For Luther, Hobbes, and Locke, as I have mentioned, politically authoritative history is biblical history, that is, the salient events of the two Testaments: Creation, Adam's fall, Abraham's faith, Moses' covenant with God, Christ and the New Dispensation, and the final Redemption. Certain of these events figure more prominently than others for each thinker, and this is of no small consequence for the political vision at which they arrive.

For Rousseau, however, politically authoritative history is a complex and transformative movement from the state of nature to civil society, the former of which (like the *Deus Absconditus* of Luther, Hobbes, and Locke) has itself all but been obscured from view. Rousseau's history is therefore a deep recollection without a Holy Book, an anamnesis not unlike that granted to Er by the gods in the closing passages of the *Republic*,[26] which recalls events outside of the "everyday" time of the civil epoch, which, in Rousseau's case, retrieves the now almost irretrievable innocent and uncorrupted Self temporally located only in the state of nature: that moment that is the *silent* counterpoint of all that transpires in civil society.

From one vantage point, of course, these two kinds of politically authoritative history bear no relation to one another. Rousseau's intention was to find the precivil foundation of human life. Because Christianity was a formulation that arose *within* the historical epoch cordoned off by civil society, humanity's true origin could not be found there. Only by going back to the state of nature, which preceded civil society—and so was *before God*[27]—could the Source be found. The state of nature precedes God and His Creation; these latter are only recollected by human memory—the objects for which are the *written* words that *mark* the outset of civil history.

The irony of this radicalization of the search for human origins is that the starkness of the contrasts Rousseau poses between the state of nature and civil society simultaneously recapitulates and radicalizes Luther's earlier contrasts between the realm of works and the realm of faith. Where Luther, with qualification, identified the realm of works with the time of the Old Testament and the realm of faith with the time of the New (thus locating the antinomies of human experience and existence *within* the biblical tradition), Rousseau locates the *whole* of the biblical tradition within one of his two epochs of history. This is at once a break from Luther's rendition of the relationship between the orders of reality and a continuity (of form, at any rate) as well. Luther's historical anti-nomies are Christian; Rousseau's historical antinomies are ostensibly *trans*-Christian.

The starkness of the antinomies of these two thinkers and the confluence of history and psyche in their work suggests that something of theoretical impor-tance is being thought through in the early modern period which has not previ-ously been adequately explored. While the content of politically authoritative history is clearly different, the form is not. This form, which conveys that the soul is at present in exile, reveals the insufficiency of everyday life and demands an attunement to a deeper level which cannot be grasped by reason alone. Er-rancy here, though understood as inevitable, is not countenanced, and the *po-litical* problematic is how to order human life so that atonement for errancy is not obstructed.

PSYCHE AND THE STRUCTURE OF POLITICALLY AUTHORITATIVE HISTORY

What is to be learned, then, from the form of the politically authoritative his-tory that both Luther and Rousseau invoke? First, that history has a structure, that there are distinct periods of history within which one set of antinomies within the soul dominates or excludes another.[28] For Luther, for example, prior to the coming of Christ human life was characterized as a kind of surface exis-tence lived in accordance with the exteriority of the Law and of works, rather than with the interiority of faith, the genuine possibility of which was only brought about by Christ's first coming. The mystery of God and of suffering is subsequently more fully revealed. Opacity gives way to translucence, and by the steely radiance of the light of grace, the contours of a new and deeper soul ap-pear and a new mode of atonement is exacted. (His profound ambivalence not-withstanding, Nietzsche saw this as Christianity's great contribution to the history of the soul.[29])

For Rousseau as well, the grand pivot point of history is a moment of transformation—a transmogrification, in fact, if the splintering fragmentation in civil society is juxtaposed to the pristine unity that preceded it. The servitude of civil society: this would have been inconceivable to the savage. The savage *is* free, in his or her very being; like the undivided soul of which Plato speaks, which *knows* the good because it *is* good,[30] the soul of the savage cannot know servitude because its nature is not servile. The commencement of the civil ep-och, however, occasions (or is occasioned by—the etiology is unclear) a corrup-tion in the human soul. Here the unity of the soul is dirempted at the grand pivot point of history.

In the thought of all four authors there is, I submit, a relationship between psyche and history, a relationship according to which the epochs of history co-incide with psyche's attributes or moments. For Luther and Rousseau, as well as for Hobbes and Locke, history is the medium by which psyche is differentiated and the antinomies of human experience comprehended. History is the structure of the soul writ large. The architecture of the psyche—think of Freud's buried city metaphor[31]—is here articulated in terms of historical epochality. The exposition of historical antinomies (whether biblical or otherwise) grants psyche a self-reflective grasp of its *then*, *now*, and *future*, and this grasp at the same moment pulls together its disparate domains, none of which can be vanquished.[32]

Recollection of *this* kind of politically authoritative history is quite different from reflections on the history of ideas—the substance of so many contemporary explorations into the origin and identity of early modern thought. The *search* for identity by returning to origin is similar, but the content is different, as I have said. Above all, perhaps, it should be noted that origin here is *not wholly immanent;* the immanent context which contemporary investigations set out to explore (cultural, political, biological, even religious!) closes off that *opening* to the domain which reason cannot grasp, but which these authors could not ignore. This similarity of form (the search for origin) and difference in content (purporting to find it *in time*) is what makes it so difficult to specify exactly what *our* relationship to early modern political thought might be. To remain true to the progenitive modern vision, to circumvent the annoying asymmetry, it would be necessary to invoke a history that would be, for us, a stumbling block.

HISTORY, DIALECTIC, AND FULFILLMENT

The narrative of history for Luther, Hobbes, Locke, and Rousseau, as I have said, is the medium through which is expressed the multiplex, articulated truth of the human soul. The mode of containing temporal and ontological difference, of possessing this multiplex truth, the principle according to which a narrative unity of a nonunity becomes possible at all, yet needs to be considered. To do this I will set aside Rousseau's (nonbiblical) history for a moment and consider the two Testaments.

When speaking of biblical history, the real events are those delineated by the two Testaments; Creation, Adam's fall, Abraham's faith, Moses' covenant with God, Christ's first coming, the Redemption, etc. The preeminent event of biblical history for Christians is, of course, Christ's first coming. Yet this central event raises questions about the relationship between the pre- and post-Incarnation epoch whose answers are far from obvious.

The Scriptural passage that is helpful in phrasing the difficulty is to be found, I suggest, in a declaration by Matthew's Christ:

> Think not that I have come to destroy the law, or the prophets: I have come not to destroy, but to fulfill.[33]

Not a destruction, but a fulfillment; something New that at the same time pre-serves the Old. There is no simple formula here for the relationship between the Old and the New, between a still binding past (the Old) and a present (the New) that annuls *and* preserves the past, between who we *are* and who we *were*, between the *already* and the *not-yet*. Understanding the relationship between identity and origin in this way is no easy matter. The specification of one's *pre-sent* identity entails the invocation of a *then* that pregnantly portends a future which subsequently supersedes and transposes the earlier moment; identity is inexorably related to origin, but in a dialectical manner. *Then* is both necessary and not sufficient to establish identity *now*.

It should not be forgotten that identity *was* spoken of in this way by Refor-mation Christians who wished to return to primitive Christianity, to Christ. The central theoretical issue of the Reformation was this question of the mean-ing of Christ's fulfillment of the Old Truth which, though still binding for Christians, had in the same breath been annulled. This is no less true of Luther than of Hobbes and Locke—and later, in a philosophical key, of Hegel.[34] The extraordinary tension and uncertainty about identity that follows in the wake of this most Christian of questions has receded with the ebb of the progenitive Protestant vision, and in its stead has reemerged the view that origin *is* identity, that to establish our identity now requires that we go back to the beginning—in political terms, to the *founding*,[35] in psychological terms, to the traumas of *child-hood*.[36] How different this is from the Reformation view should be clear.

THE INHERENT AMBIGUITIES OF FULFILLMENT: THE BASIS OF ANTIFOUNDATIONALISM

The question of the meaning of fulfillment is *the* question that informs attempts to distinguish between the Old and New Testament and to establish the rela-tionship between origin and identity. No *incontestable* reading of meaning of this fulfillment is possible, however, if for no other reason than that while one Testament may be *more* of a revelation than the other, it is still only a *partial* revelation. Different understandings of the meaning of Christ's fulfillment are therefore possible, and no doubt vary in accordance with the kinds of problems political theorists find most formidable in their own age. This does not reflect disingenuousness; rather, it testifies to the inherent open-endedness of biblical interpretation in the face of ever changing historical contingencies.

I will not consider the matter further here. More important, and before providing an overview of each author, I want to comment briefly on the *theologi-cal* reason for the antifoundationalism of Hobbes and Locke, which can be attri-buted to the only partially revealed God in the post-Incarnation epoch.

The Source, the *Deus Absconditus*, out of which originates human life and the foundation of political authority for Luther, Hobbes, and Locke, is at pre-sent obscured from full view, as I have said. The preeminently real for all three is *not here now*. Because of the absence of epiphany, the search for origin and the foundation of political authority is a twilight affair: the owl of Minerva which "spread[s] its wings only with the falling of the dusk"[37] is but the philosophical confirmation of the biblical view of the relationship between knowledge and history: what must come to pass before the truth can be fully known is not *any* particular moment but rather the *last* moment. The *true* meaning of biblical history, which bears decisively on human identity, is not within mortal grasp.

The salient events of the two Testaments, consequently, cannot but have an ambiguous meaning. Certain of these events figure more prominently than others for Luther, Hobbes, and Locke, and this is of no small consequence for the political vision at which they arrive. Nevertheless, when human genius has left its mark and eloquently said all that it may, the biblical dialectic remains unexhausted; it is open-ended and must remain so because the End is not yet known. Fulfillment, in a word, is not yet the final Revelation.[38]

For we know in part, and we prophesy in part. But when that which is perfect is come, then that which is in part shall be done away.[39]

In this light, it must be remembered that the modern political efflorescence—I speak now especially of Hobbes and Locke—hinges upon the "antifoundational" insight that human knowledge is limited and that these limits exist because human fallibilities cannot be exorcised in this moment of history after Christ's first coming and before the final Redemption. God the Son may be a mediator and guardian of the way to eternity, but the rudimentary fact remains: human beings in this moment of history are without the unmediated presence of God, and so must struggle to establish a political order consistent with His hiddenness, one which attenuates displaced and disruptive attempts by beings made in the *image* of God[40] to be *as* God or speak *for* God *in time* and before the arrival of *eternity*. Merely consult Hobbes on *Nunc-stans*[41] and Locke on enthusiasm[42] for their arguments on this matter.

This view is antifoundational, to be sure; but pander to what is lowest it does not. Rather, the early modern view is based on a view of the whole (replete with all its necessary perplexities and mysteries) insofar as it had been revealed through the biblical narrative. To generate a politics on the basis of God's *hiddenness* cannot adequately be described as building from what is lowest, but rather of constructing with a view to the mysterious though partially revealed character of the whole, with all that that entails about the limits of human knowledge. To speak of the limits of knowledge is to commit the antifoundational heresy, to be sure, but the high-low distinction has no place here. God has withdrawn His presence; human knowledge is limited in this epoch before the second coming: this is the point of departure for early modern thought, not the ancient virtues whose rejection, it is sometimes purported, occasioned a more stable though less glorious polity.[43]

It should, of course, also be clear how the antifoundational historiography of early modern thought differs from the eschatological historiography of Marxian thought. The linkage should be clear, too, between antifoundational historiography and early modern skepticism.

LUTHER'S DIALECTIC OF HISTORY

Luther's reading of the relationship between the two Testaments is a highly charged one, if only because of what it demands of the Christian who accedes to it. The active righteousness of works countenanced in the Old Testament and the passive righteousness sanctioned in the New Testament are like the two chambers of an hourglass, separate yet contiguous with the Christ event and the *second use of the Law* that unconceals God the Son to the Christian. Each realm, with qualification, corresponds to a particular historical epoch;[44] the realm of works precedes the realm of faith, historically and in terms of the psyche's experience. Again, the conjunction of history and psyche.

Because human beings *now* live in the age of faith, it is incumbent upon them not to confuse active and passive righteousness, nor to think that Christ will come to presence anywhere else but in the abyss of powerlessness when "the world" has been utterly condemned. The Catholic analogical vision of reality (a hierarchal scheme) does not, in this view, reflect the truth of the post-Incarnation epoch. The God of the Old Testament created the world, granted authority to leaders of His chosen people, and required that His people be righteous, to be sure; yet the New Testament offers eternal life through faith; this is an irruption of something *new* (yet portended) for psyche which the analogical vision does not grasp.

For Luther, the Old Law is necessary, paradoxically, so that the Christian can get *beyond* it. The instability of this dialectical formulation cannot be underestimated. Christians must get beyond the Law to attain salvation, but to get beyond it they have to go *through* it. The sense of liberation, of freedom, made possible by this going-through-and-beyond in Luther's writings is unmistakable; yet all the while it is to be juxtaposed to existing political power that has received Divine sanction.[45] The two moments of the apparent paradox, if they are to be held together at all, require the *experience* of faith; when this is lacking, when the abyss of powerlessness that yawns only when the Christian *tries to live* in accordance with the Law does not reveal itself, then the integrity of this position dissevers. Pride, not faith, results when the supersession of the Old Testament by the New is taken to mean only the annulment of it; not faith but rather pride ensues when the meaning of the fulfillment of the Old by the New is not comprehended dialectically, when the New is not understood to annul *and to preserve* the Old.

Without the *living experience* that makes this dialectical understanding possible, the identification of the New Testament alone with salvation denigrates the Old—which can offer no such promise. The realm of the Law, and of political life, made authoritative by the Old, offers no recompense equivalent to eternal life. This is what makes Christian righteousness misconstrued so volatile. Hobbes was to observe that

> no man can serve two masters; nor is he less, but rather more a master, whom we are to obey for fear of damnation than he whom we obey for fear of temporal death.[46]

This is a poignant reminder of the impotency of politics, and of the Law, in the face of promise of life eternal. While Luther did not intend to derogate the Old, the very starkness of the contrast between the New and the Old, the appeal of what was promised by the New, and, most important, the dialectical nature of the relationship between the Old and the New could be misconstrued as a devaluation of the Old—the very ground of political authority.

HOBBES'S DIALECTIC OF HISTORY

Hobbes's theoretical vision can be seen as a counterpoint to the starkness of Luther's formulation and to the politics of Christian righteousness misconstrued. I am not suggesting here that Hobbes was responding *to Luther,* but rather to the righteousness that dialectic thinking of a sort adduced first (or at least most forcefully) by Luther *may* countenance. The link is logical *not* causal.[47] Luther and Lutheran quietism are not at all the culprit for Hobbes. What *was* the culprit was a way of understanding Christ's first coming which emphasized His newness, His transformative character. God, after all, could not possibly have meant for his Son to be the occasion of a dualism that would subvert temporal life! Christian righteousness misconstrued could be vanquished by a formulation of the meaning of fulfillment that was not as oppugnant as that articulated by Luther. The constitutive ground of political authority found in the Old Testament could be reaffirmed in such a way that it softened the disjunction between the two Testaments. The notion that Christ was utterly transformative, in a word, could (and had to) be countered; for Hobbes the interpretative move consistent with God's peaceful intention was to accept the Pauline formulation that Christ is the new Adam but reject the claim that He can absolve Christians of sin or pride. Christ solves the problem of loss of eternal life, but *not* the problem of pride—a move which demands a more restrictive reading of Romans and I Corinthians than many Reformers were willing to endorse.[48]

While the details will have to wait, Hobbes argues that Christ will solve the problem of loss of eternal life at His second coming, that is, in the distant future. Until that time, the problem of pride—an almost insurmountable obstacle for human association—is mitigated by the *Christ-like* figure of the Leviathan: the king of the children of pride who, like Christ, takes their pride in upon himself. There is, for Hobbes, a *temporal* solution to the problem of pride. It should be emphasized here that this is *not* a secular government—for that term supposes already precisely the distinction between secular and religious that Hobbes wished to deny!

In addition, Hobbes grants authority to the Leviathan by *tracing* out the genealogy of authority, starting with Moses. This is not surprising, for Hobbes's recourse to the Old Testament for the ground of political authority is consistent with his attempt to soften the disjunction between the Old and the New, and thereby to further substantiate the authority of the Old. It should also be no surprise that Hobbes attributes to the Leviathan the same rights as those granted by God to Moses: the right of interpretation and the right to command obedience. Unlike Luther's dialectic of supersession, Hobbes's dialectic is one of renewal. The New Testament renews the Old, and the political form he advocates derives from this dialectic.

Above all else, perhaps, the great lesson Hobbes learns from the Old Testament was that God does not unconceal Himself to the people, but only to their mediator.

> And they said unto Moses, Speak thou with us, and we will hear: but let not God speak with us, lest we die.[49]

The message is clear; unlike Locke, for whom Christ unconceals a foundation that *all* may grasp, for Hobbes the concealment of God from the people has not be superseded. Christ's truth is contiguous with that of Moses; it does not overturn it.

LOCKE'S DIALECTIC OF HISTORY

Locke, too, softens the disjunction between the Old and New Testaments. Christ, he claims, clarifies the message of the Old. Although at first glance the difference between a dialectic of renewal and a dialectic of clarification may seem slight, the political implications of this difference are immense. A dialectic of clarification presumes that the message of the Old was correct but that it did not *know* itself to be so. While for Hobbes something was *lost* and had to be reinstantiated, for Locke something known had to be more fully authorized by Christ. This formal statement may sound abstract at this point; nevertheless, Locke's doctrine of toleration hinges on the contention that Christ merely clarified and gave authority to what was knowable, if not known, by natural reason all along.

Natural reason, of course, was given to Adam by God in the beginning. For Locke, this event rather than Moses' covenant with God is the primordial political event. Thus, while Locke and Hobbes both want to reestablish the importance of the Old Testament, Locke's return to Adam, the first Old Testament figure, allows him to conclude in favor of both toleration (which does not blot out the light of human reason) and the right of dominion: property as stewardship. Hobbes, on the other hand, was not able to generate a doctrine of property because the paradigmatic political event to which Christ is a counterpoint contains within it no referent to property. That is, Moses' receipt of the covenant is an event out of which a doctrine of property cannot be elicited. The right to command obedience and to interpret, yes; property, no. It is out of the two themes of reason and property—both of which derive from Adam—that Locke develops his liberal vision. A dialectic of clarification deriving from Adam/Christ generates a different political form and identity of the psyche, and has a different tonality altogether, than does a dialectic of renewal deriving from Moses/Christ.

I should also point out here, however, that notwithstanding their differences, Hobbes and Locke do belong together, but for reasons having little to do with their being social contract theorists. The theological problem of which they must give an account is the meaning of the dialectical preservation and annulment that Christ offers; yet their account is—one is tempted to say, so "English!" There is no *Angst*, no deep spiritual journey of the German sort to be undertaken here; faith is not a rebirth unto the world of spirit, but rather a *necessary supplement* to the Law. It is a clean and tidy affair. To overstate the point, it is almost as if Christ's proclamation: "for my yoke is easy and my burden light,"[50] were taken to be the essential teaching of the New Dispensation! The view that faith is a necessary supplement to reason no doubt disposes political thinking to traverse certain terrain to the exclusion of other territory. Precisely what the relationship might be I do not explore here.

ROUSSEAU'S HISTORY OF DIREMPTION

Rousseau's politically authoritative history is not biblical. To be sure, this fact has certain far-reaching political consequences, and consequences for the identity of the psyche. To be sure, also, the dialectical form does not appear around the question of Christ's fulfillment of the prophets. Rather, it appears in the form of that *supplement* (the written word) which *stands-in-for* what must, yet cannot, come to presence. The entire constellation out of which Rousseau's problematic arises is the historical horizon constituted by the *problem* of errancy, concealment, and atonement. He is, therefore, worthy of inclusion here.

I have insisted thus far that dialectical thinking about the relationship between history and the soul emerges in speculations about the relationship between the time *before* and *after* Christ. Rousseau's authoritative history is delineated by a transformative event that cordons off one epoch and mode of experience from another—reality from appearance, inner from outer, freedom from servitude, action from thought, natural goodness from vice, nature from civility, etc.—but Christ is absent.

His invocation of a category of experience that is foreign to what is immediate in this civil epoch and in experience is what makes his *use* of these alien modes so *Christian*, however. In Christian speculations on the meaning of history the truth of the soul is fundamentally *historical*, and cannot be understood without recurring to the transformative moment, the preeminent pivot point that is Christ. Biblical history is the record of psyche's articulation and differentiation.[51] Rousseau's nonbiblical history does nothing less. Notwithstanding his profound inversion of the relationship between God, time, and memory, Rousseau's history, like biblical history, serves to situate psyche, to orient it toward another time that is both *back* and *within*—as Saint Paul had done. While the Source may have been discerned without severe distortion in nature, or by the ancients, that *we* are called to listen *now*—to attend with great acuity to what is both *back* and *within* that our errancy may be understood—betrays a pattern of thinking that is profoundly biblical.

More explicitly, the psyche in its present moment is the *supplement* to the ancients, to nature, to natural goodness, which evasively hears the voice that can barely be discerned;[52] and this supplement to what is natural yet foreign and distant conjoins in the soul the essential and the unessential, the *not now* with the *now*, in such a way that psyche, despite its degeneracy at *this* moment, may recollect and "possess" the pristine unity of Nature. Nature requires its supplements that its voice be heard—the master concept of *Emile*. Theologically, the absent God may be called upon by the degenerate human race, and *only* by the degenerate human race, which is God's supplement. While God *must* remain a trace for the degenerated, the Divine requires something constituted by itself, that is nevertheless other than itself, something impure, in order that the Divine be known at all. Think here of Genesis:

> And the eyes of them both were opened, and they knew that they were naked; and they sewed fig leaves together, and made themselves aprons. And they heard the voice of the Lord God walking in the garden in the cool of the day: and Adam and his wife hid themselves from the presence of the Lord God amongst the trees of the garden. And the Lord God called unto Adam, and said unto him, Where art thou?[53]

Adam, created in the image of God, comes to know his separation *from* God only upon the occasion of his errancy. Concealment and self-hiding already suppose a separation that *knows* its separation from the Source, that *can have* God as an object of knowledge.[54] Only the errant one can know *of* God; in Rousseau's idiom, the corrupt soul *already* knows its errancy from Nature and yet conceals itself from Nature *because* it knows Nature is its Source.[55] The distance *from* Nature is the requisite for knowing-which-evades Nature. His criticism of the Enlightenment must be seen as a transposition of the Genesis pattern, one which is faithful to its insight about the relationship between concealment, knowing, and Source. I will add in passing that Hobbes's discussion of the first politico-religious covenant between the Israelites and God, which is *the* paradigm for legitimate authority, is no less faithful to the Genesis pattern of errancy from God, and of not wishing to be seen by God.

History, for Rousseau, is not a fulfillment but rather a perennial absence of fulfillment; nevertheless, the history which evinces only diremption, only the Egyptian darkness of captivity, *stands in for* that which is concealed. Psyche in this present epoch knows *and* conceals, and consequently grasps *and* evades, both a present lacking in substance and an uncapturable "past" overflowing with it—a "past" capable of coming to presence in the heart but *perhaps* not of being brought into life in "this" time at all. Conscience, the voice of nature, "is timid, it likes refuge and peace. The World and noise scare it,"[56] Rousseau says. The *way* is frightened of the world! And yet the world knows its own self-deception! Here is an absence of epiphany to match Luther, Hobbes, and Locke—and at the same time, in one of its valences, an explosive *demand* for an immanent and imminent reconciliation that emends the defection from Nature. This eschatological tone is absent in Luther, Hobbes, and Locke and is not without political relevance.

The matter cannot not be left at that, however. In Chapter 4 the eschatological tone will be seen to acquire a new meaning (in *Emile*) which will necessitate a significant revision. Here, the eschatological valence of Rousseau's history of the species (phylogenetic history) is transposed, subsumed, and defused by a history of individual development (ontogenetic history) that is *thinkable* only within the confines of the Adamic myth which profoundly informs the thinking of Luther, Hobbes, and Locke. But I will come to that.

Rousseau, I suggest, is in certain respects a break from the earlier speculations of Luther, Hobbes, and Locke, and in certain respects contiguous with them. I have mentioned his inversion of the biblical relation between God, time, and memory, and that this alters his horizon of history significantly. Nevertheless, he transposes, he does not write anew; what he does not break with—and this is crucial—is the thought that the *real* history of the soul is not disclosed by reason alone, that the *problem* of errancy, concealment, and atonement establish the right historical horizon, *strange* as it may seem to the soul for whom errancy, concealment, and atonement are not a problem. About this, all four authors are in agreement.

Summary Comments

In the Conclusion it will be possible to comment on several themes for which the materials in any one chapter alone will not have been sufficient.

First, there is the question of where in early modern political thought God/nature stands in relation to humankind. One of the platitudes of contemporary interpretations of early modern thought is that it purveys no vision of the Good, that it is a political view without God. This view is only partially correct.

The *Deus Absconditus* of Luther, Hobbes, and Locke is not wholly absent; biblical history is the mode of specifying the way in which God is *both* hidden and present. (Rousseau's history of the errancy from nature conveys this same profound tension.) This paradox must be grasped if early modern political thought is to be understood.

Second, I will consider the matter of whether political action of a certain sort is entailed or made imperative whenever humankind is situated within a politically authoritative history. My contention is that it is, and that early modern thought presupposes this. In early modern thought, political action is not entirely self-assumed, as so many contemporary interpretations would have it. This misconception becomes egregious when Hobbes and Locke, for example, are read solely as contract theorists. It is not possible, however, to move from contract theory by itself to the kind of politics envisioned by Hobbes and Locke without recourse to a biblical history that compels human action in certain directions. Beings whose identity is *constituted* by a history of a certain sort will more readily find certain actions ethical and others not. Neither the attributes of the Leviathan and the kind of political community Hobbes envisions nor the doctrine of property, government based on reason, and toleration Locke envisions can be derived without their respective politically authoritative histories. If they could, then Hobbes and Locke could more easily be interchanged with, say, Rawls. Their theories, however, would be vacuous formalisms without a history that interjects content—a difficultly which Rawls only circumvents by invoking something as amorphous and ill-defined as "the public culture of a democratic society."[57]

Third, the pedigree of the notion of freedom, its embodiment in early modern and subsequent thought, deserves attention. For Luther, the dialectical movement of biblical history establishes the foundation of true human freedom. In Locke, too, this dialectic engenders freedom. Toleration, required because of the New Dispensation, entails that political power be wanting in matters of faith, that one be free *of* political power to be free *to* attain salvation. Consult Hegel's *Spirit of Christianity* and a similar thought is expressed: freedom and the dialectic of history are inexorably linked. Tocqueville, too, offers a variant of this claim. These dialectics are Christian, to be sure. Most significant, it is *God the Son*, who came *in the past*, in "the fullness of time," who engenders human freedom and, just as important, allows the subsequent events of history to be understood in a certain light. On this reading, the theoretical task of defending a dialectic of history not based on God the Son, and which is *forward* looking, can only be a dubious undertaking, a project undertaken only by a "Pharisee"— by a person with the audacity to suppose that the *expected* fulfillment will be the fulfillment that comes to pass. Any forward-looking dialectic that posits the content of the fulfillment that is to come is *pre*-Christian rather than post-Christian.[58]

Fourth, some consideration will be given to the question of the early modern understanding of death. Heidegger remarks on the unauthentic attitude toward death,[59] a remark that, in one of its resonations, is a critique of the modern soul. But he is not alone.[60] Taken as critique, this is, I think, a misunderstanding—at least of early modern thought. Luther's insistence that Christians attempt to live in accordance with the Law (which attempt, of course, can only fail) is the theological equivalent of the philosophic practice of death. If a more properly political example is demanded, we need only turn to Locke's doctrine of toleration, the expressed intention of which is to assure that the path to salvation, available to all reasoning souls, not be blocked. For those who adduce a biblical history, life lived in accordance with the whole is one that assures a place in the order of things, if not in eternity. Political life must be organized such that a being-toward-death that comports with the truth of the whole can be assured. This does not change with Rousseau. The eternity that places death into relief in the biblical tradition, that refuses to elide its prospective *terror,* is certainly absent; death's "sting of strangeness,"[61] however, is no less an issue. But I will come to this.

Fifth, some attention will be given to a powerful and unifying theme that runs through the thought of Luther, Hobbes, Locke, and Rousseau: the equality of all human beings under the sovereign. This notion I take to be one of the essential elements of early modern thought, a notion that has no antecedent in the ancient world. This is quite relevant in the debate about the nature of modern political thought; it suggests that the ancients-moderns distinction is of little help in understanding the problematic the early moderns sought to think through: Christianity intervenes and cannot be dismissed.

Sixth, some thought will be given to the difference between what I will call the contemporary ecumenical horizon of history, predicated upon the *ordinary* time of which Heidegger speaks, and what I take to be the horizon of history which comes into view only for the soul for whom errancy, concealment, and atonement are *a problem.* On the ecumenical historical horizon, in its most generous moment, Christianity is but one of many possible historical artifacts from which the self may learn and be deepened. Yet if modern political thought, from whence comes the peculiar form of modern democratic sentiments, derives and can only make full sense from a nonecumenical historical horizon, the implications are vast and the conflict inevitable between a political sentiment that is particular (because predicated upon the particular religion of Christianity) and an ever increasing need to think ecumenically as different peoples around the world cease to be isolated from one another. The supposition currently in force, of course, is that ecumenism *is* compatible with democracy. I will suggest that this *may* not be the case, and that the implicit historical horizon adopted by the discipline of the history of political thought is already ecumenical by virtue of its blindness to this *other* historical horizon I bring into view here.

In all, I hope to show, among other things, that, notwithstanding Rousseau's ostensible break, early modern thought is part of an ongoing dialogue about the implications biblical history has for political identity. Its characteristics do not suggest a *break* from the medieval Christian thought that preceded it. The supposed break that early modern thought purportedly represents is, after all, the offspring of a Christian trinitarian schema in which history is divided into the ancient, medieval, and modern periods.[62] In this work I reject that formulation, paradoxically, at the very moment I endorse the view that speculations on the meaning of biblical history are the threads that hold together the fabric of early modern political thought. Less am I concerned to show the *validity* of these early modern formulations than the *way* in which they were thought through. What is at issue, I suggest, is whether situating the soul in a history confirmable through faith (Luther), Revelation that *supplements* reason (Hobbes and Locke), or the heart (Rousseau)—most emphatically, at any rate, *not* by reason alone!—was recognized to be the only way in which a foundation for politics in the broadest sense could be secured, and whether *this* is the real lesson of early modern thought which we reject at our peril.

ONE

Luther: The Dialectic of Supersession and the Politics of Righteousness

FROM THE STANDPOINT of politically authoritative history, modern political theory begins with Luther and the Reformation. This is not to say that Luther develops an elaborate and explicitly political theory, but rather that with Luther, voice is given to a view of biblical history which raises profound questions about the relationship between the post- and pre-Incarnation epochs, atonement and sin, Christian righteousness, the meaning of freedom, and the relationship between the orders of reality—all of which served to enfeeble existing views of the place and justification of political order in the economy of salvation.

It was above all the economy of salvation with which Luther was concerned. Notwithstanding his substantial theoretical divergences from the Roman Church—his belief, for example, in the priesthood of all believers—Luther shared without dispute the idea that the spiritual realm has precedence over any other. It was only the meaning of precedence that was at issue. In an important sense, then, Luther's Protestantism *continues* the Catholic supernaturally directed civilization;[1] yet it demands, as well, a profound self-reflectivity that shuns the authority of another, and in *this* respect it comports with Kant's view that,

> Enlightenment is man's release from his self-incurred tutelage. Tutelage is man's inability to make use of his understanding without the direction of another,[2]

and Mill's insistence that liberty comprises,

> first the *inward domain* of consciousness, in the most comprehensive sense; liberty of thought and feeling; absolute freedom of opinion and sentiment on all subjects, practical or speculative, scientific, moral, or theological.[3]

This conjunction of spiritual orientation and unmediated self-reflective method is what makes Luther so confounding; harbinger of a consciousness that would dissever itself from the Bible even while it purported to *be* the truth contained there (following Hegel), Luther's *inwardly searching Christian* does not take this form, yet belies the easy opposition between modern and premodern—suggesting perhaps that the terms conceal more than they reveal about the reverberations of Protestantism.

Consider more specifically Luther's theoretical differences with the Roman Church. There, the precedence of the supernatural had been articulated in such a way that the higher orders were not utterly disjoined from the other, lower orders. The whole of Creation disclosed a hierarchy. The higher orders illuminated the lower and clarified their purpose. Between the different orders of reality there is likeness, not utter difference, and this theoretical supposition undergirds the whole scheme. Luther rejected this at the outset.

Aquinas, the Church's great theoretician, constructed a systematic account of reality which drew heavily on Aristotle's vision (Luther held Aquinas responsible for the importation of Aristotle and for the abandonment of Saint Paul), a vision in which the good manifests itself ever more fully in higher and higher levels of human association.[4] Here human beings find a home in a world which intimates but does not disclose God except through *resemblance*.[5]

Positing an analogical relationship between the lower and the higher, spiritual orders made it possible, at the theoretical level, to argue that the spiritual must rule over the lower orders, that the higher orders completed the lower orders by pointing beyond them to something that fully discloses their purpose and nature. Moreover, and perhaps this is the crucial point of difference, the importation of Aristotle conduced to the understanding that the economy of salvation required that virtue could—indeed must—be acquired, and, in Luther's view, this massively distorted the nature and problem of sin, and the mode of atonement offered through Christ.[6] Against the ideas of resemblance and completion found in analogical reasoning, Luther asserts that there are *only two* realms, carnal and spiritual; that the carnal realm, "the world," is steeped in sin; and that the relationship between the two realms can only be understood in terms of Christ's atonement, the problematic for which is *already prefigured in the Old Testament!* Christ's fulfillment, His advent in history, supersedes what is prefigured in the Old Dispensation; and history is given a dialectical structure defined by the centrality of this event.

This compact formulation requires further exposition, to be sure. At this point, however, several provisional thoughts need to be brought forward. First, the Old Testament's correspondence to the era before Christ and the New Testament's correspondence to the era after Him must be understood to mean that there is a truth of the soul for each historical epoch, an order of reality associated with each period of time. Second, a related point: for Luther, *the dialectic of history, not analogy,* is the key to understanding the relationship between the (two) orders and the mystery that still pervades the whole. This is, I insist, the essence of Luther's break with the Roman Church, and the implications this theoretical position has for understanding political and social relations are vast.

Resorting to the dialectic of history offered a way to envision the relationship between the orders, or realms, of reality, and, ironically perhaps, the abiding significance of the Old Testament. *Ante adventum Christi* there had only been the carnal realm and the Old Testament, *the Law,* with which it accords.[7] Christ and the New Testament provide the basis for more fully comprehending the (now superseded, though necessary) Old Testament; and in the juxtaposition of the New and Old, along with the dialectic of fulfillment that comprehends it, Luther finds an answer to the Roman Church.

Prior to Luther's breakthrough, in the medieval period at any rate, the Old Testament had only been a *shadow* of the New Testament. Now it *foreshadowed* it; now the promise of salvation was *already there* awaiting only the *unconcealment.*[8] The pertinent question now became what is the nature of the unconcealment offered by Christ and in what way was it foreshadowed by the events of the Old Testament? These, of course, were precisely the questions taken up by Hobbes and Locke, both of whom had little patience with the abstruse scholastic debates of the Roman Church.

At the theoretical level, Luther's formulations are significant because of the *way* in which the New Testament fulfills the Old. For Luther, the dialectic relationship between the two was such that the message of the Old (the need to perform works and obey the Law), though important, was—if not properly understood—a *threat* to the life of faith made possible through Christ and the New Testament. Although the New Testament fulfills the Old, it does so by virtue of what can, with important qualifications, be called a discontinuity with the Old. Again, no analogical relationship obtains.[9] Here the superiority of the New Testament and the spiritual realm that accompanies it are comprehended in a manner quite different from the Roman Church.

The message of the Old Testament was at once annulled and preserved in the New Testament.[10] About this Luther was certain. But his persistent efforts to distinguish between the Christian righteousness, which is the possession of the new, spiritual human being, and the righteousness of the Old Testament, which is the possession of the old, carnal human being, could, without retaining dialectical vigilance, be read as emphasizing the annulment, and not the preservation, of the Old Testament. "If you want to live to God, you must completely die to the law";[11] the new Law "devours the other law that held us captive";[12] the liberty of Christ "strikes [the old] law dumb":[13] these notions accentuate the disjunction, not the continuity, between the two Testaments.

Despite Luther's dialectical understanding, his impatience with those who misunderstood the *newness* made possible through Christ became pronounced at times—to the detriment of his position. His lengthy and vitriolic polemic against the Jews[14] speaks not of a subtle mind in possession of a profound way to understand Christ and biblical history, but of a soul lost in the hubris, the bad infinity, of absolute freedom.

Although Luther did not wish to denigrate works or obedience, and thought them the *necessary* first step toward God,[15] the distance is infinitesimally small between hubris and the faith which brings the Christian close to God. Both provide security for the soul, one by standing over the world *in* God, the other by "ascending the throne of the world without any power being able to resist it."[16] Each offers a security from "the world," but the difference between the two is absolute. Bear in mind, too, that for Luther the Old Law possessed political weight only for the unrighteous and not for Christians equal to one another before the eyes of God. This was of no small consequence in light of the paradoxical affinity between faith and pride. Subsequently, Hobbes was faced with a politics of righteousness that he thought had to be quelled. The pride of confused faith that would "ascend the throne of the world" could not be countenanced;[17] to mollify it, at the theoretical level, it was necessary to reformulate the meaning of the dialectical relationship between the two Testaments in such a way that its political implications were not destabilizing—and this *could* be done by rejecting the view that faith was an utterly interior affair.[18] The attempt by Hobbes to formulate a theological-political position based upon a dialectic of biblical history that diffused the instabilities of faith by depreciating "the secret matter" provides strong evidence that his subsequent "political" theory is an answer to the *kind* of dialectic of history Luther envisions. That Hobbes should try to avert the pride of absolute freedom (which *would* denigrate the Jews) by finding in Moses the basis of political order is also suggestive. Hobbes was not simply being rhetorical; rather, it was inconceivable to him that the unity of political and religious life found in the Old Testament would have been overturned by God the Son, that God the Father would wish the covenant between Himself and His people be overturned by God the Son. But this will be substantiated in a subsequent chapter. At present the task is to consider Luther's dialectic of biblical history, an early modern dialectic which ironically precipitated the modern political debate even while it sought to return to a much earlier primitive Christianity.[19]

These are but anticipatory comments, to be sure; what now must be considered in greater detail are the two realms in which humankind dwells, after which it will be possible, with certain qualifications, to characterize each realm in terms of a Testament. The relationship between the two realms and the two Testaments is, of course, dialectical, and so no simple one-to-one correspondence can be adduced. The dialectical nature of the relationship naturally raises questions about the path Christians must follow that they may rest under the wing of Christ and find release from the unbearable burden of works. In this regard a discussion of the relationship between powerlessness, the abyss that it discloses, and Christian freedom will be especially important; for it is here that the kernel of Christian righteousness is to be found. This matter, in turn, devolves onto an exposition of Luther's vision of the structure of biblical history. Finally, it will be possible to comprehend Luther's thoughts on temporal authority and the ground of sociality in the light of his vision of biblical history. His thoughts on these matters indicate his position on the relationship between the Old and New Testaments most clearly and evince decidedly modern notions about the separation of religion and politics that come to full flower in Locke's "Letter on Toleration." By way of anticipation, Luther's notions about sociality will become important when Rousseau's claim that Christianity produces no "bonds of union"[20] among human beings emerges later, and so are considered carefully here.

In my concluding remarks I attempt to clarify further Luther's understanding of the dialectic of the Testaments and to lay the foundation for explorations into the early modern thought in subsequent and heretofore considered explicitly political theorists.

THE TWO REALMS

A Christian is a perfectly free lord of all, subject to none. A Christian is a perfectly dutiful servant of all, subject to all.[21]

With this paradox Luther begins his main argument in "The Freedom of a Christian," a work addressed to Pope Leo X which "contains the whole of Christian life in a brief form, provided you grasp its meaning,"[22] a work that attempts to reconcile freedom and servitude, faith and works, the Old Testament and the New.

The coincidence of freedom and servitude exists because of a bifurcation in human nature itself. Hobbes and Rousseau, each in his own way, would subsequently argue against this notion, of course; yet for Luther this was axiomatic—confirmed by experience and by Scripture.

I see another law in my members, warring against the law of my mind, and bringing me into captivity to the law of sin which is in my members.[23]

Human beings have both a "spiritual" nature and a "carnal" nature.[24] Each nature has a corresponding domain, spiritual to faith and carnal to works and the Law. Moreover, belonging to each domain or realm is a distinct species of righteousness: the active righteousness of works and obedience to the Law with the carnal realm and the passive righteousness of the Christian to faith. These two kinds of righteousness are utterly incompatible and must be kept within their respective bounds, lest they get confused. The body and the spirit are separable.

While faith can comprehend carnal nature, the reverse is not possible. To carnal nature, faith is incomprehensible; faith's claim is one for which *no* evidence in the carnal realm can be adduced.

> For the earth cannot judge, renew, and rule the heaven, but contrariwise,
> the heaven judgeth, reneweth, ruleth and maketh fruitful the earth.[25]

When the earth (the carnal) judges, it always condemns faith and tries to destroy it. This is the lesson of the apostles, who were accused of heresy by those
who could not understand that a spiritual realm resides within. Likewise,
Luther understands this to be the lesson of *his* life. He is condemned as a heretic
by a papacy that fails to understand that Christ's coming made possible a spiritual realm distinct from the carnal realm.[26] Hegel, too, had in mind what Luther had earlier iterated when he insisted that "only spirit grasps and
comprehends spirit."[27] The body does not understand spirit; spirit's life is of a
higher order.

The matter cannot be left at that, however, for while spirit is of a higher
order, spirit, paradoxically, *requires* the body for its height to be revealed—just
as the Law of the Old Testament is a precondition for the issuance of spirit. In
this reading the body and the Law are less derogated by the spirit and by faith
than superseded by them. This is *not* the weariness of the body about which
Nietzsche was alarmed in the *Genealogy*,[28] Luther's citations against its post-
Edenic condition notwithstanding.[29] Luther's Christians are less weary than
warring; it is the chasm between the body and the spirit that the Christian of
Rom. 7:23 must bridge, and for that both the body and spirit must make their
demands. Luther's dialectic entails both.

The supersession of spirit over the carnal realm, then, is not simply annulment. The manner in which "heaven may renew and rule the earth" entails a
passing through the carnal realm, the realm of sin, in order that Christ may come
to presence. This is, of course, another way of saying that atonement through
Christ is not made possible through virtue (as Aquinas, with qualification,
would have it), but only through sin, or rather through *accepting* one's sinfulness, and only then.

The locus of atonement here is projected, relocated, to a new "place."
Now, suddenly, works that would bring virtue do not count as righteousness,
and this raises massive questions about the status of works in the economy of salvation upon which Luther was not fearful to seize. The full implications will be
developed in a subsequent section; here I wish only to point out that on Luther's
reading, while Christ comes to presence in a realm distinct from the carnal,
from works done in "the world," this does not mean that the Christian should be
unconcerned with works. Rather, the Christian should resist the temptation to
think that righteousness and works are coincident.[30] The Christian must perform works, but should not believe that righteousness is achieved by performing
them. True (passive) righteousness cannot be attained through works.

> Since faith can rule only in the inner man . . . it is clear that the inner
> man cannot be justified, freed, or saved by any outer work or action at all,

and that these works, whatever their character, have nothing to do with the inner man.[31]

While the inner man, through faith, however, grows in the knowledge of Christ and not in the knowledge of works,[32] through this growth in the knowledge of Christ works *can* be done to the glory of God.[33] Although the active righteousness of works can lay no claim to Christian righteousness, Christian righteousness can, in effect, *sanctify* works if the righteous soul performs them.[34] Theologically, the passive aspect encompasses and supersedes the active, and not the other way around.

In this respect, there is a correspondence with Rousseau, who insists, although in a different key, that the overt, visible, dimension is less substantial than that hidden standard within. Appearances notwithstanding, the inner is always superabundant over the outer. But I will consider this position, which is the credo of all those from Plato to Augustine to Nietzsche for whom the soul must be twice born that it may come unto itself,[35] further on.

For the spiritual, passive, realm to come to presence, the Christian must overcome the propensity to remain imprisoned within the carnal, active, realm. Adjudging the spiritual realm in terms of the carnal is tantamount to construing the meaning of Christ in terms of the Law. Like the resident aliens who inhabit the cave in Plato's *Republic*, Christians must be vigilant that they not construe the world above in terms of their habitual world below. In the midst of the confusion below, where the soul is enthralled by the enticements of works, by "the world," teachers of righteousness use the *words* but are not able to grasp the thing itself because "they cling only to the righteousness of the law."[36]

The sophistry about which Plato worried is transposed here into a Christian key. Christ, who brought the message of faith, is interpreted in terms of the Law; His message, consequently, is subverted, misunderstood, violated. To avoid this confusion the two realms must be separated and "kept within their limits"[37]—an extraordinarily difficult task because in the final analysis only spirit can know the basis of its *difference* from the carnal realm. And without this knowledge, there is no antidote to words that *can* go astray, that can be *misinterpreted*. Needless to say, Luther supposes this understanding possible (though not likely) for *all* Christians or else he would not write as he does.

This egalitarian sentiment aside, however, Luther notes that the propensity to subvert the (spiritual) truth of Christ is not to be underestimated. Because of their weakness, human beings fall into the "slavery of works." Far easier it is to imagine that righteousness is attained through prescribed works than to attain a righteousness *beyond* designated activities or prohibitions.

But such is human weakness and misery that in the terrors of conscience and the danger of death we look at nothing except our own works, our worthiness, and the law. When the law shows us our sin, our past life immediately comes to our mind. Then the sinner, in his great anguish of mind, groans and says to himself: "Oh, how damnably I have lived! If only I could live longer! Then I would amend my life." Thus human reason cannot refrain from looking at active righteousness, that is, *its own righteousness;* nor can it shift its gaze to passive, that is, Christian righteousness.[38]

And elsewhere, while the spiritual man wishes to serve Christ,

> he meets a contrary will in his own flesh which strives to serve the world and seeks its own advantage.[39]

Release from this contrary will at all is possible only because God intervened in the world and wrote His new "law in our hearts."[40] The power of this contrary will to lead astray, however—its capacity to produce self-deception and errancy—is enormous. As in Augustine's search for what is "most hidden from us and yet most present amongst us,"[41] the conjunction of human errancy and Divine intervention creates an extraordinary tension in the Christian soul. The soul's virulent *denial* of what is most hidden *confirms* that it is in fact most present. Subverting the truth of Christ, here, is a kind of repression of what has been written in the heart, but which would entail a *death* of sorts were it to be allowed to emerge. Think here of Peter's betrayal . . .

Another way to understand this bifurcation in human nature and the errancy to which the soul is susceptible is to view it spatially, in terms of interiority and surface. The inner is to the carnal as interiority is to surface or exteriority.[42] Interiority is the locus of power and substance, whereas surface is vacuity and form. Those who perform works for active righteousness' sake "remain caught in the form of religion but do not attain unto its power."[43]

Words, too, as I suggested earlier, are a form of exteriority; they remain on the surface and do not capture the experience, the substance that underlies them.[44]

> All men have a *darkened heart,* so that even if they can recite everything in Scripture, and know how to quote it, they yet apprehend and truly understand nothing of it. . . . The Spirit [alone] is required for the understanding of Scripture.[45]

In addition to words, the domain of exteriority includes titles and rules—in short, *form*—which perverts the Word of God found in the New Testament. Luther argues, for example, that those with titles oppose truth with their power and cunning;[46] that knowledge of Christian faith has been supplanted by the "unbearable bondage of human works and laws";[47] and that there are "no fixed rules for interpretation of the word of God, [for the Word of God] must not be bound."[48] In each of these instances exteriority or surface misinterprets and subverts the truth of interiority, a truth it cannot comprehend. So distinct are these two from each other that Luther claims that his quarrel is not even about morals (which are external actions) but about truth, which can be found only in the interior realm of faith. [49]

The disjunction between interiority and exteriority can also be seen in the several analogies that Luther invokes. There is, for example, the model analogy. What the model or plans are to the building, so exteriority is to interiority, works are to faith. And to cite another, what the youth raised by maidens and taught by the "iron bars of ceremony" is to the adult, so is the person of works to the person of faith, bondage to freedom, the Jew to the Christian. [50] Maidens and ceremony are good for the development of the child, but must be dispensed with in adulthood. The child, though he or she can only begin from exteriority, must experience the interiority of faith as an adult.

Finally, Luther is even alarmed about the days of the week. By making many days holidays, the distinction between work days and holy days breaks down. [51] The canonization of the saints and the feasts and notoriety that surround them do not serve the glory of God. Here,

> spiritual treasures have even been misused . . . so that everything, even God Himself, has been forced into the service of Avarice. [52]

The Pope takes away the gifts that God gives freely and gives his own gifts which the Christian must buy. [53] Intending to mediate between Christian and God, the Roman Church inadvertently desanctifies the spiritual domain; it destroys the distinctions it is charged with upholding and illuminating.

TESTAMENT FOR EACH REALM, AND THE DIALECTICAL MEDIATION BETWEEN THEM

I have so far considered the several antinomies that Luther invokes to distinguish between the two realms: spiritual-carnal, passive-active, interiority-surface. The first of each of these pairs corresponds to the "Christian moment," the second to the "pre-Christian moment." Because the dialectical nature of Christianity entails that the Christian moment is already latent in the pre-Christian moment—that the Gospel is already *there* in the Law—this is an oversimplification that borders on distortion, I recognize. Precisely how this is so will be considered shortly. First, however, it should be recalled that Luther insisted that Christians be vigilant, that they be keenly watchful and not fall prey to an Old Testament reading of Christ. An Old Testament reading, which presents the relationship of God (the Father) to humankind in carnal, active, surface form, cannot comprehend the *new* relationship of God (the Son) to humankind announced in the New Testament, which presents that same relationship in terms of spirituality, passivity, and interiority. The positive danger is that the truth of Christ will be confounded without recognizing the utter *difference* between these two understandings. Citing scripture, [54] Luther notes that when the Jews asked Christ how to do works for God, he responded simply that they should "believe in him who was sent."[55] Conceiving only of their relationship to God through works, they tried to understand Christ in terms of the Old dispensation, rather than in terms of the New—and they were confounded.

Considerable caution must be observed, as I have just said, however, in claiming this direct and unwavering correspondence between realm and Testament. Although Luther claims that

> the Old Testament is a book of laws, which teaches what men are to do and not to do . . . [while] the New Testament is Gospel or book of grace, and teaches where one is to get the power to fulfill the law,[56]

he is not, nor could he be, unequivocal.

> In the Old Testament too there are, besides the law, certain promises and words of grace, by which the holy fathers and prophets under the law were kept, like us, in the faith of Christ.[57]

The Law-Gospel distinction is, of course, crucial for Luther, but his was a dialectical understanding of the relationship between the Law and the Gospel and so (as in any dialectical relationship) the Old must portend the New—it must anticipate, contain in germinal form, the Gospel that is to supersede it. The story of Abraham, for example, while found in the Old Testament, is the kernel of faith, which only becomes fully *what it is* upon the arrival of Christ. Contained in the Old Book are elements of the Gospel that are unconcealed only through Christ.[58]

The paradoxical position that must be adopted, then, is that the two realms are *utterly* different, that each corresponds to a Testament, *and* that the Old portends what is later accomplished in the New and so is not only not *radically* separable from the New but is in some sense *identical* with the New. The relationship is one of identity *and* difference.

This dialectical relationship, in which anticipation, difference, and identity are present, is best seen in Luther's understanding of the paradigmatic instance of the Law: Moses' receipt of God's commandments—the original, compact, event that establishes the Old truth and presages the New.

As in Hegel's original undifferentiated compactness of *Geist* in the *Phenomenology*, Moses' receipt of God's commandments both is and is not yet fully itself. The New here is foreshadowed, as the negation of an affirmation is presaged in any dialectical movement.[59]

Commandments from God have a double effect. First, although they *cannot* produce salvation, they are necessary for the unrighteous, who would not abstain from sin without "the [fear] of the sword and of the executioner."[60] This is, for Luther, the *first* use of the Law.[61] Because most human beings are unrighteous, there is a need for the Law. I will speak about this in greater detail in the section on temporal authority.

Second, Law can direct the human being beyond the realm of works to a place where the spiritual journey can begin.

> [Commandments] are intended to teach man to know himself, that through them he may recognize his inability to do good and may despair of his own ability.[62]

Or to put it more starkly, the law leads "us to hell and not . . . back again."[63] This second use of the Law is the bridge, as it were, between the two Testaments: between works and faith, between exteriority and interiority, between commandments and promises; it mutely announces the *insufficiency* of the Law in the very event that constitutes it.[64] Here in the archetypal instance of that message the fulfillment that is offered by the New Testament is foreshadowed, as the negation of an affirmation is presaged in any dialectical movement.

In his commentary on the Israelites at Mount Sinai, who dared not hear the Word of God directly[65] even after they had been cleansed in ceremony,[66] Luther suggests that when confronted with God (pure Spirit) the flesh is mortified. Even proper ceremonies, obedience, and works—in short, active, exterior righteousness—cannot prepare the human being for the encounter with God. The light of God, *which reveals to them their sinfulness*, frightened the Israelites, whereupon they implored Moses alone to be their representative before God. The Law of God is the light that reveals the sins of the hearer of the Law.[67]

Here in the narrative surrounding Moses' reception of God's commandments (the very core of the Old Testament) the Law is already present in its twofold form, disclosing to the people of Israel both the Law that is meant to bind the actively righteous and the interiority that the Law reveals when faced with the very presence of God, which interiority had to wait for the coming of Christ before its full meaning could be revealed.

Moses thus represents the message of the Old Testament most completely and foreshadows the message of the New Testament articulated through Christ. This foreshadowing, however, does not obscure the fact that the message of Moses was works, whereas Christ's message was faith and the promise of salvation from sin.[68]

Although the dialectic relationship between the Old and the New Testament is presaged in the narrative surrounding Moses' receipt of God's commandments, the relationship is confirmed, retrospectively, by virtue of the parallels between God's first-born and the first-born of the Old Testament; between the first-born of the Spirit and the first-born of the flesh. Here the attributes of the first-born of the Old Testament are transposed and achieve their true (spiritual) meaning in the attributes of Christ, attributes which can, through faith, become the possession of the Christian.

The first-born of the Old Testament, for example, was "a type of Christ,"[69] lord and priest over the rest; God's first-born, too, was lord and priest over the rest. Like an earthly king, Christ and the Christian are "exalted above all things

. . . so that nothing can do him harm."[70] But unlike the earthly king who has physical power over all things, Christ and the Christian do not stand *against* other powers as does the earthly king. The New dispensation provides a new kind of power, spiritual power, that parallels physical power but is not explicable in its terms. As nature cannot comprehend spirit, so, too, physical power cannot comprehend spiritual power, nor can the human being for whom God discloses Himself through commandments comprehend the God who discloses Himself through the promise of atonement in Christ. Commandments are to the first-born of earthly kings as the promise is to the first-born of God.

The parallels between the Old and New Testaments and the foreshadowing of interiority disclosed in Moses' receipt of God's commandments establish a plausible linkage between the two Testaments by at once distinguishing the predominant message of each Testament (works vs. faith) and by showing how in the kernel of the message of the Old is the seed of the New. Through these, however, the interiority of spirit that coincides with the promise (largely) of the New Testament is not yet grasped. To do this it is necessary to look more closely at the powerlessness that is the precondition of the coming to presence of Christ. Only through powerlessness is the interiority of spirit revealed.

POWERLESSNESS AND THE COMING TO PRESENCE OF CHRIST

The troubled conscience—whose true home is the interiority of the spiritual realm—cannot be appeased by dwelling on the surface, that is, by works or by the Law.[71] It must find its respite in the interiority in which it may truly dwell,[72] in the Christian righteousness that is attained only through faith.

In Hegel's estimation this insight was a portentous one which signaled a grasping of the truth of Christianity that the Catholic Church was incapable of. Above all, what was necessary was that "a brokenness of the heart [be] experienced, and that Divine Grace [enter] into the heart thus broken."[73] Theologically, what was necessary was that the Christian *reenact* Christ's suffering, fall into the abyss, into "Hell," as Christ did when He died to the "world." The "world," of course, is the everydayness with which the soul is perpetually occupied in its efforts to be *actively* righteous. This (external) world, again, the Christian must die to. In Luther's words,

> It is evident that no external thing has any influence in producing Christian righteousness or freedom, or in producing unrighteousness or servitude. . . . None of these things touch either the freedom or servitude of the soul.[74]

The faith that produces such righteousness and quells the troubled conscience comes only when the word of God is heard within the realm of interiority; that is to say, when, in Luther's words, Christ is "for you and me," when

He is "effectual in us."[75] The Christ who is encountered as an *historical fact*, as an object of historical knowledge, possesses the kind of exteriority that characterizes the nonspiritual, surface realm of the carnal; this Christ cannot be an object of faith.[76] Faith *is* only underneath the everydayness of factual history and inauthenticity—if I may invoke somewhat Heideggerian language.

The Christ who is "for us" is encountered only when Christians turn away from works or, more correctly, when, in attempting to obey the commandments of God regarding works, they realize that they *cannot* accomplish what He wills.[77] In this abyss of despair the interiority of the spiritual realm comes to presence for the Christian. Only at this point does the second portion of the Scripture speak: the promise of the New Testament. In this abyss the Christian is "truly humbled and reduced to nothing in his own eyes,"[78] and dwells far from works and commandments—from exteriority and the trappings of physical power possessed by earthly kings. Here, humbled by the Law, realizing that "he cannot find any means to be delivered from his sin by his own strength"[79] and that the world—the whole of the carnal realm—is guilty before God, the Christian experiences utter powerlessness.

This *experience* is the precondition for the "appearance" of Christ *for us*, an appearance which occurs only when the Christian is in another "world," far from disputes about works. *Only then* do we hear "the Gospel . . . that Christ died for us";[80] for *this* Gospel can only be grasped "with other eyes [than] carnal reason doth [have]."[81] Theologically, before Christians may come unto Spirit, they must, like Christ, experience the abandonment of God that is in the call, "My God, my God, why hast thou forsaken me?"[82] It is in this depth of abandonment that Christ appears. In Hegelian terms, the synthesis (Spirit) is brought about only by the negation (falling into the abyss) of the thesis (works and active righteousness). The dark brooding anticipation of each transition in the *Phenomenology* is the equivalent of this standing-before-the-abyss, which must be endured in order for spirit to come to presence.

For Luther, when Christ appears *for us*, He "swallows up" sin.[83] Here sin is abrogated, taken in by the Byss of Christ,[84] who provides the Infinite Ground underneath the abyss that utter self-condemnation occasions. In this abrogation powerlessness is linked through Christ with the omnipotence of God, a condition which gives rise to the great paradox of Christian faith: "power is made perfect in weakness."[85] Through a marriage with Christ[86] the weakness of the bride is taken in in its entirety by the bridegroom. The perfection of the bridegroom (Christ), who fought a "mighty duel" and conquered both hell and death, is, through faith in this moment of powerlessness, given over to the Christian.[87] In weakness and powerlessness the sin which utterly condemns the Christian is swallowed up by the Divinity; and this act of Christ's taking sin in upon Himself imputes a penultimate perfection back to the Christian in virtue of his or her marriage with Him.[88] Here the Christian reenacts the drama of suffering (sin) and descent into hell (the abyss) which Christ endured and over-came, and, through a marriage with Christ, overcomes them through Him. Thus, Luther is able to assert,

> [the] cross and death itself are compelled to serve me and to work together with me for my salvation.[89]

And elsewhere,

> [when you know sin] you will know you need Christ, who suffered and rose again for you . . . so that you may through faith become a new man [by being] justified by the merits of another.[90]

In the Byss of Christ the powerless Christian achieves a penultimate perfec-tion. He or she attains a stature like Christ, that is, above the Law and sin—indeed, above the whole world.[91] In powerlessness the Christian attains a power over all things.

> God our father has made all things depend on faith so that whoever has faith will have everything, and whoever does not have faith will have nothing.[92]

In possessing this "everything" which is "no-thing," the Christian attains his or her true and complete freedom,[93] a freedom which is to be distinguished from the freedom possessed by earthly kings who wield power. Christian free-dom, in contradistinction to that of kings, avails itself only in powerlessness, through an abrogation of power in the midst of the abyss which perfects and liberates.

THE PARADOX OF PERFECTION AND SIN:
UNDER THE COVER OF GOD THE SON

The relationship between *willing* (the will of God and failing) and *knowing* (the abyss into which one must fall in order to encounter Christ) has not been ex-hausted by my remarks above. My intention has been merely to outline the broad contours of the journey of the soul into the abyss and its embrace in the Byss of Christ, the *experience* of which purports to be the *only* possible validation of a faith that leaps over reason—which brings "death to reason, God's bitterest enemy."[94] A more comprehensive treatment would demonstrate the extraordi-nary tension and self-reflectivity that must attend this sojourn. Here, however, I will turn briefly to a related matter: the paradoxical coincidence of this perfec-tion and power in Christ with human carnality in this present moment of history.

In the abyss there is perfection and powerlessness, but it is not complete, nor can it be. Because human beings are of the flesh, there are "remnants" of sin which cannot be erased. These remnants are an aspect of human nature in this historical moment before the Redemption. Consequently, the perfection attained in the Byss of Christ is a provisional victory over the carnal realm which, in effect, forever *returns* merely mortal human beings to their carnal nature. The immediacy of *temptation* vitiates perfection immediately. What recompense atones for this virtual impossibility of righteousness?

> So long as I go on living in the flesh, there is certainly flesh in me. But meanwhile Christ protects me under the shadow of His wings and spreads over me the wide heaven of forgiveness of sins, under which I live in safety. *This prevents God from seeing the sins that still cling to my flesh.* [95]

Not surprisingly, the model for this imputation, for this gift of God the Son (who would hide the sins of humanity from God the Father), is found in the Old Testament—in Abraham, who anticipates the faith of the righteous under Christ.[96] Like Moses, too, who shielded the Israelites from God lest they die nakedly exposed in their sin,[97] God the Son intercedes so that the Father will not see the sin of the Christian. This not-seeing of imperfection *is* forgiveness; through it Christian faith is supplemented by Divine imputation and righteousness becomes possible, notwithstanding sin. In this moment of history, then, there is a constant battle inside each Christian between the spirit and the flesh,[98] a battle which human effort alone cannot assuage.

That the faith of the Christian is not sufficient to complete righteousness and attain salvation evinces Luther's decidedly non-Pelagian theological position.[99] The Christian can will to act in accordance with God's will (His commandments), but *always* fails in this attempt because he or she is of the flesh. It is precisely in this failing to act in the way the Christian wills to act that the abyss in which Christ swallows up this sin appears. Through the Christian's *inability* to freely will his or her salvation, true Christian liberty appears.[100] Through non-freedom comes true freedom. Likewise, were there to be truly free will, the abyss would not yawn, Christ would not appear, and salvation would not be possible.[101] Through freedom would come oblivion—a paradox about which Augustine is insistent when he speaks of the insufficiency and dependence of the created upon the Creator.[102]

It should be added that while the philosophical "problem of free will" does not arise in the Old Testament, it is *there* in representational form in the Genesis account of God's covenant with Abraham. Sarah, Abraham's wife, is barren;[103] and it is only through God's intercession that she is able to be the "mother of nations."[104] The meaning of Sarah's barren womb is clear: she represents humankind, which cannot become fecund without God. All its efforts come to naught if undertaken without God's assistance. In a perverse twist of logic, Nietzsche would agree: the God of biblical religion *did* cause the contemporary illness/pregnancy,[105] though not in the way proffered in the Old Testament or insinuated in the New!

Hardening of the Will, Providence, and the Ground of History

The yawning abyss into which one must fall is *concealed* from the human being that would insist upon its radical freedom, and, consequently, from the person who would oppose the Providential designs of God in history—from the soul that would insist that it *creates* its forward movement, its history. This is hubris of the worst sort.

> No man's plans have ever been straightforwardly realized . . . for everyone things have turned out differently from what he thought they would.[106]

The unforeseen—that which no plan can plan against—is nothing less than evidence of God's will working through all apparent contingency, sometimes with and sometimes against the will of His servants.

Human beings do, of course, participate freely in this Providential design, not by *creating* history, but by (freely) yielding to God's will or (freely) resisting it. The task of the Christian in history is not to discover God's immutable will—that is, what the course of history will be—or to create history,[107] but to discover the *interiority* that historical existence portends. Not the exteriority of the movement of history, but the interiority of the realm of true freedom is the purview of the Christian. To attempt anything other than this only confirms the *superbia* of reason. Christians are given the Word of God, with its promises of salvation through Christ, not the freedom to create history.

> It is our business, however, to pay attention to the Word and leave that inscrutable will alone, for we must be guided by that Word, and not by that inscrutable will.[108]

In freely resisting the will of God, in proceeding with plans irrespective of evidence that they have been confuted by the movement of events, the interiority of history is foreclosed and the will is "hardened."

> They become all the more averse and are made much worse when their aversion is resisted and thwarted. So it was when God proposed to wrest ungodly Pharaoh's tyranny from him.[109]

This movement away from, or against, the course of history preordained by God, who "keeps on presenting and obtruding His words and works from without,"[110] *increases* the opposition of the will that purports to be sufficient unto itself, the consequence of which is that this will that will not submit "cannot help [but hate] what is opposed to [it] and [trust further to its] own strength."[111]

And, because the inscrutable Will of God *is good,* persistent opposition to that Will increasingly takes on the character of evil.

> Free choice can do nothing but evil . . . and when confronted with a good that is contrary to it, can only become worse.[112]

The future is, as it were, a *Holzwege,* a woodpath into the darkness undiscernible to human reason;[113] without a willingness to reverentially defer to the Inscrutable Will working through history, the finite human will "absolutizes" itself, conceives of itself as sufficient unto itself, and would oppose what it encounters with a ferocity proportional to the magnitude of the opposition it receives. Like earthly kings, this will would prevail only by confronting power *with* power. Foreclosed in this confrontation is the abyss of powerlessness that is unconcealed with the self-confession that the will cannot, of its own accord, will to do good. Pelagius's position obstructs the entrance to the abyss and forecloses the interiority that history portends.

The *Ultimate* Victory of Justice and the Mystery of Evil

Hardening of the will manifests itself as evil in the world. This manifestation delays but does not prevent the triumph of justice, for the finite will is *eventually* swallowed up by the infinite will. Here evil does not confirm God's absence, but rather His awesome inscrutable presence. Evil redoubles faith in the goodness and justice of God that He *could* overcome such evil.[114] The grandeur of His goodness always exceeds the evil made manifest.

While an account of how evil is overcome by the infinite goodness of God may deepen faith, however, it in no way answers the question of why evil should exist at all. True, deep faith of this sort is (alone) capable of dispelling the belief in the freedom of the will, and by disposing of this virulent strain of Christian doctrine the path to the abyss is left open, and Christian righteousness is again made possible. But while this may avert the Christian from taking the path into oblivion, but it does not put the matter to rest.

For if God bestows grace to Christians living amidst the vicissitudes and evils of historical existence, the question arises why God should allow such evil in the first place, for here the attainment of righteousness by the Christian *requires* the prospect if not actuality of errancy. Is the loss of any number of evil souls that may coincide with the retrieval of even one soul unto complete Christian righteousness just? Why God should allow such errancy and loss is beyond comprehension. Notwithstanding the importance of God's ultimate victory over evil, and notwithstanding even its salutary effect, that evil should be present at all would seem to be absurd.

To the matter of God's ordination of some to righteousness and the condemnation of others to oblivion, Luther's answer is scriptural: that God does not alter those with an evil will is a matter shrouded in mystery; the valence of evil is transposed from absurdity to mystery by faith in the Word.

> If the flesh and blood is offended here, and murmurs, by all means let it murmur; but it will achieve nothing; God will not change on that account. And if the ungodly are scandalized and depart in great numbers, yet the elect will remain. [115]

This answer is not meant to be a subterfuge. It accords with Luther's claim that the Word of God, not the will of God, is the possession of the Christian. It is, furthermore, consistent with Luther's view of the structure of biblical history, which can now be considered more fully.

THE STRUCTURE OF BIBLICAL HISTORY

The outline of a structure of history has already been suggested by the relationship between the Old and New Testaments. The New annuls the Old, and the interior, spiritual realm (while intimated in the Moses narrative and elsewhere) is unconcealed only through Christ. Without further qualification this would suggest a structure of history that is twofold: a carnal moment and a spiritual moment, with the former preceding the latter, and the former containing the seed of the latter. [116]

This picture is complicated, however, by the fact that while Christians attain a foothold in the spiritual realm through Christ, they do not become *as* God. Christians retain a "remnant of sin" because they still possess a carnal body. The *absence* of freedom is forever and the only path to deliverance to the spiritual realm, it is true, but this constitutional absence of freedom also indicates a de facto rupture between God and humankind. Notwithstanding the righteousness attained through Christ, the Christian *remains* finite. Predestination and evil: these mysteries stagger the mind precisely because the finitude of human freedom cannot arrest their course, as only God could. In the Lutheran world Christians partially attain the treasures of the spiritual realm but do not themselves become as God. [117]

The second, penultimate spiritual moment, consequently, remains shrouded in mystery despite the depth of soul attained by the Christian. Christ and the truth of the New Testament *deepen* the Christian, but fundamental mystery still abounds. The guide, in the midst of this mystery, can only be the Word—which will finally speak again at the end of history, at the moment of Revelation. This is the third and last moment in the structure of history, one necessitated by the limitations of the second. In this final light, the mystery of God will be illuminated.

There are, then, three lights that illuminate: the first corresponds to the Old Testament, the second to the New, and the third to the moment of Revelation. The first light is the light of nature, the carnal realm in which suffering and injustice are incomprehensible. These are unsuccessfully treated as matters of offense against God. Right conduct, works, and obedience to the Law, however, fail to ameliorate them. By the light of grace (disclosed in the New Testament but already intimated in the Old) suffering and injustice become comprehensible. Here it becomes clear that God deplores not the death *of* his people, but the death *in* his people.[118] Suffering and injustice per se have no significance unless they are linked to a spiritual journey within. By enduring these hardships without opposing the inscrutable Will of God, Christians attain a *foothold* in the spiritual realm. Finally, by the light of glory the mystery of the God who has only partially revealed Himself to Christians through His Word is illuminated. Here the mystery of evil in the world becomes comprehensible for the first time. And, because this light has yet to shine, Christians have only to believe in the inscrutable justice of God insofar as it has been disclosed by His Word in the two Testaments.[119]

Each successive light, or moment of history, cannot be comprehended by the former. I have already alluded to Luther's claims that nature (the realm of works and obedience to the Law) cannot comprehend spirit (the realm of faith) and that the "terrors of conscience" animate the Christian to seek refuge in works.[120] When confronted by the higher, spiritual realm—and the terror of conscience is just such a confrontation—Christians gravitate to the lower, natural realm. Hence, Luther's unremitting attempt to battle against the tendency to fall into nature and into the perverse interpretation of the New Testament that such a fall occasions. Because Christians live in the second moment of history, and await the third, they are obliged not to live in accordance with the principles of the first.

TEMPORAL AUTHORITY AND THE GROUND OF SOCIALITY

The political implications of the inability of the carnal realm to comprehend the spiritual realm, that "secret, hidden, spiritual matter,"[121] are vast. Physical power, the very medium of politics, cannot in principle, and ought not to in practice, be used to confront the believer. Consequently, heresy can never be prevented by force.[122] Worldly government extends to life and property, but over the soul it holds no sway. Belief and unbelief are matters of conscience, not power.[123] That this arrangement should not at this moment obtain is due, not to a defect in the order of things, but rather to the fact that the carnal and the spiritual realms have been so confused *by humankind* that bishops rule over cities while lords rule over the human souls.[124] While the government that *does* rule over human souls is an invisible Christian government where "all are alike subject to each other,"[125] because the great majority of human beings will never be Christian, the invisible government that ministers to Christian souls must be supplemented by a visible government that produces peace among the unrighteous.

Luther's dialectic understanding of the relationship between the two Testaments is clearly in evidence in his thoughts on the two kinds of government. Where earthly kingship was authorized by God in the Old Testament, and given to the children of this world that there may be order, it is *not* abolished by Christ. It still applies for the unrighteous. The fulfillment that Christ offers pertains to Christians only. The sword remains—necessary for the unrighteous and justified by "divine right."[126] God the Father authorizes rule over the unrighteous with unwavering severity; God the Son rules the righteous in love. While politics and faith must clearly be separate, the political realm is decidedly *not* disenchanted. Rather, each realm (politics and faith) coincides with separable moments of the Triune God. Luther's dialectic of biblical history, as I mentioned earlier, does not disenchant the world; rather, the world is enchanted in a different manner from the Roman Church. The two realms are separable, yet dialectically related, as God the Son is dialectically related to God the Father. The Son fulfills the rule of the Father; He does not overturn it.

The inverse arrangement, however, where the spiritual usurps control of the carnal realm, is calamitous. This abolishes the distinction between the two realms that must be retained. Where the distinction is effaced and the spiritual is allowed to dominate the carnal, the result is always evil.

> Where the spiritual government alone prevails over land and people, there wickedness is given free reign and the door is opened for all manner of rascality, for the world as a whole cannot receive or comprehend it.[127]

And elsewhere,

> I say therefore that since the temporal power is ordained of God to punish the wicked and to protect the good, it should be left free to perform its office, in the whole body of Christendom without restriction and without respect to persons, whether it affects pope, bishops, priests, monks, nuns or anyone else.[128]

The work of temporal authorities is one thing, that of the spiritual kingdom another. When temporal authorities are free to take care of their affairs, obstacles to salvation are removed; when the Church has no say in secular matters, the work of this world is left to those most able and authorized to perform it. Separate the two realms and both operate without doing violence to the other.

There is an ancillary consideration as well. The pattern of social relations that recapitulates the rule of the spiritual realm *over* the carnal is hierarchical. While Luther's contempt for the Roman Church cannot be fully disentangled from his wish that *German* Christendom not be held captive by Rome, it is also clear that in principle the hierarchical system of social order that is patterned by the Church's understanding of the relationship between the orders of reality deeply offended Luther's sensibilities. What distinguishes Christians from one another is the work they do, and even this difference is almost superficial. It is a convention. There is no spiritual superiority of the priest over the farmer.[129] That the priest may possess certain capabilities (even virtues) that the farmer lacks does not make the one more important, dignified, or worthy of respect than the other. Christian righteousness *levels all difference*. The eyes of the spiritual government do not look at capability, virtue, or station. In *this* kingdom all are equal. Whatever essential difference there is in the Christian kingdom is not *among* Christians, but *between* Christ and *all* Christians.[130] Hierarchy, where it exists, is conventional, not fixed in the order of things. For Christians, hierarchical distinctions must give way to the only distinction of any gravity: that between Christ and humankind. *Lateral* relationships between human beings (*coram hominibus*) are subservient and secondary to the *vertical* relationship between Christ and the Christian (*coram Deo*). No hierarchical social order meant to portend the analogical relationship between the orders of reality can convey the truth of this direct relationship between humankind and the Divine.

THE CHRISTIAN PRINCE

Following the line of reasoning developed above, the very idea of a Christian prince would be problematic. The prince rules by the authority of God the Father. Indeed the suspicion is not easily overcome that the wrath of the prince *ought* to reiterate the wrath of the Father, for only by drawing upon it can the almost Nietzschean beast within be constrained at all.

> If anyone attempted to rule the world by the Gospel and abolish all temporal law and sword . . . he would be loosing the ropes and chains of the wild savage beast and letting them bite and mangle everyone.[131]

Christians will never be numerous; rulership by the Son can never restrain the world; the idea of a Christian prince is no less farfetched than that of a philosopher king! Though it would be the best form of government, the prospect of its instantiation is remote. As in Rousseau, the *way* will never capture the world!

In "Temporal Authority" Luther is, to be sure, more circumspect about the likelihood that a Christian prince would come forth, but this was a sober lesson learned only after the publication of his "Christian Nobility" two years earlier (1520), which did not have the result he intended. There he details a view of the Christian prince which is extraordinary in that it holds together the seemingly contradictory demand of being a Christian and of being a prince.

To understand the difficulty, it need only be noted that Christian princes must be instances in which (political) power and (Christian) powerlessness coalesce. The Christian prince must dwell in both realms because he is a Christian *and* a prince.[132] When Luther appeals to Christian princes, therefore, to liberate the German Christians who "are oppressed by distress and affliction,"[133] he is asking them to exercise their power in a way that accords with the spiritual realm that comes to presence only in the abyss of powerlessness and the denial of "the world." In the Christian prince, that locus of the extraordinary conflation of the two realms, is to be found a release from the burdens on German Christianity.

First and foremost, because physical power (of the sort possessed by earthly kings) can only be used to oppose, great evil will result if only this form of power is relied upon. The prince cannot *simply* oppose; such opposition is the way of "the world," not of spirit. We must not use our own power to oppose the Church, for

> the more force we use, the greater our disaster if we do not act humbly and in fear of God.[134]

Humility and fear, of course, act to arrest pride before the person it dominates gets lost in the temptations of "the world." But power, with all its temptations, must be exercised nonetheless, for physical power is needed to oppose the equally physical power exercised by the Roman Church over the German states.

This may seem like a trivial matter to the modern ear, yet it was not to Luther; the prince who relied only on the physical power at *his* own disposal was bound to lose sight of the *Source* of all power and so suffer hubris which would foreclose an encounter with the Byss of Christ that alone could make him a *Christian* prince. The Weberian definition of political power as "the monopoly of the legitimate use of physical force within a given territory"[135] may seem axiomatic today, but the idea would have seemed ludicrous to Luther. For Luther, the Weberian view could only countenance hubris; it is un-Christian. To which Weber would emphatically say, "Yes"!

The intractability of this situation is resolved by enjoining princes to rely on the power of God and not their own power to oppose the oppressors—much as Abraham had to trust that God would make Sarah's barren womb fecund.

> We must not start something by trusting in great power or human reason, even if all the power in the world were ours. For God cannot and will not suffer a good work to begin by relying upon one's own power and reason.[136]

The power to be used *in* the world to oppose the forces of injustice must come from beyond it; the foreign threat can be averted only with God's assistance. Defense against "the rapacious wolves who come dressed in sheep's clothing"[137] requires that they be lambs possessed of God's strength.

In domestic affairs, too, there is need of God's assistance. The Christian prince must act in a manner befitting both an earthly king and a Christian subject of the spiritual government above.[138] This is not to say that the prince is to deny himself the exercise of power; rather, that the *use* to which such power is put is informed by the prince's experience *as a Christian*. He is not powerless toward his subjects, but the abyss of powerlessness he experiences *as a Christian* discloses his true relationship with his subjects and, presumably, the boundaries beyond which in the use of his power he cannot transgress.

The pattern of Christ's relationship to the Christian, as well as the archetypal narratives elsewhere in the two Testaments, orient the prince, provide a "pattern set up in the heavens," as it were, by which he may chart a course that neither violates his charge nor naively disregards the ways of the world.

Because God once spoke as an ass, for example, the prince must respect people of even the lowest station. But because God's highest angel fell, the prince must trust no one. [139] Christian subjects, Luther enjoins, are both Christian and subjects. In their latter capacity they occasionally conspire to acquire the power of earthly kings. Respect and distrust go hand in hand—all this, from the *Word*.

Where the need for respect and distrust have scriptural support, however, the actual laws instituted by Christian princes do not. The *right* of making law is justified by the Word of God, it is true, but the *content* of such laws is not to be found in Scripture itself. The laws, simply put, cannot be bound if they are to emanate from God. To bind them is to ossify and harden them and to misconstrue their Source, which cannot be bound.

> We should keep written laws subject to reason, whence indeed they have welled as from the spring of justice, and not make the spring dependent on its rivulets, nor make reason captive to the letter. [140]

And elsewhere,

> I know of no law to prescribe for a prince, but will simply instruct him what the *attitude of his heart and mind ought to be* with respect to all laws . . . so that if he governs himself thereby, God will surely grant him the power to carry out all laws . . . in a proper and Godly way. [141]

The laws of the Christian prince, then, are not simply his own. They issue from his person but are occasioned by God acting through him. In this, finite law is not a recipe for righteousness, but rather an expression guided by God of the right relationship among all Christians.

> A prince should in his heart empty himself of his power and authority, and take unto himself the needs of his subjects, dealing with them as though they were his own needs. For this is what Christ did for us; and these are the proper works of Christian love. [142]

The *derivative* quality of sociality cannot be overlooked, though this is not at all to dismiss it as insignificant. Christian righteousness is a matter between the human being and God; yet as a consequence *of* this relationship, of this marriage with Christ, the foundation of sociality is revealed. Christians cannot have a genuine affiliation with others without the assistance of Christ. [143] Only through a marriage between a single Christian and Christ—where no others are

involved—can this happen. The obligations, if any, that bind one human being to another derive from the relationship between the individual Christian
and Christ; they are not coincident with or constituted by it.[144]

Marriage with Christ, then, is the basis of sociality. The Commandments
of God do not provide such a foundation, except perhaps negatively. That is, in
the *failure* to carry them out the Christian finds the ground of sociality through
Christ. Again, not Commandments, but powerlessness (and the pattern set
forth by Christ which reveals itself fully in that powerlessness) is the basis of
Christian sociality. This is simply another way of saying that the Commandments have no other foundation than in Christ.[145] Through a marriage with
Christ that excludes all others, the Christian is able to (indeed must) include all
others; the pattern established by the bridegroom (Christ) is reproduced in the
bride's (the Christian's) relationship to all others.

> As our heavenly Father has in Christ freely come to our aid, we also ought
> freely to help our neighbor through our body and works, and each should
> become as it were a Christ to the other that we may be Christs to one
> another and Christ may be the same in all, that is, that we may be truly
> Christian.[146]

The marriage with Christ provides the basis for the twin orientation that is the
possession of the Christian: on the one hand, toward the Divine; on the other
hand, toward all others. By "reduc[ing] himself to nothing in his own eyes,"[147]
the Christian is negated and finds the basis for a relationship with others.[148]

> A Christian lives not in himself, but in Christ and his neighbor . . . he
> lives in Christ through faith, in his neighbor through love. By faith he is
> caught up beyond himself unto God. By love he descends beneath himself
> unto his neighbor.[149]

The orientation toward the neighbor made possible through Christ, and
thus through the powerlessness of the Christian, requires of the Christian that
he or she not be powerless with respect to the neighbor, however. With regard
to self, the Christian must be powerless; with regard to the neighbor, the Christian must punish the enemy who harms. Although you do not need the secular
sword and the law

> and are not to have them, [you are] to serve those who have not progressed
> as far as you and still need them. Although you do not need to have your
> enemy punished your weak neighbor does.[150]

This twin orientation possessed by the Christian suggests that carnal life
has a twofold purpose. First, as I have noted repeatedly, it is to be used as a
stepping stone to the spiritual realm—Luther's second use of the Law. Second,
it is an occasion for reproducing the pattern established by Christ in the relationship with the neighbor. And it is in the context of this reproduction, which

is the fruit *of* righteousness, not the occasion *for* it, that the Christian is the servant to all. Submitting to the law that makes social life possible, the Christian "labors on earth not for himself but for his neighbor."[151] Here, finally, the meaning of Luther's paradox, cited at the outset, is clarified.

> A Christian is a perfectly free lord of all, subject to none. A Christian is a perfectly dutiful servant to all, subject to all.[152]

Through Christ, Christians encounter the ground of their freedom from, and supersession over, the carnal realm; they attain a freedom from all *things*, that is, everything carnal. Here, Christians reproduce the pattern established by Christ and, like Him, become a servant to all. They depart from the carnal world to return to it grounded in the spiritual realm which provides the wherewithal for their authentic return.[153]

CONCLUDING REMARKS

Dialectical thinking is a perilous undertaking; it demands an assent to an identity that both is and is not what it was. Far more difficult to comprehend than either/or is both/and. More than anything else, this accounts for the instability of Luther's thought. Luther's syncretic effort can be undercut because of the comparative ease with which the antinomies he announces could *remain* sundered in thought rather than be unified in experience. Hegel recognized this problem, in his own way, in "The Spirit of Christianity," when he discussed the immense gap between (fragmentary) thought under the Law (Hegel includes Kant here) and the unity of human being in Divine love. As *mere thought*, Luther's conclusions are extraordinarily unstable.

Posed with a picture of a carnal realm in which the soul is exiled from the interiority through which it attains the precious certainty of eternal peace,[154] Luther's vision is severe in its contrasts and unwavering in its allegiance. Although fundamental mystery remains for the Christian who dwells in the interim before the final Revelation, the spiritual homeland of the soul has no rival. Neither the incomprehensibility of predestination nor the apparent absurdity of evil countervails the promise of salvation by the God who is only partially revealed in this present moment of history.

The Old Law does speak to Luther's Christian, to be sure, but only insofar as it speaks *beyond itself* and of the spiritual realm. It is valuable only in superseding itself. The Law, like the "iron bars of ceremony,"[155] is useful only to the child. And like everything in childhood, it assists fully only when it is outgrown. Here, the adult comes to know God when he or she grows beyond the childish Law.[156] But while the adult is the goal, the goal cannot be reached without *first* being a child; childhood *must* be passed through—ironically, the same lesson Rousseau would later insist upon in *Emile*.[157] What cannot be overemphasized is the need to be a child first, then an adult.

The volatility of this formulation cannot go unnoticed. The child can and must be the father of the adult, but the adult without this child-father can only father bad infinity, hubris, pride, and the like. Dialectic draws the soul along upon the former path; absent this, there is only the oblivion of false faith.

Hobbes's explication of a psychology in which all knowledge derives from the senses[158] must be understood, I think, as an effort to disarm those who would fall into false faith, for in Hobbes's psychology the carnal, physical realm alone is real and all else is apparition or bad digestion. The Leviathan, it must be remembered, is the king of the children of pride. Given Luther's identification of children with the Law and adults with saving faith, it should be no surprise that Hobbes would find greater comfort in identifying human beings as children under the Leviathan rather than as adults under Christ. *Luther's* adults may enter the abyss of powerlessness and the subsequent marriage with Christ once they have outgrown childhood:

> Wherefore the law was our schoolmaster *to bring us* unto Christ, that we might be justified by faith. But after that faith is come, we are no longer under a schoolmaster.[159]

Hobbes's adults, however, are not so gifted; they merely attain a level of hubris unparalleled in children—and it was this hubris that he sought to counter. Hobbes saw only the fruits of the abuse of Christian righteousness, of the faith that falls too easily into pride. His materialist psychology was a rejoinder to it.

Materialistic psychology alone, however, would not be sufficient. What was really necessary was a comprehensive reformulation of the dialectic of biblical history which formulated the meaning of the fulfillment of Christ so that it solved (Hobbes) or dissolved (Locke) the problem of pride, gave greater weight to the Old Testament from which political authority emanated, and provided a theoretically coherent account of political sovereignty.

The key used to unlock these difficulties was to be found in attending to the question of the meaning of the fulfillment purported to be offered by Christ. To dispel the political volatility that surrounded Luther's reading of the supersession of the New over the Old, it was necessary for Christian thought to take the Old Testament *more seriously.* Hobbes and Locke, in their own way, do this, which suggests that they are part of the continuing dialogue within the Christian tradition, not a break from it.

It would remain for Rousseau to pose anew a vision of history with stark, though non-Christian, antinomies. In this respect he is, of course, a departure from Luther, Hobbes, and Locke. But like Luther, and unlike Hobbes and Locke (whose Christian faith was effortless and without travail), Rousseau would stir the soul from its present exile—not to observe the Christian edict to *forget* thyself, but to extol the Greek edict: *know* thyself. There is an additional twist as well. Whereas, for Christians, God reveals Himself only partially through his Word, for Rousseau the written word itself requires concealment *by the author* that the inner sanctum be protected.[160] In both cases mystery, paradox, and perhaps even the apparent injustice of Truth remain untrammeled by those not in a condition to grasp it—the decisive difference being that for Luther, Hobbes, and Locke, *no* one can fully know because of Adam's fall, whereas for Rousseau, perhaps a few can.

TWO

Hobbes: The Dialectic of Renewal and the Politics of Pride

H OBBES IS BOTH SOMETHING NEW on the horizon of political speculation[1] *and* part of a tradition concerned with biblical history and its political implications.[2] This conjunction in his thinking, which seems
not at all disingenuous or labored, is what makes his work so extraordinary—
and such a stumbling block. The easier course, of producing a coherent reading
of his work by disavowing some of its parts, is no substitute, however, for an
understanding achieved through a synthesis of all of its aspects, a view Hobbes
himself would have agreed with, judging from the hermeneutic principle he
adopted when trying to understand Scripture as whole.

> The scope of the writer . . . giveth the true light, by which any writing is
> to be interpreted; and they that insist upon single texts, without consider-
> ing the main design, can derive nothing from them clearly.[3]

The enigmatic Hobbes, who writes of science, passions, the right and laws of
nature, and of the conditions under which civil peace is possible, also writes of
prophets, miracles, the three personations of God, eternal life, the Church, and
the kingdom of fairies, among other things. Only by grasping the scope of
Hobbes's thinking is it possible to understand how these different aspects *could
have* formed a unitary thesis, and conversely, only by suspending judgment that
these things *could not have* gone together is it possible to begin to understand the
scope of Hobbes's thought.

It would be erroneous to conclude that Hobbes's politics is a testimony to
reason's capacity to supervene over the passions that lurk under the surface of civil
society and forever dispose human beings toward war.[4] For so tenuous is the hold
of reason, however, that civil peace can be maintained only at the price of submitting to a *one* who personates *all*—an arrangement that mitigates against clouded
private judgment and faction. What is more, Hobbes's unified sovereign is not
only a political figure, but a vicegerent of God as well. Political and religious
sovereignty are unified. Wishing even to supersede this false opposition in words,
Hobbes remarks, "there is therefore no other government in this life, neither of
state, nor *religion*, but *temporal.*"[5] (I will use the term "politics" throughout this

chapter when speaking of government, but it should be remembered that this term already presupposes what Hobbes wishes to deny, that, in Augustine's language, there is no separation between the "City of Man" and the "City of God.")[6]

Hobbes's theoretical location is two large steps away from the contemporary position that first separates political and religious sovereignty and then divides political sovereignty itself. This combination of steps together is not easily taken without faltering.

Reunifying *political* sovereignty is the less difficult thought experiment to perform; Hobbes on science, the passions, and the right and laws of nature is provocative even if ultimately unpalatable. And notwithstanding his recommendations, we cannot but be fascinated by this strange Hobbesian world and taken by his powerful and sobering assessment of pride, the proximity of the war of all against all, and the fear of violent death that is so often taken to be at the heart of his politics.

The fear of violent death is not, however, the final arbiter of Hobbes's political thought. The claim of a master who protects from violent (temporal) death falls mute in the face of the fear of eternal death; a politics based on the dictates of reason alone, one that mitigates the lesser fear, is impotent in the face of the greatest fear:

> no man can serve two masters; nor is he less, but rather more a master, whom we are to obey for fear of damnation than he whom we obey for fear of temporal death.[7]

The reason-based case for the unity of political sovereignty, astonishing as it may be, therefore, is only *half* of Hobbes's account of sovereignty. It is, in fact, the less significant portion.[8] What was needed, in Hobbes's view, was a demonstration of the unity of political and religious sovereignty that was *consistent with* the conclusions of reason but ultimately *confirmed* by Scripture; an arrangement necessitated by the fact that about certain crucial matters reason must remain silent and defer to a Higher Source.[9] Eternal death (a religious matter) is not a subset of temporal death (a political matter); politics can never contain or subsume religion: this is the Erastian position Hobbes cannot be understood to have taken. Tocqueville remarks that no worldly doctrine of self-interest or political obligation would have beneficent results unless it comported with what the economy of salvation required.[10] No less could be said of the politics Hobbes wished to institute.

The thrust of my argument, then, is that although Hobbes's vision is, at first blush, explicitly political, that does not at all prove that he is a break from the thought of his Christian predecessors. The politics of reason does not countermand Revelation. Reason can *clear away* false religion so that the True religion may take its rightful place as reason's necessary *supplement.* No more.[11] Hobbes's is not a bold assertion about the sufficiency of reason, nor is his project one more in a long line of secret teachings dressed up in biblical garb for

concealment—the denouement of which view would have Hobbes *really* partic-
ipating in an ancients-moderns debate without Christianity intervening.[12]
Hobbes "perverse theology"[13] must be taken seriously.

As I have suggested elsewhere, the way to understand the scope of Hobbes's
project best is as an attempt to provide a *full* account (political and theological)
of the meaning of Matthew's Christ's proclamation:

> Think not that I have come to destroy the law, or the prophets: I am not
> come to destroy, but to fulfill.[14]

Again, this is not to diminish the place of reason. The meaning Hobbes attributes to Christ's fulfillment is consistent with the conclusions of reason and,
more important, it provides a way for Christians to attain eternal life through
the *supplement* of faith that Christ offers—a supplement that (and this was crucial for Hobbes) does not detract from the obedience owed to the sovereign. The
meaning of Christ's fulfillment that Hobbes adduces, it will turn out, *buttresses*
reason's conclusion that the subject owes obedience to the sovereign. But all
this in due course.

Substantively, I begin by suggesting that pride is, for Hobbes, *the* preeminent
temporal problem and show how the political form that he recommends is, in
his view, the only security against the vagaries of pride. The etiology of pride can,
of course, be understood in several contexts: Hobbes could have enlisted the
support of Greek tragedy or Christianity in his exposition. He does not rely upon
the more conventional Reformation account, however, which would have it that
Christ takes upon Himself the sin, the pride, of humankind, and this deserves
comment. What is so astounding about Hobbes's system is that while Christ does
not take upon Himself the pride of Christians, the *Christ-like* figure of the Leviathan does. There is, in effect, a political rather than a conventionally religious
solution to the problem of pride—though, again, it would be more correct to say
that there is a temporal solution to the problem rather than a *Nunc-stans* made
possible through Christ. No bosom of Christ in which to rest when weary is offered; yet the weariness remains. And *this* cries out of the solution that the Leviathan offers, without which there can only be "death." The almost irredeem-
able pride of humankind is underscored again and again by Hobbes—as it is in
Saint Augustine[15]—but Christ does not serve as the counterpoint. Here is the
acuity of Saint Augustine on human corruption, but without Christ for
atonement!

Christ *does* figures prominently in Hobbes's account of death, however.
Christ offers a way to avoid eternal death; here, there is a more conventionally
religious solution to that other inheritance from Adam: loss of eternal life. Contrast this to Saint Paul, for whom pride and death are the *twin* problems that are
occasioned by Adam's fall and ameliorated by Christ's first coming[16]—a view

with which Hobbes no doubt was well acquainted. That Christ should only atone for the loss of life eternal in Hobbes is, I think, no accident.

As I have said, Hobbes's understanding of Christ's fulfillment of the Old Testament is crucial to comprehending the scope of his political vision. After specifying the way Christ atones for the loss of life eternal, I consider more directly Hobbes's view of the meaning of Christ's fulfillment and also *what* the content of the Old Law was that was purportedly fulfilled by Christ.

Bearing in mind Hobbes's earnest wish to unify sovereignty, it should not be surprising that the paradigmatic event of the Old Testament is, for Hobbes, Moses' receipt of the covenant. *Who* Moses was needs to be considered in some detail, for it is from Moses that Hobbes traces the genealogy of authority forward, in principle, to the Christian commonwealth and derives the sovereign's right to interpret Scripture. This feature of Hobbes's politics is perplexing, to be sure; nevertheless it becomes, if not plausible, then certainly comprehensible in light of the hermeneutic principle that guides his interpretation of Scripture: that sovereignty must be unified—or, put another way, that if God did not wish humankind to see double *before* Christ's first coming there is little reason to suspect that He changed his mind *after* it. [17] While certain interpretive turns are foreclosed by taking this tack, from the biblical narrative surrounding Moses it *is* possible to converge upon the interrelated problems of authority and interpretation. Hobbes went to great lengths to avoid the kind of linkage between Adam and Christ that would make Christ a solution to the problem of death *and* pride—thus betraying his indebtedness to this linkage while skirting or deflecting its more conventional implications. He does not at all step lightly, however, when considering either Moses or Moses' relationship with Christ.

These two relationships: Adam to Christ and Moses to Christ are the foundation upon which Hobbes's political vision rests. By specifying the meaning of Christ's fulfillment that is pre-*figured* in these figures, Hobbes is able to unify sovereignty and to carve out a domain of reason that is supplemented by Scripture—which provides what reason cannot: an avenue to life eternal. His theologico-political position is indeed complex; he is able to sympathize with the Protestant epistemological position and claim that reason cannot know God, [18] while at the same time write against it; [19] agree with the Catholics that God's Kingdom has its representative on earth, [20] while at the same time, as I have said, compare the papacy with the kingdom of the fairies; [21] agree that the New Testament fulfills the Old, while at the same time return to the Old Testament for a solution to the dualism and the political turmoil occasioned for some Christians by Christ and His message in the New Testament.

Finally, if I may anticipate what will follow in the next chapter: Locke would subsequently pay a great deal of attention to Adam's relationship to Christ, but not to Moses' relationship to Christ. His political conclusions differed markedly from Hobbes's because of this. Most significantly, because Locke paid greater attention to Adam's relationship to Christ, he was able to develop a doctrine of toleration, of property, and of government based on reason, which Hobbes could *not* have developed given his emphasis on Moses' relationship to Christ.

THE PROBLEM OF PRIDE

Pride is *the* central problem of human life, and it receives extensive treatment in Hobbes's explanation of the cause or origin of human association. His assertion that pride, along with desire for gain, is an animating principle of such association suggests the extent to which pride, in his formulation, is an overriding disposition in the human soul.[22]

In his discussion of the origin of human association, Hobbes suggests that the desire for gain can be understood in terms of the lower passions, whose object is the *conveniences* of life.[23] Important and necessary as these may be, however, in animating human beings to associate with one another, what is of greater importance is the need to think highly of themselves in the company of others.[24] Their vanity, more than their desire for gain, brings them together to associate. Such vanity Hobbes identifies with the passions of the mind—in short, with the higher passions. It is these higher passions that make human association so peculiar. It is these higher passions (which produce human pride in all its forms—envy, vanity, etc.), moreover, that make human association so deeply problematic.

The problematic nature of human association is clearly seen in Hobbes's comparison of the community of beasts with the human community. Human community, unlike the community of beasts, enjoys no natural harmony, and this for several reasons. First, "men are in continual competition for honor and dignity," which gives rise to hatred and war; second, "amongst the creatures, the common good differeth not from the private," whereas human beings, who always compare themselves with others, rarely see beyond their private good; third, because creatures have no reason, "they do not see, nor think they see any fault, in the administration of their common business"; fourth, creatures lack "the art of words," that is, rhetoric, which troubles the peace.[25]

What is significant about these four reasons is that each may be attributed, paradoxically, to what is highest in humankind—to the mind and to the higher passions that derive from it. Yet Hobbes does not stop with the conclusion that the mind and its associated passions make human association merely troublesome. Indeed he goes far beyond this to suggest that "no society can be great or long lasting, which begins from vain-glory."[26] And elsewhere, where "vain esteem" is left unchecked there will be no end to human misery.[27]

Hobbes's solution to the problem of human pride is, of course, a well-known one: "the generation of that great Leviathan, or rather to speak more reverently, of that *mortal god* to which we owe . . . our peace and defense."[28] And while he does leave open the question of what particular form such a mortal God should take (claiming that he does not wish to seem of the opinion "that there is a less proportion of obedience due to an aristocracy or democracy than to a monarchy"),[29] he provides reasons for believing that monarchy is, in fact, the best way of averting the immense threat posed by human pride.

Hobbes's consideration of monarchy begins, appropriately enough, with an inquiry into what animates those who rail against it. Are they not really envious of the one whose power elevates him far above the rest? So great is their pride, based as it is on competition with others for honor, that "such men would withdraw themselves from under the dominion of the one God" if they could.[30]

The envy that animates human beings to despise monarchy is so potent that it leads them, similarly, to reject aristocracy. Aristocracy differs from monarchy only in that it gives more humans a voice in the issues of commonwealth than does monarchy. The relative power and, hence, honor (the two are closely related)[31] that distinguishes the few from the many corresponds to the relative power that distinguishes the one from the many. That is, the difference is maintained. Thus, in spite of the fact that more human beings are of elevated status in aristocracy, aristocracy differs from monarchy in degree and not in kind. The person animated by envy recognizes this and therefore calls for the only solution that levels the differences in power and honor between human beings: the institution of democracy.

The institution of democracy, however, has the effect of reconstituting the original condition of equality found in the state of nature, a condition which proved to be so problematic that it compelled human beings to enter into a covenant wherein they submit their wills to the Leviathan and abstain from arbitrating on matters of good and evil themselves. Whereas it might be possible to institute a democracy, such a regime is inherently unstable, simply because the many will inevitably seek to secure the power and honor unavailable to them within an aristocracy or monarchy. The ensuing contestations will yield not stability, but faction, which, because "every man esteems [only] according to his own judgment,"[32] leads to civil war and ultimately to the death of the commonwealth. Far better is it that such matters of judgment be left,

> not [to] the persuasion and advice of private men, but [to the] laws of the realm, [and having done this] you will no longer suffer ambitious men through the streams of your blood to wade to their own power.[33]

The best state of affairs, then, is monarchy. By submitting to the one who in his capacity of artificial person represents the will of the many, the many lose all claims to power and honor and, thus, are equal with respect to each other. As in democracy the many under monarchy are equal. Yet unlike democracy, power and honor cannot be contested for.

As in the presence of the master, the servants are equal, and without any honor at all; so, too, are the subjects, in the presence of the sovereign.[34]

There is, of course, some question whether the many are, in fact, equal under the sovereign, as Hobbes well recognizes. The ability of the weak to kill the strong does, in a manner of speaking, level all differences among human beings;[35] but this argument alone is not convincing. What about *natural* differences among human beings? What are to be made of these? Hobbes makes little of these differences, and in fact posits something like a noble lie.

Whether therefore men be equal by nature, the equality is to be acknowledged; or whether unequal, because they are like to contest for dominion, it is necessary for the obtaining of peace, *that they be esteemed as equal* . . . [and] *that every man be accounted by nature equal to another;* the contrary to which law is *pride.*[36]

According to Hobbes, human pride is behind the rejection of monarchy and the call for liberty.[37] Yet those who call for such liberty, aside from not being aware that what they *really* seek is dominion, also do not realize that there is more genuine liberty under a monarch than within a democracy. While it is true that under monarchy only a few have power and honor, it is also the case that only those few will be involved in the contestation for it. Because of this, "the ambitious [few] only will suffer; the rest are protected from the injuries of the more potent."[38]

In a democracy, where all are involved in public matters, where each sees the opportunity to declare his or her eloquence in public life, everyone supposes that they have more liberty than those who have *no voice* in these matters.[39] Hobbes argues, to the contrary, that such liberties are actually grievances under democracy. In what do these consist?

To see his opinion, whom we scorn, preferred to ours; to have our wisdom undervalued before our own faces; by an uncertain trial of a little vain-glory, to undergo most certain enmities . . . to hate and to be hated, by reason of the disagreement of opinions; to lay open our secret councils and advices to all, to no purpose and without any benefit; to neglect the affairs of our own family: these, I say, are the grievances.[40]

The supposed liberties under democracy reveal themselves to be the means whereby pride is allowed full rein, and this situation can only end disastrously— again, in Hobbes's words, "no society can be great or long lasting, which begins from vainglory."[41] As with Augustine, without a way to ameliorate pride, the "City of Man" will perpetually aim toward dominion. Human society invariably entails certain inconveniences. Those entailed by monarchy deny power and honor to most human beings; yet in return they are provided with the liberty to secure their own preservation as well as freedom from the dangerous affliction of pride.

The additional liberty they would receive under democracy, the freedom to enter into public matters, is illusory; for, in the final analysis, it is founded on the fanciful belief that human beings possess the capacities that only that mortal god, the Leviathan, as well as the immortal God, possess. Such a belief is, itself, demonstrable proof of the vanity of humankind, of its pride.

It is possible, of course, to see in this repudiation of the liberty in a democracy a purely political motive: Hobbes simply wished to defend monarchy against democracy. Obedience, he is often inferred to have concluded, was more precious than liberty, notwithstanding his ostensible argument that "in the act of our *submission,* consisteth both our *obligation,* and our *liberty.*"[42] This latter claim is not, however, simply a piece of political rhetoric. It may just as easily be viewed as an integral part of his entire argument about how pride may be attenuated. As with many Christian thinkers, human beings are so corrupted by pride that *any* effort on their part to will their own "salvation"—here broadly conceived to include salvation from the death that awaits them in the state of nature—cannot succeed. Prideful creatures acting in freedom always succumb to greater errancy. Only by resisting their pridefulness, by *obeying* the One Sovereign and not believing in the sufficiency of their own efforts, can their undertakings be fruitful. Obedience is the precondition of *genuine* human liberty.

This is a very old thought, not one peculiar to Hobbes's purported defense of absolute government. It is to be found, for example, in the Old Testament in the narrative of Sarah's barren womb.[43] Abraham and Sarah, by themselves, could not bring forth God's chosen people. Their efforts would have only come to naught without the intervention of God. But Abraham *obeys* God's commands, and this obedience is the precondition of the beneficence that follows.

In Augustine, too, obedience is crucial as well. Deference before the Sovereign (God) arrests the pridefulness of human beings who would think their own efforts are the source of their comfort and safety.

> God's instructions demanded obedience, and obedience is in a way the mother and guardian of all the other virtues in a rational creature, seeing that the rational creation has been so made that *it is to man's advantage to be in subjection to God, and it is calamitous for him to act according to his own will.*[44]

As with Hobbes, acting in accordance with one's own will can result only in "death." Obeying the sovereign is the only way for humankind to avoid calamity.

The parallel may be confirmed without hearkening back as far as Augustine, however. Luther's insistence that obedience to the commandments of God is the precondition for the attainment of true righteousness *and freedom* under Christ comports with Hobbes's position about the need for obedience to the sovereign. No less can be said of Calvin.

For as the surest source of destruction to men is to obey themselves, so the only haven of safety is to have no other will, no other wisdom, than to follow the Lord wherever He leads. [45]

The point here is that within Reformation Christianity there are good *religious reasons* for asserting that obedience to the sovereign is the only way to establish true freedom and that the liberty that withdraws itself from under the sovereign, that claims itself sufficient unto itself, is a species of pridefulness that cannot be countenanced. Without obedience errancy is inevitable; the prideful longing for liberty can lead only to death unless it is linked to obedience. [46]

Hobbes, then, is not simply being rhetorical when he subsumes liberty to obedience; he is voicing an axiom of the Reformation—only here, because Hobbes understands Christianity *not* to have brought about a spiritual kingdom that stands *next to* the City of Man, the insight which other Reformers applied only to the Christian's relationship to God the Son here applies to the citizen's relationship to the sovereign.

THE MYTH OF IXION: GRASPING FOR THE GREEK WAY—OUT

That this vanity, this pride, is Hobbes's central concern I have tried to show by adducing evidence from his thoughts on the origin of human association and from his argument in defense of monarchy and against democracy. An additional consideration that he brings to bear (which will lead the discussion to a consideration of the Christian myths that ultimately support the whole of his intellectual edifice) is the myth of Ixion.

Despite what Hobbes says about the inadequacies, the dangers, of speaking metaphorically, [47] to understand his thoughts on the problem of pride it is helpful to discuss a specific myth to which he himself alludes in the Author's Preface of *De Cive*. This myth not only sheds light on the problem of pride but, as we shall see, it also *substitutes* for the more conventional Reformation account of the problem of pride—which account Hobbes deliberately skirts throughout his writings.

Ixion, the myth goes, was invited by Jupiter to a banquet, at which he fell in love with Juno. Attempting to embrace her, he clasped a cloud, from whence the centaurs, in Hobbes's words, "a fierce, fighting, and unquiet generation," proceeded. [48] In Hobbes's interpretation of the myth, Ixion represents the private man who was invited into the court of politics to consider matters of justice. He fell in love, not with justice but with his wife and sister instead; and embracing justice's shadow thus, gave birth to "those hermaphrodite opinions of moral philosophers, partly right and comely, partly brutal and wild; the causes of all contention and bloodshed." [49] The myth of Ixion suggests to Hobbes that the private person was incapable of embracing justice itself, that its shadow was the most that could be possessed, the consequence of which was that, none but those to whom the supreme hath committed to the interpretation of his laws [should deliberate over such matters].[50]

Hobbes's supposition here is that given the nature of the world and of the knowledge that can be acquired, human beings are not what, in their pretentiousness, they claim to be. Human beings are more than beasts, but more like beasts than like God, and it is this latter consideration that has sobering political implications. Ixion does not belong in the company of Jupiter. The political community in which Ixion lives must separate the two. To ignore this edict, to allow Ixion to try to consummate his love with justice, brings forth not a divine human being but rather a centaur—a furious man-beast, again, "the cause of all contention and bloodshed."[51]

PRIDE AND THE STRUCTURE OF HISTORY

In Hobbes's interpretation of this Greek myth, and in the text which leads up to Hobbes's presentation of it in *De Cive,* there are detectable outlines of a vision of the structure of history. There is, for example, Hobbes's observation that the ancients lived in a "golden age," a "simplicity of . . . times,"[52] an era in which the affliction that besets the present period—the tendency of human beings to take up arms against their king—was absent. Here the distant past is to the contemporary period as gold is to a base metal. History is marked by a descent, a movement away from the unblemished beginning toward a present where strife rules and where the original virtues that human beings once possessed are absent. This Greek view of history, which resonates with the central argument made in the remainder of *De Cive* is consistent with the view of history that accompanies Hobbes's observation elsewhere that God's covenant with Adam "was made void and never after renewed."[53] This latter allusion is not, of course, of Greek origin. Yet in it we can see a similar pattern: in the beginning there was harmony; after that, disorder.

THE DECISIVE EVENT

Were it not for the fact that Adam's fall acquires its fullest significance retrospectively through Saint Paul's juxtaposition of Adam to Christ and is thereafter linked almost inexorably with the question of the meaning of Christ's fulfillment, in Hobbes's allusion to Adam would be encountered the identical pattern of descent from the pristine period of the beginning that we find in his allusion to the Golden Age of the ancient Greeks. In post-Pauline allusions to Adam, however, Christ is the spoken or unspoken counterpart; Christ is the decisive event, the Personage who marks the irruption of something *new* in history; and this God the Son who intercedes could never have been taken seriously within the Greek tradition. In Saint Paul's words,

> For the Jews require a sign, and the Greeks seek after wisdom: But we preach Christ Crucified, unto the Jews a stumbling block, unto the Greeks foolishness. [54]

Christ's first coming is the event that distinguishes Greek from Christian political thought. Augustine, for example, alluding to the time before Christ, and to the transformation that occurs through Him, makes clear this idea of a decisive event when he says:

> The nations had not yet received the revelation from heaven of the teaching that would cleanse the heart by faith and turn the interest of men in humble reverence toward things in heaven, or above the heavens, and free them from the oppressive domination of demonic powers. [55]

History is a fall at the beginning, at the time of Adam, to be sure, but then it is marked by the irruption of an extraordinary event that offers atonement for the problem of pride occasioned by Adam's fall. (Adam's loss of life eternal I will not consider here.) This event turns back on the fall, as it were, and serves to heighten awareness of the centrality of the problem of pride for which Christ is the way of atonement.

It should be remembered that the centrality of Adam and of pride was first noted in the New Testament, *not* in the Old. It was Saint Paul who, in I Corinthians and Romans, contrasts the Old Man (Adam) with the New Man (made possible through Christ). It is this retrospective glance that *retrieves* Adam from the insignificant place he had had in the Hebrew literature[56] and focuses attention on the problem of pride, now ameliorable through God the Son. Although in the Greek world the problem of pride certainly looms large, divine intercession by a *deus ex machina* is not to be confused with Divine intercession by Christ. It was by seeking after wisdom that the Greeks awakened the divine part of their soul;[57] the *sin* of pride possessed no philosophical currency here; pride was error, imbalance, or immoderation—"foolishness, *not* sin! do you grasp that?"[58]

SKIRTING THE DECISIVE EVENT

The account of the problem of pride I have just considered was available for Hobbes to draw on, to be sure; it is significant, however, that he skirts it, preferring *not* to concern himself with the implications prideful human beings may draw about their salvation. And this is what is so astounding about Hobbes. While he clearly wished to retain the *focus* on pride, he did not wish to retain the notion that Christ—who brings pride into focus in much Reformation thinking—is the solution to it. This was Augustine and Luther's way; Hobbes thought this path politically disastrous. He repeatedly suggests that Christ offers a solution, not to the problem of pride but rather to the problem of the loss of eternal life, the companion problem occasioned by Adam's fall.

When Hobbes provides a mythical account of the problem of pride, he alludes to the myth of Ixion rather than to the Adamic myth prototypically articulated by Saint Paul. He does so, I suggest, in order to avoid linking the problem of pride with the relationship between Adam and Christ, even though he is quite willing to draw conclusions on the basis of this relationship in the context of the problem of the loss of eternal life. (He even goes so far as to argue that the fall did not occur because of Adam's *sin,* but rather because of God's *power.* [59] This undermines one aspect of the Pauline myth at its point of origin!) To conclude that Christ was a solution to pride, and that conventional Reformation thinking could best account for it, was precisely what Hobbes wished to avoid. Hence the myth of Ixion.

In considering the problem of pride in Hobbes, then, there is a difficulty. His recourse to Adam and Christ, though it can serve to illuminate *both* the problem of pride and the problem of loss of eternal life, occurs only for the purpose of illuminating the problem of loss of eternal life. The companion problem lurks in the shadows, never spoken of explicitly when the relationship of Adam and Christ is invoked, yet always present. Analytical light is cast on the problem of the loss of eternal life, but this light casts a shadow as well, the darkness of which serves to highlight Hobbes's omission. It is this omission and commission that I wish to consider next.

The Spoken and the Unspoken

In the *Leviathan,* a book whose very title suggests the centrality of the problem of pride, the surprise, perhaps, is that Hobbes in fact seems to be equally concerned with the problem of death. His often cited observation that the ability of one human being to kill another levels all differences between them is perhaps the best-known example of this, but this kind of death—"natural" death, if you will—is of lesser political significance to him than is the "eternal" death of which religion speaks, as I mentioned in my introductory comments. Hobbes observes, for example, that,

> it is impossible [that] a commonwealth should stand, where any other than the sovereign hath the power of giving greater rewards of life, and of inflicting greater punishments than death. Now seeing *eternal life* is a greater reward than the *life present;* and *eternal tourment* of greater punishment than the *death of nature;* it is a thing worthy to be well considered of all men that desire, by obeying authority, to avoid the calamities of confusion and civil war, what is meant in the Holy Scripture, by *life eternal* and *tourment eternal.* [60]

There is, in the *Leviathan,* the remarkable situation in which the problems of both death and pride are addressed; in which Christ seems only to be an answer to the problem of death; in which the Leviathan seems only to be an answer to the problem of pride; and in which—because both of these problems are explicable even if not fully explicated in terms of the relationship between Adam and Christ—there is an unspoken transposition of the Pauline understanding of the relationship between Adam and Christ. From the symbolic interplay of these religious figures Hobbes offers a political solution to the problem of pride, and it is this unspoken transposition that blurs the tidy distinctions between the political and the religious in Hobbes's thought about the Leviathan.

For Hobbes, Christ came exclusively to offer eternal life in the world to come. That is, Christ's message pertains to the problem of loss of eternal life and not of pride.[61] Nonetheless, the pattern established by the relationship between Christ and Adam is also the basis for his solution to the problem of pride, though he does not explicate this. Hobbes, however, does not have to explicate it, for by invoking the pattern established by Christ's relationship to Adam vis-à-vis the loss of eternal life, the problem of pride stands out in bold relief. The parallel construction of which these problems are each a part serves to heighten awareness of the problem of pride to which Hobbes will return with his political solution. Reformation currency is transposed, appropriated such that the dualism it countenances may be obviated.

The starkness of the picture Hobbes portrays is not to be underestimated: what through Adam was lost, through Christ will be regained *in the distant future*. Adam fell, lost eternity, and entered the realm of profane history, where death resides. God displayed Himself to humankind at the beginning of history, and will do the same at the end of history when Christ returns. Human beings who live in the interim between the beginning and the return of Christ must act as if God is absent; that is, act as if He is utterly transcendent.[62] Whether God exists or not cannot be known. Humankind can only wait for the resurrection of Christ. Life in history without God, in other words, is what humans beings must contend with.[63]

But this picture of humankind as dwellers in the interim of history is not, by itself, a source of trouble. The difficulty lies in the fact that in this world humankind suffers all the while from the problem of pride. This pride subverts the faculty of reason and causes great difficulty for human association. Christ's relationship to Adam vis-à-vis the problem of death yields the conclusion that mortals stand between the beginning and the redemption, without the assistance or presence of the divine. Against this picture is counterpoised the previously invoked problem of pride, for which there is no divine solution in the interim of history, and for which human beings *must* find a solution if there is to be political association at all.

This rather stark view of the human situation is attenuated by the prospect of an ultimate redemption on the return of Christ. But Christ's long-run solution does not rectify the present disorder. Notwithstanding this difficulty, however, there is a provisional solution to the problem of pride: the Leviathan; and it is Hobbes's genius that this provisional solution is *temporal* rather than transhistorical.

PARALLELS BETWEEN THE LEVIATHAN,
GOD THE FATHER,
AND GOD THE SON

The parallels between Hobbes's political solution to the problem of pride and the religious one offered through Christianity cannot be ignored. These parallels confirm that there is in Hobbes's formulation a transposition of the conventional Reformation reading of the Christ myth—or rather an awkward conflation of its aspects. While, in effect, agreeing with Luther about the bleakness of the human situation without a sovereign, Hobbes, too, finds a denouement. His, however, is not Christ, but rather a figure who is *Christ-like*.

Like Christ, for example, Hobbes's Leviathan "swallows up" (to borrow Luther's phrase) human pride in order that civil life not be subject to the torments that it produces.[64] The pride that would accompany the citizens' competition for honor and glory is defused.[65] Each citizen makes a public proclamation that living with their pride can only lead to "death," and in abject humility they *assent* to become members of a community reborn through a covenant of obedience.

Like Christ, the Leviathan, too, does not seem to suffer the sin of pride himself;[66] he is somehow *different* from other human beings. The Leviathan is, thus, like Christ, but not Christ; like human beings, but not like them. He is the shadowy, mysterious sovereign who never shows his human face.[67] He is, in Hobbes's words: "a *mortal god*,"[68] and thus, by the very conflation of the categories of the divine and human, he is a solution to a Christian dualism that had, in Hobbes's estimation, been responsible for so much civil disorder.[69]

The godlike nature of the Leviathan is not simply a rhetorical ploy on Hobbes's part. Citizens, Hobbes notes repeatedly, must be overwhelmed by the *power* of the Leviathan; they must *fear* him;[70] and they must *obey* him. Power is, of course, the central attribute of God the Father; fear is the beginning of all religion;[71] and obedience is above all what is required by God,[72] according to Hobbes.

By far the most striking parallel between the Leviathan and God the Son, however, pertains to the relationship between the many citizens/Christians and the one sovereign/Christ. Because citizens give themselves over to the Leviathan, the foundation is laid for contracting with others without the uncertainty of outcome attendant to contracting in the state of nature. Like Christians who give themselves over to Christ and find the basis for sociality in so doing, Hobbes's citizens find the basis for safely contracting with one another because of their covenant with the Leviathan. Citizens find their authentic connection with others through the Leviathan,[73] just as Christians find theirs through Christ. The pattern here is that of an equality of all under a sovereign; the decisive difference being that for Hobbes the sovereign is a temporal (and quasi-religious) figure, for Luther the Sovereign is Christ. The great leveling that Hobbes accomplishes by making the ability of each to kill every other figures prominently in the state of nature can be better understood in terms of the quasi-religious function the Leviathan performs.

In addition, to push this matter even farther, it should be noted that just as Christ comes to presence for Luther only when the Christian falls into the Abyss upon experiencing a kind of *spiritual* death, so, too, the Leviathan appears as a political solution once the inhabitants of the state of nature realize that remaining in the state of nature can only result in *their* death! The pattern is the same, but the content is different. In both cases, too, there must be a *confession*, an assent, a *voicing*, that human beings need a sovereign!

A PROVISIONAL CONCLUSION

In Hobbes's temporal solution to the problem of pride the theoretical relationship between the form of government he adduces and the Reformation categories upon which it draws is clear: invoking a vision of the structure of history in which a transhistorical solution to the problem of pride inherited from Adam was absent, a provisional and temporal solution to that problem takes the form of a personage who resembles Christ, but is not Christ. A political solution to the problem of pride is imposed in the interim of history before the return of Christ (who will bring about an end to the death that came into the world on the occasion of Adam's fall); the twofold fall of Adam—involving both death and pride—is, in a word, split into its constituent parts.

The absence of the Divine in the interim of history is the occasion for the emergence of a temporal order that imitates Reformation thinking in decisive respects, though in such a way that certain of its aspects cannot become a source of contention in temporal life.

From this vantage point, which carefully skirts (or corrects, to be more generous) certain insights of the Reformers, it would not be difficult to miss the significance of the relationship between the problem of pride and the biblical vision of the structure of history that underpins it and to see in his formulations an explicitly political theory of order. I have suggested thus far that this conclusion is inadequate, that the figure of the Leviathan is Christ-like, and that he is therefore a quasi-religious figure. In due course this provisional conclusion will have to be amended even further; Hobbes does make an *explicitly* biblical argument about the Leviathan's authority to rule (based on the relationship between Moses and Christ), and this must be accounted for. Before turning in that direction, however, a more complete account of the relationship between Adam and Christ must be provided. What remains to be discussed is what, in Hobbes's estimation, the relationship between Adam and Christ discloses about the loss of eternal life and the structure of history.

Loss of Eternal Life and the Structure of History

Christ's mission of reinstituting eternal life is yet to be accomplished. Neither in this life will the eternal moment appear, nor immediately upon our death; we are to be granted eternal life only when Christ returns again.

> The comparison between that eternal life which Adam lost, and our Saviour by his victory over death hath recovered, holdeth also in this; that as Adam lost eternal life by his sin, and yet lived after it for a time, so the faithful Christian hath recovered eternal life by Christ's passion, though he die a natural death, and remain dead for a time, namely, till the resurrection.[74]

And again,

> But the kingdom of God, for restitution whereof Christ was sent from God his father, takes not its beginning before his second coming; to wit, from the day of judgment, when he shall come in majesty accompanied with his angels.[75]

Hobbes here shifts the locus of Christ's activity from the time when he first came to the time of his return.[76] The *significance* of Christ's relationship to Adam is retained, though the historical *duration* that separates them is lengthened. The transformative activity of Christ did not occur in the past, as both Augustine and Luther would have it, but rather will occur in the future. In effect, the present human historical location is not after Christ, but *before* Him. For

> if the kingdom of God were now already restored, no reason could be rendered why Christ, having completed the work for which he was sent, should come again; or why we should pray, *Thy kingdom come.*[77]

It must be emphasized again that Hobbes's formulation is a novel reading of Saint Paul's Adamic myth in which Christ is the counterpoint to the fall: Adam fell from grace with God; death was brought into the world; Christ presents a solution to the loss of eternal life—to which Hobbes immediately adds that Christ will emend this loss only at the end of history. In Hobbes's view, consequently, no fundamental conflict exists between what is due the sovereign and what is due God. The transformation that is purported to have occurred with Christ's first coming (which occasioned the generation of a dualism within Christianity) *never really occurred*. The Christian dualism of this world and the next is based on an erroneous understanding of Christ. What Christ announced was not *another* kingdom over which he rules in addition to that one already instituted in the profane world, but rather a *literal* kingdom *at the end of history* in which Christians may participate provided the requisite faith is present.

> [Because] Christ was sent from God his father to make a covenant be-
> tween him and the people, it is manifest, that though Christ were equal to
> his father according to his nature, yet he was inferior according to the
> right of kingdom. For his office, to speak properly, was not that of king,
> but that of viceroy, such as Moses' government was; for the kingdom was
> not his, but his father's.[78]

What Christ occasions is neither a solution to the loss of eternal life in the present or upon our death, nor a kingdom of God that stands "beyond" the present earthly kingdom. He merely promises that if Christians are obedient and have faith that Christ is the Son of God, as foretold in the Old Testament,[79] then they will receive eternal life upon Christ's second coming, when God's kingdom shall again reign over the earth.[80] Moreover, it will not be as disembodied souls that the faithful shall dwell in God's kingdom then, but rather as corporeal bodies.[81]

THE NEW ADAM AND BEYOND: CHRIST AS THE NEW MOSES

For had ye believed Moses, ye would have believed me: for he wrote of me. But if ye believe not his writings, how shall ye believe my words?[82]

To be sure, the argument that Christ is the new Adam only with respect to the loss of eternal life, and that this condition will be allayed only upon the second coming, deflects the claim that Christ's first coming was utterly transformative. Yet Hobbes does not wish to deny the importance of Christ's first coming altogether. Christ was, for him, redeemer, king, teacher, and renewer of the covenant with God.[83] Two of these four (teacher and renewer of the covenant) pertain to Christ's first coming,[84] and so should be considered here.

In his capacity as teacher Christ came to show human beings a new way to absolve sin. Not by making sacrifice, as in the Old Testament, but rather by accepting Christ who sacrificed himself for humankind can sins be absolved;[85] and in accepting baptism human beings affirm their belief that Christ will redeem the faithful upon His resurrection.[86] Here, through Christ's teaching, a new age is initiated: the age of faith,[87] characterized not by the coercive attempt to convert, but rather by the attempt to teach men and women to have faith in Christ.[88]

The astonishing fact about *this* formulation is that the claim that we live in a new age, an age of faith, could have come from Luther—with the massive difference that for Hobbes, faith is a *supplement* to obedience that requires the mere "believ[ing] that *Jesus is the Christ*"[89] in order to be saved. Absent is the spiritual journey of the soul entailed by the faith of Luther; gone is the abyss of powerlessness into which the Christian must fall: here, faith allows "the world" to remain intact. The faith of Luther, which would damn "the world," has no place. Hobbes's Christ, Christ the teacher, appends obedience—but does not supersede it. Christ does not teach of another realm, a realm of faith; He left the world intact—and this means, of course, that He does not confute the rule of the rightful sovereign.[90]

In Christ's capacity as renewer of the covenant the more profound *temporal* significance of Christ emerges; and it is here that Christ can be spoken of as the new Moses. Through renewing the covenant with God first fully instantiated with Moses, the legitimate authority of the sovereign is assured. Hobbes's argument on this point will become clear shortly. First, however, I would like to amend the provisional conclusion I reached several sections ago.

THREE ARGUMENTS ABOUT SOVEREIGNTY

Hobbes's quest for a justification of political authority can be seen in terms of the three distinct arguments on which he relies: the first is found largely in Parts I and II of the *Leviathan*; the second pertains to the quasi-religious symbolism of the Leviathan who, like Christ, solves the problem of pride; and the third relies upon the Mosaic covenant.

The first argument, the justification for the authority of the sovereign by comparing it to its alternative,

> continual fear, and danger of violent death; [in which] the life of man [is] solitary, poor, nasty, brutish, and short,[91]

can be understood as a something of a negative justification. Though it is in some measure compelling, it is cannot stand alone. (If this justification were enough, why would Hobbes have written Parts III and IV of the *Leviathan*?) True, uncertainty and the fear that the fruits of one's labor will be appropriated are eliminated.[92] But these "incommodities" are just that; they can never be the basis of a full-blown positive theory of political authority. Moreover, this argument is made on the basis of reason alone—what most commentators focus upon.

With the second argument, Hobbes goes part way toward providing a positive theory of political authority by acutely attending to the problem of pride; by transposing in the very act of relying upon Saint Paul's Adamic myth that gives it coherence; and by characterizing the Leviathan in such a way that his functional resemblance to Christ lurks under the surface. This novel and strange reading, however, is not explicit enough to provide a substantive—that is, positive—theory of authority.

The first argument, then, is based upon reason; and the second relies upon an unorthodox reading of Adam/Christ. Hobbes's positive theory of authority (his third argument) is one that turns explicitly to the two Testaments to find support for the Leviathan. But here—and this is the decisive change—the reference point is not the New Testament which contains the Pauline understanding of relationship between Adam and Christ. Rather, Hobbes's reference point is the Old Testament event in which God forms a covenant with His people through His intermediary, Moses, and the subsequent fulfillment of that "event" by Christ. Here, largely in the Old Testament, Hobbes finds a solution to the problems of authority and the right of interpretation. First, reason; second, Adam/Christ; third, Moses/Christ.

CHRIST: RENEWER OF THE COVENANT

Having divested Christ of all *temporal* import thus far, Hobbes now breathes life back into Him in an attempt to find a basis for the authority of the sovereign. Simply put, Hobbes asserts that not in his capacity as redeemer, king, and teacher does Christ have political significance, but rather in his capacity as renewer of the covenant.

It would be good to recall here that for Hobbes the kingdom of God is to be understood in its literal sense. Those who formed a covenant with God—the people of Israel—are of His kingdom.[93] Furthermore, it is only by covenant with God that the right of kingdom can be constituted at all.[94] This right of kingdom, when legitimately passed down, is, in effect, the way in which God's presence in the world *continues* despite His literal absence,[95] despite the fact that His *voice* can no longer be heard.[96] Most significant, it is through this right, this covenant, that a counterpoint is established to the absence of God in the world we have seen so far in Hobbes's vision of biblical history. Wholly absent from this moment of history in the life of humankind, now the *trace* of God appears—the consequence of which appearance is that a positive theory of sovereign authority comes at last into view.

Hobbes's positive theory of sovereign authority can really be broken down into two interrelated components. On the one hand there is the narrative that surrounds God's original covenant with the people of Israel, its loss, its preparation for renewal through Christ, and finally its realization in Christian commonwealths. This narration involves a genealogical tracing from the present back to the time of the Old Testament. And on the other hand, there is the derivative matter of interpretation, which takes the form of a claim that the responsibility for interpreting law and sacred documents is within the purview of the sovereign alone. First, Hobbes's genealogy of authority.

THE GENEALOGY OF AUTHORITY: FROM MOSES TO SAUL

The origin of the legitimate authority of the sovereign lies with Abraham, who was the first to form a covenant with God after the deluge. Ameliorating humankind's "passion-clouded reason," this covenant, though significant, does not, however, make up for the loss of the original pristine relationship between God and Adam.[97] For Hobbes's purpose, however, it represents the first instance in which God's relationship to humankind is mediated through a sovereign, and so amounts to a point of departure that establishes a right pattern which finds its culmination in the Old Testament in Moses.[98] Here the sovereign interprets all law, the people are obedient, the people do not judge in matters of good and evil, and there is a sign that defines them.[99]

After the initial covenant with Abraham[100] God renews his covenant with Isaac,[101] Jacob,[102] and with Moses.[103] Thereafter it is the priests who rule.[104] Next, because the Israelites were "a people greedy of prophets,"[105] power was transferred to them, though rightly it still remained with the priests. Finally, the people of Israel rejected God and instituted a succession of kings "to judge [them] like all other nations."[106] The kings retained their right to judge in matters both sacred and profane, like Moses and the prophets before them, but because the people no longer understood the reason for it, the covenant disintegrated.

> Notwithstanding the government both in policy and religion, were joined, first in the high-priests and afterwards in the kings, so far forth as concerned their right; yet it appeareth by the same holy history, that the people understood it not . . . [and] they took occasion, as oft as their governors displeased them, by blaming sometimes the policy, sometimes the religion, to change the government or revolt from their obedience at their pleasure: and from thence proceeded from time to time the civil troubles, divisions, and calamities of the nation.[107]

This situation was not, however, rectified during or after the exile; for although the covenant was technically renewed, the people of Israel did not promise obedience, which, for Hobbes, is a central feature of a covenant. After this pseudo-renewal, the situation further deteriorated because of the conquest by the Greeks.[108] Christ then prepares the way for a renewal of the covenant with God, for the instauration of sovereign authority anew, for a situation in which the people obey their sovereign in all matters and know the reason for it.[109] Christ, in other words, prepares the way for a time when human beings do not contest with their sovereign as the Israelites did when they no longer knew why they owed him obedience. The story of the Israelites—their *forgetfulness* and lapse into errancy when they were without the guidance of Moses their intermediary—is the story of all humankind, both historically specific and universally applicable. Without "Moses" there is only forgetfulness and errancy—so powerful, in fact, that it required that God send his only Son into the world to *re-mind* humankind! The physical sign of circumcision (that first reminder) required a Divine supplement, and this supplement alone has the awful authority to compel attentiveness—and obedience.

The end of Christ's coming was to renew the covenant of the kingdom of God, and to persuade the elect to embrace it, which was the second part of his office. If then Christ, while he was on earth, had no kingdom in this world, to what end was his first coming? It was to restore unto God, by a new covenant, the kingdom, which being his by the old covenant, had been cut off by the rebellion of the Israelites in the election of Saul. [110]

The lesson is clear: when the Jews instituted a king who would "judge them like all other nations," their passion-clouded reason received no corrective. A "secular" state, one ruled by Saul, offers no antidote for the inevitable errancy of its subjects. The political problem of order can only be solved, it would seem, through the intervention of God!

Hobbes, no less than Luther, is a "preacher in the wilderness of Judea." [111] Where Luther preached that human beings might abandon the righteousness of works, Hobbes preaches that they would be Jews under Moses rather than Jews under Saul—the latter being the *natural* disposition to adopt!

THE ARCHETYPAL PATTERN: EVIDENCE OF RENEWAL

For Hobbes, the archetypal pattern expressed in God's covenant with Moses represents itself in the pattern surrounding Christ's renewal of the covenant. This is, for him, evidence that Christ does indeed renew the covenant, that there is a continuity between the Old and New Testaments.

For as Moses chose twelve princes of the tribe, to govern under him so did our Saviour choose twelve apostles, who shall sit on twelve thrones, and judge the twelve tribes of Israel. And as Moses authorized the seventy elders, to receive the Spirit of God, and to prophesy to the people . . . so our Saviour also ordained seventy disciples, to preach his kingdom and salvation to all nations. . . . Again, our Saviour resembled Moses in the institution of *sacraments,* both of *admission* into the kingdom of God, and of *commemoration* of his deliverance of his elect from their miserable condition. [112]

The juxtaposition of a figure from the Old and New Testaments has already been encountered in an earlier treatment of the problems of pride and loss of eternal life. In Hobbes's discussion of covenant a similar pattern obtains; only here Christ and Adam are not juxtaposed, but rather Christ and Moses. And instead of redeeming or transforming human life, the meaning of the Christ/Moses relationship is renewal. Not only salvation (upon the occasion of Christ's second coming), but the *recovery* of the constitutive ground of authority is the lesson of the juxtaposition of Christ and Moses. While human beings must await their rebirth at the end of time, a temporal "rebirth" unto a community of ascent that *remembers* its errancy and need for an intermediary is made possible by Christ's renewal—and by Christ's renewal alone.

THE DARKNESS BEFORE THE DAWN

The true renewal of the covenant, however, could not occur until sovereigns adopted the Christian religion. Prior to that time, and after Christ's death, there is no one authorized interpreter of the Gospels and, consequently, no real Christian commonwealth or church.[113] This is a period in which the covenant is uninstituted, even though Christ provided the ground for its renewal. The theoretical difficulty posed is the following: if the Christian commonwealth was not instituted upon Christ's death, how was Christ's truth carried forward in coherent form without a sovereign who had the legitimate authority to interpret that truth for the many? Saint Paul, speaking to the church at Thessalonica,[114] points up the difficulty of the situation. In preaching to the Jews that Jesus was the Christ, he lacked authority, and so could only try to persuade. And since the authority of interpretation on this matter of Christ was vested in each individual person, every one could agree or not agree for their own reasons.[115]

This situation in which every human being is judge (of the teachings of the apostles who spoke without authority), which for Hobbes is perilous for collective life, was rectified, however, by what can only be called an inner transformation of those who hear the message of the Gospel.

> But in that time, when not the power and authority of the teacher, but *the faith of the hearer,* caused them to [embrace Christ], it was not the apostles that made their own writings canonical, but every convert made them so to himself.[116]

This inner transformation seems to have been aided by that third moment in the Holy Trinity, the Holy Ghost. It is the Holy Ghost, according to Hobbes, who carries forward the work of the one God in the person of the apostles,[117] and this provides a bridge that spans the dark age between the time of the loss of the covenant and the time of its renewal with the Christian commonwealth.

For Hobbes, however, the era of the Christian commonwealth did not arrive with the conversion of Constantine,[118] with the situation in which Christianity and sovereign authority finally merge after the work of the Holy Ghost (through the apostles) is completed. Rather, the very success of the early Church in gaining adherents was the occasion for its ossification and for the consolidation of authority within the Church—where it did not belong. This consolidation of authority occurred when the Church began to demand obedience, and the inversion of the Christian message (that human beings owed obedience to the sovereign alone) was "the first knot upon [their] liberty." The second knot was the consolidation of power in the hands of one church; the third was the extension of that power over the whole of the Roman Empire.[119]

Thus, where it could have been the case that the locus for the renewal of Christ's covenant might have been Constantine, the efflorescence of the Roman Church (which appropriated the sovereign's spiritual authority) subverts

Christ's message and unwittingly defers the true instauration of the covenant by placing three knots upon the liberty of humankind.

These three knots were, however, recently cut, and in the reverse order; first Queen Elizabeth broke with the Roman Church; next the Presbyterians undercut the religious monopoly of the Episcopalians; and finally, power was taken away from both.[120] Here, in this final act, the great Reformation hope is fulfilled: human beings are at last able to return to the primitive Christianity that inspired the faithful before the Roman Church usurped spiritual authority from the sovereign. It is finally in England, then, that the kingdom of darkness comes to an end. Not at the time of Constantine, but at the present moment can Christ's covenant be properly renewed.[121] In matters of faith no Church can intercede; in matters of obedience the sovereign has complete authority: this is the meaning of Christ's covenant fulfilled in Hobbes's England. Here is a *recovery* of Christian truth predicated upon an *enlightenment* in which *both* skepticism and faith play crucial roles, in which the drive to destroy the theologico-political underpinnings of the kingdom of darkness reflects an attempt to supplant false Christianity with true Christianity. The kingdom of darkness gives way to the kingdom of light, to Christianity recovered—to *Enlightenment*.

AUTHORITY AND INTERPRETATION

When Hobbes says, "not till kings were pastors, or pastors kings" could there have been authorized interpretation,[122] he is suggesting that interpretation and authority are inextricably linked. The *meaning* of Scripture—to get to the central issue—is subject to interpretation; and in order for a city to remain in existence without faction[123] there must be an authorized interpretation. In the final analysis, authorized interpretation makes possible the unity of voice that distinguishes a people from a multitude.[124] The task of the authorized interpreter for the city is to provide an interpretation to which all must accede.

Regarding dissent, Hobbes is quite clear on this. The city is instituted to protect the people, not *this* or *that* person.[125] Those who dissent from the single voice of the people constitute a city unto themselves; and in this situation the city retains its "primitive right . . . that is, the right of war, as against an enemy."[126] As to those for whom natural death is a small concession for the righteousness—read: dissent—that brings eternal life, Hobbes cites Romans 13:1, 2.[127]

> Let every soul be subject unto the higher powers. For there is no power but of God: the powers that be are ordained of God. Whosoever therefore resisteth the power, resisteth the ordinance of God: and they that resist shall receive to themselves damnation.

This does not mean there is no place for righteousness, for obeying the word of God; only that while human beings must obey God's commands, *the interpreta-*

tion of their meaning must be decided by the city.[128] In Hobbes's words, "there is need of an interpreter to make scripture canon."[129]

The interpreter, however, is not merely the translator who understands the language in which the Scriptures were written; above and beyond the translator's task interpretation falls to one with the authority to interpret.[130] That is, whoever holds the place of Moses in a Christian commonwealth represents God to the people and is thereby authorized to interpret His word.[131] Not only knowledge, but legitimate power is necessary for right interpretation.

WHY ONLY ONE INTERPRETER: AN HISTORICAL REFRAIN

Perhaps the best way to understand why Hobbes thought there was a need for one and only one interpreter is to recall the view of biblical history he endorses. In the future Christ will come again (at the end of history), at which point the universal Church will appear.[132] At that time there will be no need for interpreting Scriptures written long ago, for the kingdom of God that they portend will be at hand. Interpretation of the revealed Word will give way to the Revelation itself.

In the past, prior to the need for interpretation of the Revelation, the voice of God spoke through particular individuals, the prophets. Prophecy then ceased and Scripture took its place.[133] Here, the point of mediation between humanity and God shifts from the prophet who reveals to the sovereign who interprets; from the individual to the "public person" of the sovereign.[134] In other words, the individual in this Age of Scripture, if you will, is not the medium of God.[135] For this reason Hobbes claims that it "belongs not to the private man, but to the Church [that is, the sovereign] to interpret Scripture."[136] Because of the position human beings now occupy in (biblical) history the right of interpretation belongs solely to the sovereign.

Additionally, because God does not at present speak through individual human beings, questions of good and evil are not within their purview. Consequently, Hobbes can say that the thing that "disposeth men to sedition, is [the idea] *that the knowledge of good and evil belongs to each single man.*"[137] This position is consistent with Hobbes's conclusion about the centrality of human pride; though in this context we see, not the reason why the private person cannot sit at Jupiter's table (to return to the myth of Ixion), *but why the sovereign can.* Biblical history justifies the sovereign's right to do so. Because the sovereign stands *between* man and God—and this standing-between brings new meaning to the Leviathan's status as a "mortal god"—he is not, *qua* sovereign, like the private person whose pridefulness receives such acute treatment in Parts I and II of the *Leviathan.* The sovereign is a public person; the person whose authority and interpretive prerogative are justified by virtue of Christ's renewal of the covenant first fully instantiated in Moses' relationship with God and with His chosen people.

CONCLUDING REMARKS

Who was Adam? Who was Moses? Who was Christ? Who is the Leviathan? In Hobbes's thought, these are seminal and interrelated figures, simultaneously political and theological—or rather, *temporal*. In his attempt to construct a coherent theory of temporal government Hobbes thinks through the problem of pride and of death (both temporal and eternal), to the relationship between Adam and Christ, to the relationship between Moses and Christ, and to the problems of authority and interpretation that are illuminated and, in Hobbes's estimation, rectified by recourse to Moses' covenant with God. In all of this the central question remains what it was for Luther: what is the meaning—theological and political—of Matthew's Christ's proclamation:

> Think not that I have come to destroy the law, or the prophets: I am not come to destroy, but to fulfill. [138]

Hobbes understood the meaning of Christ's fulfillment in a way quite different from Luther. Christ's message of the New Testament was less a disjunction than a *continuation* of the truth of the Old Testament. Moses, to whom was owed obedience and to whom was granted the right of interpretation, emerges as the most prominent political figure in Hobbes, and Christ, who for Luther represents the irruption of something utterly new in history, recapitulates the truth of Moses. Christ is politically significant because He renews what was lost after Moses: Divine authority to rule and the right to represent the Word of God to His people. The Leviathan has this authority and right.

In this formulation, which softens the disjunction between the Old and New Testaments, faith does not have the meaning it did for Luther. The *inwardness* of faith, of which Luther spoke, which provides *all* Christians with their link to God the Son, makes no appearance. Hobbes's faith, consonant with theology from Saint Augustine to Luther and Calvin, "is a gift of God." [139] Unlike theirs, however, Hobbes's faith is not transformative; this is not the faith that staggered Saint Paul at the crossroads. No one may be staggered by God the Son at this moment of history. At this moment only the Leviathan is touched by the hand of God—or rather, is able to *impersonate* God. The Christian commonwealth: what is this but a political body in which God has withdrawn from all but the Leviathan—as He did from all the Israelites except Moses? Faith, that "secret, hidden, spiritual matter," [140] that place where Christ intervenes, where a manifestation of the partially obscure God is present for Christians, is foreclosed. God's trace in history *is* the Leviathan who takes the pride of the citizens in upon himself—and so attenuates *the* problem of temporal life. [141] And this trace, because constituted through covenant between those who verbally renounce their pride out of fear of "death," offers a rebirth of sorts, not unlike that offered when Moses returned from Mount Sinai to find the Jews lost in frenzy. [142]

The "social contract" thus forged is the *choice* made by the sons of Levi[143] to *assent* and *listen* to the Word of God as *spoken* through Moses!

While in Hobbes's formulation, as in Luther's, all are equal under the one sovereign, the one sovereign for Hobbes is not Christ, as it was for Luther, but rather the Leviathan. True, the Leviathan is Christ-like, but through him there is no possibility of possessing the interiority of faith. While the Leviathan may be Christ-like, his explicit connection to God is through Moses;[144] and in *this* connection there is no haven for the Christian faith of the sort Luther imagined that is purported to be available for all. Under Christ all are one in faith; under Moses all are one in obedience.[145]

Hobbes's formulation, in short, fails to provide an adequate account of how Christian faith (of the sort not explicitly linked to obedience to a *temporal* authority) can be respected while the integrity of a governed community can be maintained, which is simply to say that his attempt to make human beings stop seeing double by insisting that faith meant obedience could not hold. The dialectic of renewal that Hobbes provides countermands Luther's dialectic of supersession, it is true, but it does so by turning mostly toward the relationship between Moses and Christ in order that continuities between the two Testaments may be emphasized and temporal order safeguarded. The interiority of faith has no place in Hobbes's Christian commonwealth. Perhaps Luther's reference to the Leviathan as a "perverse notion concerning works"[146] was prophetic: the Leviathan is a figure for whom faith is a stumbling block.[147]

> Then Jesus said unto them, Verily, verily, I say unto you, Moses gave you not that bread from heaven; but my Father giveth you the true bread from heaven.[148]

Hobbes supposes, of course, that the bread Moses gave was bread enough and, in fact, drew a harsh lesson from this looming Old Testament figure:

> there is no nation in the world, whose religion is not established, and receives not its authority from the laws of that nation. It is true, that the law of God receives no evidence from the laws of men. But because men can never by their own wisdom come to the knowledge of what God hath spoken and commanded to be observed, nor be obliged to obey the laws whose author they know not, they are to acquiesce in some human authority or other.[149]

A Moses, a king of the Jews, is necessary in every commonwealth. While Scripture *is* authoritative, the subject can *never* hear its Voice without the authority of the sovereign, the public person of the nation. The silence is pierced not by *listening within*, as Luther, Locke, and Rousseau, each in their own way, would have it, but rather by *listening to* (the sovereign). Locke would subsequently find that this formulation offers not bread enough from heaven, that Christ was more than a renewer of the covenant. Rather, Christ unconceals and clarifies a foundation that was there all along but not fully known *to all*. And while Locke's reformulation of the dialectic of biblical history countered Luther's dialectic of supersession, it supported the distinction between the two realms that Luther wished to make and upon which the entire Christian claim, from Augustine forward, rests. To that dialectic, in which Adam and Christ are the central figures, I now turn.

THREE

Locke: The Dialectic of Clarification and the Politics of Reason

THE EFFLORESCENCE OF THE SEEMINGLY PURE liberal political vision is to be found in the thought of Locke. To comprehend it fully, this flowering, this enlightened clarification, this seemingly explicit political vision in which reason, property, and toleration play so large a part, must be understood as an attempt to grasp the meaning of biblical history and the place of humankind within the particular moment of history in which it dwells. As such, Locke's vision, like the vision of Luther and Hobbes that preceded it, is best understood as a political theology.

Locke's interpretation of the meaning of biblical history differs significantly, however, from that of Luther and Hobbes. The question of the right relationship between the two Testaments is still to be thought through, but the rather labored effort to establish the discontinuities between the Old and the New by Luther, and the equally energetic attempt by Hobbes to show the continuities between the two Testaments, are simply absent in Locke. A stark reading of fulfillment that Matthew's Christ purports to offer is neither affirmed (as it is in Luther) nor deflected (as it is in Hobbes), and this is worthy of note. The theoretical whirlwind that surrounds Luther and Hobbes is absent in Locke. The New fulfills the Old, to be sure, but that dialectic is not a turbulent one. Luther's notion of the interiority of Christian religion and the exteriority of the Law—a notion which Hobbes found so deeply problematic—does not trouble Locke. Christianity and politics can (and theoretically must!) peacefully coexist. An almost Tocquevillean calm reigns about the prospect that politics and religion can be harmonized. What Christ offers does not disturb political life, but neither does it provide its ultimate foundation; the dialectic of biblical history neither destabilizes (Luther) nor restabilizes (Hobbes) political life. The theologically abrupt precipices and chasms Luther constructs and Hobbes bridges, Locke circumscribes; his project neither traverses the hills and valleys, nor attempts to level them. His theological terrain is, from the outset, without stark contours.

The landscape of Locke's political theology, however, is not *entirely* different from that of Luther and Hobbes. Locke's attempt to separate the realms of politics and religion, for example, allies him, at the theoretical level, with Luther, rather than with Hobbes. Yet while affirming this distinction, the burden of Locke's faith, like Hobbes's, is light. Luther's notion of a radical separation between the two realms is retained; but as in Hobbes, Christ does not attenuate the problem of pride. Theoretically, Locke stands in a peculiar relationship to Luther and Hobbes. Embracing aspects of both, he develops a new understanding of the meaning of biblical history; a liberal vision in full flower which neither Luther nor Hobbes could have come to on the basis of their reading of biblical history and the Christ event.

I begin, as with Luther, with a discussion of the two realms; one concerned with spiritual matters,[1] the other concerned with power. The discussion will center around Locke's "Letter on Toleration," which illustrates his understanding of the two realms quite well. In Locke's call for toleration in the "Letter" there is an entirely different understanding of the political consequences of religious *difference* from the one found in Hobbes, and it is one of the more interesting features of Locke's thought that religious faction is a problem that can be solved without imposing orthodoxy. How this can be done, theoretically, is illuminated by a consideration of what causes and sustains religious difference, or heterodoxy, in a political community, and how this difference can be obviated without doing violence to the spiritual realm.

After an initial consideration of Locke's two realms, I turn to a motif in Locke's thought that helps to clarify his notion of toleration. This motif, *unity and difference,* helps to clarify the argument in the "Letter" and sets the stage for the problem that Locke addresses in the *Second Treatise of Government*: how to justify a representative government based on the fundamental unity of all in Adam which refutes Filmer's claim that God established a legitimate authority (itself a mark of difference between the ruler and ruled) right from the beginning.[2]

The motif of unity and difference is, as I have said, to be found in Locke's thoughts on toleration and on the origin and right of government. With respect to government, of course, Adam plays a central part, *not Christ.* The centrality of Adam, therefore, will receive a thorough consideration in a section of its own.

Although Christ is not the essential political figure, He is, nonetheless, important. This will become clear when, in the next section, I consider *The Reasonableness of Christianity.* Here, the fulfillment that Christ purports to offer of the Old is expressed in terms of reason and unconcealment. The dialectical relationship between the two Testaments is less an annulment than a *clarification.* Christ and the New Dispensation do not supersede the Old. The Law of Works remains intact, though now faith is a *supplement* to obedience that counts as righteousness.[3]

Finally, I turn to a general discussion of Locke's view of the meaning of biblical history, and then offer some provisional conclusions. In these sections I consider the extensiveness of the historical "space" between the politically salient events of Adam's fall and the redemption. It is important to note that, because Christ is not the essential political figure, no turbulence accompanies his first coming. There is the possibility of an harmonious continuity, even a peace, in the whole of creation between the events of the fall and the redemption. Even the fall itself loses the sting that it has in Luther's formulation. This tone marks a decisive shift away from that found in Luther and even in Hobbes. Were it not for subsequent eruptions of potentially eschatological thinking—notably in Rousseau, Hegel, Marx, and Nietzsche—it could be said that in Locke's liberal vision was achieved a peace in and with history, a peace according to which it was possible to live contentedly without the premonition of an imminent and utterly transformative cataclysm that occurs only in the "fullness of time" about which all eschatological accounts of the structure of history speak. But more on this in due course.

THE TWO REALMS—AND THEIR ORIGIN

> The care of souls cannot belong to the civil magistrate because his power consists only in outward force; but true and saving religion consists in the inward persuasion of the mind, without which nothing can be acceptable to God. [4]

The distinction between the interior realm of faith and the exterior realm of power is not new; it is found in Luther's thought as well. In Locke this distinction is present, though modified somewhat. Moreover, the justification for his call for toleration is founded upon this distinction. [5]

As with Luther, too, an essential distinction between the two realms revolves around the issue of power. [6] For Locke, power belongs to the realm of "outward things," not the interior realm in which reasoned conviction is the judge. Power cannot change conviction; the two operate in different dimensions. While under compulsion, reason can neither comprehend nor disclose for itself the requirements for salvation. Even if it were true that the power and compulsion could effect a change, the resultant conviction, which puts human beings

> under the necessity to quit the light of their reason, and oppose the dictates of their consciences, and blindly to resign themselves up to the will of their governors and to the religion which either ignorance, ambition, or superstition had chanced to establish [could never assure salvation]. [7]

Reasoning human beings must be allowed to come to their own convictions without outside interference. Magistrates, therefore, should not exercise their power in matters of religious conviction. The use of power would blot out the light of reason, which alone can illuminate the path to salvation. All this, of course, is well known.

While Locke's claim that the imposition of exterior power blocks the path to salvation is well known, not enough attention has been given to what Locke says about the relevance of Christ's first coming for his doctrine of toleration. Locke argues, for example, that prior to the coming of Christ the use of power for religious purposes *was* condoned (in the Old Testament), as a way of extirpating idolatry—a situation in which reason is unenlightened and worships a false God.

Locke, in fact, provides two complementary reasons for this earlier situation. First, the injunction to root out idolatry does not apply to Christians. The Old Testament message pertains only to a *particular* people isolated in a small corner of the world, not to all peoples now under the sway of Christ's *universal* message. In Locke's words, "'Hear, O Israel,' sufficiently restrains the obligations of the law of Moses only to that people."[8]

Second, while the Jewish commonwealth was a theocracy, necessitated by the tendency of inadequately enlightened reason to go astray,[9] the New Dispensation revealed to reason the true foundation of duty, whereafter the use of power—that is, political power—subverted rather than aided its disclosure. Because of the New Dispensation, political power and religious duty could and, indeed, had to be separated. Only after Christ's first coming, in other words, *were there two realms.* And it is because of this radically new situation that Locke concludes that religious affairs ought not to be impinged upon by political power.

> For the commonwealth of the Jews, different in that from all others, was an absolute theocracy; nor was there, or could there be any difference between that commonwealth and the Church. . . . But there is no such thing under the Gospel as a Christian commonwealth. . . . [Christ], indeed taught men how, by faith and good works, they can obtain eternal life; but He instituted no commonwealth.[10]

After the New Dispensation, then, externally imposed power was anathema to the discovery of duty. The earlier (and necessary) relationship between power and religious truth was sundered by Christ's illumination of the foundation of duty. Thereafter, attempts to channel conviction, to destroy heterodoxy, by the use of power must be seen in their true light:

> These things, and all others of this nature, are much rather marks of men striving for power and empire over one another than of the Church of Christ.[11]

Power should never be used to convert one person to the orthodoxy of another. The light of reason can only shine from within each person's soul, which (enlightened by the reason it possesses) is always orthodox unto itself. When the light of reason is subverted the universal message brought by Christ—in contradistinction to the particular message brought by God to the people of Israel[12]—*never gains hold.* The universal message brought by Christ can only gain hold when the reason is unimpinged upon by exterior force. To persecute the heterodoxy of others ossifies the relationship of "otherness," which the universality of the Christian message *can* overcome, provided reason is given the latitude to discover it.

Christian truth, then, demands that Christians accept heterodoxy, that they be tolerant. This paradox: that universality and heterodoxy are not inconsistent, derives from what Locke considers to be the truth of the New Dispensation, a truth according to which reason must not be inhibited by external power.[13]

UNITY AND DIFFERENCE: WHY HETERODOXY REMAINS

Locke's tolerance of heterodoxy, of difference, has so far been attributed to his conviction that the universal message of the New Dispensation requires it. By virtue of a revealed truth which provides the foundation for a morality and duty discoverable by the light of reason and which applies to humankind as a whole, local differences must be tolerated.

The underlying conviction of his call for toleration is, as I have said, that by not intervening with the use of external power, these differences will *diminish* because the revealed truth of Christ *now*—in this moment of Reformation enlightenment—provides humankind with a foundation which, prior to His first coming (and after it in the hands of the Roman Church!), had not been fully clarified. This conviction I will have occasion to consider in greater detail when I turn to a discussion of the significance of Christ.[14] In the interim, however, what must be considered is why, if the New Dispensation provides the foundation for a universal concept of morality and duty, heterodoxy remains in the world. Locke's answer to this question makes it clear why the religious factionalism which, for example, so troubled Hobbes is, for him, an overrated problem: it is an artifact of a misunderstanding which can be easily rectified.

"THE YOKE THAT GALLS THEIR NECKS"

The misunderstanding that contributes to the continuation of heterodoxy stems from a confusion about the right relationship between the two worlds. Misconceiving their purview, the magistrates have used political power to quell religious heterodoxy.[15]

> The stirs that are made proceed not from any peculiar temper of this or that church or religious society, but from the common disposition of all mankind, who when they groan under any heavy burden endeavor naturally to shake off the yoke that galls their necks.[16]

It is not religious difference in itself that is the cause of civil contention. Rather, external power instills enmity in the hearts of those who are threatened by it, who through their natural resistance become threats to civil order. Political power impinging upon the religious domain occasions civil resistance. The supposed causal connection between religion and civil disorder is, therefore, spurious. It is because of differential treatment or partiality that heterodoxy persists in a form that is threatening to civil order.

> It is not the diversity of opinions (which cannot be avoided), but the refusal of toleration to those that are of different opinions (which might have been granted), that has produced all the bustles and wars that have been in the Christian world upon the account of religion.[17]

Leaders of this world who have attempted to eradicate heterodoxy, to create within a civil community an orthodox religious community as well, have created a situation in which the partiality they employ has turned mere difference into a difference which is menacing to society. The "other" who is merely different becomes the "other" who is socially *evil*. By confusing the two worlds, religious difference, which should have no detrimental effect on civil life, erupts in civil life and takes on a socially demonic form.[18] Separate the two worlds, allow each its own affairs, and the evil that accompanies religious difference in a world where the civil and the religious are conflated will disappear. Eliminate partiality and what manifests itself as evil once again becomes mere religious difference, and the virulence associated with religious faction dissipates. In a word, the human attempt to bring God into the world results not in good, but rather in evil, and conversely, to eliminate evil from the world, humankind must not conflate the two realms.

> [If the commonwealth and church would each] contain itself within its own bounds—the one attending to the worldly welfare of the commonwealth, the other to the salvation of souls—it is impossible that any discord should ever have happened between them.[19]

Religious difference, then, need not take on a demonic quality. Provided that forces exterior to religious heterodoxy do not impinge upon it, it will remain different, yet that difference will not be one that makes a difference.[20] Civil peace is possible in a Christian commonwealth—proximally, by instituting a separation between matters of true religion and matters external to it, and ultimately, by Christians *coming to understand* that the path to salvation requires this separation.

INTERNALLY GENERATED DIFFERENCE

While this explanation may satisfactorily account for a certain amount of difference or heterodoxy (which, with time, will be ameliorated because of the universal message brought by Christ), it provides no account whatsoever of those heterodoxies that are self-generated, that is, of those generated from *within* a particular religious community and not attributable to the imposition of power from without. To explain these, Locke writes a postscript to the "Letter" on the matter of heresy and schism, two internally generated sources of difference.

Thus far Locke has accounted for the political danger of religious heterodoxy by recurring to the truth of the New Dispensation: by separating the two worlds, he claims, each can act properly within its own purview, and as a corollary, Christianity contributes to, rather than detracts from, civil peace.[21] Not Christianity, but rather Christianity misconceived, has led to religious factionalism and warfare. And like all misconceptions, this one can be corrected. Heterodoxy is ultimately benign; it does not bespeak an irreconcilable difference that matters politically.

The more difficult case of which to give such a benign account, however, is precisely the case which so troubled Hobbes, *viz.*, where the interpretation of the meaning of the two Testaments yields different conclusions about the right relationship between the political and religious realms and where such politically disastrous interpretations cannot be attributed to external power,[22] to "the yoke that galls their necks." Locke clearly believes, as will become apparent in the discussion of the significance of Christ, that the revelation of the foundation of duty by Christ *does* provide enough light now—at this moment of history after His first coming—to produce something of a consensus about the meaning of Christian duty among reasonable men and women.[23]

Because of this conviction, the most significant problem for Locke is externally generated difference, if you will, rather than internally generated difference.[24] The foundation of duty having been revealed, differences of interpretation not attributable to external power can be obviated provided "what is manifestly contained in the sacred text"[25] serves to guide. This kind of certainty about the content of Scripture can be found in Luther's formulations,[26] though, significantly, not in those of Hobbes. And the reason for this difference in conviction between Locke and Hobbes can be understood quite simply in terms of what they account Christ to have brought into the world.[27] Because of the clarity that Christ brought into the world, heresy and schism are not politically significant problems for Locke. The internally generated difference that they occasion can be obviated by adhering to what is there, in Scripture.

DIFFERENCE IS NOT PROBLEMATIC

At the theoretical level, then, the two kinds of difference are not, for Locke, inherently problematic politically. In the final analysis, both externally generated difference and internally generated difference can be attenuated by a right reading of the Gospel—a reading made possible by the light of the New Dispensation. Far from being the source of political turmoil and religious faction, the New Dispensation provides the ground for civil peace. The New Dispensation does not undermine political life, it supports it. Rather than exacerbate difference, it diminishes it—because toleration is made necessary by the New Dispensation itself. Although this seems to contradict the claim that there is but one true God, toleration is, in fact, consistent with it; for only through the use of unimpeded reason can the one God's truth be known and salvation assured.

> [In the event that I am not persuaded of the truth of a religion] in my own mind, there will be no safety for me in following it. No way whatsoever that I shall walk in against the dictates of my own conscience will ever bring me to the mansions of the blessed. [28]

Although I will not dwell on it here, the implication that this rudimentary fact has for worship and community is, for Locke, almost self-evident. While a common form of worship within a community gives the *appearance* that the one true God is being worshiped, unless inner belief is present among the worshipers, outward appearance will be deceptive. It is inner belief that gives substance to outward worship;[29] without the former, a common form of worship is vacuous. Unicity of worship under exterior compulsion does not necessarily indicate a worship of the one true God. God's truth makes its way into the mind of the person whose reason is unconstrained. Proper worship can only follow from this. Insist on a common form of worship and God's light is lost; accept the paradoxical notion that all may worship as the light of their reason informs them, and God's light once again enters the world.[30] The one true God is revealed to and in a heterodox world.

THE ORIGIN OF GOVERNMENT IN THE EQUALITY OF ALL

The motif of unity and difference does not only arise in Locke's thoughts on toleration. It is present in his discussion of government as well. The assumption in the "Letter" is that heterodoxy is a difference that does not make a difference; that the light of reason, which *all* human beings possess, levels religious differences that manifest themselves as political difference. The "Letter" is a call to recognize this.

In the *Treatises*, Locke argues that the right and origin of government derives from the unity, or equality, of all in the beginning; here the question is how to move from primordial unity to legitimate difference. Locke does this by defending a certain view about who Adam was. Against Filmer, who claims that Adam is *one man* who inherits the right of rule over other human beings, Locke claims that Adam is *all human beings* who inherent the right to rule over all creatures. In Locke's view, all are equal in Adam; in Filmer's view, God ordained *difference* among human beings with Adam.

Adam is central to both *Treatises.* I will, therefore, consider Locke's interpretation of Adam in depth, moving from his refutation, in the *First Treatise*, of Filmer's idea of the grant of rulership by God to the one Adam and his heirs, to a discussion of property, broadly understood, granted to Adam by God (which idea is only fully developed in the *Second Treatise*). Through Adam the notion of the equality of all human beings finds its support; and from this original equality, this nondifferentiated state, legitimate difference emerges.

THE SIGNIFICANCE OF ADAM

For Locke, humankind is not entirely lost and without God's *gifts* after the fall of Adam. Something does, in fact, survive. While Adam was cast out of the garden and lost eternal life, his reason was left intact, and he retained the right of dominion over the creatures of the earth. These two residuals of the fall are the basis of Locke's notion of the equality of all human beings,[31] and together constitute the kernel of Locke's liberal vision.

Because Adam is a crucial biblical figure for Locke, he must address Filmer rather than, say, Hobbes—who also defends the idea of rule by grant from God. Filmer is the real target here;[32] and this because Locke agrees with the formal thesis Filmer advances: that Adam is politically important and that something survived his fall. They differ only with regard to *what* survived. Although his conclusions are reminiscent of Filmer's, Hobbes does not rely on Adam to articulate his positive theory of governmental covenant. Locke and Filmer are allies of a sort, as well as antagonists. It is to rebuff Filmer while at the same time defend the notion of the political importance of Adam that the *First Treatise* is written.

THE DIALECTIC OF PROPERTY

Of the two residuals that survived the fall, I turn first to the right of dominion.

> Whatever God gave by the words of this Grant [of Dominion], 1 Gen. 28, it was not to *Adam* in particular, exclusive of all other Men: whatever *Dominion* he had thereby, it was not a *Private Dominion*, but a Dominion in common with the rest of Mankind.[33]

Adam's right to rule was the right of *all* human beings to rule over the creatures of the earth. Made in the image of God, human beings were set above all creatures and given the right of property in common that they may secure through its use "subsistence and comfort" in this life.[34] The truth of Adam does not establish legitimate difference between human beings, as Filmer claims, but rather establishes a legitimate basis for differentiating the human community *as a whole* from everything else created, and for the dominion over all those things created. The hierarchy of dominion is not God–Adam–other human beings–other created things, but rather God–*humanity*–other created things. The "other" over which dominion can be justifiably exercised is other created things, not other human beings within a differentiated human community. God did not differentiate the human community with Adam. All are still one in Adam. Adam is the undifferentiated human; God did not choose him to have dominion over others. Paternal dominion and the right to rule cannot be derived from the truth of Adam. It is impossible

> that the rulers now on earth should make any benefit, or derive even the least shadow of authority from that, which is held to be the fountain of power, *Adam's private dominion and paternal jurisdiction.* [35]

This does not mean, however, that the original of *political* truth cannot be found in Adam. It can. It must, however, be derived from the correct understanding of the hierarchy of dominion, which Filmer failed to grasp. [36] Political power must derive from the justification that all human beings have to rule over other created things and, thus, must derive from a consideration of the right of property that obtains in the state of nature. What requires an account is how primitive undifferentiated property (which has no fence[37] around it) becomes the differentiated and private property government is instituted to protect. This is one of the important projects of the *Second Treatise:* to move with justification from the equality of humankind in Adam to property differences in his progeny; to provide an account of the genesis of differentiation from nondifferentiation.

In the beginning there was common property. This property was, of course, *used;* for only in this way could the earth *be for* humankind, as God had ordained.

> God, by commanding to subdue, gave authority so far to *appropriate.* [And this] necessarily introduces *private Possessions.* [38]

The use or appropriation of this common property by all initially took the form of an aggregate of individual appropriations; appropriations which did not thwart others in their efforts to secure subsistence and comfort. Simply put, the initial condition is one in which what one uses does not affect what is available to others. In this primitive condition there are no fences that constrain appropriation. In this primitive appropriation a particular self extends itself to include the object appropriated. Yet this extension of the self does not yet impinge on the extensiveness of other selves who similarly appropriate. [39] With primitive property the self has a dominion over created things; private property has not yet appeared.

At this point the bounty of nature is sufficiently ample that the right to property granted by God does not cause a conflict between particular property claims. The right to property does not, consequently, require the consent of all; for the appropriation by one does not impinge on the right or capacity of another to do the same. Nature, the "common mother of all,"[40] and God the father provide the wherewithal and justification for appropriation unconstrained by others among the children of Adam.

> Though the Water running in the Fountain be every ones, yet who can doubt, but that in the Pitcher is his only who drew it out? His *Labour* hath taken it out of the hands of Nature, where it was common, and belong'd equally to all her Children, and *hath* thereby *appropriated* it to himself.[41]

Furthermore, in this primitive condition, though property exists, there is not yet a fixed fence around the self; the border of the self still wanders with the movements of those who appropriate. Thus, for example, although the water drawn from the fountain is possessed by a single person (who moves from one fountain to the next), the particular fountain is not yet possessed in the way that the part of it drawn into the pitcher is. Because human beings are perpetually in motion, their particular claim is limited to the fruits of nature's tree, as it were, and not to the tree itself—which is stationary.

This changes, however, when human communities settle down.[42] Now a new arrangement transpires; boundaries between neighbors are fixed in the ground; human beings appropriate and claim as their own what is itself stationary—the fountain, and so forth.

Yet while this differentiates the earth into parcels that are one's own and another's, equanimity is maintained, and the claims of private property do not yet transgress upon the right of others to their share of what is common. Fences become fixed for the first time, it is true, but this does not yet constrain the appropriation by others.

This second stage of property's development involves a more pronounced exclusion of others. This a more differentiated world, where physical space for the first time is used to mark off property. But even in this greater differentiation and concretion of property claims, the common stock remains ample enough to provide for the others who are excluded by a fixed property claim. (A fixed property claim, in fact, *increases* the common stock available to the rest, for by putting labor into property its productiveness increases—thus making even more of the earth available to others outside the fence.)[43]

Fixed property claims, however, have ordained limits. The increase in productivity that fixed property affords makes it possible, for the first time, to produce more than is needed by the property holder. Were this to occur, the original grant by God to have dominion over the earth for the purpose of human *use* would be violated. In Locke's words,

> the exceeding of . . . *bounds* [lies not] in the largeness of [one's] Possession, but in the perishing of anything uselessly in it.[44]

The legitimate extent of property is limited by the criterion of use. Further differentiation and exclusion is arrested by what the individual property holder can use before it perishes. The grant by God to property has found its fullest articulation.

This articulation, however, like the two before it—"mobile" property and that "fixed" property whose productivity has not yet reached its ordained limit—is simply a culmination of a movement in which not only have particular property claims not been inimical to one another, but particular property holders have not had the occasion to *exchange* with one another. While the relationship of the one to all the rest has been central to Locke's argument, the relationship of the one to the single other—the dyadic relationship—has not.[45] The single other who stands outside the fence delineating a property claim has not been needed to explain the particular property claim itself or its extensiveness. Differentiation has occurred without recourse to that single other. When the possibility of goods uselessly perishing arises, however, this changes, for through exchange, useless perishing can be avoided—and more to the point, further differentiation of property can proceed apace.

In the early stages of this new dyadic situation exchange takes the form of barter, the trade of items with use value, one for another, such that no waste occurs. In this way, if a man

> bartered away Plumbs that would have rotted in a Week, for Nuts that would last good for his eating a whole Year, he did no injury; he wasted not the common Stock; destroyed no part of the Goods that belonged to others, so long as nothing perished uselessly in his hands.[46]

Through exchange the problem of goods perishing because the property holder produces more than can be used is overcome. What would be excessive and illegitimate property for the one alone is made legitimate anew because of the possibility of exchange with the single other. Because the single other appears, at the edge of the property holding, the extent of that property may now justifiably increase. The very increase in the immediate social density justifies a further expansion of private property, which itself further excludes others.

From the vantage point of scarcity this increase in social density and exclusionary property might suggest a diminution of nature's bounty for others; for Locke, however, no such diminishment occurs. More correctly, spoilage does not occur and therefore nature's bounty is not reduced. There is room, in fact, for further differentiation, and this happens when the currency of exchange is pushed to its logical limit.

In the early stages of exchange items of use are exchanged. By exchanging items that will perish if left in the charge of one property owner, with things that last longer but are still perishable, the size of private holdings may increase. But here there is a limit set on the size of the holding; a limit set by the fact that all things of use do perish. Because items with use value do not last indefinitely, the size of a property holding extended through exchange cannot increase indefinitely. In this situation where the extensiveness of property holdings vastly exceeds the amount justifiable for a single, nonexchanging property holder, neither nature nor God's grant has been violated. Because the world of nature created by God is such that there is enough for all (provided humankind does not violate the terms of His grant), property holdings of large size—where the currency of exchange is still items of use—is not excessive or out of balance.

Neither is the next, and culminating stage, of property excessive or out of balance. Here, the currency of exchange reaches its logical limit: it *no longer perishes.* The effect of this is a further increase in the extensiveness of property.

> Find out something that hath the *Use and Value of Money* amongst his Neighbors, [and] you shall see the same man will begin presently to *enlarge* his *Possessions.* [47]

And further on,

> Men have agreed to disproportionate and unequal Possession of the Earth
> . . . having by a tacit and voluntary consent found out a way, how a man
> may fairly possess more land that he himself can use the product of, by
> receiving in exchange for the over surplus, Gold and Silver, which may be
> hoarded up without injury to any one. [48]

At this final stage of property development, humankind is still in compliance with the terms of God's grant. Even extraordinary differences in property holdings do not affront. The criterion not of extensiveness, but rather of useless perishing determines whether the property of one is excessive. By recourse to money, which does not perish, the limit to the extensiveness of property encountered when exchange is by barter, is overcome. Here, finally, the differentiation of property can proceed to no higher, more articulated stage, though within this final stage there is no longer any theoretical limit to the extensiveness of a property holding. [49]

FROM PROPERTY TO REASON

The fence around the self that property represents finds its justification in Holy Ordinance. The supposition throughout Locke's discussion has been that peace exists, that the development of property proceeds without foreign invasion or malevolent contestation; the equality of all in Adam and right of dominion eventually yields differentiated property—all this, again, without violence. The genesis of differentiation, the appearance of fences around the self, has occurred in harmony with God's grant and nature's bounty. In this movement there has been an

> *Equality,* which all Men are in, in respect to Jurisdiction and Dominion over
> one another, [and an] *equal Right* that every man hath, *to his Natural Freedom,* without being subjected to the Will or authority of any other Man. [50]

Although for the purpose of exchange the other has appeared in close proximity, the other has not yet been *hostile*. In due course I will explore the perturbations of this peace. Prior to that, however, I will consider another fence that surrounds the self. This fence does not enclose material property, but rather the interior space of the self that possesses reason. As with property, it is government's charge to protect against violation of this boundary as well.

THE DIALECTIC OF REASON

> Adam was created the perfect Man, his Body and Mind in full possession of their Strength and Reason, and was so capable from the first Instant of his being to provide for his own Support and Preservation, and govern his Actions according to the Dictates of the Law of Reason which God had implanted in him.[51]

The grant of reason is given to *adults* in whom it was either present at the beginning (in Adam) or in whom the faculty has had time to mature (in the adult descendants of Adam). For all human beings subsequent to Adam, the self-sufficiency of reason *must develop*. The movement from childhood to adulthood, consequently, from potential reason to actual reason, is of theoretical importance. Through education reason can become self-sufficient[52] and, *by right*, escape the parental constraint—of family *and* paternal government.

Locke's theoretical challenge is to demonstrate the *difference* between the child (for whom parental dominion is justified) and the adult (for whom it is not) and then to show how paternal dominion (in political life) of the sort Filmer envisions *thwarts* the reason originally granted. Within Filmer's schema, Locke argues, human beings are presumed not to be free adults but rather unfree children.[53]

> The Law that was to govern *Adam,* was the same that was to govern all his Posterity, *the Law of Reason.* But his Off-spring having another way of entrance into the World, different from him, by a natural Birth, that produced them ignorant and without the use of *Reason,* they were not presently *under that Law:* for no Body can be under a Law, which is not promulgated to him; and this Law being promulgated or made known by *Reason* only, he that is not come to the Use of his *Reason,* cannot be said to be *under this Law;* and *Adam's* Children being not presently as soon as born, *under this Law of Reason* were not presently free.[54]

Filmer failed, first, to recognize the qualitative leap that the movement from childhood to adulthood occasions and, second, to distinguish between paternal and political power. Paternal power, which presides over children until they can preside over themselves,[55] must be distinguished from political power. To make paternal power the model of political power presupposes that adult human beings are as yet still children. To return to what is perhaps the central concern of Locke's entire theoretical edifice, by treating adults as children the light of reason, which only adults possess, is extinguished. Adults must be distinguished from children, reason and freedom from their absence. Reason and the politics of adulthood must be the basis for legitimate government. The politics of childhood must be reserved for the family alone, which is the only arena where this kind of dominion can be practiced without doing violence to God's grant.[56]

FROM CHILD SOCIETY TO ADULT SOCIETY

The possession of reason by adults makes it possible—even more, makes it *right*—for political society to be ordered in a certain way. Locke must account, however, for the many instances where political society has been paternally ruled, where adults have been treated as children. If reason is the possession of adults, why has paternal rule been so prevalent? This difficulty is answered by jumping scale, by applying his insights about the distinction between child and adult *to society itself.* Here—a perennial Christian theme to which even Rousseau would later recur in *Emile*—ontogenetic development is recapitulated in phylogenetic development.[57]

Societies, Locke claims, can be childlike or adultlike. Furthermore, just as the child develops into an adult, so, too, do child societies mature into adult societies. Patriarchy was the original of government because the *difference* was ever so small between rule of the child by the father and rule of the child society by the patriarch. Here the *logical* distinction between political and paternal rule for human beings is not yet clear; *accustomed* to it from infancy,[58] political rule seemed to the child society the natural extension of rule by the father in the family.

The patriarchal arrangement served the original of human society well because in its infancy the father (figuratively and literally) could best protect it against foreign invasion.[59] Here the foreign *other* who threatens the tenuous hold on life that early society possesses cannot be repulsed by "the children." Like the father-kings of Israel who once protected children-subjects,[60] the father fends off the other, and society's hold on life becomes less tenuous; the fence around society becomes more secure. The child society is able to mature into an adult society.

The fence around society that the father secures, however, provides the "space," as it were, for the less than benign forces within society to come to the fore. Unimpinged upon by the foreign other, potentialities internal to society are unleashed, and these ultimately divulge the contingent nature of paternal dominion. The integrity of the society begins to weaken; the corruption resulting from vain ambition and concupiscence of the father-ruler "increases the Power without doing the Business, for which it was given,"[61] and the people begin to distrust the privilege of the magistrate. The destabilizing force of these higher passions (to borrow Hobbes's term), which themselves emerge when protected from foreign threat, now menace from *within* the fence that borders society. The child society was safeguarded from forces without; now the maturing adult society threatens to explode from forces within.

There are intimations that Locke found in the development of material property the beginning of an explanation for this domestic turmoil. Because in its final stage the accumulation of property has no logical limit (on account of the emergence of money), great differentials of property and power can arise, differentials that despite their justification by the original divine ordination have less than beneficent side effects.

> [Earlier in history human beings] had neither felt the Oppression of Tyrannical Dominion, nor did the Fashion of the Age, nor their Possessions, or way of living (which afforded little matter for Covetousness or Ambition) give them any reason to apprehend or provide against it.[62]

This explanation is still external to the problem, however. Money makes it possible to justify possessing great tracts of land, but *why* human beings should *want* extensive land holdings and the power that would go with them is not clear. The grant to use the natural world rationally and industriously is part of the answer, to be sure, but over time the *application* of these virtues produces "matter for covetousness and ambition," and so is implicated.

An account Locke does not give is that the relationship to and appropriation of nature is *not* primordial; that is, there is in human beings a latent potential for disharmony that is *ontologically prior* to the grant of dominion, but which emerges into consciousness only as a consequence of living in society and developing private property. Although the propensity for disharmony is ontologically prior to the grant of dominion,[63] it may be epistemologically subsequent to it.

Locke is, I think, aware of the difficulty. He alludes, for example, to "the Golden Age"[64]—that time before the problem *developed*—but he is not prepared to say that the problem has been there, *latent,* from the very beginning. This would have brought him perilously close to attributing to Adam's fall not only the loss of eternal life, but also the receipt of spiritual corruption, of sin; and this he was not prepared to accept. Sounding almost Greek, Locke recurs instead to a Golden Age rather than to a Reformation account that would have linked the problem to the very constitution of humankind.[65]

Nevertheless, for Locke, the maturing society gradually realizes in what the true foundation of government consists—a realization that dawns when domestic tranquility becomes more and more elusive. The Golden Age explanation suits his purpose because the emergent difficulties that succeed the Golden Age reveal not the original (though latent) corruption in humankind, but the true foundation of government.

The Golden Age explanation cannot, however, account for the foreigner who wished to invade and who was repulsed by the father *before* domestic tranquility was threatened from within. One of the responsibilities of paternal government, recall, is to oppose the *other* who might invade the child society. The threat of the foreign other is present right from the outset. The original condition is not so harmonious after all; it has within it the seeds of disharmony, violence, and invasion.

Locke, again, does not wish to go in this direction. His glance is not backward, to the nature of the problem, but forward to its resolution. Beginning from paternal dominion, of child society accustomed to the father who protects, an adult society develops. And because of this development the true (adult) basis of government comes into view. Again, this becomes clear only when certain excesses are unconcealed.

> Yet when Ambition and Luxury, in future Ages would retain and increase the Power, without doing the Business, for which it was given, and aided by Flattery, taught Princes to have distinct and separate interests from their People, Men found it necessary to examine more carefully *the Original* and Rights of Government. [66]

This reconsideration pierces the veil of accustomization that is the foundation of the contingent authority of the father; the true foundation of government is unconcealed: the grant of reason to Adam—the *adult* in whom reason reigns. Accumulated experience now conspires to overcome custom and habit and to reveal the original grant. *Now* reason may shine.

As with Hobbes, there is a sense that the present moment is a privileged one, one where what has been so long concealed is finally established on firm footing. (Recall Hobbes's argument about the recent removal of the three knots upon Christian liberty.)[67] As with Luther, there is the sense that we have moved from childhood to adulthood. In this case, reason cannot penetrate the unfathomable mysteries of the whole, yet it *is* capable of sufficient light and power to be able to form a government that will not fall into the darkness of childhood and rule by the father.[68] And for each, a rebirth of sorts, an end to the old ways that bring neither peace nor true happiness, is made possible by covenant which reaffirms what had earlier been lost or obscured from view.

THE TASK OF GOVERNMENT

> The great and *chief end* . . . of Men's uniting into Commonwealths, and putting themselves under Government, *is the preservation of their Property.* [69]

The task of government is to protect property—broadly understood. In the development of material property disharmony had not yet appeared; its articulation did not violate God's ordination; appropriation posed no threat. Government was not as yet necessary, which is to say property is prepolitical.

With God's grant of reason, however, it is otherwise. While *there* from the beginning, reason emerges only when child societies develop into adult societies, when the adult outgrows the need for the father patriarch. *Now that societies are adult societies,* property—again, broadly understood to include God's grant of reason and dominion to Adam—must be protected. The task of government is, in effect, to protect all who *are* one in Adam and *know* themselves to be one in Adam.

The *sanctification* of the adult person, the belief that the many are one in Adam,[70] is the foundation for Locke's rejection of absolute monarchy. By allowing monarchs to rule over citizen-adults, no fence secures the integrity of the person in whom reason reigns from the *will* of the monarch;[71] the personhood of the adult is obliterated by a relationship to the monarch that presupposes that the adult is a child bereft of reason. Absolute monarchy, by its very nature, is an invasion of the person of the adult; it gives license to the one for the purported purpose of protecting each from the other. The real threat, however, is not from the one solitary individual who would oppress another (for these are all united in Adam), but from the ruler who would eclipse reason by his or her act of willfulness against citizens.

> [To misunderstand this] is to think that Men are so foolish that they can take care to avoid what Mischiefs may be done to them by *Pole-Cats,* or *Foxes,* but are content, nay think it Safety, to be devoured by *Lions.*[72]

What is necessary is that reason not be thwarted—more than that, that family, church, and education nurture it;[73] that its light be allowed to shine; that there be standing rules that are not arbitrary, and that allow "everyone to know what is his."[74] In this way uncertainty can be alleviated[75] and reason nurtured. The fence around the self is finally respected—as it should be, according to Holy ordinance.

With this form of government, moreover, there is a *supplement* to the Heavenly Judge who granted reason and the original right of dominion to Adam. Government based on reason is a judge on earth which can redress the grievances of those who heretofore could only appeal to heaven.[76] With the assistance of the law of legitimate government (based on the truth of Adam) the sanctity of the self, now fully understood, is honored—not by God, but by humankind. God's creation itself now honors its Holy ground by constituting a political order of a certain sort.

THE SIGNIFICANCE OF CHRIST: OF OBEDIENCE AND FAITH

Christ's truth is not the foundation of political order, though in important respects He buttresses it.[77] Christ neither supersedes Adam's grant nor the need to obey the Law of Moses. Christ rather *clarifies* what yet remained obscure in the Old Testament. Consequently, the political truth established there is not threatened by Christ's first coming. The crucial question for both Luther and Hobbes, what is the *political* meaning of Christ? is, of course, important, but Locke's genius is that he understands the meaning of the fulfillment offered by Christ in such a way that it mostly deflects the question.[78]

More is at issue with Christ's first coming than politics, however. Recall that the Old Dispensation required works and the Law for righteousness sake. Obedience to God's commands is essential; what is required of the faithful is the "exact performance of every title";[79] this means that righteousness is measured, not by faith, but by actions. With Adam perfect obedience was lost,[80] however, and with it the human claim to eternal life. Human beings were subsequently doubly cursed; not only was death brought into the world, but righteousness— and with it, salvation—became impossible.

The impossibility of righteousness, of acting in accordance with God's command, is not, however, a sign of spiritual corruption, of original sin. Locke is very careful to avoid this conclusion, and he attempts to find the middle ground between those who,

> would have all Adam's posterity doomed to eternal infinite punishment, for the transgression of Adam . . . [and others who saw this to be] so little consistent with the justice and goodness of the great and infinite God, that they thought there was no redemption necessary.[81]

Locke, in other words, denies in Adam a spiritual corruption, yet envisages Christ as an answer to the impossibility of Adam's heirs attaining salvation. Christ is an answer to Adam, not because He takes in upon Himself the spiritual corruption of His bride, the human being (as Luther might have argued), but because the faith He brings *completes* the active righteousness associated with the righteousness of works. Thus, although Locke never spells out why perfect obedience is not possible once Adam fell,[82] he nevertheless argues that with faith in Christ it is possible to complete the active righteousness called for in the Old Testament.

The completion made possible through Christ compensates for the fact that *any* infraction against the Old Dispensation costs the human being eternal life.

> The difference between the law of works and the law of faith is only this;—that the law of *works* makes no allowance for failing on any occasion. Those that obey are righteous: those that in any part disobey, are unrighteous, and must not expect [eternal] life, the reward of righteousness.[83]

Faith in Christ, in a word, makes up for the inability to act righteously without fail. Through a belief in Christ, which supplements but does not replace what is called for under the Old Law, eternal life comes within the grasp of the Christian. The Law of the Old Testament still makes its claim; only now, in conjunction with faith, righteousness is again possible. Here the interiority of faith does not supersede the exteriority of the Law (to borrow from Luther), but is an adjunct to it that corrects for the loss of obedience and righteousness in Adam. Christ supplements; he does *not* reconstitute the foundation of righteousness.

Locke is indeed quite adamant about this reading of the meaning of fulfill-ment. The seemingly more generous and nondialectical alternative, one which might have Christ annul the Old Dispensation, undermines the Law that God first ordained. Without this Law the order of the world is turned on its head.

> The law [cannot] be taken away or dispensed with, without changing the nature of things, or overturning the measures of right and wrong; and thereby introducing and authorizing irregularity, confusion and disorder in the world.[84]

In spite of the fact that the Old moral Law still calls, however, there are two senses in which the New is necessary. First, there is prophetic anticipation of the New in the Old Testament that requires the very fulfillment that retrospec-tively transforms and fixes its significance. Here, the central figure of the dialec-tic who anticipates the New is not Moses, as it was for Hobbes, but rather Abraham; it was he who, when far too old to have children, had faith— *believed*—that when God said he and Sarah would yet have a son, it would come to pass.

> He *staggered not* at the promise of God through unbelief; but was strong in faith; giving glory to God . . . [And this teaches us] that as Abraham was justified for *his* faith; so also *ours* shall be accounted to us for righteousness, if we believe in God as Abraham did.[85]

Although the particular proposition that Abraham was required to believe per-tained to him alone, the general form of the proposition is that everyone should "believe *what God requires him to believe*";[86] and in the post-Incarnation epoch this means believing that Christ was the Messiah. In this, faith attains its highest form and retrospectively illuminates the faith of Abraham. The faith that brought forth a particular people gives way to a saving faith available to all.

The second sense in which the New is necessary, in spite of the still reign-ing Old Dispensation, is that Christ's mission of reinstantiating what was lost with Adam's fall (eternal life) would not have been possible without a way for human beings to be righteous once again.

> This then being the case, (that whoever is guilty of any sin, should cer-tainly die and cease to be;) the benefit of life restored by Christ at the resurrection would have been no great advantage . . . if God had not found out a way to justify some.[87]

Faith in Christ *restores* righteousness and makes possible eternal life. Through this restoration Christians are able to live eternally upon the resurrection at Christ's second coming. Although the Old Dispensation still reigns, the New remedies the loss of righteousness under the Old and points beyond itself to a resurrection in the future. Faith is necessary here not because it fulfills the Old, but because it makes possible human participation in what is to come. Not the dialectical relationship of the Old and the New (with its intimation of the truth of Christ in the truth of Abraham), but the precondition of regaining the eternal life lost by Adam is the message here.

THE UNCONCEALMENT

The relationship between the Old Dispensation, the New, and the final redemption brings into focus the central theme in Locke's understanding of the meaning of Christ: the gradual *unconcealment* of His truth to those who expected in Christ not a final redemption but a renewal of the earthly kingdom. Anticipating a literal kingdom, the hearers of Christ were unprepared, Locke claims, for His message of the heavenly kingdom to come, and the unconcealment of this truth to them is the story of Christ's first coming.[88]

Recall that Adam was granted natural reason by God, a natural reason which, as part of the Old Dispensation, is still regnant. What I want to suggest now is that Christ's message, which supplements the Law of obedience that still reigns, was, in Locke's view, revealed only gradually. Although reason is *present* from the beginning, it was not sufficiently enlightened prior to Christ.

> Though the works of nature, in every part of them, sufficiently evidence a deity; yet the world made so little use of their *reason*, that they saw him not where even by the impressions of himself he was easy to be found. Sense and lust blinded their minds in some, and a careless inadvertency in others; and fearful apprehension in most . . . gave them up into the hands of their priests; to fill their heads with false notions of the Deity.[89]

In this unenlightened mode societies ruled by priests were concerned with the accouterments of religion but not with virtue and moral duty, the real cement of a society. Barely retaining their integrity, societies continued with just enough of this cement to "tie [them] together in subjection."[90] Lacking a foundation in Christian virtue, they were held together—but not in freedom.[91]

The illuminative truth of reason *did* rule the minds of a few human beings prior to Christ, notably the philosophers, but it was

> too hard a task for unassisted reason, to establish morality, in all its parts, upon its true foundation; with a clear and convincing light.[92]

Moreover, philosophers, assisted by natural reason, which "makes but a slow progress and little advance in the world,"[93] had no way to make the laws of reason authoritative. The great majority of human beings do not have the leisure to enlarge their knowledge; hence, they cannot know, but must *believe*.[94] And because belief is predicated on authority,[95] even the law of reason discovered by the philosophers could not be disseminated.

A fortunate attribute of the faculty of reason, however, is that while it discovers for itself only slowly, "nothing seems hard to our understanding, that is once known."[96] And because of Christ's revelation, the true foundation of virtue and moral duty has been disclosed. By its authority, revelation was able to accomplish what the philosophers could not: extend the rule of reason to those who previously could not have attained it; cure the defects of local versions of morality and supplant it with a universal morality;[97] and, finally, level differences in knowledge between those who once had the leisure to know and those who did not. Now both groups stand before the revealed truth and are informed by it.[98]

CHRIST'S THREE-PART REVELATION

Christ, then, gradually revealed the truth to those who had believed what the priests had told them: that the Messiah would renew the earthly kingdom. This gradual revelation by Christ was actually tripartite: first, miracles He performed; second, intimations that He was the Messiah; and third; open declarations to that effect.[99]

The performance of miracles was designed to convince without speech that Christ was the Messiah.[100] Although chronologically farthest removed from the revelation of who Christ was, miracles are, in an important sense, the foundation upon which the second and third parts of Christ's revelation rest. Without miracles there could be no proof that a divine *interruption* in the regularities of nature had occurred. In Locke's words, miracles are "that foundation on which believers of any divine revelation must ultimately bottom their faith."[101]

Intimations in speech (parables) come closer to open declaration but are not yet that. By intimations Christ still conceals himself in order that He may fulfill His mission.[102] Had Christ declared openly who He was, He would have been set up as an earthly king,[103] for the children of Abraham had no other thoughts of the Messiah, "but of a mighty temporal prince."[104] This was not Christ's mission. His hearers, therefore, had to be prepared for the truth "in degrees,"[105] through intimations initially, and then, when more fully prepared, through parables.[106]

Finally, prior to His death, and after He had fulfilled His mission on earth, Christ openly declares His kingdom. But significantly, it is only after Christ's death that His truth (now openly declared) is fully understood,[107] though not immediately. Even after Christ died his disciples could not bear the truth of the kingdom He professed, though they more than anyone else had been prepared for it and had received open declarations of it. Because they could not bear it, there was the need for the Holy Ghost, which gave the apostles "full persuasion."[108]

With the advent of the Holy Ghost the meaning of Christ's kingdom is fully revealed: He came to "give a full and clear sense" to the Law and of the kingdom (and to what was necessary to enter into it), "free from the loosening glosses of the scribes and the pharisees."[109] This clarification reaffirmed the need to do good works; only now such works had to be conjoined with the need for faith. The full effect of this conjunction was to bring the world out of the "Egyptian darkness" and into the light of God initially possessed by the people of Israel alone; only now it is not one people who may claim it, but the whole of humanity.[110]

At that point the movement from concealment to unconcealment reaches its conclusion. The authority of God, once given only to the people of Israel, and the foundation of virtue and moral duty in reason, once possessed only by the philosophers, are now united in the full revelation and enlightenment accomplished by the Holy Ghost.[111] Now the light of reason, first granted to Adam, shines *with authority.*

The Structure of Biblical History

The reason of Adam is more fully authorized, or rather comes to *know* itself to be authoritative, upon Christ's first coming. Thus, while reason *was there from the beginning,* it is not yet *conscious of its authority* until the death of Christ.[112] From the truth of Adam derives the truth of government, but only in the truth of Christ is the truth of (Adam's) reason substantiated and clarified. While reason was an ontological fact from the beginning (in the primordial time of Adam), its epistemological foundation (what humans know of it) emerges only later. Here essence precedes existence ontologically, but existence precedes essence epistemologically.

Human beings stand, then, between Adam and the redemption. Aided by Christ, who clarifies the truth of Adam, they are now able to set government authoritatively on its true foundation. In this, Christ neither supersedes the Old Dispensation nor destabilizes political life. This latter point Hobbes, too, would have argued; yet this difference remained: Hobbes wished to conflate the two realms, Locke to separate them.

The space surrounding the self that finds its justification in the grant by God to Adam remains intact, and in fact is further authorized by Christ. Although death conquers the self for a time in this moment of history prior to the redemption, death itself is conquered in the end. The self, protected, insulated, and enlightened by reason, achieves an ultimate victory over death and nonbeing. An integrity of the self for the interval of present history under legitimate government, then the darkness and nonbeing of death, and finally the renewal of life and light: this is the imagery of Locke's reading of biblical history.

The task of human beings who dwell in this present moment of history is to make sure that the integrity of the self is maintained. While death cannot be overcome by humankind, in respecting the self and its borders, by living in accordance with the Old and New Dispensation, preparation is made for the victory of eternal life over death. Government of the sort Locke envisions (along with the institutions of family, education, and church)[113] is an essential part of that preparation.

FROM THE EXTENSIVE SELF, TO NONBEING, TO ETERNITY

Insofar as reason and the right of property that inheres in all are protected by government, the sanctity of the self is not violated. This has been most pronounced in Locke's insistence that reason be allowed to shine. Locke's "Letter," the *First* and *Second Treatises,* and the *Reasonableness* are testimonies to this concern. But that it *ought* to be allowed to shine because of the very truth of biblical history already implies the possibility that it will not, that human beings will obliterate this truth by misunderstanding what is necessary for its illumination. The "Letter" is quite revealing in this respect; there, Locke repeatedly points out that attempts to quash the reasoning soul with external force obscure the light of reason and violate the fully revealed truth of Christ.

Also in the "Letter," and in the *Second Treatise* as well, Locke's assertion that all association be voluntary must be seen as an effort to let reason take its course without external impingements. That government, the highest form of human association, is to be formed by consent, is the obvious conclusion of Locke's theological position.[114]

Then there is the matter of fences around the self. Here, there is the possibility of invasion—as I have pointed out on several occasions. This threat of invasion also represents a way in which the space around the self, the self in which reason resides, can fall into darkness and death.

In Locke's exhortation to let reason shine and to protect the self, there is the tacit acknowledgment that light can give way to darkness, that everything can come apart.[115] This almost Post-Modern theme lurks under the surface of Locke's writings, to be sure; but remember, too, that the victory of death over life is only a temporary victory. While everything may fall apart, it is ultimately put back together, provided the requisite faith is present, at the redemption. As with Luther, death is only an "aweful *intermediate* event."[116] And this solution to the tendency to disintegrate is what transposes what could be seen in Post-Modern terms back into the key of Christianity, where it belongs.

CONCLUDING REMARKS

For Luther and Hobbes an encounter with the Divine was an awesome affair; the moments or personations of God confronted the Christian either in the abyss of powerlessness (Luther)[117] or through that mortal-God, the Leviathan (Hobbes).[118] How different this is from Locke. Locke neither accentuates the disjunctions between the two Testaments by elevating Christ's significance (Luther), nor does he minimize the disjunctions by seeing a continuity between Moses and Christ (Hobbes). Locke is different, in a word, because he locates the nexus between God and humankind in Adam, and Adam, unlike Luther's Christ or Hobbes's Leviathan, is not an awesome figure.

There is more at stake here than the tonality of theology. The ease with which Locke proceeds—the sense that the nexus *is already* established and that no massive effort is needed, either by the individual (Luther) or the political community (Hobbes), to grasp what forever threatens to recede from view— cannot help but be noticed. The change in tone from Luther and Hobbes to Locke is unmistakable. For Locke, the sanctity of humankind, the link with the Divine, is established by virtue of *who we are,* not *what we must yet do;* it is fore-gone, not yet to be achieved[119] through the intercession of God the Son or through that mortal-God, the Leviathan. Human beings are all one in Adam. The Christ of Luther and the Leviathan of Hobbes give way to the Adam of Locke, on the basis of whom the link with the Divine is *already* secure.

Finally, at the outset of this chapter I noted that after Locke (in Rousseau, Hegel, Marx, and Nietzsche), thought which is eschatological in tone becomes prominent. In these formulations the fullness of time is at hand, and the politi-cal implications that follow are unlike any that have been considered up to this point. These latter eschatological (and politically authoritative) histories must be starkly contrasted with Locke's vision of biblical history.

For Locke, human beings stand between the beginning with Adam and the redemption at Christ's second coming. The human task before God is rigorous yet within reach. God requires only an "application of mind and sincerity of heart."[120] In the interim of history, they are illuminated by reason,[121] able to establish government that respects the self, and are content to know that after the death that obliterates comes eternal life.[122] How this changes when the po-litically authoritative history recurred to is no longer biblical history, that is, just how closely political and historical speculation are linked, becomes appar-ent when the transposition of content *but not form* occurs.

FOUR

Rousseau: The History of Diremption and the Politics of Errancy

ROUSSEAU'S IS A SEARCH for what is "most hidden and most present,"[1] for that silent measure which confirms our errancy even while, in its hushed tone, it urgently implores us to return to the home ground of the soul. Politics, broadly conceived, corresponds not to verities corroborated by the partial presence of God in history, but rather to concealments which must be attended to. Less does his thinking point to practical solutions than to problems rooted in the (albeit strange) history of the human soul. Above all, for Rousseau, it is the *failure* to attend to concealment that has disastrous political consequences—the central motif of Plato's *Republic*, though here transposed into Rousseau's inimitable key.

The theme of concealment and errancy is found in Luther, Hobbes, and Locke, of course, but it is mitigated there in one way or another by Christ, and this is decisive. Whether the soul finds Christ's solace in the *Nunc-stans* that comes to presence in the abyss (Luther) or at the end of history because it merely *assents* that Jesus is the Christ (Hobbes and Locke),[2] the Mediator assures that the faithful will be reprieved. There may be postponement, but not abandonment. Absent Christ, Rousseau's exiled soul restively searches, now this way, now that, *almost* lost to itself, *almost* incapable of its own deliverance. Deliverance, if it may be called that, does not come by way of a Mediator, but rather through an anamnetic recovery of foundations which have all but been concealed from view, foundations which are, again, "most hidden and most present." Where Luther would wrestle with sin, with his carnal nature, that he may find himself in Christ, and Hobbes and Locke would confidently employ reason within an envelope circumscribed by Revelation (which reason does not confute), and assent to Christ, Rousseau would expose one life, the life of illusion, that he may be oriented, even if not disposed, unto another. *Decipimur specie recti:*[3] the credo of the soul that must pass through the realm of appearance in order to come unto itself.

Expressed this way, of course, the journey of the soul resembles that described by Luther. This parallel is not without relevance, though it ought to be invoked with care: for both Luther and Rousseau the soul must be twice-born in order to reach its home ground.[4] The vacuity not of the "world" but of the "city" must be *fully* comprehended in order to live in its midst. Only this fully comprehending is the antidote to the Thrasymachean temptation. Here is a denial of one world which is at once insubstantial *and yet a temptation* in favor of another that is difficult but absolutely necessary to attain—a guiding thought in certain Christian and anti-Christian souls alike.

What *is* different with Rousseau, of course, is that biblical history is not politically authoritative history. Absent is the central event of Christ's first coming, the event around which dialectical thinking revolves in Luther, Hobbes, and Locke. *This* manner of preserving and annulling is not to be found in Rousseau.

Nevertheless, the movement from the state of nature to civil society is a grand pivot point of history which, like the Christ event in Christianity, entails a kind of ontological transformation of the human situation.[5] The history is different; the linkage of identity and history not confirmable by reason alone, however, remains. Nevertheless, having said this, the theoretical challenges that arise in Rousseau are somewhat different from those found in Luther, Hobbes, and Locke. Errancy, concealment, and atonement remain; it is their structure which is different—which difference overshadows the conventional conclusion that, say, Hobbes, Locke, and Rousseau are best understood to be contract theorists working within roughly the same wholly disenchanted and thoroughly ahistorical worldview.[6]

Briefly, because the valence of *assent* in Hobbes and Locke must be understood as a *religious* articulation inexorably bound to the insufficiencies of human reason in the face of a world which confronts the soul with the prospect of death (in the state of nature), the social contract entered into by virtue of assent reiterates the proclamation of rebirth of the natural man (Adam) unto the body of Christ. Once reborn, there is stability and genuine human health. Ascent here is not *mere* words; it is the occasion of rebirth.

Rousseau, on the other hand, does not privilege the word. Prior to the word is the voice of nature, and it is for this reason that he *must* be worried about the *decline* of the social contract made by assent in *The Social Contract.* Unlike Hobbes and Locke, the word offers no assurance; it itself has no deeper ground—hence Rousseau's perturbed efforts and occasionally frantic worries about linking the social contract with other institutional arrangements that will slow but not arrest its inevitable decline. The voice is the source, but the voice is not the word—for the word betrays errancy and concealment. And so the social contract of Hobbes and Locke (which is such a clean, tidy, and transformative affair) can offer little hope of *sustaining* a political community for Rousseau. Hobbes, Locke, and Rousseau each offer a "contract theory," to be sure; yet without looking at their respective histories of errancy, concealment, and

atonement, the context into which these theories fit and the nature and sufficiency of the political project remains obscured.

I begin by considering both the content of Rousseau's politically authoritative
history and some of the issues that arise because of its peculiar character. In dis-
missing Christianity, along with any politics that might be derivable from it,
Rousseau radicalizes the search for origins and, in effect, accuses Christianity of
not going back far enough. The *real* beginning is the state of nature. Professing to
have found it, he contrasts it to civil society in such a way that the starkness of
the oppositions he announces rivals even Luther's distinctions between the two
realms. Next I turn to Rousseau's two realms: natural and civil, and to the many
antinomies he invokes in order to infuse them with content. Rousseau, of
course, eulogizes the natural, free, active, solitary human being who resides in
the state of nature. The very remoteness of that realm, however, attests to the
difficulty of grasping it in this present, civil, moment of history. With modifica-
tion, what Luther said of the pre-Edenic condition Rousseau could have said of
the state of nature:

> All these things we have lost through sin to such an extent that we can
> conceive of them only in a negative and not a positive way. From the evil
> which we have with us we are forced to infer how great the good is that we
> have lost.[7]

This paradox, in which primitive unity is confirmed all the more by the magnitude of errancy, goes to the very core of Rousseau's thought, and introduces a
tension into his work that is absent in Hobbes and Locke. The source of this
tension cannot simply be traced to an historicization that brings into focus the
magnitude of human errancy (in this case, within civil life) yet which forecloses
the prospect of returning to the primordial, unalienated state. This thought is to
be found in Luther, Hobbes, and Locke. In Rousseau's work the mode of atonement has a different temporal horizon.[8] The unalienated state was *then,* this is
now. Theologically, Saint Paul's Adamic myth, by which Edenic sin *then* is
counterpoised by Christ's intercession *now,*[9] is reproduced here, but without a
"Christ" who "saves" the soul from errancy. Rousseau's history illuminates what
has been lost, but does not seemingly permit that it be regained in this present
moment. To explore how this difficulty can be overcome, how life can be made
substantial again, I turn in the next sections to various modes of atonement that
Rousseau proposes. There are several: famed societies; the general will; civil religion; and education. In the section on education I will significantly alter what
I have said thus far about the place and meaning of history in Rousseau's
thought. Before concluding, I consider the complexities of Rousseau's vision of
history and then his transposition and rejection of Christian political theology
as well as his final arrival at a position that is, in certain respects, Platonic.

Politically Authoritative History in a New Key

I have already noted in a preliminary way the theoretical challenge that Rousseau faces in his effort to ground political authority on other than biblical sources. His cautious remarks in the *Second Discourse* about the relationship between the origin *written of* in Scripture and the origin of which he will speak is suggestive.

> It is evident from reading the Holy Scripture that the first man, having received enlightenment and precepts directly from God, was not himself in that state.[10]

This is not entirely opaque: the state of nature *precedes* the Bible. It is *before God*, as it were.[11] The Old Testament beginning corresponds to the time that can be easily *remembered*, because written down.[12] The real beginning, however, cannot easily be remembered. It has been covered, obscured, almost obliterated from memory.[13] Rousseau's task, therefore, is to uncover what has been lost to memory (of which no previously written words *can* remind us), to recover that primordial truth which antedates the written word, and yet convey it *in* words, despite their being implicated in the very concealment which he would wish to expose.

This act of recovery is of a special sort. It entails a kind of listening within, an attending to a voice that does not speak the language of facts, of science. The faculty which trains upon facts is of no use here. The *Word* of nature indeed speaks, but in a voice which has long been silenced, and history, the movement from an almost obliterated *then* toward an everyday and inauthentic *now*, can only be known through this listening within.

> Let us therefore begin by setting all the facts aside, for they do not affect the question. The researches which can be undertaken concerning this subject *must not be taken for historical truths*, but only for hypothetical and conditional reasonings better suited to clarify the nature of things than show their true origin.[14]

The state of nature, "which no longer exists, which perhaps never existed, [and] which probably never will exist,"[15] is the standard by which civil society must be measured. Notwithstanding its obscurity, inaccessibility, and perhaps even its unreality, the state of nature, of which only the meagerest *trace* still remains, is nevertheless the heretofore unknown thing by which all known things must be understood and judged.[16] By this light, the light of nature, the true nature of civil society is revealed and the ground for a critique of political authority is secured.

Having cleared the way, having disposed of both the facts (because they are not a register of *human* truth) and biblical myth (because it is written down, and therefore an artifact of civil society),[17] Rousseau delivers a prologue.

O man, whatever country you may come from, what ever your opinions may be, *listen:* here is your history as I believed it to read, not in the books of your fellowmen, which are liars, but in nature, which never lies.[18]

Already in these remarks is the conjoining of country, opinion, books— the multiplicity of things about and with which human beings squabble, fight, and die—and the suggestion that *listening* may reveal the unity that is drowned out by the din and discord. Rousseau continues,

The times of which I am going to speak are very far off: *how you have changed from what you were!* It is, as it were, the life of your species that I am going to describe to you . . . which your education and habits have been able to corrupt but have not been able to destroy.[19]

Here is a supplication to return to the point of errancy, to that *silent* wisdom which does not write. Opening reference in the Preface of the *Second Discourse* to the Great Pronouncement at Delphi would suggest that this silent wisdom is akin to Socratic wisdom; for Socrates, like a woman, does not write. I will briefly consider the importance of Socrates at a later point. Here, I only want to indicate that the metaphysical position that underlies his claims about the relationship between the written and the unwritten is that the silent, the hidden from view, has a kind of substantive preeminence over the explicated, the visible. The *First Discourse*, of course, unrelentingly conveys this. The thought is no less present in *Emile.*

[I give my pupil] the art of being ignorant, for the science possessed by him who believes that he knows *only what he does in fact know* amounts to very little. You give science—splendid. I busy myself with the instrument fit for acquiring it.[20]

The concealed is the real; the hidden from view is the ground out of which all brilliance—and this would include scientific knowledge—appears. The transitory and dazzling artifacts of human effort betray an antecedent which, like the Good spoken of in the *Republic*, "is the chief object in the pursuit of knowledge."[21] For both Rousseau and Plato the hidden appears weak and frail, appears to be *nothing,* next to artifacts, which exude a kind of strength and potency.

Yet this is deceiving, for while "the stronger appears to be master [it] actually depends on the weaker."[22] Here is the metaphysical position embedded in the relationship of Pharaoh to Moses; Plato's tyrant to those over whom he rules; Augustine's City of Man to the City of God; Luther's active righteousness to passive righteousness; Hegel's master to slave; Nietzsche's Ancient noble soul to the Jew/Christian/Democrat—the list could be extended to the antinomies invoked by all twice-born souls! In short, Rousseau's move toward the timid voice that precedes the word, which seems to radicalize the search for origins at the same time that it dismisses Christianity altogether, is more of an idiomatic expression rather than a new language altogether. It should not be forgotten, after all, that Augustine and Luther, too, worried about the power and temptation of words which can all too easily obfuscate the truth to those who are without the antidote of moral perspicuity—here, perhaps, the central motif of the *First Discourse*.

The truth that *appears* insubstantial, worried and restive about the prospect for its own confirmation, is alluded to over and over again in the antinomies that distinguish nature from civil society—reality and appearance, inner and the outer, freedom and servitude, action and thought, and natural goodness (not to be confused with *virtue*) and vice.[23] One element of each pair is the more substantial, and at the same time the more passive and liable to conceal-ment by the noise that would actively drown out nature's timid voice. Although these pairs of antinomies interpenetrate to a remarkable degree, and taken to-gether constitute a nonbiblical vision of politically authoritative history, in the next several sections I will consider each pairing separately.

REALITY AND APPEARANCE

The natural is to the civilized human being as reality is to appearance. Civilized human beings, consequently, dwell only in the realm of appearance. Civilized human beings are, for example, *clothed;* that is, veiled to each other and to themselves. In commerce with one another, human beings are covered up and their nakedness concealed; there is semblance without substance. Here "one no longer appears as he is."[24] Clothing precludes human beings from "seeing through each other," and this concealment, which for Rousseau is a metaphor for the human soul, has made it possible for undetected vices to proliferate.[25]

In civilized life everything is "reduced to appearances," to "frivolous exte-rior."[26] Not really being good, one may nevertheless appear to be so;[27] not hav-ing talents (something necessary when civil society emerges), "it [is] necessary to appear to be other that what one in fact [is]."[28] Here the reality is masked to hide the ugliness, the hypocrisy, the lack of depth, that in fact is to be found under the veneer of civilized life. We have become, in Rousseau's words, "re-spectable men,"[29] surely a premonition of Nietzsche's "last man."[30]

INNER AND OUTER

The inner-oriented (natural) human being, the one who lives "within himself," is to be distinguished from the person, the persona, who lives "always outside himself,"[31] in the opinions of others and in the possessions that they themselves have. Those who are esteemed by others or who have much, in fact, possess nothing of value, for no external thing can be the measure of true worth.[32] And reciprocally, those who possess *no-thing* possess the very thing which is required for true strength of soul.[33]

This thought is expressed most forcefully, and at the same time in the midst of the greatest despair, in the *Reveries of the Solitary Walker*. There, faced with condemnation from his contemporaries, lost to them and forced to live "unto himself" as did the natural human being of which he had written with reverence some twenty-one years earlier (in 1755), Rousseau explores the meaning of strength of soul, of the simultaneously powerless and powerful position the soul occupies when utterly without consolation.

Rousseau's detractors and antagonists had been so severe with him, he claims, that the very strength of their arsenal has "deprived themselves of any power" over him.[34] The magnitude of the difference in power leveled the difference: a paradox. Gross inequality produced absolute equality. In their unmitigated attacks they stripped him of even the will to resist, to defend himself before their court. This was their error. Had they loosened their absolute hold on him, given some small hint that he would not be destroyed, Rousseau would have met their challenge and opposed them; and in this opposition would have remained in a *relation* of power with them. "If they had been clever enough to leave me some glimmer of hope, they would still have a hold on me."[35]

But they did not. "By stripping me of everything they have left themselves unarmed."[36] Sinking beneath the sea of social relations, of the interplay of power *relations* that keeps one at its surface, Rousseau resigns himself to his fate and discovers the true basis of happiness *within himself*, a happiness which cannot be taken away by the power of others,[37] a happiness encountered in the interior abyss of solitude which the good or evil of another cannot alter.

> Everything is finished for me on this earth. Neither good nor evil can be done to me by any man. I have nothing left in the world to fear or hope for, and this leaves me in peace at the bottom of the abyss, a poor unfortunate mortal, but *as unmoved as God himself*.[38]

In all this, Rousseau claims, "my heart has been purified by the crucible of adversity."[39] He has found both the depth in the interior realm that constitutes his true self and a distance from the exterior realm in which contestation reigns. The severity of the outer realm has led Rousseau to experience a break, a fissure, which opens up to an inner realm where, he contends, a respite can be found and a purity obtained.

This purity, of course, had been tainted by madness by the time he wrote of it in the *Reveries*. His wish in *Emile* (1762) that his pupil not be "a savage relegated to the desert," but rather that he be "made to inhabit cities [and] to live, if not like them, at least with them";[40] his claim in the *First Discourse* (1750) that famed societies are the institutional forum in which virtue can reign *within* society; the sense that there was room in society for the soul that was not lost unto itself had, by the time of *Reveries* (1776–78), been thoroughly expunged. Rousseau had come to dwell in the desert. In the bitter purity of heart he attained, however, there is, amidst a resignation to his fate, a longing to return, a suffering that betrays a still brooding conviction that an utterly interior purity of heart without one's fellow beings amounts to little. While the individual may find respite on the margins of society, the interior space uncovered in the abyss of powerlessness (if I may borrow from Luther) does not provide a purchase for human beings qua social beings; it provides no nourishment for human beings who *must* live in society.

FREEDOM AND SERVITUDE

There are two senses in which civil life is a life of servitude for Rousseau. First, there is a uniformity attributable in large measure to the presence of rules or standards to which everyone conforms. Second, there is the paradox (and this is the much stronger claim) that the real nature of the apparent freedom attained in civil life is actually a form of slavery. Civilized life is not an emancipation from the state of nature but rather a condition of sophisticated enslavement.

Regarding the servitude of uniformity within civil life, Rousseau's *First Discourse* makes perhaps the most eloquent case. There, Rousseau claims, society has tamed the human soul; it has provided its members with well-refined manners, with a veneer, again, that veils an interior vitality. Here the problem is not merely the disjunction between reality and appearance, discussed earlier, but rather that the *human* being will be obliterated by the taming forces of society.

The danger society poses to the human soul derives from its very evolution, an evolution in which ever more refined taste and manners develop, and along with them rules and standards of conduct that conduce to their maintenance. The result is a human being whose real nature is more and more stultified, crippled, and obscured from view.

> Before art had moulded our manners and taught our passions to speak an affected language, our customs were rustic but natural, and differences of conduct announced at first glance those of character.[41]

And further on,

> Today, when subtler researches and a more refined taste have reduced the art of pleasing to a set of rules, a base and deceptive uniformity prevails in our customs, and all minds seem to have been cast in the same mould.[42]

That the real danger of conformity is that the vitality of the human soul is extinguished can be seen in the manner by which Rousseau suggests conformity can be overcome. What is necessary is that there be "stronger motives"[43] than those possessed by human beings in ordinary situations. The soul, constrained from uttering itself in civil life because of the countervailing power of rules, must utter itself with greater strength to be heard, if it is to break out of the conformity in which it is entrenched.

Rousseau is not, however, optimistic about the prospect that such motives can be of much benefit. Civil society produces certain *kinds* of human beings:

ones that conform. The emergencies that might lead to a display of stronger motives occur only when civil life is threatened or annihilated,[44] for here the countervailing power of society's rules is temporarily or permanently annulled, and the soul may utter ("outer") itself without constraint. But precisely in the instant when one must know with certainty *who* the other is, that he or she may be counted on, this knowledge is least available because the other has heretofore only shown the mask of conformity. Stronger motives may appear only in emergencies, but the unfettered soul that appears during an emergency is the unknown soul, and this exacerbates rather than alleviates the danger at hand.

While conformity is a problem without a viable solution, civil freedom is a deception the reality behind which is initially obscured from view. As a deception it poses a special danger. Not knowing that civil freedom is servitude is more foreboding than being aware that conformity is a problem for which there is no solution. With conformity at least the difficulties are posed, are brought into consciousness. Self-deception is not possible. Conformity has not the allure which freedom has; one does not embrace it willingly and with a spirited eagerness.

Consistent with his thesis that freedom is absent in the civil state, Rousseau argues that dominion and servitude are unknown to the savage.[45] The other, though there, though present, is not yet *for* the natural human being in the way that he or she is for the civilized. Not entering into a certain kind of relationship with the other, there is no possibility of being enslaved by or enslaving that other.

> It is impossible to enslave a man without first putting him in the position of being unable to do without another; a situation which, as it did not exist in the state of nature, leaves each man there free of the yoke, and renders vain the law of the stronger.[46]

Freedom gives way to servitude when relationships between natural human beings are based on exclusive claims of one over the other or over what the other can provide. When human beings attempt to fulfill their needs by turning to one *particular* other that they may find in him or her something specific to that person, then humankind begins the march toward servitude. While the natural human being turns to *any* other to fulfill his or her needs, civil society develops in its members tastes and imagination which are yet slumbering in the savage. Any person cannot fulfill, *this* or *that* person is required. The savage man

> heeds solely the temperament he received from nature, and not the taste he has not been able to acquire; any woman is good for him.[47]

The development of civil society over time refines the human being ever more. Yet in this refinement, this civility, there is a perverse twist. The more the refinement, the more human beings are enslaved by their need for particular persons or things. The unrefined are spared this servitude; their needs can be met with relative ease. The beloved of the refined man—the Helen who is without equal—occasions great suffering when absent or taken by another. Here enslavement is the reward of civilized taste. Need, which by nature can be fulfilled by many different objects, now can be fulfilled by only one; a thirst which can be easily quenched now demands to be sated in only one way. [48]

An equally insidious form of this unnatural fixation upon a particular object occurs because of the very inequalities that develop within civil society. Unlike the situation considered immediately above, however, where a particular person is the object desired for the traits that he or she alone possesses, this second form of servitude can be attributed to structural inequalities that arise because of property—itself a claim over this or that particular thing. Here, one group of human beings needs another not for their attributes as persons but because of their comparative ranking. This is servitude of a different sort.

> Rich, he needs their service; poor he needs their help; and mediocrity cannot enable him to do without them. He must therefore incessantly interest them in his fate, and to make them find their own profit, in fact or in appearance, in working for his . . . [the net effect of which is] ambition, the fervor to raise one's relative fortune less out of true need than in order to place oneself above others. . . . In a word: competition and rivalry on one hand, and opposition of interest on the other. [49]

The servitude based on relative differences, though linked to structural inequalities, in fact arises because of the way human beings respond to these differences. Not the mere fact of difference causes servitude. Something more is needed, and that something more is the desire emanating from within the human being to be better positioned than others. Relative social rank or position is a necessary but not sufficient cause of the servitude that arises when one human being begins to compare him or herself with another. Competitiveness, the tendency to evaluate oneself in accordance with standards set by others, is the leaven which turns mere difference into a difference that matters.

While Rousseau's analysis of the injustice of inequality is as compelling as any, and as sympathetic to the poor as one is likely to find, it is clear that he is more concerned with the servitude of the soul educed by this structural inequality than with the objective facts, and even the suffering, that surround it. It is the disposition of the soul that concerns him first and foremost, for there, in the interiority of the soul, the foundation of human freedom is to be found. [50] Without grounding freedom there, no measure of structural equality will secure it; and as a corollary, any attempt to secure freedom through structural arrangements alone will only lead to greater enslavement. [51] Not knowing what true freedom is, efforts to instantiate it necessarily fail. The objective articulation of freedom is without substance unless accompanied by this interior foundation.

This indeed is the source of the difficulty. It is precisely because there is the appearance of freedom that true freedom is so difficult to acquire. Focusing only on its trappings, human beings are (self-)deceived in thinking that they possess it. Yet all the while they are, in this pseudo-freedom, ensnared and enslaved by it. They consider themselves free if they attain a relatively higher rank than others, and so are captivated by making "comparisons between themselves."[52] Because of this, "those who think themselves the masters of others are indeed greater slaves than they."[53] In civil society the appearance of freedom keeps human beings from truly attaining it. Freedom is servitude, despite appearances to the contrary.

ACTION AND THOUGHT: FIRST EPISTEMIC CONSIDERATION

The case for the antinomy between action and thought in Rousseau is to be found largely in the *First* and *Second Discourses* and in *Emile*. I will consider *Emile* in due course. Here I wish to focus on the two *Discourses*.

Consistent with his general view that civilized human beings are tame and without natural vitality, in the *First Discourse* Rousseau disparages the idea that the advance of science, of knowledge, has benefited humankind. "Advancement" in science has been achieved by, among other things, the labor of a certain *kind* of human being: the civil human being, for whom thought has supplanted action.

> As all the progress of the human species moves it farther away from its primitive state, the more new knowledge we accumulate, the more we deprive ourselves of the means of acquiring the most important knowledge of all; so that it is, in a sense, by dint of studying man that we have made ourselves incapable of knowing him.[54]

Self-knowledge cannot come through study, through consideration of ideas *about* the self. Such study and consideration is external to the self. Real self-knowledge cannot be acquired by thought alone; action, too, is necessary. Indeed, it is the precondition of all self-knowledge. Considering the case of Rome, that much more natural civilization predicated on action, Rousseau sees the problem even there.

> "Since learned men have begun to appear among us," [Seneca tells us], "good men have disappeared." Until then, the Romans had been content to practice virtue; all was lost when they began to study it.[55]

Rome here represents a kind of pivot point of history, where action gave way to thought, substance to superfluity. Modern society (or rather post-Roman society) privileges thought, privileges the brilliant superfluities it can produce, but fails to grasp that just as nature antedates civil society, so, too, action precedes thought.

The meaning of the precedence of action to thought must be made clear, for it is the basis of the epistemological theory developed later in *Emile*,[56] as well as of his warning to civil society about the dangers of privileging thought. The best way to do this is to consider Rousseau's observations about imbecility. Here is a condition in which thought has been dissevered from natural "instincts" (which for illustrative purposes can be understood as the analog of action), and becomes impotent when its root has withered from disuse.

> Why is man alone subject to becoming imbecile? Is it not that he thereby returns to his primitive state; and that—while the beast, which has ac-quired nothing and which has, moreover, nothing to lose, always retains its instinct—man, losing again in old age or other accidents all that his *perfectability* had made him acquire, thus falls back lower than the beast.[57]

Human beings develop and then discard the "instincts" they possess at birth. Civil society fosters this complex development in which the apparent self-sufficiency of the result seemingly justifies cutting the umbilical cord to nature. Then, when the complex human being begins to falter with age, there are no instinctual supports left to rely on.[58] There is no dialectical preserving and an-nulling here; the original plenitude has withered away. It may appear (for a time at least) that nature has been superseded by civil society, that knowledge ob-tained in action is superseded by knowledge obtained by thought and study; the reality, however, is that *all* knowledge derives from or rests upon action and, ultimately, the bodily passions. Theologically, though it may wish and appear to be able to, spirit can never do away with the flesh.

> Whatever the moralists may say about it, human understanding owes much to the passions. . . . It is by their activity that our reason is per-fected; we seek to know only because we desire to have pleasure; and it is impossible to conceive why one who had neither desires nor fears would go to the trouble of reasoning.[59]

The social consequences of this development deserve comment. The per-fection of reason obscures one of the two principles anterior to reason, namely, the "natural repugnance to see any sensitive being perish or suffer."[60] The devel-opment of reason isolates one from another by concealing the natural pity that is the bond holding a society together.[61]

The political implications of Rousseau's epistemological position are even more stark. Because the success of the state depends on virtuous action on the part of its citizens, that is, it requires that citizens draw on their natural passions to defend it, civil society (with its emphasis on thought and study) does not produce the kind of citizens necessary for its defense.[62]

> [When] living conveniences multiply, arts are perfected and luxury spreads, true courage is enervated, military virtues disappear, and this too is the work of the sciences and of all those arts which are exercised in the shade of the study.[63]

And further on,

> The Romans admitted that military virtue died out among them to the
> degree that they became connoisseurs of painting, engravings, jeweled
> vessels, and began to cultivate the fine arts. [64]

Once civil society emerges, thought overlays and supersedes action. Yet this development is in conflict with the epistemological foundation of knowledge. Knowledge depends on the natural passions (and the actions they animate) for it to emerge at all. *Most* of those who would wish to advance the sciences do not possess the kind of self-knowledge that only the right training *of the body* can provide, which alone can yield science of a beneficent sort (the outline for the training for which *Emile* purports to provide). Absent a genuine love of truth, science becomes only a forum for gaining distinction, and this, as it were, *motivational* problem, raises a second epistemic consideration which is structured by an additional (historical) antinomy Rousseau posits.

NATURAL GOODNESS AND VICE: SECOND EPISTEMIC CONSIDERATION

Goodness is to natural life as vice is to civil life. The movement from natural equality toward civil inequality is, therefore, a movement from goodness toward vice. [65] Civil society, being far removed from the state of nature, is corrupt through and through.

> Excesses of all kinds, immoderate ecstasies of the passions, fatigues and
> exhaustion of the mind; numberless sorrows and afflictions which are felt
> in all conditions and by which souls are perpetually tormented: these are
> the fatal proofs that most of our ills are our own work, and that we would
> have avoided almost all of them by preserving the simple, uniform, and
> solitary way of life prescribed to us by nature. [66]

The diremptive move toward vice from original goodness is not, however, without its recompense. While I will not consider the matter here, Rousseau claims that virtue is *possible* only because of the propensity to fall into vice. Virtue is the correlative of vice—both of which are to be distinguished from *natural* goodness. [67]

My immediate concern is with the relationship between scientific knowledge and vice. Scientific knowledge, civil society's great mark of distinction, is clearly implicated in movement from natural goodness to vice. Claiming that the origins of the sciences owe their birth to the vices of civil society, [68] Rousseau asserts that the "heavy veil" which makes knowledge so difficult to attain provides ample warning of the costs of its acquisition. [69] Nature apparently wished to keep humankind out of harm's way. "Our souls have been corrupted in proportion to the advancement of our sciences and arts toward perfection," he says. [70] The cost is high, almost too high. Truth does not disclose itself readily. A thousand errors are necessary to reach one truth; and even if one truth is found, who can make good use of it?[71] The civilized human being knows little of use, of appropriation which is genuinely human. The one truth found is of dubious value.[72]

But there is more. The great leveling of humankind, the conformity that annihilates all difference, militates against the prospect that truth will make its appearance. Truth is for the few, those who simultaneously possess the strength to "walk alone" and who have been thrust into "great events."[73] The rest have not the fortitude to embrace it. They fall short, succumb to the *temptation* of using science (and art) to serve their weakness. Humans become enslaved to what enables them to perpetuate their illusion.

> The sciences, letters, and arts . . . make them love their slavery, and turn them into civilized peoples . . . [who possess] the semblance of all virtues without the possession of any.[74]

The few who do have the talent—Socrates of Athens and Cato the Elder of Rome provide historical examples of such persons[75]—are those who need no teachers. Possessing what they need by nature, they are not susceptible to the corrupting influence of society.[76] Those who do not, ought not enter into science. They should be content with obscurity. The alternative for them is not greatness, but rather the endless search for the reputation and honor which gives only a semblance of virtue.[77] The alternative to the abyss that *not* seeking reputation would be for the soul that is wholly other-related is a certain *kind* of science that perhaps has luster but not depth, power but not true potency. (Think here of Heidegger!) An impure motivation is the gatekeeper of the truth. Better, then, that most not even approach it. Only true greatness, which is without the "passion to gain distinction,"[78] may embrace science worthy of its name and charge.

> Without envying the glory of those famous men who are immortalized in the republic of letters, let us try to put between us that glorious distinction noted between [Athens and Sparta] long ago: that one knew how to speak well, the other to act well.[79]

Toward Atonement

I have focused so far upon the diremptive aspects of Rousseau's thinking. These are not to be underemphasized, yet neither are his efforts to point out the importance and necessity of atonement, the general question surrounding which I wish to consider here.

Not having a Christian way of atonement, alternatives must be found. Without a way of atonement, and with only the barest trace of nature visible, the situation would be unendurable—not simply because of the *fact* of errancy, but because the errancy would not end in some unknowable future after a death which is patiently endured. The temporal horizon is not constructed to accommodate such patience easily. The exile of errancy *may* foment revolution when passivity and patience offer no recompense, when there is a longing with a short(-lived) fuse. Conjoin this longing with the systemic corruption of the soul in civil society,[80] and the difficulty is compounded.

The irony, of course, is that Rousseau rejects the idea that biblical history is authoritative, but not the necessity of what religion purports to provide: a *rebinding* of what is sundered. Accepting that atonement is necessary,[81] he nonetheless rejects the biblical schema which purports to make it possible. Re*orientation*, looking to the East (to the Jerusalem of Nature), is necessary: this atavism remains despite the rejection of the Jerusalem of the Book.

The first innocence of Nature, however, is irretrievably lost—"Eden" is behind us; the urge to conceal, the discomfort with unconcealment, betrays our distance from it. Biblically, Adam hides when he has lost his innocence;[82] and invoking Locke, humankind is still one in Adam—though not in the way Locke imagined. The paths of atonement Rousseau proffers must accommodate the verities of the civil moment of history and yet countermand them in one way or another. Consider, for example, a passage from *Emile:*

> There is a great difference between a natural man living in the state of nature and the natural man living in the state of society. Emile is not a savage to be relegated to the desert. He is a savage made to inhabit cities. He has . . . to live, *if not like them, at least with them.* [83]

I will consider *Emile* in due course. This work is crucial because it transposes all of Rousseau's historical antinomies, antinomies that pertain to the *species,* onto the life of the individual. This will require special treatment. First, however, I will consider three other modes of atonement: famed societies, the general will, and the civil religion.

FAMED SOCIETIES: ATONEMENT AS DISSEMINATION

The theoretical problem for which famed societies are a mode of atonement arises from Rousseau's characterization of the difference between civil society and the more natural period which antedates it. Civil society, recall, is that moment of history in which action has given way to thought and natural goodness given way to vice. These both have epistemic implications, as I have shown. What is necessary is that a *kind* of thinking which needs no teachers, which is virtuous, come to presence in civil society. *Virtuous thought* must be institutionalized and disseminated.

The difficulty, of course, is that human beings in civil society are, for the most part, without virtue; history, in effect, conspires against it. All is not lost, however. There is an antidote for this disease. Louis XIV, learning from the wisdom which places

> healthful herbs beside various harmful plants . . . drew out of the very bosom of the sciences and arts, sources of a thousand disorders, those famed societies simultaneously responsible for the dangerous trust of human knowledge and the sacred trust of morals—trusts which these societies protect by the attention they give both to maintaining within themselves the total purity of their trusts, and to requiring such purity of the members they admit.[84]

Here an institution instantiates the virtue of which only a few human beings are capable. These institutions "serve as a check." Those admitted are worthy because of their "useful works and irreproachable morals."[85] These societies are the light amidst the darkness, a supplement of virtue that provides the antigen necessary to keep vice at bay, but not eradicate it. Famed societies can revive "love of virtue in the hearts of citizens" and "disseminate throughout the human race not merely pleasant enlightenment but also salutary teachings."[86] The few who possess the "strength to walk alone,"[87] who have the requisite virtue, hallow the halls of the famed societies. These few provide the light by which the many may be guided.

In order for this dissemination to have a beneficent effect, however, political power must be marshaled in the service of intellect. Kings must place intellect under their wing for the felicity of the whole community. Reminiscent of Hobbes's thought that the many must be kept away from the wellsprings of political power because their pride would lead them to abuse it,[88] Rousseau here adduces a parallel argument, formulated not to keep the people from power, but rather to keep them from a kind of knowledge that their corrupted (but not corrupt) souls are incapable of using well. Securing science *under the wing* of the king makes corruption unlikely. A clear reformulation, this is, of a thought from *The Republic,* as the following passage shows; yet it is no less a Christian thought about the *hiding* of sin under the wing of Christ.[89]

> But so long as power is alone on the one side, intellect and wisdom alone on the other, learned men will rarely think great things, Princes will more rarely do noble ones, and the people will continue to be vile, corrupt, and unhappy.[90]

THE GENERAL WILL: ATONEMENT AS CHRISTOLOGICAL REENACTMENT

The fundamental responsibility of government is to form a social contract in which all people "unite their wills into a single will."[91] The form this unification takes, theoretically, is the general will, which reconciles the will of the one and the will of the sovereign so that the freedom of the one is not diminished by virtue of submitting to the will of the sovereign who stands over the one who submits. The complexities—perhaps even the intractable difficulties—that surround this idea of the general will can be traced to the paradoxical notion of freedom attendant to it.

> The difficulty . . . may be expressed in these words: "How to find a form of association which will defend the person and goods of each member with the collective force of all, and under which each individual, while uniting himself with all others, obeys no one but himself, and remains as free as before." This is the fundamental problem to which the social contract holds the solution. [92]

There is in this formulation, of course, a paradox that rivals those pointed out earlier in Luther[93] and in Hobbes.[94] In their thought, recall, the paradox revolves in one fashion or another around the relationship between Christ and the Christian, and the Christ-like figure of the Leviathan and the citizen, respectively. These paradoxes are quite central to theological speculation; yet it is one of the supreme ironies of Rousseau's thought that when explicating his notion of the general will it should be expressed in terms of paradoxes which recall those surrounding the Christian's relationship with Christ.[95] The irony is that at this most political of moments the symbol to which Rousseau tacitly recurs is one that derives from the biblical source he wished to supersede.

When Rousseau speaks of the articles of association, themselves the kernel of the social contract, he suggests that they entail "the total alienation by each associate of himself and all his rights to the whole community."[96] Here the one gives him or herself entirely to the whole community. The relative differences between persons are consequently negated; persons become equal with respect to one another and subservient to the whole. Moreover, this equality is achieved by a leveling of sorts; a person gives up the power he or she possesses as a natural being. In Rousseau's words, "each individual gives himself *absolutely*, [and] the conditions are the same for all."[97] This, of course, militates against human beings judging in their own case, and, just as important, human beings judging and having power over each other.[98] There is a higher authority that judges. Because each gives him or herself over to no one but rather to the sovereign, not only is the problem of self-judging solved but also relative differences in power are eliminated. Each becomes powerless with respect to the other (citizen), but becomes utterly powerful by virtue of the power of the sovereign whole of which he or she is a part. Here is a *rebirth* unto civil peace through a covenant in which all lose their corrupted particularity and come unto universal citizenship.

> [Since] each man gives himself to all, he gives himself to no one; and since there is no associate over whom he does not gain the same right as others

gain over him, each man recovers the equivalent of what he loses, and in the bargain he acquires more power to preserve what he has.[99]

This alienation and recovery, this giving up and receiving back, has clear implications for lateral relations between human beings. Structurally, they are similar to those found in Luther. The right orientation toward the sovereign produces a "remarkable change in man."[100] To submit to the one (sovereign) *makes it possible* to work for others; under this condition "a man cannot work for others without at the same time working for himself." Here, again, lateral relations between the all who are powerless and who orient themselves toward a powerful one who stands above the all is the foundation for relations between the all.[101] Because of this vertical orientation a lateral one is possible, in theory at least. In Rousseau's words:

> in making a contract, as it were, with himself [each person] finds himself doubly committed, first, as a member of the sovereign body in relation to individuals, and secondly as a member of the state in relation to the sovereign.[102]

As I have said, the parallels to Luther's formulation cannot be overlooked here. Luther's Christian, for example, must enter the abyss of powerlessness in order to be enveloped by the saving power of Christ (who possesses a power over all things). By giving him or herself over completely to Christ the Christian becomes both powerless, and therefore equal to all others, and powerful, because enveloped by Christ. One is enveloped, too, in Rousseau; though not by the Spirit of Christ, but rather by the social body—which Durkheim was later to observe was personified *as God.*[103]

Not wishing to develop the point fully here, I should point out, however, that the relationship between Hobbes's citizen and the Leviathan also bears a close resemblance to that found between citizen and sovereign in Rousseau. The equality of all under the sovereign and the paradox of power and powerlessness: these notions are present in Hobbes and are, as in Rousseau, transpositions of Christian symbols. Hobbes's citizens, for example, are to be "esteemed as equals"[104] and are to submit to the "public person"[105] who stands above them that true liberty may be secured for the many.[106] Rousseau, of course, thought that Hobbes's political form merely reinstituted a perverse form of the equality of all found in the state of nature.[107] He simply failed to see that his argument with Hobbes was an interdenominational one!

The similarities I have considered suggest that at this critical juncture in Rousseau's political thought the atonement Rousseau propounds, the way to institute freedom in this age of its absence,[108] is explicated in terms which resonate with Christian symbols that convey the paradox of the relation between Christ and the Christian. The paradox of freedom and servitude that stands at the core of the general will required of Rousseau a symbolic language capable of expressing it. That symbolic language, that pattern of thought, though radically transfigured, is a kind of Christology.

THE CIVIL RELIGION: ATONEMENT AS COMPLIMENTARITY

Where the general will purports to instantiate a freedom heretofore absent from civil society, the civil religion purports to reinstantiate the outwardness and vitality of the Roman ethos which may supplant the wholly inner-oriented and politically inadequate ethos of Christianity. What is called for—and it is unmistakably a *longing* for a new kind of soul—is the human being who possesses the attributes of both, who is able to become part of the social body, but without ceding the utterly interior dimension that Christianity produced; what is called for is a human being who participates in the civil religion (the Roman component) while possessing a personal religion (the Christian component). Rome produced *citizens*; Christianity, which deepened the soul, produced *men* who knew the (interior) source of their freedom.[109] Where is the soul capable of both?

Rousseau's admiration of the Romans is only too apparent: "they were the freest and strongest people of the world."[110] Roman vitality was undiminished by other allegiances; the citizens' political life was not distinguished from their life of worship. *The two were one.* This left their souls undivided and capable of greatness. Rome is prior to the diremption wrought by Christianity.

> [Because] a God was placed at the head of every political society, it follows that there were as many Gods as peoples. . . . National divisions produced polytheisms, and this in turn religious and civil intolerance. . . . Political war was just as much theological war; the provinces of Gods were determined, so to speak, by the frontiers of nations.[111]

This primitive unity, however, was shattered. First the Jews refused to submit to the Gods of the people who conquered them,[112] then Jesus came and separated the political realm from the religious.[113] This divided what should have remained unified, and the result has been enfeebled government.

Efforts to return directly to the ancient unity, however, are doomed to fail. "The spirit of Christianity has won completely."[114] There is no return. And since the present state of affairs is "at bottom more injurious than serviceable to a robust constitution of the state,"[115] the vitality and unity of Rome must be combined with the truth of this (Christian) epoch to form a new synthesis, one detrimental to neither the interiority of true religion nor to the exteriority of a vital political life. The Cross once drove out the Eagle;[116] the new civil religion must accommodate both. (Ironic though it may be, here is a twist upon Augustine's admission that Rome is *necessary* for the economy of salvation!)

While Rousseau does identify precisely what the positive and negative pronouncements[117] that constitute the articles of faith of the civil religion would be, and suggests that there is also a place *next to* this civil religion (hence the notion of complementarity) for an utterly personal religion which would neither bolster nor detract from the "sentiments of sociability" the civil religion produces,[118] the higher unification he hopes for remains only that—a hope, a longing fueled by his sense that Christianity as well as civil society had somehow lost its way.

EMILE: ATONEMENT AS SUPPLEMENTARITY

Rousseau's *Emile* can be understood to contain the whole of his teaching[119] in the form of an educational treatise, the meaning of which is not easy to grasp. The historical antinomies of the *First* and *Second Discourse* which orient the soul to something seemingly irretrievably lost are here recapitulated in a new idiom; the antinomies between nature and civil society that ostensibly described the history of the *species* now are transferred to the development of soul: one *individual* soul. The history of the species (phylogeny) is supplanted by the history of an individual (ontogeny). The unabsolvable tension between the self-relatedness of human beings in nature and the other-relatedness of their counterparts in civil society,[120] which could not be mitigated because the original unity manifested itself only *then*, in some hypothetical beginning before *our* time, is circumvented, in principle, through an education of the soul which arrests the development of *amour-propre* for as long as possible, and then only awakens its salutary forms. The authentic self-love of the savage, *amour de soi* (which fortifies its possessor and is self-related) falls away, to be sure, but it is supplemented by an *amour-propre* that keeps the soul *within itself*. Unity gives way to diremption as it does in respect to the history of the species, but a higher unity amidst others—one, in fact, constituted *through* a relation to others—supplants it. The unified soul unveiled in *Emile* lives as Robinson Crusoe lived: on an island;[121] here, however, the self-sufficiency of island life is not purchased at the price of marginality, of living *away* from others. A respite from civil society does not entail a withdrawal from it, as the frontispiece of the *Second Discourse* intimates; rather, here the unified soul is able to reside *within* it. The mode of atonement here is not institutional (as were famed societies, the general will, and the civil religion), but rather confessional-therapeutic; what is offered is nothing less than a narrative recovery of the childhood that does not go astray.

The preliminary sketch of the problem was traced earlier, in the discussion of freedom and servitude. There, the apparent freedom of the human being in civil society was characterized as a kind of servitude in which human beings incessantly compare themselves to others, and by this their happiness is tied up with the happiness of others. Content with their relative standing, they consider themselves free and happy; disconcerted with their position, the true ground of their freedom is concealed. Unhappy with what they find outside themselves, they think their hardship can only be redressed in that realm, in their relations with others.

The phylogenetic basis of this servitude is to be found, of course, in the movement from the state of nature to civil society. Prior to civil society human beings were sufficient unto themselves; the other was not *for* them. Yet in *Emile,* as I have said, the presumption is that the history of the species is *not* implicated in the etiology of the disease. The account in *Emile* is another history, as it were, one which *parallels* the history of the species in certain respects, yet is not to be conflated with it.[122]

Consider, for example, the wellspring of *amour-propre.* While Rousseau's history of the species may suggest that it arises only within the civil age, he also claims that there is a propensity to fall into perverse self-love right at the beginning, as it were; in the prelinguistic[123] cries of the infant.

> The first tears of children are prayers. If one is not careful, they soon become orders. Children begin by getting themselves assisted, they end by getting themselves served. Thus from their own weakness, which is in the first place the source of the feeling of their dependence, is subsequently born the idea of empire and domination.[124]

At first the child cries out of genuine self-love, out of the desire for self-preservation. The child learns, however, that by crying he or she may manipulate the adults who are there to provide. Original self-love, which is wholly within itself, can (but need not) be supplanted by a self-love oriented toward and by those around the child. The one gives way to the other when the "secret intention" of the child[125] has not been managed properly. The pristine unity of the self, interrupted by a projected void that is filled by the adult, gives way to a pseudo-unity that needs another. The pristine unity is shattered once the child realizes that through his or her willfulness the adult can be controlled. Now, in the name of self-preservation, the child commands; he or she desires not the necessities of life but rather *dominion.*[126]

What must be done to ameliorate this disposition (which does *not* betray original sin!) is to dissuade the secret intention from emerging. Because *amour-propre* develops in the human child before the faculty of reason, which later can guide the soul away from its dangers, children must be made to believe that their wills have little control over events. In this way the secret intention lies dormant. If events around them seem to occur according to necessity, they do not learn that other wills *can* be dominated.

> [Self-love] becomes good or bad only by the application made of it and the relations given to it. Therefore, up to the time when the guide of *amour-propre,* which is reason, can be born, it is important for the child . . . to respond only to what nature asks of him, and then he will do nothing but good.[127]

And when reason is finally able to serve as a guide, children will not have been corrupted by *amour-propre*. They will possess the antidote before the disease consumes them. Here, in effect, is an answer to Hobbes: the antidote for the pride, envy, vanity, etc. is *not* political at all; rather, it is educational![128]

Prior to the time when the antidote can be effective, however, indeed in order to develop the faculty of reason fully, it is necessary that the child who is still wholly dominated by *amour de soi* next be given an education of the body that will serve as the foundation for the subsequent education of reason. This education in practice, so important for the healthy development of the soul—of which Tocqueville thought he discovered living confirmation in America[129]—involves not book learning but rather *doing*. I will not rehearse the argument here, but simply note, again, that in Rousseau's theory of knowledge, doing precedes knowing. That "the Athenian babblers feared [the Spartan's] words as much as their blows"[130] suggests that education and development of the body does, in fact, give rise to vigor of the mind.

This education of the body, like the earliest education based on necessity, is intended to keep the self wholly within itself. *Amour-propre* is yet "keep secret." Eventually, however, *amour-propre* does appear, and when it does, the soul now under the sway of this other-related passion must, above all, not be exposed to those whom it can *envy*. Pity (Nietzsche's final sin!),[131] not envy. With pity other-relatedness does not foster the development of envy or pride, both of which are a disaffection with self that, in their most elevated forms, can only be appeased by bringing God Himself down to the human level so that the self may be raised above its station.

> I was carried along by the prejudices of education and by that very dangerous *amour-propre* which always wants to carry man above his sphere, and, unable to raise my feeble conceptions up to the great Being, I made an effort to lower Him down to my level. I reduced the infinite distance He has put in the relations between His nature and mine.[132]

This remark, of course, is made in the "Profession of Faith of the Savoyard Vicar." This extraordinary section, in which pride reaches a pitch that can only be conciliated through a humility that would reestablish the right relationship between God and humanity, between Creator and created, purports to reveal the religion beneath all religions, the source of faith beneath all dogma.

Any *account* of Revelation is a human account, subject to human infirmary and predicated only upon the authority of the conveyor,[133] which can carry no weight for the truly religious soul. No matter how awesome the *account*, it is but words; these are as removed from God as spirit is from flesh in Luther.[134] Words—the entire contents of *the* Book—is a blasphemy against God! Only the heart can hear the *voice* of God; there alone is the interiority of faith.

As soon as peoples took it into their *heads* to make God *speak*, each made him speak in its own way and made Him say what it wanted. If one had listened only to what God says to the heart of man, there would never have been more than one religion on earth.[135]

Not without exaggeration it can be said that *if* the inner kernel of Protestantism is the self-certainty of conviction arrived at without the aid of a human intermediary or authority, then, notwithstanding his derogation of the New Testament (which ostensibly authorizes just such a view), even his severe criticism of it confirms him to be Protestantism's deepest voyager![136] Here the authority of the Book is rejected. God's message is revealed only to humankind in a form anterior to the mediative faculty that would give an account of God in words. The true religion is available to all, but only in the search for the God *beneath* the God conveyed by words;[137] the multiplicity of religious forms that *must* arise once God is adorned with words can give way to a unitary understanding attained only in the heart. Locke's religious unanimity may be achieved, but by a mechanism entirely different from the one he had imagined.

The sanctum of the "Profession of Faith," however, is not the final word. That portion of it concerned with why evil should exist in a world created by a beneficent God, the account of which would have it that human merit and dignity consists in the *capacity* to fall into errancy and yet *not* to do so, can be seen as a prolegomenon to Book V, where Sophie (wisdom) is won only when Emile demonstrates his merit, his worthiness before her.[138] Here wisdom is a woman. She has need of her reputation;[139] she does not seek the courtship of those who are not earnestly interested in *her* (the sophists), but wants a lover who would honor her (a true philosopher, one who has earned the right to be her consort).[140] As with the withdrawal from the Pireaus at the outset of *The Republic*, here, too, wisdom finds its ally only in a secluded forum, not in the "city." In this place, and throughout *Emile*, the city is the site of corruption, of stain. Biblically, Cain, the founder of cities, was a murderer, an impure one.[141]

> [In the city, men's] superficial minds, their vanity, their jargon, their unruly morals, and their frivolous imitations disgusted [Sophie]. She sought a man and found only monkeys; she sought a soul and found none. . . . My heart rejects all those who attract my senses.[142]

Critically placed allusions to *The Republic* inform the reader of Rousseau's reverence for the Platonic *way*. There is, however, a difference in *this* ascent of the soul. Sophie's consent to marry is exacted only when, after Emile fails to appear for a prearranged meeting because of his pity for the poor and sick, he declares:

> Do not hope to make me forget the rights of humanity. They are more sacred to me than yours. I will never give them up for you.[143]

The meaning is clear. Wisdom is received in the soul, not when the Divine element stirs, but rather when the *human* heart is rousted from its slumber—or, in Emile's case, when it *remains* attentive to the voice of conscience that timidly yet imploringly speaks. Here the principle of sensitivity to the suffering of other sentient beings, which is anterior to reason, about which he spoke in the *Second Discourse*, [144] is elevated to a level to which Plato never would have acceded.

Consent is not yet marriage, however, and in the journey Emile must make before he is able to return to embrace her, he must overcome a last stumbling block: not Nietzsche's final sin (pity), but rather attachment to the object of his passion: Sophie herself! The paradigm established in the "Profession of Faith," of finding the One True God of the heart *beneath* the God mediated to human-kind through the *Word,* is recapitulated in the journey toward wisdom. "The fear of losing everything," Rousseau says, "will prevent you from possessing everything."[145] When Emile and Sophie part, "they separate as if they were never to see each other again."[146] Wisdom is revealed only when the soul who longs for her is able to die to her. The conformity of this view to that offered in the *Phaedo* is unmistakable.[147]

Upon the return from his journey Emile has become a man. He has learned that no earthly cities are attuned to the eternal laws of nature, and so has oriented himself to the City of Nature of which he is a citizen. Emile, the modern day Glaucon in search of Justice, proclaims himself a citizen of the city whose "prototype can be found somewhere in heaven."[148] The profound paradox of politics found in *The Republic,* that notwithstanding the impossibility of it,

> unless philosophers becomes kings of our cities, or unless those who are now kings and rulers become true philosophers, so that political power and philosophic intelligence converge . . . there can be no end to troubles[149]

is here recapitulated in a slightly modified form.

> Men say that the golden age is a fable; it will always be for those whose feelings and taste are depraved. People do not really regret the golden age, for they do nothing to restore it. What is really needed for its restoration? One thing only, and that is an impossibility; we must love the golden age.[150]

Not the soul that does not know the good because it is not yet ruled by reason, but rather the depraved heart is the source of this paradox. The difficulty is *prephilosophical.* Errancy occurs first in the heart. Depravity mutes the timid voice of nature, which alone could entice it back to the Source. To love it, the heart must already hear that voice; not hearing it, it cannot be loved. Errancy disposes only to further errancy. That which is most present remains most hidden.

THE STRUCTURE OF HISTORY

The starkness of the historical antinomies between the state of nature and civil society, the veracity of which is confirmable only by a silent listening within, authorizes a view of Rousseau according to which he is the first if not most profound critic of the modern age. Alienated from authentic existence, the modern soul experiences pleasure without happiness, security without repose, and power without genuine potency. The civil period of history is without recompense or vitality; something more is needed. That the vitality lacking *was* to be found once, in an antecedent stage of history, I have considered in some detail. From primitive unity to diremption and loss: as with political theology, the present condition is one of exile and concealment.

Having said this, however, a crucial difference remains. In the biblical view the reunification of the soul with its home ground is in some future moment known only to God.[151] Here the temporal distance between the present and God's redemption of the world is inconsequential, for no matter how distant, it compensates, as it were, for the travails and mysteries, the exile, of this moment of history. Human beings die and never unravel the mystery of God. This, however, is of no ultimate consequence. The return of the Divine into history, no matter when, relieves the burdens of the faithful. The Divine return conquers death, broadly or narrowly understood. What can the uncertainties, the suffering, the darkness, the absence of sustenance, mean when the countervailing force of God can overcome all the vicissitudes of temporal existence—when suffering is an argument *for* God, not against Him?[152]

The irony of these political theologies is that while they are otherworldly, it is precisely this otherworldliness that enables their adherents to endure, even reconcile themselves to, the bleakness of existence in time and to live in accordance with the imperatives of this historical period. Politics need not be a forum of great hopes and deep longings when another avenue, *and another time,* promise their fulfillment. The faith that conquers the world is confirmed and deepened only by suffering in the world.[153]

Rousseau's politically authoritative history, however, has no place for the glory of God at the end of history. The soul does not easily wait in patience; it wants reconciliation: hence the near-revolutionary timbre of Rousseau's history. "Man was born free, and he is everywhere in chains"[154]—and to be free again the *illegitimate* fetters must be eliminated. The tone is one of urgency. While great suffering can be endured for prolonged periods if there is respite in eternity, recompense (*should* it be demanded) must be imminent if the whole of history is immanent. There is an eschatological vision lurking beneath Rousseau's condemnation of an impotent present.

But the matter cannot be left at this. The ascension of the soul in *Emile* toward Sophie, toward wisdom, subsumes the whole of the history of the species within the history of one soul's ascent toward wisdom and unification. Here errancy is circumvented, *amour-propre* is guided down channels by that necessary supplement, education, which can produce a truly moral being, and the potentially explosive wish for a transformation of *epochal* proportion is defused and supplanted by this modern "pattern set up in the heavens" whose purpose is not to change the world, but to offer the soul an antidote to the allures of civil society, allures which constitute the greatest threat to its ascent.

> The multitude will always be sacrificed to the few, and the public interest to the particular interest. Those specious names, justice and order, will always serve the instruments of violence and the arms of iniquity. . . . In order for each of us to know how to judge his own lot, it remains to be seen whether the rank these men have grabbed is more advantageous for the happiness of those who occupy it. This is now the study which is important to us. But to do it well we must begin by knowing the human heart.[155]

This history, which both amplifies upon and supersedes his historical speculations on the movement from the state of nature to civil society, accepts the inevitability of corruption, its *eternal* character as it were, and is unyielding in its conviction that the Socratic question: "whether the just have a better life than the unjust,"[156] has not lost its currency.

In this key, of course, the question is whether, appearances notwithstanding, the soul whose nature has not been corrupted by society, whose heart has not yet grown cold, is happier than the one whose heart has. Here Rousseau's thoughts about the vacuity of brilliance and the logic of tyranny in the *First* and *Second Discourse*, respectively, are brought to bear on this decisive question—and answered as Plato did. The rebirth about which Plato speaks at the end of *The Republic*[157] has its counterpoint in the issuance of Emile and Sophie at the conclusion of *Emile*, and in both cases, after a long journey, this rebirth *is* the profound *re*-cognition that while the soul must live in the world, it is not truly of the world. The revolutionary tenor of Rousseau's history of the species is transformed into a heartfelt though esoteric call to attend patiently and without pomp to what each soul has lost and to what a few souls, at any rate, may regain.

CONCLUDING REMARKS

One of the great ironies in the history of political theory is that Rousseau's multifaceted and paradoxical thought, which purports to set political theory on a new and more secure foundation than politico-theological inquiry could, results in the same measure of ambiguity and complexity that the politico-theological speculations he claims to supersede so often display. The first irony.

Second, as I suggested in the preceding section, the valence of his history is not unambiguous. At times there is a revolutionary fervor that would challenge any and all injustice.[158] Elsewhere the warning is sounded that *the* political act is to return to nature; then and only then can politics be other than the perverse longing for power that *will* end in tyranny unless arrested.

The pedigree of this is unmistakably Platonic. And so the matter could be left if after having said this, the correspondence between the history of the species and the history of the soul did not betray an affinity with Saint Augustine, who initiates phylogenetic and ontogenetic historical speculations that would be inconceivable within Platonic thought,[159] or outside of Christian thought!

> The experience of mankind in general, as far as God's people is concerned, is comparable to the experience of the individual man. There is a process of education, through the epochs of a people's history, *as through the successive stages of a man's life,* designed to raise them from the temporal and visible to an apprehension of the eternal and invisible.[160]

While Rousseau's history of the species is ultimately subsumed within the history of the soul's ascent, thus differing from Augustine, this species history nevertheless possesses immense rhetorical force—due, no doubt, to its affinity with the biblical theme of exile from God. Rousseau, this nonbiblical prophet, charges his people with errancy, and it was this charge that not only fostered a longing for revolution[161] which would release "the people" from exile, but also began the critique of the Enlightenment in earnest. That this species history (and its explosive implications) is subsumed to the ascent of the soul in *Emile* was for the most part ignored, that *Emile* was relegated to the dusty shelves along with other antiquated educational treatises, is something to be pondered. Had it been understood otherwise the eschatological fervor of his early writings (which so influenced Marx) would have to have been transposed, and could *not* have served the ideological function they did. What that might have meant, we can only speculate.

Third and finally, an at once epistemological and ontological point. While Rousseau rejects the biblical account of human origins, he too felt the need to recur to a history that is partially obscured and veiled to the corrupted but not corrupt human soul. In that history the antinomies of human existence are thrown into stark contrast. Rousseau's history of diremption, inappropriately called a conjectural history, is confirmed only by a faculty more powerful than reason, which reason can neither understand nor, without assistance, confirm. Expressed in this way, Rousseau and Luther embark on identical projects, the remaining but nonetheless decisive theoretical differences being that while for Luther the antinomies within the psyche are expressed in terms of the two Testaments, for Rousseau they are not, and that while Luther silences reason that he may listen in faith to the Word, Rousseau silences reason that he may listen with his heart[162] to the timid voice of nature that precedes the word. The historical form is similar, the content is different, and in both cases this listening that silences reason disrupts any world that listens to reason alone.

CONCLUSION

HISTORIES THAT SITUATE THE SOUL, that *orient* it toward its home ground while specifying the nature and duration of its present exile, avail themselves of becoming politically authoritative histories under the condition that they speak when reason has reached its limits and *must* silence itself or at the outset *before* the presumption is made that reason is capable of any measure of clarity about ultimate matters.

Under these conditions reason *defers;* it passively acquiesces when its activity has brought it to a border which it cannot transgress—and only then. On this reading the extraordinary efforts of Hobbes and Locke to carve out an unassailable domain for reason do not reflect a foundational impulse, but rather an attempt to find out precisely *where* reason must defer, where it must be silent.[1] It is not difficult to imagine them condemning, as hubris of the most elevated sort, the suggestion that "two thousand years of training in truthfulness . . . finally forbids itself the *lie involved in belief in God.*"[2] The light of reason, however enlarged by a dialectical slight of hand, never achieves the clarity it might wish to attain. What is authoritative in ultimate matters is *forever* over reason's horizon. "Religion," Hobbes says, "can never be abolished out of human nature."[3] By this he means that no matter how brightly the light of reason shines, there will always be a boundary to reason's luminescence—and a beyond that can neither be abolished nor ignored without peril. Following both Hobbes and Locke, religion *is* the account of this beyond which reason cannot illuminate, and is only *religion* when this boundary has been reached.

> Religion is the vision of something which stands beyond, behind, and within, the passing flux of immediate things; something which is real, and yet waiting to be realized; something which is a remote possibility, and yet the greatest of present facts; something that gives meaning to all that passes, and yet eludes apprehension; something whose possession is the final good, and yet is beyond all reach; something which is the ultimate ideal, and the hopeless quest.[4]

It is often said that Hobbes and Locke, unlike their ancient counterparts, were *not* concerned with questions of God/the Good. Their observations about reason *alone*, of course, gives *prima facie* confirmation of this view. They, however, had the good sense to realize that political theory—especially in moments of crisis, when reason holds so little sway—must include some account of what reason alone cannot grasp. Reason's eventual (or initial) silence does not announce the threshold beyond which *theory* cannot go; rather, it marks a boundary that theory must traverse in order to be compelling when reason may no longer speak. Spinoza well understood the issue:

> Men would never be superstitious, if they could *govern all their circumstances by set rules,* or if they were always *favored by fortune:* but being frequently driven into straits where rules are useless . . . they are frequently, for the most part, very prone to credulity. The human mind is readily swayed this way or that in times of doubt.[5]

And being prone to credulity, they sometimes fall back onto superstition or religion. In times of crisis, Spinoza seems to intimate, the real alternatives are not reason and religion, but rather religion or superstition—I am tempted to say biblical religion or paganism.[6]

Political theory, then, must take account of the *whole;* this is hardly an insight possessed only by the ancients and lost to early modern thinkers. Only a self-confident age that would believe human life can be governed in all its circumstances by set rules, only an age favored by fortune, could read its originaries with such aplomb. "If only prosperity, while affecting my conduct, would leave my judgment free!"[7]

Not only Hobbes and Locke, but Luther and Rousseau theorize about the whole as well. Each of them has an abiding respect for what reason alone cannot grasp: for the *un*-thinkability of faith (Luther), the *supra*-thinkability of Revelation (Hobbes and Locke), or for the *pre*-thinkability of the heart (Rousseau). Even in Freud's thinking, to move seemingly far afield, human beings must silently, passively, and deferentially listen to what authoritatively calls out to them from what is beyond thought's purview (hence, in Freud's case, the designation: the *Id,* for that which calls out). Yet where, in contemporary theorization, is there a place for this deferential listening—aside, perhaps, in feminist theory?

In a self-confident age the notion of that which is unconfirmable yet more authoritative than reason alone has "conscience *against* it," in Nietzsche's words.[8] Here, without disquietude, Wittgenstein's injunction "whereof one cannot speak, thereof one must be silent"[9] is embraced—and Heidegger whispers:

> by disavowing [what is forgotten, this] mystery leaves historical man in the sphere of what is readily available to him, leaves him to his resources. Thus left, humanity replenishes its "world" on the basis of the latest needs and aims, and *fills out* the world by means of proposing and planning. From these man takes his standard.[10]

It should be remembered that Wittgenstein only intended by his maxim to suggest what Hobbes had earlier insisted, *viz.,* that reason must defer; yet his statement is often taken to mean that we need not even *listen* when reason must be silent! Heidegger implores us to listen anew to that which is concealed from reason's world of light. *Not* listening, he says, leads us to fill out the world, to suppose erroneously that the whole *can* be lit up by reason. The *ineluctable* whole matters no more—and we (busily) blink.

The contemporary tendency to treat early modern political thought entirely under the rubric of reason, to dismiss or ignore portions of texts which try to comprehend the mystery that unassisted reason cannot grasp, evinces this (worrisome) tendency to dispose of talk about what is beyond the boundary of reason. It is a portentous development. Reason can become more precise, to be sure, but it becomes ever less compelling in proportion as it achieves precision. Its capacity to orient is compromised by its very exactitude.

What I have tried to suggest here is that Luther, Hobbes, Locke, and Rousseau were decidedly not under the sway of this contemporary impulse and that *how* they conclude politically involves a listening to an historical narrative which can orient in a way that reason alone cannot. To the extent that *we* depart from this, to the extent that theory has come to mean what can be concluded from reason alone, it is not without warrant to suggest now that early modern thought does have conscience against it and that the "liberalism" that is now derided or defended is interstitial. The authoritative history that *defines* the space it occupies is left out—and the dialogue becomes vacuous.

WHERE IS GOD/NATURE? THE PARADOX AND "PLACE" OF PRESENCE AND HIDDENNESS

What, precisely, may be concluded about the location of God/nature in the thought of Luther, Hobbes, Locke, and Rousseau? *Where* is God/nature, and what political implications does this have? The answer provided by each author, without fail, has been that humankind stands in a paradoxical relationship to its Source: at once "most hidden and most present."[11]

For Luther, God comes to presence for human beings through the Son, who, though standing *outside* of time, would enshroud Christians living *in* time. God is hidden to the Christian who would try to find Him through active righteousness, in the everydayness of works. This inauthentic mode conceals rather than reveals—and when faced with the terrors of conscience that would reveal the abyss, the Christian would hide ever more intransigently in works.[12] God is present, to be sure, but *only* in the inwardness that appears upon the disclosure of the "world's" corruption.

The *Nunc-stans* which grasps the Christian is the Moment of moments, the eternity beneath the history of earthly kings and kingdoms, yet the power *over* the world so attained is a qualified one; it is attenuated by the propensity for errancy that in fact *makes* the appearance of the *Nunc-stans* possible at all. In Heidegger's terms, the concealment and revelation of Being is always already a possibility of Dasein.[13] (The structure of Rousseau's argument is similar.) The dialectical relationship between carnality and spirit, brought to a feverish pitch in Saint Paul and deeply embedded in Luther's understanding, suggests none other than that it is only *from* a condition of carnality—with all that this means about errancy, hubris, and concealment—that the move can be made *to* spirit. The *Nunc-stans* is *there* only for the soul that *wrestles with* its carnal nature. As Augustine discovered, the path to God must pass through Rome and the temptation of corruption it offers. [14]

The political ramifications of this warrant attention. Until God returns at the end of history, until the dialectical tension between carnality and spirit is finally put to rest, politics must take full account of both the corruptions of spirit *and* the victory of spirit over the "world." Because human beings often lose their wrestling match with sin, they must not be trusted; because they occasionally win, they must be accorded a stature no mere earthly king may merit. The hiddenness of God in sin and the presence of God (the Son) in spiritual achievement demand a politics both distrustful of humankind and accommodating to the "secret, hidden, spiritual matter." [15] Politics must arrest the excesses that accompany corruption, yet it dare not transgress the border of spirit. This has a very familiar ring to it, to be sure. It is, again, the paradox of God's presence and hiddenness that sets up this problematic, one that will not give way until the final Redemptive moment, the time of which is known only to God.

For Hobbes, too, the historical period within which humankind now dwells is marked by the hiddenness of God. Yet in this interim God is present, as it were, through the covenant renewed by Christ and carried on in the Christian commonwealth. There is both a presence and hiddenness of God, but in a manner different from Luther.

Where the presence of God is to be found, for Luther, in the *Nunc-stans* of wrestling with and overcoming sin through Christ, for Hobbes, the presence of God is to be found in the trace of God that is legitimate sovereignty. Here the presence of God takes the form of the rightful *impersonation* of God along the lines set forth in the Exodus account. God *speaks* through Moses; His presence is withdrawn from the people.

> And thou shalt set bounds unto the people round about, saying, Take heed to yourselves, *that ye* go *not* up into the mount, or touch the border of it; whosoever toucheth the mount shall be surely put to death. [16]

The "place" of God's presence here is decidedly not the *experience* of wrestling with and overcoming sin through Christ which *all* Christians may have. God's presence is revealed on the mountain. The people are to be kept away. (Recall that the myth of Ixion, invoked at the outset of *De Cive*, conveys the same thought.) What the people may know of God's presence comes down to them in the saying of the Word of God by Moses, [17] by the sovereign—hence the importance of the right of interpretation. Here the "place" of God's hiddenness is not *within*, not, as it was for Luther, in that place were the terrors of conscience must be faced. *That* place is only bad digestion for Hobbes.

God is not hidden within, but rather hidden *from* the people. The distance from the mountain to the plain is considerable; the voice that speaks on the mountain, therefore, must be *conveyed* to the people—by a sovereign. The "place" of the hiddenness of God is that location where the people wait for the Word's conveyance through the sovereign, and there alone. The presence of God is made manifest when the people deferentially obey, when they *assent* to the sovereign who conveys the Word, when Moses, upon coming down from the mountain, *is listened to.* [18] (That Hobbes should write a great deal about speech in the *Leviathan*, while Locke should say very little about it in the *Second Treatise* is, I suggest, no accident.) For Hobbes the paradigm for the presence of God is the Exodus narrative of the speaking of God through Moses, and this paradigm will not be supplanted until the second coming. "There is," in his words, "no covenant with God, but by mediation of somebody that representeth God's person." [19] The presence of God comes by way of the *one*.

The matter is otherwise with Locke. The tenor of Locke's writing, so different from Hobbes's, can be attributed to the central theological proposition that informs the entirety of his work, *viz.*, that Adam is always already there in *all* Christians. Politics is not an *achievement* made possible by a deferential obedience to the voice of God's mediary, but rather an arrangement that does not obliterate the grant bestowed at the beginning. Politics must accommodate what is prepolitical: reason and the right of dominion granted to Adam in the beginning.

The presence of God *is* that grant that is already there; government based on reason and the right of property is authorized because of this. Political order is not made possible because of a right relationship to what is *said* (Hobbes), but rather because of an unconcealment of what human beings *are*: the children of Adam. The *First* and *Second Treatises*, of course, offer precisely that unconcealment; yet as I have said elsewhere, unconcealment is also the message of his "Letter on Toleration" and *Reasonableness of Christianity*. There, the presence of God is revealed in the miracles and teachings of Christ, teachings which now fully authorize what could only be known by a few prior to the first coming. There, too, the unconcealment reveals the truth in and for all Christians. It is because, in principle, *all may now know* this truth (provided reason is not disturbed by political power) that tolerance is countenanced.

Taken together, these thoughts suggest that the "place" of God's presence is in a government based on the original grant to Adam and in a tolerant comportment based on the unconcealment by Christ. Reject such a government and such a comportment and the truth of Adam and of Christ is violated and God's partial presence sequestered. Human beings have a responsibility in the post-Incarnation epoch to orient political life to truths which can easily be known because of *who* human beings are and *what* Christ revealed. It is not, therefore, merely to appease that Locke says, "the taking away of God, though but even in thought, dissolves all."[20]

For Rousseau, of course, the paradox of presence and hiddenness pertains not to God but to nature. More like Hobbes and Luther, the balance is tipped toward hiddenness than presence. There is a much more Augustinian tone here than in Locke. Self-deception, the intransigence of souls that are frightened, unable, or too taken by the transitory brilliance of the "city" to turn toward nature: this thought dominates Rousseau's thinking.

The "place" where nature comes to presence is, of course, in the heart, that place which all human beings possess but few dare to recognize as authoritative. Errancy begins here. The hiddenness of nature follows from this dereliction in which the heart is hardened, and the result of continuing in errancy is injustice, violence, and unnatural inequality. The *inevitable* decline without justice, the inevitability of tyranny without returning to the Source, about which Plato writes in the *Republic,* could certainly be invoked as a model here; yet more fit-ting, in light of the hardening of the heart Rousseau has in mind, is Pharaoh's resistance. Human beings, to use biblical language, stand accused of being Pharaoh.

> And Pharaoh said, Who *is* the LORD, that I should obey his voice to let Israel go? I do not know the LORD, neither will I let Israel go.[21]

Let the Lord be nature, and Israel be the soul in bondage, and the words could be Rousseau's.

Not recognizing nature, Pharaoh suffers, and, following Luther, Pharaoh becomes *more* hardened as evidence accumulates that the life lived is one of errancy.[22] The more the presence of nature comes to the fore, the more this is threatening—the more Pharaoh seeks to *remain hidden* from nature. This wish-ing to remain hidden from nature, from the Source, *can* be understood in terms of the drama surrounding the death of Socrates, to be sure (he was killed pre-cisely because no polity can bear the Truth!); an account of the almost systemic distortion in the soul that would above all *not* wish that God/nature be revealed is not provided there, however. The temptation is to invoke Nietzsche's dictum about the difference between the Greek and the biblical tradition: "foolishness, *not* sin! do you grasp that?"[23] With the biblical tradition, errancy, wishing to remain hidden, is built into the human constitution because of sin. Hiddenness has a certain kind of preeminence over presence; human life is more exile than dwelling in the land of milk and honey.

Further complicating the matter of presence and hiddenness, as I have said elsewhere, is the temporal horizon Rousseau invokes. While the temporal hori-zon of presence and hiddenness in Rousseau may, arguably, go back further and deeper than Luther, Hobbes, and Locke's biblical temporal horizon, it does not effectively extend into the future at all. There is no second coming *in the future* that resurrects the dead unto the kingdom of God. Errancy is not *forgiven* by a Christ who would *hide*—not eliminate—"sin."[24] There is no *gift*. The hiddenness of God(/nature) is no less acute in Luther and in Hobbes (Locke seems out of place here), yet the gift of God offsets the errancy, even if only at the end of history. God the Son hides sinful Christians under His wing so that the Father may not see their sin. An indictment of errancy that may appeal only to the errant one for deliverance from it foreshortens the temporal horizon, extends it only until the errant one's own death. *Afterlife* can mean nothing here.[25] Where hiddenness is accepted as an aspect of the post-Incarnation epoch for Luther and Hobbes (and even, in this respect, Locke), to be superseded *at the end*, no such solution is countenanced by Rousseau. The valence of hiddenness is, consequently, *reversed* in Rousseau; hence the often impatient tone. The more than occasionally imploring urgency can be understood to follow from his thinking about presence and hiddenness within the temporal horizon he invokes. This conjunction occurs in Marx's thought as well.

The case of Luther and Rousseau aside for a moment, the genius of Hobbes and Locke is that they locate God close enough to authorize a form of political life, yet distant enough to assure that political conflicts are never ultimate conflicts. Until *that time* of the Redemption, which is different from *this time*, God remains hidden. It is impossible therefore to justify religious warfare in the present moment of history. God may be present, but in such a way that no political conflagration in His name can be justified now. While it *is* true that the thought of Luther, Hobbes, and Locke lowers its sights, asks of government that it abstain from attempting to resolve ultimate questions, it is not true that these ultimate questions are not implicated in the very formulations of political order they offer. What is significant is the *way* in which ultimate questions are implicated. The argument for keeping God at a distance is itself a *theological* argument about where God resides, about the whole.

Much more could be said about Luther, Hobbes, Locke, and Rousseau on this matter of presence and hiddenness. I merely suggest here that an important aspect of politically authoritative history is the way in which it specifies the presence *and* hiddenness of God/nature, and the "place" where this paradox is located. Certain political implications follow from this aspect and cannot be ignored if the depth of early modern thought is to be grasped.

Not grasping this paradox, however, makes it unlikely that our understanding will advance beyond the half-truth that early modern thought understood God to be outside of the purview of political life[26] or that more than the *hiddenness* of God is needed to sustain it.[27] In any effort to find in early modern thought a political vision that does not recur to the whole, only one-half of the truth is captured. The politically authoritative history adduced by Luther, Hobbes, Locke, and Rousseau suggests that they do have a vision of the whole—but one which paradoxically entails that the content of that whole remains partially hidden from human view.

Plato observes that there can be no advantage "in possessing everything except what is good, or in understanding everything else while of the good and desirable we know nothing."[28] Nietzsche notes that "without esteeming, the nut of existence would be hollow."[29] No world can be sustained or created (or defended)[30] without God/the Good. This thought was not lost to Luther, Hobbes, Locke, and Rousseau—notwithstanding the unfamiliarity of their formulations. The paradox of presence and hiddenness in politically authoritative history yields neither an enfeebled self mired in a relativistic morass of a disenchanted world, nor a self capable of both great accomplishment and hideous transgression. Between the supposed weakness of the liberal soul and the ghastly force used by those possessed by the *manifest* God is the early modern alternative. There is an extraordinary tension in this vision, to be sure; yet the easy alternatives which we suppose today—God wholly absent or God wholly present, the liberal without God or the anti-liberal too comfortably enshrouded by Him—are not countenanced here. Politically authoritative history allows us to compass these alternatives without falling into a vicious polarity from which we cannot withdraw—even if we would wish to.

THE FALLACY OF SELF-ASSUMED ACTION

In the contemporary debate about early modern thought the point of departure of proponents and detractors alike is often the view that political action is self-assumed, that community is an achievement of persons who themselves are *not* constituted through the community they together achieve. The alternative, non-self-assumed action, is most often taken to mean action which originates from a socially constituted self. And so the debate about action devolves into one about the self—whether it is self-constituted or socially constituted. This I take to be the fundamental point of contention of the liberal/anti-liberal debate.

The belief that holds the debate together, that gives proponents and detractors something in common *from* which they may disagree, is that the ontological foundation of human life must rest on one or the other of these polar alternatives, and the fate of the theory of liberalism (the kernel of which, it is claimed, is self-assumed action and the self-constituted self) is understood to hang on which of these two is indeed primordial.

Neither one of these alternatives is primordial, however. The procrustean reflex that alleges otherwise, that would urge early modern thought to lie down between these alternatives that it may be coddled or defiled, violates the spirit of the entire enterprise; it infuses into early modern thought a contemporary polarity not present there as a philosophical *category* and assures that in reading its texts the horizon of thought is *not* expanded beyond what is comfortably provincial. What is primordial for early modern thought is neither the individual nor society, but rather the history of God/nature's concealment and unconcealment. From this history the present human condition, in the fullest sense, is understood. On this view the self is constituted neither by itself nor by the community, and action is decidedly not wholly self-assumed.

Politically authoritative history, which discloses the constitutive ground and situation in which human beings find themselves, implores that *this* action be taken and not *that,* in order that the truth of the partially revealed and concealed God/nature not be violated. Certain actions are obliged because they are revealed to comport with verities that the self dimly intimates to be true yet cannot by itself confirm. Politically authoritative history reveals the ultimate foundation upon which human life rests, notwithstanding initial or longstanding resistance to it.

Politically authoritative history, then, implores that human beings act from a vantage which, at first blush, is *not* their own, for it conveys what they initially do not know, or remember, or wish to remember, or wish to do or refrain from doing. It is the authoritative account of what the self is and must do, yet would wish it could reject, even while it knows or dimly intimates that it cannot. Action is guided along a course that would *not* be chosen were it not for a history which draws the self outside itself, away from the persistent temptation for the self to narrow its horizon, to act *only* from a self that is, when all is said and done, *dead* unless oriented to God/nature.

The Augustinian problem of the self-enclosure, so preponderant in his *Confessions* (and arguably, *the* political problem for Tocqueville),[31] is countermanded by a history which is remembered and which reorients the self toward God/nature. Politically authoritative history is anamnetic; in the recovery of what is forgotten, the self is, if not drawn beyond itself, then at least placed into a tension with an authoritative truth that it cannot ignore without peril, without death. While the self might, of its own accord, wish to act one way, politically authoritative history says, in effect, "thou shalt do otherwise than immediately inclined."

Representationally, this thought is conveyed by Adam and Eve's *hiding from* God;[32] here is a diremption that would construe its constitutive ground to be Other than itself even while it "knows" it is not. Were action self-assumed they would continue to hide from God; were action non-self-assumed they would come out of hiding because they know they are bound by an obligation to do so. In a "thin" sense Adam and Eve's coming out of hiding because of God's call to them[33] is non-self-assumed action. They wish, after all, to remain hidden. Yet in a "thick" sense their action *is* self-assumed, for the *real* ground of their choice is the command of the God who *constituted them.* The historical narrative authoritatively conveys to the self who it is, and implores it to do otherwise than it is inclined to do; it conveys to the self that it is other than it would wish to think it is. Had Adam and Eve thought they were truly not bound by the Other, by God, they would not have come out of hiding; yet they dimly intimated that they were, and so they came out. God's command was, in effect, *their* choice.

What is at issue here is the status of a self that is *like* God[34] yet dirempted from Him, a self apart from God and unto itself, yet like and bound to Him at the same time—and in a way that the self would, in its errancy, wish to forego. In Hegel's words,

> the unity of Man with God is posited in the Christian religion. But this unity must not be superficially conceived, as if God were only Man, and Man, without further condition, were God. Man, on the contrary, is God only in so far as he annuls the merely Natural and Limited in his Spirit and elevates himself to God. That is to say, it is *obligatory* on him who is a partaker of the truth, and *knows* that he himself is a constituent [Moment] of the Divine Idea, to give up his merely natural being.[35]

The self left unto itself would not wish to grasp its Ground; it would deny what its authoritative history only reconfirms, what it knows already but would wish to deny. Politically authoritative history conveys what the self *already* knows, and would rebind it to its Ground.

It is this *bound-by* quality of action that permeates early modern thought. The self, left to itself, would choose a different course of action were it not for a politically authoritative history that discloses to the self its boundedness, a constitutive ground which appears, at first blush, to demand what the self would not wish to do.

In Luther's thought, for example, there is an abiding concern that the two realms be kept separate, an alacrity which betrays his worry that left to itself, the self would *not* wish to face the "terrors of conscience" that must be faced in order for the spiritual realm to yawn, for that other realm to be unconcealed. The end of history *is* the overcoming of the dialectical relationship between flesh and spirit; yet in this moment of history Christians must not abrogate their charge of wrestling with sin that the spiritual realm may come to presence. They must not, in a word, *only* succumb to *temptation*—which is what the self would choose were it left entirely to itself. God is partially obscured, fundamental mystery remains; nevertheless, what *has* been revealed by history requires an attunement to something other than the carnal world into which the self is thrown— and would wish to remain, unperturbed, in. Atonement requires doing what the self would not wish to do. Here is non-self-imposed obligation where the constitutive ground is God, *not* "the social."

For Luther, action is not self-assumed in any conventional sense. It is compelled in certain directions by the God who is in one important sense an Other, if only because of the self's wish not to comply with His mandate, and *not* an Other because He is the Creator, the constitutive Ground which creates the self. The Christian must annul the Old that he or she may live in accordance with the truth of this historical epoch. This is not simply a *moral* imperative; it is a necessity dictated by the structure of biblical history, of reality, itself!

In the case of Hobbes the question of whether action is self-assumed hinges

upon the notion of covenant to which he recurs. That he uses the term covenant rather than contract suggests already that obligations incurred or promised
have a sacred character about them. Indeed, while reason may supervene over
the passions and may discover that should they be left alone to rule there can be
only death, that "covenants exhorted by fear are valid"[36] suggests that something else more primordial than reason's foresight is at work in the making of
covenants. Locke, after all, would never have acceded to this view. Moreover,
Hobbes's continual insistence about the need for obedience seems disingenuous
or somehow out of place should he be viewed as a theorist for whom action is
wholly self-assumed.

The reason *why* fear and obedience figure prominently in Hobbes's notion
of covenant is that the model for it is biblical; more precisely, it is based on his
reading of the covenant between God, his mediary Moses, and the Israelites in
Exodus. *This* covenant, unlike the earlier covenant between God and
Abraham,[37] requires that the people *obey* God's commandments in exchange
for passage out of exile and into the land of milk and honey.

In the Exodus covenant the problem, in a word, is the perpetual backsliding of the Israelites, their murmurings against Moses,[38] their tendency to fall
into idolatry, to be led astray, when Moses (the voice of God) is absent.[39] On
their own their actions would violate God's injunctions. And it is the *obedience*
to these injunctions that assures the Israelites that they will be led out of Egypt
(the state of nature where left to themselves they will die?). Obedience to God,
to the Other who would command them under the threat of wrath to do otherwise than they would do on their own, guides their action *this* way rather than
that. So unattuned to God are the Israelites that only fear can draw them unto
God, can draw them outside of themselves. Errancy is inevitable,

> when there is no visible power to keep them in awe, and tie them by fear of
> punishment to the performance of their covenants. . . . Covenants with-
> out the sword, are but words, and of no strength to secure man at all.[40]

This passage, of course, comes from the *Leviathan,* not from Exodus. The message, however, is similar. A covenant of the Exodus sort is necessary precisely
because self-assumed action would take the Israelites back to Egypt, not to Canaan. There is the need for an Other, for a Leviathan who is God's mediary.
And in the final analysis, it is *because* he is God's mediary that the people obey.
They obey because God, while Other, is in some deeper sense the Ground from
which action must spring.

The Leviathan, to whom obedience is owed, is (recall) the trace of God. In
obeying the Leviathan (and in accepting his interpretation of the word of God),
human beings are drawn outside of themselves upon the *authority* of God. The
Leviathan to whom the self must submit is the intermediary of the God through
whom the self becomes what is promised: a self living amidst peace (the land of
milk and honey) who, in giving itself over to the Leviathan, loses Egypt and

gains Canaan in the same moment. Wholly self-assumed action would intern the self in Egypt. Precisely because the self cannot, of its own accord, enter into Canaan, God's trace (the Leviathan) is necessary—as Moses was!

Consider Locke. The call for toleration is authorized by a history that is structured by a dialectic of clarification. By being tolerant human beings act in accordance with the God who is disclosed in biblical history. The person who is tolerant is *called upon* to be so, not by Locke, but by the very truth of the post-Incarnation epoch. This is much less a moral matter than an ontological one. Because of what Christ did *then*, human beings must act *this* way rather than *that*. Being tolerant is not a matter of expediency, or self-interest; rather, being tolerant entails that the self attend to a (biblical) history which binds it, which implores that it comport itself toward other (reasonable) human beings in a way that they would perhaps not be otherwise disposed were their actions wholly self-assumed. Not because they are *different* must Christians tolerate those who espouse different thoughts, but because they are the *same* underneath their differences. It was this thought that prompted Lord Acton to observe that the

> great *political* idea, sanctifying freedom and consecrating it to God, teaching men to treasure the liberties of others *as their own,* and to defend them for the love of justice more than as a claim of right, has been the soul of what is great and good in the progress of the last two hundred years.[41]

The boundedness of the self and of its actions in Locke is nowhere made more apparent than in his understanding of the linkage between *all* Christians and Adam.[42] This linkage, this mode by which *any* difference between selves is encompassed by a manifest *original* identity that unites them, is the basis of government by law and reason—the latter of which was granted to Adam *ab origine*. It is precisely because human beings are not *just* isolated selves that they may act in concert. Underneath their difference is a unity (Adam) which politically authoritative history discloses, and it is this unity that makes government of a certain sort possible.

Without laboring the point it should also be added that Locke's thinking about property reinforces what is implicit elsewhere. Action is not wholly self-assumed. Property here is *stewardship;* it may not be treated in any which way, for any purposes the self might deem desirable for itself. "Nothing was made by God for Man to spoil or destroy," Locke says.[43] The self must act in accordance with, and within the parameters set by, the truth of its authoritative history. This is a far cry from a bourgeois theory of property, where all things (permitted by the market) are permitted. Property is for humankind, but the *authority* of this claim directs humanity's *use* of it back toward God.

Of Rousseau it may be said that action is non-self-assumed as well, though in two different senses. His indictment of the civilized human being in the *First Discourse* can be understood in a variety of ways, not the least of which is that the person who resides *there*, in that epoch, is motivated by envy. He or she is other-related, not self-related, as the savage *was*. Here the *others* are the author of the self's action. Having the source of its action outside of itself, it loses itself in transitory brilliance, in the temptations of public opinion, in bustle of the Pireaus.

This kind of non-self-assumed action is, of course, rooted in the soul's errancy from nature. In civil society the self that acts does not, properly speaking, *yet* act because it *is* not yet. Not yet being itself, *it* does not yet really act. The actions that emanate from this other-related self may win honor, fortune, and power; yet these are as ephemeral as the soul who would pursue them is lost to itself—as Glaucon comes to know in *The Republic*.

To act from itself the self must, then, come unto itself, or, in Emile's case, never defect from nature. Yet this coming unto nature is precisely to be bound by nature, to act upon the counsel of that timid voice that would shun what is brilliant, transitory, and above all a *temptation* to the self that has *already* betrayed nature in its heart. [44] Nature, the Source from which the self would hide itself amidst clothing and other encumberments, does speak, but to the errant self it is as a voice that calls from a foreign place. To the self "deceived by the appearance of right" [45] the *appearance* of right goes unnoticed, or worse yet, is scorned. Wholly left to itself, the (bourgeois) soul scoffs at bread and water— nature's offering [46]—preferring more elegant fare. [47] Indeed these are seen as the wages of dereliction from civil society, of crime against it.

There are two senses, then, in which action is non-self-assumed in Rousseau. Lost to itself in civil society the self is other-related; coming unto itself it listens to the counsel of the timid voice of nature—and is Other-related. The first sense is, of course, absent in Luther, Hobbes, and Locke. For them, the epochs of politically authoritative history are differentiated around the Christ event, not around the fall into civil society and other-relatedness. This (massive) difference notwithstanding, however, Rousseau does not defect from the fundamental insight: for the self to be what it most fully is it must defer to an authoritative voice that guides it *this* way rather than *that*.

All this is to say that whenever a politically authoritative history is invoked, ethical implications are entailed. [48] Wholly self-assumed actions can only begin to be thought of outside of this context. [49] So, too, may its antithetical partner, socially constituted action. This latter form of action, however, is not to be confused with the non-self-assumed action of Luther, Hobbes, Locke, and Rousseau.

GOD THE SON AND THE PEDIGREE OF FREEDOM

The early modern problematic of freedom arises out of the Reformation question about the meaning of Christ's fulfillment of the Mosaic law given by the

Father, and hence about the dialectical relationship between God the Father and God the Son. In Luther's "Freedom of a Christian" and Locke's "Letter on Toleration" it is God the Son who punctuates history and offers a new way of atonement which demands attunement to a spiritual realm upon which no worldly power may impinge. Because of a dialectical movement that has *already* occurred, the Ground of freedom is already *there* to be grasped by the soul who would be taken under the wing of God the Son.

Attunement means, among other things, that human beings not conflate the spiritual and worldly realms. These must be separated that God the Son might come to presence—either in the abyss (Luther) or in Reason's clearing (Locke). Without that separation: no Christ, no freedom. The ground for the separation is already there, for the *event* has already happened; the failing would be, like the Romans about whom Augustine wrote, to "worship perishable defenders,"[50] to be tempted to find in worldly power the wellspring of true freedom now that the decisive event has occurred.

The event that *has* occurred *did* occur in the "fullness of time."[51] About this something should be said, for precisely the conditions which it expresses serve to specify the substance of the dialectical fulfillment Christ offers. For illustrative purposes, I will turn not to Luther, Hobbes, or Locke, but rather to Hegel and Tocqueville—two thinkers no less convinced of the inexorable relationship between God the Son and freedom than were Luther, Hobbes, and Locke.

For Hegel, for example, the fullness of time is anticipated by the withdrawal of the corrupted Greek world into itself, the reemergence of the self as (still natural, though Universal) Personality in the Roman world in the form of Legal right,[52] and finally the contradiction of this principle in the person of the Emperor whose Private Right rules and negates the rights of citizens. "The supposed condition of Right turns out to be an absolute destitution of it," Hegel says.[53] Rome ends, for both Hegel and Augustine, in the longing for dominion.[54]

Yet this longing that brings suffering in its wake is not yet internalized. For that the Jews are necessary; they alone see suffering as an internal attribution, as explicable in terms of a spiritual disposition toward errancy. Discerning the root of suffering to be Subjective, its external attributes are shed and Universal Subjectivity returns, only now spiritualized.[55] This was the pregnant Moment, the "fullness of time" into which Christ came. Now Subjectivity utters ("outers") itself in a *particular* being (God the Son). Spirit becomes Flesh, Universal becomes particular, God the Father becomes God the Son: "a Man who is God— God who is Man."[56]

The "fullness of time" is the moment at which it becomes possible for the first time for the unity of God and man to appear. This first-time appearance is, of course, the *only* appearance; and yet it is the pattern for the whole of history: the dialectic itself is the recapitulation of this pattern.

In [Christ's] death, and his history generally, [is] presented the eternal history of Spirit—a history which every man has to accomplish in himself.[57]

In Hegel's view, Luther's genius was to have grasped this Truth, and grasping it as he did, he prepared the way for true freedom—where the Christian recapitulates Christ's life and so becomes as Christ: Spirit made Flesh. The errancy of Adam gives way to Christ's irruption into the world—which *is* humanity becoming as God again in spiritual freedom. Hegel was compelled to say of Luther, who he thought truly understood what the Catholic Church did not, that "the essence of the Reformation is this: that Man is in his very nature destined to be free."[58] The Reformation is hallowed because it is the world-historical utterance, though still understood in the representational form, of a dialectical truth whose substance is able to specify *retrospectively* the content it fulfills in the "fullness of time," in Hegel's view, the principle of Subjectivity which the Romans (more than the Greeks, but less than the Jews) evinced.

It is the retrospective element that above all needs to be emphasized here. Precisely what this means will perhaps require another example, after which it will be possible to comment on the general problem faced by any *forward-* rather than backward-looking dialectic.

Consider Tocqueville. Though certainly not a dialectical thinker, Christianity, and therefore Christ, figures prominently in his narrative of American identity and exceptionalism. Unlike Rousseau, for whom America represents the past, savage, condition,[59] for Tocqueville, America is the future; it is, in effect, the vanguard of providential design, and so, worthy of study by Europe.

The grand thought that orients his *Democracy in America* is that providence has dictated that there will be equality, but that the *kind* of equality that obtains is in the hands of humankind. This is made clear in Tocqueville's opening remarks,[60] and in the last paragraph of the book:

The nations of our day cannot prevent conditions of equality from spreading in their midst. But it depends upon themselves whether equality is to lead to servitude or freedom, knowledge or barbarism, prosperity or wretchedness.[61]

So while providence, the Christian God, has dictated that there will be equality, it will be either an equality of all in freedom or an equality of all *under a one* in servitude, he says.[62]

The pattern of the equality of all under the one I have discussed in the thought of Luther, Hobbes, Locke, and Rousseau; it is a fundamentally Christian pattern, as Tocqueville well knows. What is fascinating about his treatment of it, however, is that unlike Hegel, for whom Christianity is about Spirit become Flesh, the import of Christianity for Tocqueville pertains to the *habits* of thinking and acting in political and social life that derive from it. Consciousness here determines life's habits.[63]

> There is hardly any human action, however private it may be, which does not *result* from some very general *conception* men have of God, of His relations with the human race, of the nature of their soul, and of their duties to their fellows.[64]

The matter cannot be left at this, however, for there are passages only a little farther along where, in Tocqueville's subtle fashion, the causality is reversed: life's habits determine consciousness, and it is this thought to which I wish to attend. Consider the following lengthy passage:

> At the time when Christianity appeared on earth, Providence, which no doubt *was preparing* the world for its reception, had united a great part of mankind, like an immense flock, under the Caesars. The men composing this multitude were of many different sorts, but they all had this in common, that they obeyed the same laws, and each of them was so small and weak compared to the greatness of the emperor that they all seemed equal in comparison to him.
>
> One must recognize that this new and singular condition of humanity *disposed* men to receive the general truths preached by Christianity, and this serves to explain the quick and easy way in which it then penetrated the human spirit.[65]

As a sociology of knowledge this passage suggests that the real life condition of the Romans (where, as in Catholicism, all are equal under the pope/emperor) "disposed" the people toward a religious idea that recapitulates what their habits confirm. They could easily come to *think* Christianity because the life they *lived* already evinced the Christian pattern. Being precedes consciousness; real-life conditions of equality conduce to the acceptance of certain religious notions. (Notwithstanding several centuries of turmoil, and contrary to the secularization thesis, as the world becomes *more* equal, Christianity will make *increasing* sense!)

The notion that "Providence *was preparing* the world for Christianity's reception," however, is a more intriguing entrée into the matter. Put into theological rather than sociological terms, the suggestion here is that the Roman unification under the Caesars *was* the fullness of time into which Christ came. The Christ event, in effect, brought into thought what had, in the fullness of time, been only in habit. Christ's fulfillment in the fullness of time confirmed in thought what had been portended but not anticipated—hence the "no doubt" clause before "was preparing." Christ's fulfillment is the idea of the equality of all—not under a one because the pope/emperor is absent—*now* reflected back onto the habits of that most democratic people in the world: the Americans.[66]

The general conclusions that can be drawn here, from both Hegel and Tocqueville, are, first, that the dialectical event of Christ that occurred long ago is the determinant agency of post-Incarnation history on the basis of which it is possible to specify which institutional form best comports with its truth (for Hegel, the Reformation; for Tocqueville, America), and second, and more to the point for the purpose at hand, that the events that constitute the fullness of time *in no way* allow a prediction of precisely what will be entailed by the dialectical fulfillment. Rome, after all, occurs in both Hegel and Tocqueville's account;[67] yet precisely what it was about Rome that *portended* the fulfillment by Christ can only be known upon the actual event of fulfillment. Only a looking-backward in hindsight grants thought its grasp of both the anticipatory conditions and the substance of the fulfillment. There may be differences in respect to *how* the fulfillment is understood, but this does not at all alter the condition under which even different understandings *can be achieved.*

This ineluctable condition, of course, makes it quite clear that the idea of a *forward*-looking dialectic which purports to comprehend what the fulfillment *will be* even while it stands in its darkest hour of negation can only be a deception and dangerous obstruction to it. Locke makes this clear when speaking of the unconcealment of Christ's truth. The fulfillment *expected* was not the fulfillment that came to pass; for that very reason Christ had to prepare His hearers by degree so that they would not kill him *before* His truth could be revealed.[68] Luther, too, notes the problem of the anticipatory look forward that would wish for atonement, *yet not wish to be startled or dislodged.*[69] Consider also Saint Mark:

> And when the centurion, which stood over against him, saw that he so cried out, and gave up the ghost, he said, Truly this man was the Son of God.[70]

The centurion, the one who did not expect the Messiah at all, the outsider to the whole painful affair of anticipation, was the *only* person who came to recognize Christ; all the rest failed to understand because they purported to know *already* what the fulfillment would be.[71]

Many more examples could be adduced. The insight of the New Testament about dialectic, recapitulated elegantly by Hegel, is that the Pharisees were wrong. The *expected* king does not come. While Marx, for example, is at times circumspect about the precise *content* of the communism to come,[72] it would be more than generous to say that elsewhere he comes precipitously close to specifying what communism/the Messiah would actually look like.

Marx purports to have shown that Christianity was the "spirit of the past," that he has developed an adequate language to understand "the new scene of world history."[73] Rather than being post-Christian, however, his insistence that he *knows* what the outcome of the dialectic of history will be makes him a pre-Christian figure—in biblical terms, akin to the Pharisees. Luther, Hobbes, and Locke, ostensibly nondialectical thinkers, display a subtlety of thought absent in Marx; they at least recognize that dialectical fulfillment annuls and pre-serves, and that it is the *unexpected* nature of the fulfillment that brings into bold relief the question, at once political and theological, that they urgently sought to answer: *Who* was Christ? From the vantage of the totality of their thinking, Luther, Hobbes, and Locke are more properly dialectical than is Marx. The "Messiah" is portended but always unexpected; hence for "the Jews" (those who await the new kingdom with great hope and expectation), the "Messiah" (what actually fulfills that hope) will always a "stumbling block."[74]

THE POLITICS OF DEATH

The only death to which politics understood as "the monopoly of the legitimate use of *physical* force within a given territory"[75] can pertain is, of course, *physical* death, the threat of which can compel and guide in ways that mere words can-not. In a passage which has come to be seen as paradigmatic of the modern rela-tionship to death, Hobbes observes that it is the "continual *fear*, and danger of violent death"[76] that prompts human beings to enter into civil society. The modern soul, it would seem, is fearful of death, and politics is the arena in which physical life is protected or taken away by the legitimate power that can (easily) animate that fear.

Less wrong than only partly correct, the veracity of this view demands the dismissal of the Reformation question that compels Luther, Hobbes, and Locke to consider biblical history in the first place, *viz.*, who is the Christ that came to fulfill the old Law, and what is necessary in order to attain salvation—*eternal* life? This question is a *political* one precisely because of the Reformers' insistence that in order to attain eternal life it was necessary either to separate the two realms, carnal and spiritual, that each may have its due, that *obstructions* to sal-vation be removed, or that they be unified in a particular manner. While the politics of Luther and Locke are an attempt to specify the way in which they must be separated, and the politics of Hobbes is an attempt to show that, ap-pearances to the contrary, they are indeed *not* to be separated, for all three the problem is the same. The first, physical, death is not so much discounted as put in its place in the overall economy of salvation. Above all, it was how to avoid the second, eternal, death that *orients* their politics. As Hobbes says,

> no man can serve two masters; nor is he less, but rather more of a master, whom we are to obey for *fear* of damnation than he whom we obey for fear of temporal death.[77]

It is this *real* fear of eternal death that drives political theory to specify a form of political life which does not arrest the prospect of receiving Christ's *gift*. Making Hobbes into an Erastian betrays a shrinking from the real fear.

For Luther, because Christ's gift comes to presence in a "place" beneath "the world," worldly power must never purport to mediate faith. For Hobbes, because Christ's gift demands assent and obedience, the sovereign must *always* be obeyed—hence no right of revolt. For Locke, because Christ's gift requires assent and the use of reason's light (granted initially to Adam), toleration is countenanced and government must be based on reason—hence the right of revolt if reason's law is transgressed. In all three instances, *who* Christ is, the manner in which the real problem of eternal death may be overcome, serves to specify the appropriate form of political life.

For Rousseau, there is no *gift*, as I have said. Nevertheless, the politics of death is no less an issue. God the Son is not the way of atonement for the errant soul, but nature is. The import of the *Second Discourse* is to show that when human beings fall away from the state of nature, lose their innocence and come upon death *as something to be feared,* the unfolding logic would lead them back to a second equality—only this time one in servitude under a tyrant.[78] In *Emile,* fear of death is less overcome than not awakened. It is in the imagination of the restive, errant soul that the fear of death comes to rule. And so ruled, it cannot come unto life, unto nature. "I am not able to teach living to one who thinks of nothing but how to keep himself from dying," Rousseau says.[79] Just *who* it is that is fearful of dying is clear throughout: the person lost in civil life. Not knowing how to die, no person can know how to live; not knowing how to live, no person can come unto the city of nature[80]—the only alternative to which, following Augustine, is the City of Man which aims only at dominion.[81] Not facing the politics of death leads inexorably to tyranny.

While the "how" of confronting that most fearful thing is clearly different in Luther, Hobbes, Locke, and Rousseau, they each address it nevertheless— and not as mere "idle talk."[82] It is to be wondered whether the contemporary reflex that in the same breath would disavow talk of eternal death, insist *with certainty* that persons die with their first and only death,[83] and read early modern thought without regard to its overriding fear, evinces the evasive concealment of the *terror* of death, following Heidegger,[84] that "eternal damnation" conveys.

Furthermore, while Rousseau decries this sorry state in which the fear of death abridges life, it is also to be wondered whether his insistence that the terror of death is an artifact of errancy from nature, that it advances like a cancer in the *unchecked* imagination,[85] does not in the end countenance a self-deception about death even as it urges the soul to live authentically. "*Not* fear; rather that we no longer have anything left to fear in man," says Nietzsche:[86] that is the real danger.

Yet even in Nietzsche's pithy blast that would shatter the whole of Rousseau's fragile, sensitive edifice, the death to be joyously feared is at the hands *of others.* It is *temporal* death, faced with an honorable nobility, to be sure; but it is a death without the terror of eternal death. *That* death is historicized, relegated to a cultural form animated by hidden springs of envy and now suffering from weariness. *That* death is a projection of a wounded *animal*—whose preeminently biological identity demands that it *feel* fear again that it may be itself again.

This homecoming, though a more precipitous one than Rousseau's, comes no closer to the problem—even in its sanction of fear. Hobbes, it seems, is closer to the truth in recognizing the power of the fear of temporal death—and the superabundant fear of eternal death for which atonement is necessary.[87] Should this be the *real* danger, then the scholarly denial of eternal damnation *as a problem* would be demonstrable evidence of its misapprehension of the horizon of early modern political thought. Here I suggest that not because there *is* a Hell, but because the conveyance of such a *representation* is perhaps adequate to a terror that cannot be mollified by attending to the mere *fact* of death, the notion of eternal death ought to be given serious consideration—as it is by certain early modern thinkers.

THE EQUALITY OF ALL UNDER THE ONE

Christianity and not ancient political thought is the pedigree of the modern notion of the equality of all under the one, in whatever its manifested form. I will not rehearse the differences and similarities here, but simply note for the purpose of contrast that Aristotle would find this notion quite foreign.

Not the equality of all under the one (sovereign), but rather the association of all *who have something in common* is his driving thought. This having-in-common is the basis of unity among many.[88] Here, too, the friend who is capable of being a friend to and for another plays an important part.[89] In contrast to the quasi-friendships based on pleasure and use (which, contra Smith,[90] can never be the basis for an enduring society),[91] the true friend loves what is most noble in himself; therefore he *can* love others. Self-love properly understood is the ground of being with others;[92] love of self occasions the possibility of forming friendships with other selves like our own.[93] Here equality between selves is possible only if souls have the requisite *hexis*, which develops out of right training. There is no idea of the equality *of all* within this philosophical schema; nor is the equality achieved comprehended as being *under* the sovereign and, in some decisive respect, attributable *to* the sovereign. The theoretical edifice on which Aristotle's notion of equality rests is quite different from the one which underlies the thought of Luther, Hobbes, and Rousseau.[94] Tocqueville remarks, contra Aristotle, that the political form into which democracy can fall is not a perverted form of the rule of the many, but rather a tyrannical rule by the one.[95] The very logic of the notion of the equality of all under the one dictates that modern democracy is disposed to fall into what Aristotle thought the worst kind of tyranny: dominion under the one. That even Rousseau (whose *Second Discourse* seems to offer a different history from that offered by the Bible) arrives at the same conclusion, *viz.*, that the corrupted political form which follows the equality of all is the equality of all (in servitude) under the one (tyrant), suggests that this pattern of thinking has not been expunged even in his work. Tocqueville, after all, found it very easy to readapt Rousseau's conclusion in the *Second Discourse* and issue a warning to America—that without *faith* the logic of the pattern *will remain intact* and this nation will be lead unwittingly toward the equality of all under the one tyrant![96]

This sobering prophecy aside, it can be said that the beneficent though by no means unequivocal result[97] of this notion of the equality of all under the one in modern political thought has been a general endorsement of democracy, whose underlying support in the modern period, as Tocqueville remarked, is Christianity.

> Christianity, which has declared all men equal in the sight of God, cannot hesitate to acknowledge all citizens equal before the law.[98]

The pedigree of modern democracy—by which is meant here the institutional arrangements which comport with the sentiment that *all* human beings are, in the most important ways, equal—can be traced to the Christian notion of the equality of all under God.[99] The precise meaning of this notion that all are equal under a One may be understood in a variety of ways, to be sure; yet notwithstanding permutations and contestations, the notion endures: the general pattern remains unassaulted even while its articulations do not. Contradictions and difficulties do not force the abandonment of the notion itself, but rather occasion different formulations of it which betray an effort to continue to comprehend the vagaries of experience in its terms.

This perennially resurrected pattern suggests, but by no means proves, that viable political forms cannot be constructed from whole cloth and given to (or even willingly appropriated by) peoples whose religious traditions do not, in effect, *allow* those political forms to make sense.

This should not be taken to mean that the labors of Luther, Hobbes, Locke, and Rousseau, which with hindsight appear as way stations along the path to attaining a set of stable *sentiments* of democracy, can only come to Christian nations, perhaps even only to Christian nations of a certain sort, but rather that *if* democracy is to be a viable form, it will have to find its support in still thriving or in residual patterns of religious thought which conduce toward it; alternatively, if *other* thriving or residual patterns of religious thought still abound, the most viable political form may *not* be democracy.[100]

Tocqueville observes that "every religion has some political opinion linked to it by affinity."[101] We could do no better than to attend earnestly to the full implications of this thought.

My invocation of Aristotle has not been purely for the purpose of contrasting ancient and early modern Christian views of government, however informative this might be. Aristotle too often surfaces in the debate between liberals and communitarians. In this debate, it is often supposed, Aristotle offers an antidote to the community of strangers that liberal political thought seems to countenance, and so it is appropriate to show that he (and by extension, the communitarians who would recur to his thinking) might misapprehend the foundation upon which theorists for whom the equality of all under the one is the paradigm for community build.

Communitarians *are* right, for example, in their view that community is not primordial in Hobbes;[102] yet they miss the theoretical significance of the relationship between Hobbesian citizens and their sovereign: *all* are prideful, *all* are ruled by passions—yet all accede to a *one*. While our particular passions may differ, while we may be *strangers* to each other, Hobbes, like other reformers, saw community in biblical terms. That is, community was the result of a covenant through which all stand before the one. Human beings *are* all strangers to each other except through a sovereign. Transposed to pertain to Christ the Sovereign, Luther would say no less. Only through the Sovereign can there be community. Augustine, perhaps writing *against* Aristotle—certainly, at any rate, against the idea that community can have an immanent foundation—would agree:

> [Although friends may] cling together, no friends are true friends unless you, my God, bind them fast to one another through that love which is sown in our hearts by the Holy Ghost.[103]

It is a considerable misrepresentation, then, to suggest that because Hobbes did not subscribe to some sort of organic view of society (from which, it is purported, individuals spring), he is an "individualist." The two alternatives, "communitarian" and "individualist," are not pertinent categories for Hobbes. Communitarians would do well to heed this point. Community is a unity (made possible by the one) of the many strangers, who are not by disposition prone to form a community together. To put it succinctly, human beings are not by nature social, they are by nature *prideful*, and this is a massive obstacle to community which can be overcome only by the equality of all under the one. The question of the ontological preeminence of the community or of the individual is a nonissue for Hobbes. The problem of pride, in a word, does not map onto the contemporary liberal-communitarian debate!

When the progenitive Protestant vision (which insisted upon the theological notion of the equality of all under the one) ebbs, *then* perhaps it begins to make sense to speak of the frailty and instability of a community of strangers.[104] But not until then. What happens hypothetically without a sovereign in Hobbes's commonwealth happens empirically in a Reformation culture without Christ the sovereign: all the strangers lose their basis for unity. The *community* of strangers now become—*mere* strangers. This is a profound difficultly, to be sure, and it is at present impelling more and more people to search for a less *scandalous* basis of unity than through a Sovereign, to search for ways in which they may *have something in common* (by affirming their *membership*, say, in a racial, ethnic, linguistic, or national community).

Alternatively, they simply retain their status as strangers, alone and unto themselves, and fail to be drawn beyond themselves and back toward others through the one sovereign, as Augustine, Luther, Calvin, and Hobbes would insist was necessary—whether in fear, love, or both.

This does not mean that the communitarians are right about Hobbes and, by extension, liberalism; rather, it suggests that the *discreditation* of the sovereign destroys the basis for the strangers to be anything else but strangers to one another, something the communitarians perhaps *now* rightly see, even while they misapprehend Hobbes and indeed much of the Reformation thinking in which the pattern of the equality of all under the one makes possible the community of strangers.

The post-Reformation project, if I may call it that, of finding a basis for community, not among strangers whose basis for unity *transcends* them—of the sort that Paul alluded to:

> There is neither Jew nor Greek, there is neither bond nor free, there is neither male nor female; for ye are all one in Christ[105]

—but rather, by being a part of an *immanent* community is, I take it, an inevitable step once the notion of the equality of all under the one (a liberal Protestant notion, through and through) "has conscience *against* it." The politics of immanent community, I suggest, cannot alone forge a unity of the different; the Reformation understanding of the equality of all under the one proffers one vision of the unity underneath multiplicity *which reason will never grasp;* other paths will no doubt be needed in the future if the one I have considered here is increasingly misunderstood and forgotten. Whether the forging of a new path based upon overcoming our status as strangers, upon attaining a "genuine" community, will yield anything other than the *idolatry* that communities whose identity is wholly immanent tend to generate (with the propensity for violence that that seems always to involve) remains to be seen. From the perspective of Reformation thinking *this* basis of community, though less scandalous, can only yield factionalism, fanaticism, and finally, great suffering. We *are* strangers except through a Sovereign. To construct a community on any other grounds is to fancy that being strangers to one another and to ourselves is *not* linked to our pridefulness—a naïveté which confirms ever anew our wish to evade and deny the magnitude of the problem of pride and the centrality of the figure of Adam.

IDENTITY AND HISTORY

An ecumenical disposition, such as one possessed by, say, Emerson, would have it that "there is properly no History, only Biography."[106] As with Rousseau, for whom the past becomes *history* only insofar as it illuminates the human heart,[107] history can only be *for us,* and *is* most effectively *for us* when its yield is moral development. In true ecumenical spirit, Emerson's historical method would constitute each soul in its depth through an appropriation of the world-historical record of the One Mind. Entering into it authentically is not mere study, it is an *enactment* through a *reenactment*—a grand recapitulation of the liturgical year, now comprehended on a cosmic scale as the totality of manifestations of the One Mind. Understood this way, "history no longer shall be a dull book," he says.[108] The self is taken out of itself and brought unto Itself by history rightly read; its horizon is expanded, its identity is fully grasped only when the "wild, savage, and preposterous There or Then [is done away with], and in its place [is introduced] the Here and Now. [This banishes] the *not me* and [in its stead supplies] the *me*."[109]

This is no overt recipe for solipsism. The horizon of self that comes unto Itself is expanded through an historical archaeology which discovers its own depth in the artifacts it unearths. "I once lived *there* too," the self comes to proclaim. The alien becomes the familiar. As with Hegel, difference is perpetually subsumed by identity in a drama that is alternatingly restively anticipatory and confidently self-enclosed—as it must be.

"What a shallow village tale our so-called History is," Emerson confesses.[110] It need not, however, be provincial. It may be outwardly expansive. In time and with humility we may come to comprehend worlds, whole realms of being, which at present remain alien to us—even the worlds of rat and lizard that know nothing of precious Rome, Paris, and Constantinople![111]

This is, as I have said, an ecumenical spirit, one that would reconstitute identity ever anew in proportion to its ever increasing *deep* grasp of the multiplex articulations of the One Mind in history. Christianity, the self-proclaimed universal,[112] is revealed to be but one particular manifestation amidst a plurality of articulations, less *true* than deepening, all of which intimate the depth of the One Mind in which human beings participate. History reveals the multiple forms of Unity to the self whose identity is enlarged in the act of grasping history's revelation.

The history that *is* revealed, however, is *not* the history of the hiddenness of God/nature from humankind as it is received and thought through in Luther, Hobbes, Locke, and Rousseau. From one vantage, of course, the horizon of Emerson's history is far more expansive, for it would purport to place their insights *next to* the insights of other thinkers from other times *in* history, all to be plumbed by a cosmopolitan soul and truly world citizen.

Yet from another vantage, this history that deepens has a *less* expansive horizon, for it is predicated wholly upon an *ordinary* conception of time (to invoke Heidegger's term),[113] upon that time which *evades* the centrality of the question of death that comes into view *only* in those (politically authoritative) histories that concern themselves with the whole distasteful matter of errancy, concealment, and atonement. "What light does [history] shed on those mysteries which we hide under the names of Death and Immortality?" Emerson asks.[114] The supposition that underlies *his* question is that while this unexplored domain is hidden from view, it is not, in principle, unviewable from the vantage of ordinary time. A recognized constitutional disposition toward errancy that would invite the soul to listen, not to ordinary history, no matter how brilliant and deepening, but instead attend to a history which speaks authoritatively *of that errancy* which is *a problem* has no place or meaning here. The horizon of that history which speaks of errancy, concealment, death, and atonement is definitively foreclosed.

I do not invoke Emerson lightly here, for the purpose of mocking either the horizon of ordinary time he seems to be comfortably working within or the deepened identity made possible because of it. On the contrary, to the self for whom errancy, concealment, etc. *can have no meaning,* Emerson's notion of history has much in its favor. The pluralism countenanced by this ecumenical view of identity and history would include as candidates for reverence and review not only members of the *entire* human community but the community of all living and inanimate things as well.[115] Moreover, since the notion (present from Hebrew through Protestant thought) that history discloses something about the soul's identity *cannot* seemingly be expunged, no matter how great the effort of historians to do so,[116] Emerson seems uniquely suited for the contemporary disposition that would link history and identity but which finds the biblical mode of doing so a stumbling block. Even Rousseau, who appears initially to be such a break with Luther, Hobbes and Locke, only serves to confirm that "it is biblical thinking, and not its poison, that repels us."

What I *do* wish to suggest, however, is that as appealing and timely as this or any other ecumenical linkage of history and identity may be, early modern thought was not as ecumenical as Emerson in its view of the relationship between identity and history. Throughout this work I have, in accordance with this insight, resisted the temptation to place these authors in their *historical context* and instead focused upon what for each of them is the *context of history.* Here is a context that, while immanent, opens upon a domain not graspable by reason alone, one that cannot but remain elusive in an inquiry that wishes only to situate authors in their political, social (and even religious!) context. For Luther, Hobbes, Locke, and Rousseau, the history of errancy, concealment, and death pointed to a mode of atonement that—and this is crucial—entailed a politics of the sort that does not obstruct Christ's gift or nature's rightful claim. Both come from *beyond* the everyday world that reason may grasp. How far this is from Emerson, who, while a friend of democracy to be sure, was a friend only to certain dispositions of Christianity, but not the historical horizon it proclaims. The notion of the equality of all under the one (which orients Luther, Hobbes, Locke, and Rousseau) only *need* be thought through in the event that errancy, concealment, and death are taken seriously; and this Emerson did not do. To think these through seriously entails that, to put it strongly, *sin* be taken seriously; for the supposition of sin is that of "a relation broken off"[117] which is the *cause* of errancy, concealment, and death. Only by taking sin seriously does the horizon of history that is proffered by the Bible become at all plausible; it becomes compelling at all only to the soul for whom errancy, concealment, and death are *a problem*. Even Rousseau belongs here, of course; for while he may have rejected the authoritative history of the Bible, the horizon he unveils nevertheless takes sin (in the sense mentioned above) seriously.

What can sin mean today, however? The efforts to think sin through anew in recent years[118] have not at all increased its general comprehensibility. Not wishing to enter into the question of whether this is to be deplored or celebrated, I simply want to reinforce here that the "relation broken off" with Adam's sin is the counterpoint to the relation reestablished by Christ's first coming; that modern political thought sought either to comprehend the political meaning of this emendation (Luther, Hobbes, and Locke), or that where this emendation was rejected (Rousseau), errancy, concealment, death, the need for atonement, the pattern of the equality of all under the one, and an historical epochality delineated by a *decisive event* are nevertheless on hand as a close and functional relative.

The historical horizon predicated upon an acceptance of the "relation broken off" is the basis of early modern political thought—true no less of Luther, Hobbes, Locke, than of Rousseau. There is no ecumenical disposition here. Hegel's claim, echoed by the others in their own way, that "the Fall is . . . the eternal Mythus of Man,"[119] that it is the *true* account, applicable to all, can only be met with patronizing indulgence by an ecumenical spirit. And yet there it stands: the seemingly *particular* supposition about the universality of this point of departure in Adam (or Rousseau's equivalent, the Natural human being) to which modern political theory is so indebted, and without which the democratic sentiment of the equality of all under the one—the political relative of the priesthood of all who believe in the atonement offered by Christ *for sin*— would have no referent. The Christ under whom all are one must, after all, be regarded "'as foolishness' [if there is no sin] for which Christ is the answer."[120]

It may well be that the ecumenical historical horizon is capable of sustaining democratic sentiments, that the tolerance of *difference* which undergirds it supposes already the equality of all historical articulations of the One Mind— all of which are capable of deepening the self. But *this* equality supposes the ground of a higher unity only to be in the One Mind, and it remains to be seen whether the *political* implications of this amount to anything more than a vacuous formalism about intolerance not unlike that found in Rousseau,[121] easy to abide by when, as in Tocqueville's America, there are no *fundamental* disagreements,[122] yet difficult to sustain unless (like Marx's communism) it is a world-around phenomenon.

The politics of an ecumenical horizon is a grand experiment that on its surface *does* comport with the sentiments of democracy. Unclear, however, is whether the survival of democracy requires a notion of unity undergirding difference that is, from the ecumenical horizon, particular rather than universal, infused with a *content* that would be an affront to it, of the sort, say, Locke had in mind when he derived property and government based on reason from the *concrete figure* of Adam—the Adam of the Bible. All of this is simply to say that while the cosmopolitan world we live in may cry out for an ecumenical horizon capable of encompassing all difference, which accords every voice its say *because* it is different, early modern thought privileges unity rather than difference, privileges the originary event of Adam (or his equivalent) from whom all are derived. In Augustine's words, it should be remembered that Adam

> was created by God with this intention: that from that one individual a multitude might be propagated, and that this fact should teach mankind to preserve a harmonious *unity in plurality.* [123]

This "universal" is from one vantage merely a particular, to be sure; yet from this particular can be developed a political framework that is not susceptible to what, ironically, may be the greatest threat to a politics based on the ecumenical horizon: the prospect that seemingly relevant differences may so proliferate that politics becomes impossible. The relevant political datum for Luther, Hobbes, Locke, and Rousseau is that the *foundation* of politics is unity rather than difference. The ecumenical horizon that has superseded it would, at best, have unity based upon the mediation of difference, based upon cultivating "agonistic respect between interlocking and contending constituencies." [124]

Between the two is a world of difference. Should this ecumenical movement falter, of course, all will not be lost: community will be maintained—if not in the hearts and minds of a citizenry receptive to a transcendent unity, then by virtue of an overarching (yet perhaps gentle) power in the world. It was Locke's claim, recall, that prior to Christ's first coming communities *were* held together, but *not* in freedom! [125] Who now takes this *particular* claim seriously?

How, then, is the study of the history of political thought implicated in this matter?

The refusal to take seriously the historical horizon of modern political thought, to treat it under the heading of "the history of ideas" which are to be compared, contrasted, and made *interesting,* rather than as an earnest effort to decipher the political meaning of the history of errancy, concealment, and atonement, whose horizon reason alone cannot grasp, already betrays a commitment to an ecumenical horizon. From this vantage, the foundation of modern political thought can only remain hidden from view, and the reason-based case for politics ostensibly drawn from it (which is, in a manner of speaking, only the visible portion of the iceberg) will appear to be superficial or distorted—or, when defended, selectively read to disregard those aspects of its case that seem strange, disingenuous, or "merely rhetorical."

Whether the pronouncements of academic scholarship for or against the modern political thinkers I have considered here will help forge the future is, of course, an open question. Luther, Hobbes, Locke, and Rousseau may, as I have suggested, now only be anachronisms, vestiges belonging to a past in which *errancy* was a problem, to whom we return for a thought here, a thought there. If, as I suggest, however, the historical horizon delineated by the problem of errancy, concealment, and atonement must be recurred to in order for early modern political thought (and ultimately democratic sentiments in the broad sense I have defined) to make sense, then in time it will become clear that the early modern horizon cannot be juxtaposed with the contemporary ecumenical horizon. *Should* democracy wish to be defended—perhaps it will no longer be wanted—then the future will be forged in the crucible of the contradiction between a particular universalist claim whose horizon is, when all is said and done, biblical, and an ecumenical universalist claim that would accord respect to all but not deferentially *accede* to any particular claim. The historical horizon then adopted by a discipline now almost wholly under the sway of the ecumenical spirit will become a political act par excellence—no less so than it is already, of course; only then the political implications of embracing *this* historical horizon rather than *that* will be ever more clear.

> Only a horizon ringed by myths can unify a culture. The forces of imagination and of the Apollonian dream are saved only by myth from indiscriminate rambling. . . . Over against this, let us consider abstract man stripped of myth, abstract education, abstract mores, abstract law, abstract government; . . . a culture without any fixed and consecrated place of origin, condemned to exhaust all possibilities *and feed miserably and parasitically on every culture under the sun.* Here we have the present age . . . [126]

A disquieting picture indeed. Yet it is worth pondering whether we *have* awakened from the first naïveté which would allow us to say, remorsefully but with a proud and sober self-confidence, that "our eyes are now opened,"[127] that the biblical horizon, the mythical horizon, is behind us, or whether the whole somber business of awakening only further corroborates that we are ever still within its horizon, and that even the universalist aspirations of the ecumenical spirit merely confirm anew that, in Nietzsche's words, "it is the church, and not its poison, that repels us."[128]

NOTES

Introduction

1. The debate about the founding is so highly charged precisely because of the tacit assumption that the founders somehow determined *our* identity. The ascendancy of economics over politics in Charles A. Beard's *Economic Interpretation of the Constitution* (New York: Macmillan, 1913); the anti-democratic assessment of the evils of human nature in Richard Hofstadter's *American Political Tradition* (New York: Vintage, 1948); the solid but low horizons of modern liberalism adduced by Martin Diamond in "Democracy and *The Federalist:* A Reconsideration of the Framers Intent," *American Political Science Review* 53, no. 1 (1959), pp. 52–68: these interpretations of the founding period are not simply reconstructions of *a past* which came before us, but rather reconstructions of *our* past. While at once reconstructions of our past they are simultaneously *constructions* of our identity, hence their peculiar valence.

2. In the constitutional interpretation literature, for example, this kind of argument is often adduced. See Robert Bork, "Neutral Principles and Some First Amendment Problems," *Indiana Law Journal* 47, no. 1 (1971), pp. 1–35; and Henry Monaghan, "Our Perfect Constitution," *New York University Law Review* 56, nos. 2–3 (1981), pp. 353–96, for attempts to derive what ought to be done in the present from the principles purportedly established at the founding.

3. See Eldon J. Eisenach, "John Stuart Mill and the Origins of A History of Political Thought," in *Essays in the History of Political Thought: Studies in Honor of Ferran Valls I Taberner,* ed. Manueal J. Peláez and Miguel Martínez López (Barcelona: Promociones Publicaciones Universitarias, 1988), vol. VIII, pp. 2347–62, for the argument that the idea of a history of political thought—the horizon within which *we* work—is inaugurated by Mill, for whom the appropriation of the history of ideas *by* consciousness occasions the development *of* consciousness and of freedom. In Mill's essay, "On Genius" in *Collected Works of John Stuart Mill,* ed. John M. Robson and Jack Stillenger (Toronto: Toronto University Press, 1981), vol. I, pp. 329–39, for example, the claim is made that genius involves not *belief,* but *knowledge*—which is a discovery made for oneself (p. 332). Modernity is encumbered with ideas amassed by the sheer additive weight of cumulative effort. The ancients, by contrast, were unencumbered. Consequently, belief rather than knowledge is a more likely outcome in the modern era; for how many have the courage to expend the effort necessary to make thoughts *their own* when they can easily believe on the authority of the great thinkers who have come before them. The study of the history of ideas, authentically performed, involves the *simultaneous* discovery of the past and of the self in the present. The past, consequently, is brought forward into the present, and identity is constituted by this looking *back* and looking *in.* This way of conceiving the

relationship between history and identity can be found in Emerson as well, whose think-ing I will consider in the Conclusion.

4. I Pet. 1:18–19.

5. See David Hume, *The History of England* (Indianapolis: Liberty Press, 1983), vol. 1, p. 4: "the only certain means, by which nations can indulge their curiosity on researches about their remote origins, is to consider the language, manners, and customs of their ancestors, and compare them with those of neighboring nations." Hume be-lieved that "convulsions . . . and revolutions . . . [were] guided [only] by caprice" (ibid., vol. 1, p. 3). These periods (which for Rousseau would have been founding periods and, therefore, authoritative) were more accident than essence for Hume. See also David Hume, "Of National Characters," in *Essays, Moral, Political, and Literary*, ed. Eugene Miller (Indianapolis: Liberty Press, 1985), pp. 197–215.

While Hume's seven-volume *History* is predicated on the notion that there is such a thing as a stable cultural identity which can be known, in his *Treatise* he jettisons the idea of a stable *personal* identity which can be known and demonstrated. See David Hume, *A Treatise on Human Nature* (Oxford: Clarendon Press, 1978), Book I, Part IV, Section VI, pp. 252–53: "I may venture to affirm . . . of mankind, that they are nothing but a bundle or collection of different perceptions, which succeed each other with an inconceivable rapidity, and are in a perpetual flux and movement. . . . [There is no] single power of the soul, which remains unalterably the same."

6. Voltaire's *Essay on the Manners and Mind of Nations*, written in 1756, some thirty years before Hume's *History*, was an effort to emancipate history from theology and to suggest that history is the story of human progress. More particularly, his *Essay* was an attack on Boussuet's *Discourse on Universal History*, a work defending a providential view of history. See Karl Löwith's *Meaning in History* (Chicago: University of Chicago Press, 1949), Ch. 5, pp. 105–14, for a synopsis of Voltaire's philosophy of history.

I am inclined to believe, with Hayden White (*Tropics of Discourse* [Baltimore: Johns Hopkins University Press, 1978]), that the failure of Enlightenment historians lay "in their incapacity to conceive of historical knowledge as a *problem*. . . . [They tended] to draw the line too rigidly between *history* on the one side, and *fable* on the other" (p. 140, emphasis in original). The motive behind this willful forgetfulness of fables, which may bring *either* clarity or ossification in its wake, is to be commended in an epoch where they stupefy and produce rigidity. But the cost of *categorical* condemnation is high: the failure to grasp the "otherness" of one's own distant history as well as the history and present identity of other cultures not yet "liberated" from fables.

7. Think, for example, of Hobbes's translations of Thucydides' *History of the Pelopon-nesian Wars*, of which Strauss makes much in *The Political Philosophy of Thomas Hobbes*. That history does not figure at all in Parts III and IV of the *Leviathan*. There, Hobbes is concerned with adducing conclusions about the authority of the Leviathan who would rule the Christian commonwealth, from a consideration of biblical history. It is from this *trace of God* that Hobbes derives political authority. Thucydides and other ancient au-thors do not provide Hobbes with the foundation he needs.

J. G. A. Pocock, in "Time, History, and Eschatology in the Thought of Thomas Hobbes," in *Politics, Language, and Time* (New York: Atheneum, 1973), quite rightly points out that biblical history is crucial to Hobbes's overall argument, though Pocock overemphasizes God's absence in the world, and does not heed the way in which, for Hobbes, God *continues* to be present in the form of a politico-theological covenant modeled (necessarily) after the covenant between the Israelites and Moses their mediator.

8. Löwith, *Meaning in History*, p. 2.

9. Gen. 3:5.

10. Jean-Jacques Rousseau, *Emile*, trans. Allan Bloom (New York: Basic Books, 1979), Bk. IV, p. 229.

11. Theologically, reason is at the *center* of the Cross for Hegel. Rather than *countering* Hegel's joy with a plaintive cry that this rationalized and disenchanted world is to the Christian era what skeleton is to living body, here I suggest that both alternatives suppose what Luther, Hobbes, Locke, and Rousseau do not, *viz.*, that reason in one or another guise is at the center. For a brief contrast between Luther and Hegel see Karl Löwith, *From Hegel to Nietzsche*, trans. David E. Green (New York: Columbia University Press, 1964), pp. 18–19. Löwith is, I think, incorrect in suggesting that "through Rousseau's meditation, in the French Revolution the European spirit determined for itself the content of its goal" (ibid., p. 34). Rousseau's self, like Luther, Hobbes, and Locke's, is not sufficient unto itself. In a word, Löwith fails to account for Rousseau's insistence that the self is concealed from itself, that the disposition of the self is to drown out the Voice to which it must attend if it is to be happy. Rousseau's self *hides itself* from the Source. True, it *wishes* to set for itself the content of its goals; but does so in order *to avoid* listening. Its apparent self-sufficiency always already betrays its errancy!

12. For Calvin, on the contrary, God is *manifest*, not hidden. See John S. Dunne, *The City of the Gods* (Notre Dame: University of Notre Dame Press, 1978), pp. 186–87. Max Weber's *The Protestant Ethic and the Spirit of Capitalism* (New York: Charles Scribner's Sons, 1958) addresses the economic repercussions of the idea of a manifest God; here I attempt to show the political implications of the hidden God. Calvin does not figure in this study. See Ralph C. Hancock, *Calvin and the Foundations of Modern Politics* (Ithaca: Cornell University Press, 1989), p. 141: Calvin transforms "Christian inwardness into outward *activity*" (emphasis added).

13. Rousseau, *Emile*, Bk. IV, p. 268. See also John Locke's Censor's Valedictory Speech of 1664, entitled, "Can Anyone by Nature Be Happy in This Life? No," in *Essays on the Law of Nature*, ed. W. von Leydon (Oxford: Clarendon Press, 1954), pp. 221–23; "philosophy holds out many riches, but they all are mere words rather than the property of men. Those pointed and shrewd discourses concerning the highest good do not heal human misfortunes any more than fist and sword cure wounds. . . . Philosophers in their search for happiness have not accomplished more than to tell us that it cannot be found."

14. See Michael Sandel, *Liberalism and the Limits of Justice* (Cambridge: Cambridge University Press, 1982). Arguing against the deontological view of Rawls (for whom the self may be abstracted from its historical, cultural, and social particularity), Sandel calls for a notion of the self with "constitutive attachments." See ibid., p. 179, *passim*. While focusing on contemporary liberal theory, Sandel assumes that a politics based on Hobbes and Locke is more akin to a group of strangers than to a true community.

15. See Quentin Skinner, *The Foundations of Modern Political Thought*, 2 vols. (Cambridge: Cambridge University Press, 1980). See also J. G. A. Pocock, *The Machiavellian Moment* (Princeton: Princeton University Press, 1975). Both Skinner and Pocock take

the view that the political significance of the Reformation was that it induced a political vacuum into which a vital Renaissance political spirit flowed. See Skinner, *The Foundations of Modern Political Thought*, vol. 2, p. 349, *passim*; and Pocock, *The Machiavellian Moment*, pp. 31–48, 545, *passim*. They both suppose, like Aristotle but unlike Augustine, that politics is a realm where theology has no real pertinence.

16. See Sheldon Wolin, *Politics and Vision* (Boston: Little, Brown & Co., 1961). Wolin sees in Hobbes a renewed awareness of the centrality of "the political," an awareness which was lost when Locke discovered society and prepolitical property. See ibid., p. 310, *passim*.

17. See Leo Strauss, *The Political Philosophy of Thomas Hobbes* (Chicago, University of Chicago Press, 1963), p. xix, *passim*. Hobbes does not found his politics on the ancient virtues, it is true, but he is concerned with humankind's relationship with God and the biblical dialectic in which the relationship is disclosed. To disregard the fact that the issues which inform the political thought of Hobbes are not of Greek origin is to miss the extent to which, like Plato and Aristotle, Hobbes *was* concerned with the implications God and the Good have for political life. Contrary to the thesis advanced here, Strauss claims that Hobbes's political philosophy can be characterized as, among other things, a "movement away from the recognition of a superhuman authority—whether of revelation based on Divine will or a natural order based on Divine reason—to a recognition of the exclusively human authority of the State" (ibid., p. 131).

18. See C. B. Macpherson, *The Political Theory of Possessive Individualism* (Oxford: Oxford University Press, 1962). Macpherson saw in the thought of Hobbes and Locke an attempt to provide a justification for the emerging bourgeois ethos.

19. See Michael Oakeshott, "The Moral Life in the Writings of Thomas Hobbes," in *Rationalism in Politics* (New York: Basic Books, 1962), pp. 248–300. Oakeshott's Hobbes argues that "it is reasonable to expect that, having been reasonable enough to have made a covenant, enough men at any given time will be reasonable enough (that is, free enough from avarice and ambition and the like to recognize where their interests lie) to be disposed to keep it" (ibid., p. 299). This said, however, Oakeshott is well aware of the limits of reason.

20. See Ernst Troeltsch, *Protestantism and Progress* (Philadelphia: Fortress Press, 1986). Troeltsch's argument is that Protestantism prepared the way for the emergence of the autonomous and disenchanted world of liberal politics.

Max Weber's work is also pertinent here. His "Politics as a Vocation" and "Science as a Vocation," for example, are attempts to specify the substantively rational principle which obtains within each of these separate spheres. His *Protestant Ethic*, on the other hand, offers an account of religious roots of the disenchantment of the economic sphere. Weber notes that in early Protestant thought the world is not disenchanted; quite the contrary, it is enchanted in a way different from the way it had been under the Catholic Church. In his words, "the Reformation meant not the elimination of the Church's control over everyday life, but rather the substitution of a new form of control for the previous one" (*Protestant Ethic*, p. 36). My argument parallels Weber's, though my interest is not with the economic sphere but with the political. I explore the way in which the political sphere *remains* enchanted within Protestant thought.

21. See Alasdair MacIntyre, *After Virtue* (Notre Dame: University of Notre Dame Press, 1984). MacIntyre understands the modern world as a lapse from the Aristotelian Catholic world of Saint Thomas. The beginning of the end he locates with Luther. See ibid., p. 165, *passim.*

22. See J. W. Gough, *The Social Contract* (Oxford: Oxford University Press, 1957). Gough saw Hobbes and Locke as part of a long tradition of social contract theory. He does not allude to their religious writings at all.

23. See Harvey C. Mansfield, Jr., *The Spirit of Liberalism* (Cambridge: Harvard University Press, 1978). Mansfield sees in Hobbes the beginnings of a theoretical justification of representative government in which the central issue is not substance but rather process. Here the question is not whether government is good, but whether it represents well. See ibid., p. 45, *passim.*

24. See Albert O. Hirschman, *The Passions and the Interests* (Princeton: Princeton University Press, 1977). Hirschman sees in Locke the attempt to eliminate the uncertainties of passion and substitute for it the certainties of interest. See ibid., pp. 53–54, *passim.*

25. Eldon Eisenach's *Two Worlds of Liberalism: Religion and Politics in Hobbes, Locke, and Mill* (Chicago: University of Chicago Press, 1981), and Henning Graf Reventlow's *The Authority of the Bible and the Rise of the Modern World* (Philadelphia: Fortress Press, 1985) are excellent treatments of the idea that interpretations of biblical history were immensely important to early modern thinkers. Their work cannot be criticized for what it does not purport to do. Eisenach's task is, in some sense, my own: to bring to bear the side of modern thought concerned with God's providential history. Reventlow intends to show that biblical interpretation in England begins long before Hobbes and Locke, is evident in their thought, and is important after them as well.

26. Plato, *Republic,* trans. Richard Sterling and William C. Scott (New York: W. W. Norton & Co., 1985), Bk. X, 621a–b.

27. Augustine, recall, theorized about the relationship between God and memory. See *The Confessions of Augustine,* trans. R. S. Pine-Coffin (New York: Penguin Books, 1961), Bk. 10, Ch. 25, p. 230: "truly, you (God) dwell in [my memory], because I remember you ever since I first came to learn of you, and it is there that I find you when I am reminded of you." But where Augustine saw memory as a creation of God, Rousseau saw the Christian God as a creation of memory.

This provocative inversion which makes God the offspring of the human rather than the other way around is also found in Marx, who claimed that "the gods . . . are not the cause but the effect of man's intellectual confusion" ("Economic and Philosophical Manuscripts of 1844," in *The Marx-Engels Reader,* ed. Robert C. Tucker (New York: W. W. Norton & Co., 1978), p. 79). See also ibid., p. 92, where, in response to the question of who created humankind and nature, Marx says, "since for the socialist man the *entire so-called history of the world* is nothing but a begetting of man through human labor, nothing but the coming-to-be of nature for man, he has the visible, irrefutable proof of his *birth* through himself, of this *process of coming-to-be*" (emphasis in original).

28. Consider, in this light, Augustine, for whom the period after Christ's arrival was different from the time before. See, for example, *City of God* (New York: Penguin Books,

1984), Bk. I, Ch. 31, p. 42, where Augustine speaks of the fear that motivated human action prior to Christ: "the nations had not yet received the revelation from heaven of the teaching that would cleanse the heart by faith and turn the interest of men in humble reverence toward things in heaven . . . and free them from the oppressive domination of demonic powers."

R. G. Collingwood, in *The Idea of History* (Oxford: Oxford University Press, 1956), notes that Christian historiography "will set itself to detect an intelligible pattern in [the] general course of events and in particular it will attach a central importance in this pattern to the historical life of Christ (p. 50). These characteristics are present in the historiographies of Luther, Hobbes, and Locke, and, with considerable qualification, Rousseau.

29. See Friedrich Nietzsche, *On the Genealogy of Morals*, trans. Walter Kaufman (New York: Vintage Books, 1967), Third Essay, §28, p. 162: "the meaninglessness of suffering, not suffering itself, was the curse that lay over man so far—and the ascetic ideal *offered man meaning*" (emphasis in original).

30. See Plato, *Republic*, Bk. IX, 580d–583a. There, the truest pleasures are only known to the soul that veritably is—the soul of the philosopher which is unified in accordance with the eternal pattern set up in the heavens (Bk. IX, 592b).

31. Sigmund Freud, *Civilization and Its Discontents*, ed. James Strachey (New York: W. W. Norton & Co., 1989), Ch. I, pp. 16–18.

32. See Paul Ricoeur, *Time and Narrative* (Chicago: University of Chicago Press, 1984), vol. 1, p. 6: "speculation on time is an inconclusive rumination to which narrative activity alone can respond." See also ibid., p. 52: "time becomes human to the extent that it is articulated through a narrative mode, and narrative achieves its full meaning when it becomes a condition of temporal existence." Politically authoritative history, of course, is such a narrative.

33. Matt. 5:17. The question of the meaning of Christ's fulfillment is perhaps the central one posed by that most prominent of early theologians, Saint Augustine. See Augustine, *City of God*, Bk. VII, Ch. 32, p. 293: the "symbols and predictions [of the Old Testament] that find their fulfillment on Christ . . . give eternal life to those who believe. We believe that they have been fulfilled; we observe that they are being fulfilled; we are convinced that they will go on being fulfilled." See also Jeremiah 31:31–34.

Nietzsche, too, was not lost to the question of the significance of Christ's fulfillment. "This Jesus of Nazareth, the incarnate gospel of love, this 'redeemer' who brought blessedness and victory to the poor, the sick, the sinners—was he not this seduction in its most uncanny and irresistible form, a seduction and bypath to precisely those *Jewish* values and new ideals?" (*Genealogy*, First Essay, §8, p. 35, emphasis in original). Here Christianity is the victory *of* Judaism! Not wishing to press the point too far, might his remark, "but some day, in some stronger age than this decaying, self-doubting present, he must yet come to us, the *redeeming* man of great love and contempt" (ibid., Second Essay, §24, p. 96, emphasis in original), suggest that the Messiah has not yet come! Zarathustra is the fulfillment! See also ibid., p. 95, where Nietzsche playfully transposes the idea of the fulfillment of the law: "If a temple is to be erected *a temple must be destroyed*; that is the law—let anyone show me a case in which it is not fulfilled" (emphasis in original). Nietzsche's call for fulfillment is, ironically, the call to supersede Judaism-

Christianity-Democracy, those *three waves of resentment* which have insinuated themselves into the modern soul.

34. Hegel, who it is often claimed originated modern speculation on the meaning of dialectic change, actually comes relatively late in the history of this kind of speculation. In his early writing he, too, was concerned with the dialectical relationship between the Testaments. Significantly, his understanding of Christ's fulfillment is deeply influenced by Luther. (He, in fact, considered himself to be a Lutheran all of his life.) For both, the Law is a form of bondage, and yet, as with his master/slave dialectic of the *Phenomenology*, the soul that would come unto freedom must pass through bondage. The *Phenomenology* is, of course, a philosophical articulation of the inner truth of Christianity; the young Hegel, however, wrestled with the question of the relationship between bondage and freedom in more conventionally religious terms. See G. W. F. Hegel, "The Spirit of Christianity," in *Early Theological Writings*, ed. Richard Kroner (Philadelphia: University of Pennsylvania Press, 1971), where Hegel claims, among other things, that "over against commands which required a bare service of the Lord, a direct slavery, an obedience without joy, without pleasure or love . . . Jesus set their precise opposite, a human urge and so a human need" (p. 206). Here Hegel is attempting to provide an explanation of the fulfillment offered by Christ. While later he would transpose this notion into a philosophical key, his interest in dialectical thinking about history begins much earlier, with his theological investigations. While novel in their conclusions, his theological work is only one relatively late formulation in a long tradition of theological speculation. This connection between Luther and Hegel is important, for if the link can be shown to exist between Luther, Hobbes, and Locke, then by extension Luther, Hobbes, Locke, and Hegel can *all* be seen to be involved in the same kind of project, *viz.*, that of deriving the political implications of a biblical history which can only be understood as being dialectical.

Finally, I think Warren is incorrect in locating the origin of dialectical thinking in the modern period in Kant. It is already present much earlier in the dialectic of (biblical) history developed by Luther. See Scott Warren, *The Emergence of Dialectical Theory* (Chicago: University of Chicago Press, 1984).

35. Think here of Plato's discussion of the fall of the ideal state in the *Republic*, Bk. VIII, 534a–568c; Jean-Jacques Rousseau's claim that "the right of laying down rules of society belongs only to those who form a society (*The Social Contract*, ed. Maurice Cranston [New York: Penguin Books, 1984], Bk. II, Ch. 6, p. 83); Niccolò Machiavelli's assertion that the maintenance of any institution requires that it periodically return to its originating principles (*The Discourses*, ed. Bernard Crick [New York: Penguin Books, 1970], Bk. III, Discourse I, pp. 385–90); and of the claims of those who endorse one or another version of the "founding fathers thesis." Consider also Alexis de Tocqueville's observations about the relationship between origin and identity. In his view, the nation, like the whole man, "is there, if one may put it so, in the cradle" (*Democracy in America*, ed. J. P. Mayer [New York: Harper & Row, 1969], Ch. 2, p. 31).

36. The matter is not unambiguous in Freud. The concept of "organic repression" (*Civilization and Its Discontents*, Ch. VI, p. 54n) is meant to account for aspects of development—both phylogenetic and ontogenetic—that both remain *and* have been superseded and foregone. The proof that a superseded stage *still remains* is the experience of being repulsed by what once gave pleasure. Certain implications of this are made clear

further on: family (the forum of erotic love) is prior to community (the forum of aim-inhibited love); yet family must be superseded in order for a large community to become possible at all (ibid., p. 58). If the notion of "organic repression" is brought to bear in this matter, it *may* be that truly world-around community would require persons who were *repulsed* by the idea of family!—a thought confirmed in novel form by Aldous Huxley in *Brave New World* (New York: Harper & Row, 1946).

37. G. W. F. Hegel, *Philosophy of Right*, trans. T. M. Knox (Oxford: Oxford University Press, 1967), Preface, p. 13.

38. See Reinhold Niebuhr, *The Nature and Destiny of Man* (New York: Charles Scribner's Sons, 1964), vol. II, pp. 3–4, where *sin* is understood as the hubris of finite beings who would attempt to grasp the meaning of history that can be known only by God. For Niebuhr, antifoundationalism, as I have called it here, can only be thought within the confines of original sin.

39. I Cor. 13:9–10.

40. Gen. 1:26.

41. Thomas Hobbes, *Leviathan*, ed. Michael Oakeshott (New York: Macmillan Publishing Co., 1962), Part IV, Ch. 46, p. 486.

42. John Locke, *An Essay Concerning Human Understanding* (Oxford: Oxford University Press, 1975), Bk. IV, Ch. 19, pp. 697–706.

43. See Tocqueville, *Democracy in America*, Author's Introduction, p. 15, *passim*.

44. This is in marked contrast to Augustine, for whom history is not simply a movement from the truth of exteriority and the Law (the Old Testament) to the truth of interiority and faith (the New Testament). Rather, history is a seven-stage affair, with each epoch corresponding to a day of God's creation. See Augustine, *City of God*, Bk. XXII, Ch. 30, p. 1091; and Augustine, *Confessions*, Bk. XIII, pp. 311–47, where creation is interpreted allegorically, not historically. The meaning of Christ's fulfillment is crucial to Augustine as well, of course, but his sympathies with allegorical thinking would not allow him to focus upon historical interpretation alone—as Luther certainly attempted to do.

45. Hence the apparent incongruity of his earnest defense of the freedom of a Christian and his repudiation of the peasant's cause against the political status quo in the War of 1525. See Martin Luther, "Against the Robbing and Murdering Hordes of Peasants," in *Luther's Works*, ed. Helmut T. Lehmann (Philadelphia: Fortress Press, 1967), vol. 46, pp. 49–55. Notwithstanding this tract, his sympathies were generally with the poor. See Martin Luther, "Treatise on Good Works," in *Luther's Works*, vol. 44, p. 51.

46. Thomas Hobbes, *De Cive*, in *Man and Citizen*, ed. Bernard Gert (Gloucester, MA: Humanities Press, 1978), Ch. VI, p. 179. See Matt. 6:24.

47. For an account of the dissemination and reception of Luther's thought in England between 1520 and 1600, see William A. Clebsch, "The Elizabethans on Luther," in *Interpreters of Luther: Essays in Honor of Wilhelm Pauck*, ed. Jaroslav Pelikan (Philadelphia: Fortress Press, 1968), pp. 97–120. Clebsch concludes, "the spirit of Luther's religion and theology began to settle on Elizabethan England like a London fog; hauntingly unspecifiable, and with real welcome only after his death, it just seeped into the atmosphere" (p. 116).

48. See I Cor. 15:21–22: "For since by man came death, by man came also the resurrection of the dead. For as in Adam all die, even so in Christ all shall be made alive"; and Rom. 5:18–19: "Therefore as by the offense of one judgment came upon all men to condemnation; even so by the righteousness of the one the free gift came upon all men unto justification of life. For as by one man's disobedience many were made sinners, so by the obedience of one shall many be made righteous."

49. Exodus 20:19. (See Hobbes, *Leviathan*, Part II, Ch. 26, p. 213.) Consistent with Hobbes's general view that errancy from God is the way of humankind, see Michael Walzer, *Exodus and Revolution* (New York: Basic Books, 1985), p. 120, where, "the Exodus texts . . . almost seem designed to teach that the promises will never definitively be fulfilled, that backsliding and struggle are permanent features of human existence." Both Hobbes and Walzer wish to avert the danger of Messianism and to show that God's *presence* takes the form of a promise for a future of milk and honey that will be fulfilled only if the covenant is obeyed. See Hobbes, *Leviathan*, Part III, Ch. 43, p. 425, where, "all that is NECESSARY *to salvation*, is contained in the two virtues, *faith in Christ*, and *obedience to laws*" (emphasis in original). Obedience, for Hobbes, is not purely political.

50. Matt. 11:30.

51. See Martin Luther, "Bondage of the Will," in *Luther's Works*, vol. 33, pp. 139–40, where, in the time before Christ, God deplored the death *of* his people; after Christ, God deplores death *in* his people. The first is a physical death, the latter, a spiritual death. From the pre- to the post-Christ epoch the soul is deepened.

52. Derrida's allusions to writing as the supplement to speech are not without relevance here. See Jacques Derrida, *Of Grammatology* (Baltimore: Johns Hopkins University Press, 1976), Part II, Ch. 2, pp. 141–57, *passim.* The situation of writing with respect to speech is analogous to that of psyche *now* to psyche *then;* both are the necessary and dangerous supplement—necessary because distantiation from the source is a precondition of knowing, dangerous because in this knowing is the seed of errancy. The danger of this knowing is that it pretends a sufficiency unto itself; standing in for what is absent, it countenances an abandonment of what is, in its standing apart, now foreign to it. As Derrida notes (ibid., Ch. 3, pp. 216–26), Rousseau works this idea out in terms of the geography of language in his *Essay on the Origin of Language.* The dialectic Rousseau works through is structured by the reality of the premediative (and prelinguisitic) Voice knowable with the heart, and the difficulty and need to point with words to what words cannot encompass; this dialectic spawns problems and regions of inquiry which Luther, Hobbes, and Locke do not place at the center of their thinking.

53. Gen. 3:7–9.

54. See also Jacques Derrida, "Plato's Pharmacy," in *Dissemination*, trans. Barbara Johnson (Chicago: University of Chicago Press, 1981), Part I, §3, p. 80: while there is a father of *logos* "it is precisely *logos* that enables us to perceive and investigate something like paternity." The supplemental relationship between father and *logos*, God and humankind, confers a peculiar dignity upon what stands apart from "the Father."

55. See Martin Heidegger, "The Essence of Truth," in *Martin Heidegger: Basic Writings* (New York: Harper & Row, 1977), p. 134: "the forgotten mystery of Dasein is not eliminated by forgottenness; rather, the forgottenness bestows on the apparent disappearance of what is forgotten a peculiar presence." Heidegger goes on to say that this living amidst

errancy and refusing to grasp the Ground of Being thrusts human beings into a certain kind of relationship with the world, one of proposing and planning, of using and using up. Errancy produces a peculiar kind of relationship to the world—a thought not lost to Rousseau, for whom human beings in civil society are lost to themselves and incessantly want enlightenment and progress. Heidegger's insight can be found already in the thinking of Luther, as I shall show.

56. Rousseau, *Emile*, Bk. IV, p. 291. See also ibid., Bk. V, p. 362n, where Sophie (wisdom), too, is timid; *Second Discourse*, p. 107, where, "nothing is so timid as man in the state of nature"; and I Kings 19:11–14, where God addresses Elijah not amidst wind, earthquake, and fire, but as "a small voice."

57. John Rawls, "Justice as Fairness: Political not Metaphysical," *Philosophy and Public Affairs* 14, no. 3 (1985), p. 250. The vacuity of Kantian formalism can be amended, as Hegel's work attests, only by an historical narrative.

58. Think also of Marcuse, who construed the problem of modernity as one in which the future is arrested because the dialectic is unable to proceed. His deepest worry was that in advanced capitalist society, "the space for the *transcending* historical practice . . . is being barred by a society . . . that has its *raison d'être* in the accomplishments of its overpowering productivity" (Herbert Marcuse, *One-Dimensional Man* [Boston: Beacon Press, 1964], p. 23; emphasis added). To be fair to Marcuse, he is less dogmatic about what the content of the future fulfillment will be than Marx, in part because he is less certain that the future would be genuinely different. Marcuse's overarching thought is already portended in Rousseau: society has become a total system. (This latter insight is something about which Tocqueville worries, as well; see *Democracy in America*, vol. I, Part II, Ch. 7, pp. 254–56.)

59. See Martin Heidegger, *Being and Time*, trans. John Macquarrie and Edward Robinson (New York: Harper & Row, 1962), Division II, Ch. 1., §52, pp. 299–300: "everydayness confines itself to conceding the 'certainty' of death . . . just in order to weaken that certainty by covering up dying still more and to alleviate its own thrownness into death. By its very meaning, this evasive concealment in the face of death can *not* be *authentically* 'certain' of death" (emphasis in original). If the intent of modern political thought were merely to provide rudimentary security free from the events which disrupt everydayness, then it would be, among other things, an attempt to mask death.

60. Bloom, too, makes this criticism of the modern soul in his Introduction to Rousseau's *Emile*, p. 5.

61. Rousseau, *Emile*, Bk. II, p. 131.

62. See Löwith, *Meaning and History*, pp. 145–59, for the view that Joachim of Floris was the first to give explicit form to this idea. See also Eric Voegelin, *The New Science of Politics* (Chicago: University of Chicago Press, 1952), pp. 110–14. Voegelin argues that Joachim's "trinitarian eschatology . . . created the aggregate of symbols which govern the self-interpretation of modern political society to this day" (ibid., p. 111).

CHAPTER ONE

1. See Troeltsch, *Protestantism and Progress*, p. 47, *passim*. Troeltsch argues that Luther retained Catholic questions but provided new answers (this is Hans Blumenberg's argument, too, about modernity's relationship to the preceding epoch in *The Legitimacy*

of the Modern Age, trans. Robert M. Wallace [Cambridge, MA: MIT Press, 1983], p. 65, *passim*). Troeltsch saw in Protestantism a path for the emergence of the various autonomous spheres of human life. The temptation of this position is to see subsequent political theory as wholly secular. The later political thought of Hobbes and Locke, however, is not a "disenchanted view of the political world" and a "value-neutral politics," to borrow from Weber, but rather a *continuing* effort to make sense of political life in terms of the dialectic of biblical history.

R. H. Tawney, who argues in *Religion and the Rise of Capitalism* (London: John Murray, 1936) that capitalism arises largely out of the Catholic tradition, subscribes to the same view of Luther that Troeltsch and Weber do. In his words, Luther's Protestantism contained "a dualism which, as its implications were developed, emptied religion of its social content, and society of its soul. Between light and darkness a great gulf was fixed. Unable to climb upwards plane by plane, man must choose between salvation and damnation. If he despairs of attaining the austere heights where alone true faith is found, no human institution can avail to help him" (ibid., p. 101).

2. Immanuel Kant, "What is Enlightenment," in *Kant's Political Writings*, ed. Hans Reiss (Cambridge: Cambridge University Press, 1970), p. 54.

3. J. S. Mill, "On Liberty," in *Three Essays* (Oxford: Oxford University Press, 1975), Ch. 1, p. 18; emphasis added. Mill brings the tension between spiritual orientation and self-reflective method to a high point with his defense of atheism in the name of the self-certainty that can only obtain when belief encounters its counterposition. See ibid., Ch. 2, p. 45, where, "if the intellect and judgment of mankind ought to be cultivated, a thing which Protestants at least do not deny, on what can these faculties be more appropriately exercised by any one, than on the things which concern him so much that it is considered necessary for him to hold opinions on them."

Notwithstanding Nietzsche's contempt for Mill (see *Beyond Good and Evil*, trans. Walter Kaufman [New York: Vintage Books, 1966], Part 8, §253, p. 191), it is not far from this position to Nietzsche's observation that "it is the awe-inspiring *catastrophe* of two-thousand years of training in truthfulness that finally forbids itself the *lie involved in belief on God*" (Nietzsche, *Genealogy of Morals*, Third Essay, §27, p. 160; emphasis in original).

4. See Aristotle, *The Politics*, trans. Ernest Baker (Oxford: Oxford University Press, 1958), Bk. I, Ch. 1 1252a: "all associations aim at some good; and we may also hold that the particular association which is the most sovereign of all, and includes all the rest, will pursue this aim the most, and will thus be directed to the most sovereign of all goods. This most sovereign and inclusive association is the polis." See also Aristotle, *Nicomachean Ethics*, trans. Martin Oswald (New York: Macmillan, 1986), Bk. I, Ch. 1 1094b: since the science of politics "uses the rest of the sciences . . . its end seems to embrace the ends of the other sciences. Thus it follows that the end of politics is the good of man."

Luther has great contempt for Aristotle. See, for example, Martin Luther, "To the Christian Nobility of the German Nation Concerning the Reform of the Christian Estate," in *Luther's Works*, vol. 44, p. 201, where, "this dead heathen [Aristotle] has conquered, obstructed, and almost succeeded in suppressing the books of the living God. I can only believe that the devil has introduced this study." Hobbes, who also breaks with Aristotle, does so not to oppose the Greeks, but to register quasi-Protestant objections against the Aristotle of the Catholic Church. (See, for example, Thomas Hobbes, *Be-*

hemoth or the Long Parliament, ed. Ferdinand Tönnies [Chicago: University of Chicago Press, 1990], Dialogue 1, pp. 16–17, 40–44; Hobbes, *Leviathan,* Part IV, Ch. 44, p. 438; Ch. 46, pp. 478–83, *passim.*) Strauss, in *The Political Philosophy of Thomas Hobbes,* is correct in seeing Hobbes as a break from Aristotle, but does not see that break as part of a debate *within* the Judeo-Christian tradition. See also MacIntyre, *After Virtue,* for the contention that Luther is implicated in "setting the tone" for the repudiation of Aristotle in the modern world (p. 165). Given MacIntyre's position on liberal thought, which I claim begins with Luther, it should not be surprising that he would see in Luther the beginning of the end.

5. See, for example, Thomas Aquinas, *Summa Theologiae* (Garden City, NY: Image Books, 1969), Question 4, Article 3 (Can Creatures Be Said to Resemble God?), pp. 94–95. "Creatures are said to resemble God . . . only analogically, inasmuch as God exists by nature, and other things partake existence." The scriptural passage Aquinas cites is Gen. 1:26, where man is said to be made "in our image, after our likeness." Luther considers this passage in his "Lectures on Genesis" (in *Luther's Works,* vol. 1, pp. 55–68). There he concludes that, "since the loss of this image through sin we cannot understand it to any extent" (ibid., p. 61), and that, "not only have we no experience of [this likeness to God], but we continually experience the opposite; and so we hear nothing except bare words" (ibid., p. 63). Here and elsewhere, Luther has no patience for analogical reasoning. Significantly, Locke grants this Genesis passage considerable political weight.

See also the Bull, *Unam Sanctam,* of Boniface VIII, written in 1302. "The way of religion is to lead the things which are lower to the things which are higher through the things which are intermediate. According to the law of the universe all things are not reduced to order equally and immediately; but the lowest through the intermediate, and the intermediate through the higher" (cited in R. H. Tawney, *Religion and the Rise of Capitalism,* pp. 20–21).

6. See B. A. Gerrish, *Grace and Reason: A Study in the Theology of Luther* (Oxford: Clarendon Press, 1962), pp. 127–36, for an excellent treatment of Luther's divergences from Aquinas.

7. I take it that Calvin's sentence: "by the Law, I understand not only the Ten Commandments, which contain a complete rule of life, but the whole system delivered by the hands of Moses" (John Calvin, *Institutes of the Christian Religion,* trans. Henry Beveridge [Grand Rapids, MI: Wm. B. Eerdmans Publishing Co., 1989], Bk. II, Ch. VII, p. 300) is a succinct but not inaccurate restatement of what Luther has in mind. Throughout these chapters I will use "Law" when referring to "the whole system of Moses," and "law" when referring to more explicitly political laws. Luther (and other authors) who refer to the Law often do not adopt this convention; the context, however, should make their meaning clear.

8. See James Samuel Preus, *From Shadow to Promise* (Cambridge: Harvard University Press, 1969), for a superb exposition of this thesis. Because the Old Testament now foreshadows the New, it takes on an extraordinary significance for Protestants. Luther's commentaries on the Old Testament, for example, comprise roughly three times the number of pages in his *Works* than do his commentaries on the New Testament.

9. This is perhaps overstated. When Luther speaks of the basis of Christian *commu-nity* he argues that the relationship between one Christian and another must be *like* the relationship between Christ and each Christian; Christian community is an analog of the relationship between the Divine Mediator and the faithful servant.

In addition to analogical reasoning, allegorical interpretation, too, should be shunned. See Martin Luther, "Lectures on Isaiah," in *Luther's Works*, vol. 16, p. 327, where, "faith must be built on the basis of *history,* and we ought to stay with it alone and not so easily slip into allegories . . ." (emphasis added).

10. Taylor describes Hegel's dialectic in precisely these terms. See Charles Taylor, *Hegel and Modern Society* (Cambridge: Cambridge University Press, 1979), p. 49, where, "*Aufhebung* [is Hegel's term] for the dialectical transition in which the lower stage is both annulled and preserved in a higher one." As I mentioned in the Introduction, thinking about history dialectically does not begin with Hegel. See Hegel, "The Spirit of Chris-tianity," in *Early Theological Writings*, §2, pp. 212–14, *passim,* for a brief interpretation of the theological meaning of dialectic.

11. Martin Luther, "Lectures on Galatians," in *Luther's Works*, vol. 26, p. 156. See also Luther, "Lectures on Genesis," in *Works*, vol. 1, p. 234, where, "the tree of death is the Law, and the tree of life is the Gospel, is Christ."

12. Luther, "Lectures on Galatians," in *Works*, vol. 26, p. 157.

13. Luther, "Lectures on Galatians," in *Works*, vol. 26, p. 161. Also see II Cor. 5:17: "old things are passed away; behold, all things are become new."

14. See Martin Luther, "On the Jews and Their Lies," in *Luther's Works*, vol. 47, pp. 137–306. Hegel, too, was unequivocal about the Jews in his early works, notably *The Spirit of Christianity and Its Fate.* Some thirty years later, however, when his *Philosophy of History* lectures were compiled, he had already long known that any dialectical position could have no room for the denigration of the Jews. In his words, for a higher condition to emerge, man "must feel himself as the negation of himself. . . . This state of mind, this self-chastening, this pain occasioned by our individual nothingness—the wretched-ness of our [isolated] self, and the longing to transcend this condition of soul—must be looked for elsewhere than in the properly Roman World. It is this which gives to the *Jewish people* their World-Historical importance and weight. . . . [In this people] is the thirst of the soul after God" (G. W. F. Hegel, *The Philosophy of History* [New York: Dover, 1956], Part III, Sec. III, Ch. II, p. 321; emphasis in original).

15. See Luther, "Treatise on Good Works," in *Works*, vol. 44, pp. 21–114. Here Luther defends the need to do good works, but insists that faith is the "master-workman and captain of all works, [without which these works] are nothing at all" (ibid., p. 34). By way of anticipation, theologically, the soul must be "Jew" before it can be Christian. Luther's charge, in effect, is that Christians are still "Jews." Like John the Baptist in Matt. 3:1, Luther no doubt considered himself a "preach[er] in the wilderness of Judea." This self-understanding which would call the soul beyond its native "Jewishness" is not, perhaps, unique to Luther. Hegel understands Kant in this way in his "Spirit of Chris-tianity and Its Fate"; Nietzsche charges us all of this in the *Genealogy*; and Heidegger wonders about the soul's propensity to be caught up in the everyday world of "works" in

Being and Time, and about the authenticity made possible by his equivalent to Luther's *passive* righteousness!

16. G. W. F. Hegel, *The Phenomenology of Spirit,* trans. A. V. Miller (Oxford: Oxford University Press, 1977), §585, p. 357. See also Rousseau, *Emile,* Bk. IV, p. 292.

17. Koselleck expresses Hobbes's problem well. "The Reformation and the subsequent split in religious authority had thrown man back upon his conscience, and a conscience lacking outside support degenerates into the idol of self-righteousness. No wonder this very conscience imbued the embattled parties with the courage and energy to keep fighting. Mere conscience which as Hobbes put it, presumes to mount the throne is not a judge of good and evil; but is the source of evil itself" (Reinhart Koselleck, *Critique and Crisis: Enlightenment and the Pathogenesis of Modern Society* [Cambridge, MA: MIT Press, 1988], p. 28).

18. Much later Marx would note that Luther had "shattered the faith in authority by restoring the authority of faith. . . . He liberated man from external religiosity by making religiosity the innermost essence of man." See Karl Marx, "Contributions to the Critique of Hegel: Introduction," in *The Marx-Engels Reader,* p. 60. Although Marx recognized this shift toward the interiority of faith, he saw in Luther not a destabilizer but a harbinger of the new who "conjured up the spirits of the past" for lack of an adequate language to understand "the new scene of world history" ("The Eighteenth Brumaire of Louis Bonaparte," in *The Marx-Engels Reader,* p. 595). Questions about the political meaning of faith in God the Son, however, were at the foundation of much subsequent early modern political thought. Luther was not the last gasp of a now superseded self-understanding.

19. In tracing the emergence of early political thought back to primitive Christianity, I bypass Machiavelli altogether. Machiavelli's motifs are fortune and fate, and the necessity of prudent rather than moral action. That he offended the sensibilities of Christians there can be no doubt, but this does not make him the first modern political theorist. Fortune and fate are pagan themes; modern political theory arose within the tradition of the two Testaments, as a response to the political volatility that inheres in Christian righteousness. Early liberal political theory is an answer to the politics of righteousness; the Christianity that Machiavelli writes against is not caught up in such righteousness, for it had no such political vigor. Hegel expresses the difference well: "opposed to the universal *Fatum* of the Roman World, we have here the consciousness of Evil and the direction of the mind Godwards" (*Philosophy of History,* Part III, Sec. III, Ch. II, p. 322). Machiavelli is the last Roman, not the first Modern.

20. See Rousseau, *The Social Contract,* Bk. IV, Ch. 8, p. 186. Rousseau believed that Christianity produced no bonds, and therefore that there was a need for a civil religion which would hold a community together. For Rousseau the relationship between human beings and society is at issue, not the relationship between human beings and God. This is a decisive difference.

21. Martin Luther, "The Freedom of a Christian," in *Luther's Works,* vol. 31, p. 344. See I Cor. 9:19; Phil. 2:7.

22. Luther, "Freedom," in *Works,* vol. 31, p. 343.

23. Rom. 7:23.

24. Luther, "Freedom," in *Works*, vol. 31, p. 344. See II Cor. 4:16; Gal. 5:17. Also see Paul Ricoeur, *The Symbolism of Evil* (Boston: Beacon Press, 1967), pp. 331–36. In Saint Paul there is almost an equivalence between the notion of the exile of the soul and the carnal realm—a theme, Ricoeur notes, Luther also draws upon. Subsequent Calvinist thought would further develop this notion of exile. In the American context especially, the theme of exile and the creation of a new Israel, a perfect land, was a powerful religious image which shaped the identity of the American consciousness. See Sacvan Bercovitch, *The Puritan Origins of the American Self* (New Haven: Yale University Press, 1975).

25. Luther, "Lectures on Galatians," in *Works*, vol. 26, p. 8. See also Martin Luther, "Temporal Authority: To What Extent It Should Be Obeyed," in *Luther's Works*, vol. 45, p. 92: "the world as a whole cannot receive or comprehend" the spiritual domain; ibid., p. 113: "the world is God's enemy"; and Luther, "Freedom," in *Works*, vol. 31, p. 363: "nature of itself cannot drive out [faith] or even recognize it."

26. Luther, "Freedom," in *Works*, vol. 31, p. 377. See also Luther, "To the Christian Nobility," in *Works*, vol. 44, p. 217, where Luther asserts that although his cause is just and will be rewarded in Heaven, it will be condemned on earth.

27. Hegel, *The Spirit of Christianity*, §iv, p. 255. See also Matt. 9:17; Mark 2:22; John 3:6.

28. Nietzsche, *Genealogy*, Second Essay, §7, p. 67, *passim*. Nietzsche's emphasis upon the body is not wholly anti-Christian; nor later would Rousseau's be in *Emile*. In one respect their insistence upon granting the body its due is a *reaffirmation* of the path the Christian must follow: *through* the body unto something higher. See I Cor. 15:46 (the first is not spiritual, "but that which was natural; and afterward that which is spiritual"). Humanity comes unto Christ (spirit) *through* Adam (nature)! While heaven is home, there can be no arrival there without first passing through nature.

29. See Luther, "Lectures on Genesis," in *Works*, vol. 1, p. 110: "in the state of innocence no part of the body was filthy. There was no stench in excrement, nor were there any other execrable things. Everything was most beautiful, without any offense to the organs of sense."

30. Luther, "Freedom," in *Works*, vol. 31, p. 363. See also ibid., pp. 372–73: "our faith in Christ does not take us from works, but from false opinions concerning works," and "in this world we are bound by the needs of our bodily life, but we are not righteous because of them."

31. Luther, "Freedom," in *Works*, vol. 31, p. 347. At that same place, Luther also contends that no "work can make [a human being] guilty and a damnable servant of sin," and that a belief in Christ saves a man from every evil. Hegel understood Luther's significance in terms of this utter disjunction between the two realms. See Hegel, *The Philosophy of History*, Part IV, Sec. III, Ch. I, p. 415: "Luther's simple doctrine is that the specific embodiment of the Deity—infinite subjectivity, that is true spirituality, Christ—is in no way present and actual in an outward form, but as essentially spiritual is obtained only in being reconciled to God—*in faith and spiritual enjoyment*" (emphasis in original).

32. Luther, "Freedom," in *Works*, vol. 31, p. 347.

33. Luther, "Freedom," in *Works*, vol. 31, p. 353.

34. Luther, "Freedom," in *Works*, vol. 31, p. 353. See also Luther's allusion to the good man bearing good fruit in "Temporal Authority," vol. 45, p. 89; and Matt. 7:17–18.

35. See William James, *The Varieties of Religious Experience* (New York: Penguin Books, 1982), Lecture VIII, pp. 166–67: there are those who might be called "the healthy-minded, who need to be born only once, and [then there are] the sick souls, who must be twice born in order to be happy. [They each have] different conceptions of the universe of our experience. . . . [For the twice-born] the world is a double-storied mystery . . . . Natural good is not simply insufficient in amount and transient, there lurks a falsity in its very being. . . . [The] renunciation and despair of it are our first step in the direction of truth. There are two lives, the natural and the spiritual, and we must lose the one before we can participate in the other."

36. Luther, "Lectures on Galatians," in *Works*, vol. 26, p. 9, *passim.*

37. Luther, "Lectures on Galatians," in *Works*, vol. 26, p. 7. See also ibid., p. 8: "between the active righteousness of the Law and the passive righteousness of Christ, there is no middle ground."

38. Luther, "Lectures of Galatians," in *Works*, vol. 26, p. 5 (emphasis added). Here Luther worries about the reluctance of human beings to break out of the safe world of the Law, within which the charge of righteousness falls squarely upon humankind. See Thomas M. McDonough, *The Law and the Gospel in Luther* (Oxford: Oxford University Press, 1963), p. 30: "for Luther, the human will is somehow curved in on itself . . . and bent ineluctably on earthly goods. This is the concupiscence or carnality that Luther identifies with sin." McDonough rightly notes that the Law-Gospel distinction "is not a mere aspect of Luther's theology but the very heart and core of his basic convictions" (p. 146).

I have already mentioned that portion of Heidegger's essay, "The Essence of Truth" (in *Martin Heidegger: Basic Writings*, p. 134), which suggests that "filling up the world" intimates a hiding-from-Being. Luther has the same insight, viz., that the terror of conscience, the terror of looking below the everyday world of works, leads Christians to "look at nothing except . . . works." See also Rousseau, *Emile*, Bk. IV, pp. 229–30.

39. Luther, "Freedom," in *Works*, vol. 31, p. 359. Again, an allusion to Rom. 7:23.

40. Luther, "Freedom," in *Works*, vol. 31, p. 376. See also Augustine, *City of God*, Bk. I, Ch. 31, p. 42. Rousseau would later claim that this law written in our hearts makes the Bible itself unnecessary, indeed a positive threat to the one true religion. See Rousseau, *Emile*, Bk. IV, pp. 295–97, *passim.*

41. Augustine, *Confessions*, Bk. I, Ch. 4, p. 23.

42. Luther, "Freedom," in *Works*, vol. 31, p. 362: discussion of works without faith "remains on the *surface*, however, and very many have been deceived by this *outward appearance* . . ." (emphasis added).

43. Luther, "Freedom," in *Works*, vol. 31, p. 376.

44. Luther, "Lectures on Galatians," in *Works*, vol. 26, p. 9. Hobbes, too, spoke of the dangers of words and of reason, though for him faith did not dispel their danger. A lawful sovereign who alone had the right of interpretation: this was the only way to avert the problem. See also Rousseau, *Emile*, Bk. II, p. 109: "unless one has the ideas of the

thing represented, the representative signs are nothing"; and ibid., p. 125: "books . . . teach us to know the reason of others, . . . to believe much and never know anything." As with Luther, words entrap unless they have corresponding experiential referents. See also Augustine, *Confessions*, Bk. III, Ch. 5, p. 60.

45. Luther, "Bondage," in *Works*, vol. 33, p. 28 (emphasis added). While Hobbes and Locke do not speak much of the heart, Rousseau does; and this is not to be overlooked. As with Luther, for Rousseau the heart must not be hardened if it is to receive the knowledge appropriate to it. Luther's heart receives God; Rousseau's heart hears the voice of nature.

46. Luther, "Freedom," in *Works*, vol. 31, p. 333.

47. Luther, "Freedom," in *Works*, vol. 31, p. 356.

48. Luther, "Freedom," in *Works*, vol. 31, p. 341. See II Tim. 2:9. The corollary is, of course, that the Pope ought not to have exclusive right in interpreting the Word of God (ibid., p. 342). While Hobbes would later agree that the Pope had no right of interpretation—he likened the papacy to a fairy kingdom—he argued that the sovereign must have the right of interpretation in order for civil life to be free of debilitating strife.

49. Luther, "Freedom," in *Works*, vol. 31, p. 335. See also ibid., p. 343: "many people have considered Christian Faith an easy thing, and not a few have given it a place among the virtues. They do this because they have not experienced it and have never tasted the great strength there is in faith."

50. Luther, "Freedom," in *Works*, vol. 31, p. 375. Hegel would later further develop this distinction and claim that even the person of faith is still a child if grounded on the authority of Christ's miracles. Unless faith is given oneself by oneself, one is as a slave is to a lord: faith based on the authority of God has not yet attained its truth. In Hegel's words, human nature "is too dignified to be placed at this level of nonage where it would always need a guardian and could never enter its status of *manhood*" ("Positivity of Christian Religion," in *Early Theological Writings*, Part I, §9, p. 80; emphasis added). Compare this to the master/slave dialectic of the *Phenomenology*, §194, p. 117: "servitude has the lord for its essential reality; . . . its whole being has been seized with dread; for it has experienced the fear of death, the absolute Lord. In that experience it has been quite *unmanned*" (emphasis added). In both its theological and philosophical expression the movement toward manhood is a movement beyond *fear* (by the Jews/the slave) of a Lord. This step is a necessary one, in much the same way as for Luther the Christian must pass through the Old Law (the Jews) in order to attain Christian freedom. The Old Law portends but does not disclose the truth of the New Testament. The argument of Rousseau's *Emile* is analogous: the soul must pass through childhood, must be a child, *before* it is possible to be an adult—to unite with Sophie; the child must first be subject to the necessity of *things* before coming unto the level of moral development (see *Emile*, Bk. II, p. 85, *passim*). No less could be said of Lessing, though for him the human race itself must pass from childhood to adulthood. See Gotthold Lessing, *The Education of the Human Race* (New York: Columbia University Press, 1908), §16, p. 37; §51, p. 47, *passim*. Finally, with Freud (*Civilization and Its Discontents*, Ch. 2, p. 22, *passim*) there is a reluctant resignation to the fact that most human beings will be unable to face reality and so remain in *perpetual* childhood—here is monotheistic religion!

51. Luther, "Christian Nobility," in *Works*, vol. 44, pp. 182–83.

52. Luther, "Christian Nobility," in *Works*, vol. 44, p. 188.

53. Luther, "Christian Nobility," in *Works*, vol. 44, p. 189. See also "Lectures on Galatians," in *Works*, vol. 26, p. 135, where Luther remarks that the Pope has made the mass a piece of merchandise.

54. John 6:28, 29.

55. Luther, "Freedom," in *Works*, vol. 31, p. 347. Hobbes, too, cites this passage (*Leviathan*, Part III, Ch. 43, p. 429), though for him the meaning of belief is quite different. Not a search after righteousness that ends in the abyss of powerlessness, but rather a simple *verbal assent* to the claim that Jesus is the Christ. Belief does not supersede the law; it is, rather, the law's *supplement*.

56. Martin Luther, "Prefaces to the Old Testament," in *Luther's Works*, vol. 35, p. 236. See also Martin Luther, "Prefaces to the New Testament," in *Luther's Works*, vol. 35, p. 358.

57. Luther, "Prefaces to the Old Testament," in *Works*, vol. 35, p. 237.

58. See Luther, "Lectures on Galatians," in *Works*, vol. 26, p. 138, where, "it was the Law when Abraham was commanded to sacrifice his son Isaac. . . . And yet he was not justified by this work; he was justified by faith." Here the inner truth of the New Testament is *already presaged* in the Old. See ibid., pp. 226–40, where Luther provides a commentary on Gal. 3:6–7 ("Thus Abraham believed God, and it was reckoned to him as righteousness. Know we therefore that they which are of faith, the same are the children of Abraham").

59. See Preus, *From Shadow to Promise*, p. 209, where, in Luther's reading, the Israelites were "caught, as it were, between the 'already' and the 'not yet,' [and this] is replete with theological significance for Christians. . . . The tension of old and new, present and future, grips them as it does Christians."

60. Luther, "Lectures on Galatians," in *Works*, vol. 26, p. 308. See also Luther, "Freedom," in *Works*, vol. 31, p. 349 where, "the law is not laid down for the just" (I Tim. 1:9).

61. Luther, "Lectures on Galatians," in *Works*, vol. 26, pp. 308–9.

62. Luther, "Freedom," in *Works*, vol. 31, p. 348. See also "Lectures on Galatians," in *Works*, vol. 27, p. 74, where, "it is very beneficial if we sometimes become aware of the evil in our nature and our flesh, because in this way we are aroused and stirred up to have faith and to call upon Christ." See Rom. 7:7 ("What shall we say then? *Is* the law sin? God Forbid. I had not known sin, but by the law: for I had not known lust, except the law had said, Thou shalt not covet").

63. Luther, "Freedom," in *Works*, vol. 31, p. 364. Because the law leads to hell humankind is lost without the New Testament. See also ibid., p. 345, where, without the New Testament, "there is no hope at all for the soul."

64. Significantly, Calvin endorses these two uses of the law, *but adds a third*: that the law has a *positive* value as well. The law, in other words, does not simply "lead us to hell," it is also "the best instrument for enabling [Christians] daily to learn with greater truth and certainty what that will of the Lord is which they aspire to follow" (Calvin, *Institutes*, Bk. II, Ch. 7, §12, p. 309). Servants, he says elsewhere, while they may *despair* of their inability to perform the will of their master, must perform it nevertheless. Luther does

not suggest that Christians *simply* despair, to be sure; yet the difference here is significant: with Calvin the Law is not simply *passed through;* it is *dwelt in* as well. For Calvin's thinking on the meaning of the fulfillment of the Law spoken of in Matt. 5:17, see ibid., §§14–16, pp. 311–12.

65. Exodus 20:18, 19

66. Exodus 19:10

67. Luther, "Lectures on Galatians," in *Works*, vol. 26, p. 311. The first instance of this light that would reveal sin is to be found in Gen. 3:8, where Adam and Eve conceal themselves from God because they know they have sinned. See Luther, "Lectures on Genesis," in *Works*, vol. 1, p. 172.

68. While Luther finds a dialectical relationship between Law and Gospel in the juxtaposition of Moses to Christ, Hobbes sees in this relationship evidence of continuity. He understands the narrative in terms of the covenant with God that is established with Moses and *reestablished* with Christ. Like Luther before him, Hobbes would have it that the Gospel offers the promise of salvation, but only in the distant future *when Christ returns.* No deepening of the soul in the post-Incarnation epoch—as both Luther and Nietzsche would have it—occurs!

69. Luther, "Freedom," in *Works*, vol. 31, p. 353.

70. Luther, "Freedom," in *Works*, vol. 31, p. 354.

71. Luther, "Lectures on Galatians," in *Works*, vol. 26, p. 5.

72. See Luther, "Lectures on Galatians," in *Works*, vol. 26, p. 5, where "there is no comfort of conscience so firm and so sure, as this passive [Christian] righteousness is."

73. Hegel, *Philosophy of History*, Part IV, Sec. III, Ch. I, p. 424. Cf. Hobbes, *De Cive*, Ch. XVIII, pp. 372–73, for whom faith "is evermore a *proposition,* that is to say, a speech affirmative or negative, which we grant to be true."

74. Luther, "Freedom," in *Works*, vol. 31, pp. 344–45.

75. Luther, "Freedom," in *Works*, vol. 31, p. 357.

76. To this even Locke accedes. See John Locke, *The Reasonableness of Christianity*, ed. George W. Ewing (Washington, DC: Regnery Gateway, 1965), §164, p. 123, *passim*. See II Cor. 5:7 ("for we walk by faith, not by sight"). Faith cannot be "seen" with the carnal eye that knows history.

77. Here the flesh acts in the service of the spirit; the Old in the service of the New. The Old is thus annulled yet preserved in the New. See Luther, "Lectures on Galatians," in *Works*, vol. 27, p. 87, where, "a Christian struggles with sin continually, and yet in his struggle he does not surrender but obtains victory."

78. Luther, "Freedom," in *Works*, vol. 31, p. 348.

79. Luther, "Lectures on Galatians," in *Works*, vol. 26, p. 131. See also Luther, "Freedom," in *Works*, vol. 31, pp. 346–47, where, the moment you begin to have faith, "you learn that all things in you are altogether blameworthy, sinful, and damnable."

80. Luther, "Lectures on Galatians," in *Works*, vol. 26, p. 234.

81. Luther, "Lectures on Galatians," in *Works*, vol. 27, p. 86. See I Cor. 2:9. Gerrish notes that Luther accorded reason its place in matters pertaining to the "world," but insisted that "reason stumbles at the doctrine of the Incarnation, . . . not because reason

refuses to believe in God, but rather [because] it does not understand who God is; consequently it invents a God after its own fancy" (*Grace and Reason*, p. 14). As Hobbes (and even Rousseau, in *Emile*, Bk. IV, p. 255, *passim*) would later argue, reason concludes *that* there is a God (*quod sit Deus*), but not *what* God is (*quid sit Deus*). In insisting that reason cannot comprehend the mystery of faith, the labor of reason is directed entirely and with legitimacy toward the "world," Gerrish suggests. Luther's insistence that reason cannot understand salvation frees reason from a burden it is not capable of bearing. In this one respect Luther, Hobbes, Locke, and Rousseau agree: *philosophic* knowledge must be subordinated to another, higher, knowledge.

Tocqueville remarks about the peculiar way in which Christian faith and reason can work together and, in fact, argues that, unlike Islam, Christianity and Enlightenment are not contradictory impulses precisely because Christian faith demands that reason defer *only in matters of salvation* (see *Democracy in America*, vol. II, Part I, Ch. 5, p. 445).

82. Matt. 27:46, Mark 15:34. From Psalm 22:1.

83. Luther, "Freedom," in *Works*, vol. 31, p. 357.

84. Byss: the alpha privative of abyss; it is the bottom underneath the apparently bottomless. The term is first used by Jacob Boehme (1575–1624), a Lutheran mystic. More recently, Tillich's theology is predicated on the experience of the abyss and of the Byss beneath it. See Paul Tillich, *The Courage to Be* (New Haven: Yale University Press, 1951).

85. Luther, "Freedom," in *Works*, vol. 31, p. 355. See II Cor. 12:9.

86. This metaphor is found in both the Old Testament (Ps. 19:5) and the New (Rev. 19:7–9). The marriage spoken of there was interpreted by the Church fathers to be the marriage between Christ and the Church, *not* between Christ and the Christian—Luther's interpretation. Cf. Mark 2:19; John 3:29.

87. Luther, "Freedom," in *Works*, vol. 31, p. 352.

88. In the Divine-human equation, then, human beings are the passive, feminine principle, while God (the Son) is masculine. This is further confirmed by Luther's insistence that Christian righteousness is *passive* righteousness, not active. See Rom. 7:2–4.

89. Luther, "Freedom," in *Works*, vol. 31, p. 355.

90. Luther, "Freedom," in *Works*, vol. 31, p. 347.

91. Luther, "Lectures on Galatians," in *Works*, vol. 26, p. 134.

92. Luther, "Freedom," in *Works*, vol. 31, p. 349.

93. Immanuel Kant's "starry heavens above and the moral law within" (*Critique of Practical Reason*, trans. Lewis Beck [Indianapolis: Bobbs-Merrill, 1956], Part II, p. 166): what are these if not analogs of the two realms of which Luther speaks. Kant's twofold division of reality in which the soul finds a respite from the storm of the sensuous world without is as severe in its lines of demarcation between the two realms as is Luther's. Richard Kroner, in his Introduction to Hegel's *Early Theological Writings*, notes that the "philosophic decision [to deny knowledge of things as they are in themselves] and the method of reflective subjectivity which it entailed are, according to Hegel, fruits on the tree of Protestantism. The reformers made an end to the confident rationalism of the Scholastics. They cut the bond between knowledge and faith, between human intellect and divine revelation, between the temporal and the eternal. By denying philosophy the

power of penetrating into the essence of things, Kant and his disciples gave their blessing to this separation" (p. 37). See Otto Wolff, *Die Haupttypen der neueren Lutherdeutung* (Stuttgart: W. Kohlhammer, 1938), for the argument that Luther discovered the categorical imperative three centuries before Kant!

94. Luther, "Lectures on Galatians," in *Works,* vol. 26, p. 229.

95. Luther, "Lectures on Galatians," in *Works,* vol. 26, pp. 231–32 (emphasis added). See Ps. 17:8. God the Son, in effect, protects the soul from the wrath of God the Father. Consider, for example, the symbolism of leprosy. When Miriam speaks against her brother Moses, in His wrath God the Father makes her leprous (Num. 12:1–10). Leprosy is a symbol of God's wrath, of the *decay* that is the life which turns from God. In the New Testament, of course, Christ *cures* leprosy (cf. Matt. 8:2–3). The symbolism is clear: Christ *forgives* errancy from God, hides it from Him, makes the sinner *clean* again. Treating it as a miracle obscures its symbolic meaning.

96. Luther, "Lectures on Galatians," in *Works,* vol. 26, p. 229. See Exodus 15:6.

97. Exodus 20:19.

98. See Luther, "Freedom," in *Works,* vol. 31, p. 359. Luther here again cites Rom. 7:22–23: "For I delight in the law of God, in my inmost self. But I see in my members another law at war with the law of my mind and making me captive to the law of sin."

99. Pelagius's doctrine that human beings have free will was condemned at the Councils of Carthage in 416 and 418 upon the insistence of Augustine. Pelagius held that grace merely helps the Christian accomplish what is already in his own power. Neither Augustine nor Luther believed that the Christian could achieve salvation without the assistance of Christ. See Augustine, *City of God,* Bk. IX, Chs. 14–15, pp. 359–61; Luther, "Bondage," in *Works,* vol. 33, p. 107, *passim.*

100. When Luther argues that there is no free will he means only that human beings are not free with respect to what is "above," to salvation. With respect to what is "below" (possessions, etc.), human beings do have freedom. See Luther, "Bondage of the Will," in *Works,* vol. 33, p. 70.

101. Luther, "Bondage," in *Works,* vol. 33, p. 69.

102. See Augustine, *City of God,* Bk. IV, Ch. 12, p. 152, where the attempt to make God the Soul of the world—which would deny the difference between created and Creator—is condemned as "blasphemous and irreligious"; and ibid., Bk. XIV, Ch. 4, p. 552, where, "it is God who has said, 'I am the Truth.' By contrast, when [man] lives by his own standards . . . then he lives by the standards of falsehood. . . . man should live by the standard of his Creator, not his own."

103. Gen. 16:1.

104. Gen. 17:16.

105. Nietzsche, *Genealogy,* Second Essay, §19, p. 88.

106. Luther, "Bondage," in *Works,* vol. 33, p. 41.

107. These two alternatives, historical necessity and human creativity in history, are both to be found in Marx's writings, and contemporary scholars of Marx have moved back and forth between them. In the contemporary literature Marx is interpreted largely from the vantage point of human agency. A good example of this latter interpretation is

found in Jon Elster's *Making Sense of Marx* (Cambridge: Cambridge University Press, 1985). Elster concludes his book with the thought that while much of Marx is theoretically incoherent—including his notions of historical necessity—Marx's values are worth retaining. Marx's claim, of course, was that history unfolds according to an inner logic originating in the opposition between nature and humankind, expressing itself in the opposition between human beings, and ending when productive forces are finally able to provide adequately for human needs. See Karl Marx, "Private Property and Labor," in Erich Fromm, *Marx's Concept of Man* (New York: Frederick Ungar Publishing, 1978), p. 127: communism "is the *definitive* resolution of the antagonism between man and nature, and between man and man. It is the true solution of the conflict between existence and essence, between objectification and self-affirmation, between freedom and necessity, between individual and species. It is the solution to the riddle of history and it knows itself to be so" (emphasis in original). Again, neither one of these alternatives comports with Luther's understanding of the *Christian* dialectic.

108. Luther, "Bondage," in *Works*, vol. 33, p. 140.

109. Luther, "Bondage," in *Works*, vol. 33, p. 177. See Rom. 9:17–23.

110. Luther, "Bondage," in *Works*, vol. 33, p. 179.

111. Luther, "Bondage," in *Works*, vol. 33, p. 179.

112. Luther, "Bondage," in *Works*, vol. 33, p. 180.

113. For a brief discussion of Heidegger's *Holzwege*, see David Farrell Krell's "General Introduction: 'The Question of Being,'" in *Martin Heidegger: Basic Writings*, pp. 34–35. Heeding Heidegger's caution that "often it seems as though one [woodpath] were identical with another" while in fact it is not (ibid., p. 34), there is, nevertheless, something to be said about the resemblance between Luther's way and Heidegger's. Heidegger notes that theology "is slowly beginning to understand once more Luther's insight that the 'foundation' on which its system of dogma rests has not arisen from an inquiry in which faith is primary, and that conceptually this 'foundation' is not only inadequate for the problematic of theology, but conceals and distorts it" (Heidegger, *Being and Time*, Introduction I, §3, p. 30).

114. Luther, "Bondage," in *Works*, vol. 33, p. 183.

115. Luther, "Bondage," in *Works*, vol. 33, p. 180. See also Luther, "Lectures on Genesis," in *Works*, vol. 1, p. 144; Rom. 11:33. This apparent cruelty was, for Nietzsche, evidence of a continuing vibrancy in the human soul which Christianity has been unable to eradicate. See Nietzsche, *Genealogy*, First Essay, §7, p. 69.

116. See Luther, "Lectures on Genesis," in *Works*, vol. 1, p. 57, where, "Adam had a two-fold life: a physical one and an immortal one, though this was not yet clearly revealed, but only in hope."

117. See Luther, "Lectures on Genesis," in *Works*, vol. 1, p. 65, where, "the new creature *begins* to be restored by the Gospel in this life, but it will not be *finished* in this life" (emphasis added).

118. Luther, "Bondage," in *Works*, vol. 33, pp. 139–40. See also Augustine, *City of God*, Bk. I, Ch. 8, p. 14: "what matters is the nature of the *sufferer*, not the nature of the *sufferings*" (emphasis added).

119. A discussion of the three lights can be found in Luther, "Bondage," in *Works*, vol. 33, p. 292.

120. See Luther, "Lectures on Galatians," in *Works*, vol. 26, p. 5. See also Luther, "Freedom," in *Works*, vol. 31, p. 370: in most works, "we seek only our profit, thinking through them our sins are purged away. . . . In this way Christian liberty perishes altogether."

121. Luther, "Temporal Authority," in *Works*, vol. 45, p. 108.

122. Luther, "Temporal Authority," in *Works*, vol. 45, p. 114.

123. Luther, "Temporal Authority," in *Works*, vol. 45, p. 108. This is not an innovation of Luther's. As he notes at the same place, it was Augustine who said "no one can or ought to be forced to believe." (Later in his life, of course, Augustine *did* assert that the Church could coerce.) Locke's "Letter on Toleration" is perhaps the most eloquent modern plea for separating the two worlds, religious and political, and in certain respects it covers no new ground. By insisting, however, that reason was not utterly corrupt, he not only took matters of belief out of the hands of the state, but out of the hands of the church as well. This significant difference aside, his is a theological argument about the political implications of Christ's first coming. See Joshua Mitchell, "John Locke and the Theological Foundation of Liberal Toleration: A Christian Dialectic of History," *Review of Politics* 52, no. 1 (1990): 64–83.

124. Luther, "Temporal Authority," in *Works*, vol. 45, p. 109; see also ibid., pp. 115–16.

125. Luther, "Temporal Authority," in *Works*, vol. 45, p. 117.

126. Luther, "Christian Nobility," in *Works*, vol. 44, pp. 131–32; see also Luther, "Temporal Authority," in *Works*, vol. 45, p. 87. The case Luther makes for the divine authority of worldly government was not strong enough for Hobbes, for it extends only over the unrighteous and is annulled for the righteous. Hobbes claims that the covenant that authorizes earthly government applies to all, Christian and non-Christian alike. This is a central theoretical difference between their positions.

127. Luther, "Temporal Authority," in *Works*, vol. 45, p. 92.

128. Luther, "Christian Nobility," in *Works*, vol. 44, p. 130.

129. Luther, "Christian Nobility," in *Works*, vol. 44, p. 129. See also p. 134, where Saint Peter gives the keys to the Church to all Christians, and p. 168, where no one should kiss the pope's feet.

While all Christians are equal in the eyes of God, and while the work a Christian does is a mere convention, Luther did have contempt for those who were idle and yet reaped wealth from the work of others. That work is a mere convention does not mean that it is irrelevant. See ibid., p. 190, where, "if a man wants to be rich, let him put his hand to the plough and seek his fortune in the land." This sentiment is not yet temporal equality, however. The injunctions of Luke 20:25 and Rom. 13:1 remain intact, as he points out in "Against the Robbing and Murdering Hordes," in *Works*, vol. 46, p. 50, *passim*.

130. Luther, "Temporal Authority," in *Works*, vol. 45, p. 117. Hobbes's formulation of the relationship between the Leviathan and all those under him with whom a cove-

nant is formed is the functional equivalent to this relationship between Christ and all Christians, as I will show in chap. 2.

131. Luther, "Temporal Authority," in *Works*, vol. 45, p. 91.

132. The importance of the person in whom two disparate realms are unified is a venerable theme, found first in Plato's *Republic*, Bk. V, 473d; later in Hobbes's *Leviathan*, Part III, Ch. 42, p. 376; and in Rousseau's "First Discourse," pp. 63–64. Luther's Christian prince differs from Hobbes's Leviathan in that matters of scriptural interpretation are not within the purview of the former. Although for Luther certain mysteries about God remain, the Word of God is understandable to those who are pure of heart. In the abyss of powerlessness and in the marriage with Christ the meaning of God's Word becomes transparent. Christian righteousness clarifies the Word of God. Hobbes, of course, detects in Christian righteousness a recipe for unbridled enthusiasm and political chaos.

133. Luther, "Christian Nobility," in *Works*, vol. 44, p. 124.

134. Luther, "Christian Nobility," in *Works*, vol. 44, p. 126. See ibid., p. 125: we "must tackle this job by renouncing trust in physical force."

135. Max Weber, "Politics as a Vocation," in *From Max Weber*, ed. H. H. Gerth and C. Wright Mills (New York: Oxford University Press, 1946), p. 78.

136. Luther, "Christian Nobility," in *Works*, vol. 44, p. 125. See also Augustine, *Confessions*, Bk. IV, Ch. 16, p. 89: "when you are our strength we are strong, but when our strength is our own we are weak."

137. Luther, "Christian Nobility," in *Works*, vol. 44, p. 145. In the full passage from which this is taken, Luther clearly believes that the princes are Christian and not rapacious wolves. The prospect that the princes themselves might be the "wolves in sheep's clothing" did not occur to him here. (Later, Locke would argue against Hobbes for making the same error about the Leviathan's relationship to the people of the commonwealth. See John Locke, *Second Treatise*, in *Two Treatises of Government*, ed. Peter Laslett [Cambridge: Cambridge University Press, 1988], Ch. VII, §93, p. 328.) Luther's subsequent "Temporal Authority" attempts more to carve out a domain for conscience that would be impervious to the machinations of either the Roman Church or the state.

138. Hence, Luther's claim at the beginning of the "Temporal Authority" that Christian princes are incorrect in believing that because the two realms are separated they may do what they please in the earthly kingdom. See "Temporal Authority," in *Works*, vol. 45, p. 83.

139. Luther, "Temporal Authority," in *Works*, vol. 45, p. 121.

140. Luther, "Temporal Authority," in *Works*, vol. 45, p. 129.

141. Luther, "Temporal Authority," in *Works*, vol. 45, pp. 119–20 (emphasis added). See also Luther H. Waring, *Political Theories of Martin Luther* (New York: G. P. Putnam's Sons, 1910), pp. 163–84. Waring's chapter, "The Objects of the State," is especially good at showing that Luther believed that Christian princes must be Christians in order that their power be used well. Waring contends that, for Luther, "the duty of the prince is fourfold: (1) toward God, with confident and devout prayer; (2) toward his subjects, with Love and Christian service; (3) toward his counselors and his mighty men, with clear mind and unprejudiced judgment; and (4) toward evil-doers, with dis-

criminating earnestness and firmness" (p. 177). See also pp. 276–77, for Waring's summary of Luther's political principles.

142. Luther, "Temporal Authority," in *Works*, vol. 45, p. 120. The difficulty faced by Luther and subsequent reformers was what to do when princes derogated their Christian charge. When princes do not treat subjects in a Christian manner, when is it acceptable to resist? See Skinner, *The Foundations of Modern Political Thought*, vol. 2, pp. 189–238, for a discussion of the idea of the right to resist in Reformation thought. Skinner contends that "the main influence of Lutheran political theory in early modern Europe lay in the direction of encouraging and legitimating the emergence of united and absolutist monarchies" (vol. 2, p. 113).

143. Freud also notes the utter inability to uphold God's commandment to love one's neighbor. "What a potent obstacle to civilization aggressiveness must be," he notes, "if the defense against it [the commandment to love] can cause as much unhappiness as aggressiveness itself" (Freud, *Civilization and Its Discontents*, Ch. VIII, p. 109). For Freud, of course, there is no Byss underneath the abyss of despair and unhappiness capable of enveloping and overcoming it.

144. Later, Rousseau understood the utter interiority of Christian religion to mean that human beings are left "without bonds of union." See Rousseau, *The Social Contract*, Bk. IV, Ch. 8, p. 186. Failing to grasp Luther's claim that *through Christ* the Christian discovers the foundation of his or her relation with others, Rousseau calls for the inception of a civil religion to compensate for the absence of social bonds within the Christian community.

145. Luther, "Treatise on Good Works," in *Works*, vol. 44, p. 23. See John 6:28–29.

146. Luther, "Freedom," in *Works*, vol. 31, pp. 367–68. See also p. 371, where as Christ "puts on" the Christian, so, too, the Christian must put on his neighbor.

147. Luther, "Freedom," in *Works*, vol. 31, p. 348.

148. There are traces of the notion that one must enter into another for there to be civil peace in the thought of Adam Smith as well. Luther's Christ, of course, is not important for his theory of the foundation of civil life; nor is Hobbes's Leviathan. For Smith the key that connects humans together is the imagination. See Adam Smith, *The Theory of Moral Sentiments* (Indianapolis: Liberty Press, 1982), p. 9: "by the imagination we place ourselves in his situation, we conceive ourselves enduring all the same torments, we enter as it were into his body, and become in some measure the same person with him." See Rousseau, *Emile*, Bk. IV, p. 223.

149. Luther, "Freedom," in *Works*, vol. 31, p. 371.

150. Luther, "Temporal Authority," in *Works*, vol. 45, p. 95.

151. Luther, "Temporal Authority," in *Works*, vol. 45, p. 94. This is Luther's interpretation of Rom. 13:1: "Let every soul be subject unto the higher powers. For there is no power but of God; the powers that be are ordained of God." Christ and Christian righteousness come first, sociality follows. Hobbes also cites this same scriptural passage but does not interpret it in terms of the derivative quality of sociality; rather, he sees in it a refutation of the claim that the relationship between the Christian and Christ is primary in the present moment of history. For Luther, "we are named after Christ, not because he is absent from us, but because he dwells in us" ("Freedom," in *Works*, vol. 31, p. 368). For

Hobbes, Christ will be present for the Christian only at the end of history, and therefore the Christian must submit to temporal authority.

No treatment of Rom. 13:1, 2 would be sufficient without considering Nietzsche's interpretation. The soul dominated by the ethic of resentment, the weak soul, the liberal soul, is one that shuns its primary instincts and, along with them, the state of *fear* which makes the soul feel most alive. Saint Paul's insistence that we defer to earthly powers because *God commands* Christians to do so is the effort of the sick soul to deflect fear, to grant the suffering one might experience at the hands of the ruler-beast a meaning that *justifies* weakness. See Nietzsche, *Genealogy*, First Essay, §14, p. 47.

152. Luther, "Freedom," in *Works*, vol. 31, p. 344.

153. This spiritual journey and return is analogous to the journey of which Plato speaks in the *Republic*, Bk. VII, 514a–521c. In both cases what is involved is an encounter with what veritably *is* and yet which is absent and concealed from the soul that is unable to embark upon the dialectical journey. The issue here is not the similarity between Plato and Christianity but rather that for Plato and certain Christian thinkers the soul must be twice born before it *really* exists. See James, *Varieties of Religious Experience*, Lecture VIII, pp. 166–88.

154. See Luther, "Bondage," in *Works*, vol. 33, p. 22: "what is more miserable than uncertainty?" While I have not considered the subject in this chapter, it should be noted that uncertainty is the experience which corresponds to the religious symbol of purgatory for Luther. Purgatory is the uncertain "place" in which Christians find themselves when they do not know if the works they do are done in accordance with the truth of the Old Testament or the New. See John S. Dunne, *A Search for God in Time and Memory* (Notre Dame: University of Notre Dame Press, 1977), pp. 76–117, for an excellent treatment of Luther and the experience of Hell, Purgatory, and Heaven.

155. Luther, "Freedom," in *Works*, vol. 31, p. 355.

156. Contrast this to Locke, who says, "the law [cannot] be taken away . . . without changing the nature of things, or overturning the measures of right and wrong" (*Reasonableness*, §180, p. 136). The supplementarity of faith to the law, not the spiritual journey through which the law is superseded by faith, would preoccupy both Hobbes and Locke.

157. In this light, both Luther and Rousseau would be concerned about the *arrest* of the soul's progress that would occur if it did not pass through certain preparatory stages of development. See Rousseau, *Emile*, Bk. II, p. 79, where, perhaps alluding to that Christian education which would wish to condemn the soul to oblivion in the act of (prematurely) trying to save it, he says, "what, then, must be thought of that barbarous education which sacrifices the present to an uncertain future, which burdens a child with chains of every sort and begins by making him miserable in order to prepare him from afar for . . . a pretended happiness which it is to be believed he will never enjoy."

158. Hobbes, *Leviathan*, Part I, Chs. 1–13, pp. 21–102, *passim*.

159. Gal. 4:24–25.

160. See Rousseau, *Emile*, Bk. III, p. 205: "the goal is less to teach him the truth than to show him how he must always go about discovering the truth. In order to instruct him better, you must not undeceive him too soon"; and ibid., Bk. IV, p. 259: "let us refrain from proclaiming the truth to those who are not in a condition to understand it." All this

could be seen as coming from the Gospel of John, who writes extensively of Christ's unconcealment, or even from Locke. If Rousseau were transposed into a theological key, however, he would be more akin to Hobbes, for whom the unconcealment (by Christ) of a moral truth to which *all* could easily accede *never occurs*.

CHAPTER TWO

1. See Hobbes, *Leviathan*, Part II, Ch. 31, p. 270: "neither Plato nor any other philosopher hitherto, hath put into order, and sufficiently and probably proved all the theorems of moral doctrine [I have put forth here]."

2. See Reventlow, *The Authority of the Bible and the Rise of the Modern World*, for the argument that biblical criticism originates not in Germany but rather in England, notably in the thought of Wycliffe (1320–84). Reventlow claims Hobbes is but one of a long line of thinkers in England whose biblical interpretation and political thought are intertwined. For a succinct and provocative presentation of the importance of biblical history for Hobbes, see Eldon Eisenach, "Hobbes on Church, State, and Religion," in *History of Political Thought* 3, no. 2 (1982): 215–43. See also David S. Katz, *Philo-Semitism and the Readmission of the Jews to England, 1603–1655* (Oxford: Clarendon Press, 1982), p. 9: there was an "interest in Hebrew studies which blossomed in England during the late sixteenth and early seventeenth centuries as a consequence of the emphasis that Reformation theologians placed on the reading and understanding of the text which recorded the word of God. The validity of the Old Testament commandments for Christians was an issue of crucial importance during the Reformation."

3. Hobbes, *Leviathan*, Part III, Ch. 43, p. 436; see also Part IV, Ch. 44, p. 444, and Review and Conclusion, p. 509. See also Locke, *Reasonableness*, §248, p. 186: "we must look to the *drift* of the discourse; observe the coherence and connection of the parts; and see how it is consistent with itself, and other parts of Scripture" (emphasis in original).

4. Hobbes, *Leviathan*, Part I, Ch. 13, p. 100.

5. Hobbes, *Leviathan*, Part III, Ch. 39, p. 340 (emphasis added). See Matt. 12:25.

6. Koselleck argues that while this separation goes back to Augustine, in fact it only becomes politically problematic in the Reformation, when the "visible Church no longer held the two [realms] together" (*Critique and Crisis*, pp. 29–30, n. 27), and that a unification of sorts was necessary in order to stabilize political life. While Koselleck's footnote in many ways captures the differences between Luther and Hobbes, he vastly overestimates the place of reason in Hobbes's thought and suggests that reason comes to the fore in the face of religious warfare, which then becomes disencumbered of its religious substrate. See ibid., p. 34: "reason, rising from the turmoil of religious warfare, at first remains under the spell of that warfare and founds the State. This is how we are to understand Hobbes's failure to see that the spirit of Enlightenment enables reason to emancipate itself. Hobbes did not know that reason has a gravitation of its own."
Koselleck's argument is, of course, a variant of the secularization thesis, a thesis which, I suggest, falls flat when it attempts to account for Hobbes's political thought.

7. Hobbes, *De Cive*, Ch. VI, p. 179. See Matt. 6:24; Augustine, *City of God*, Bk. XIX, Ch. 4, p. 852. Stephen Holmes's Introductory Essay to *Behemoth* is quite clear on this point. See especially pp. x–xi, and 14–15.

8. See Hobbes. *Leviathan*, Part III, Ch. 43, pp. 424–25: "but if the command be such as cannot be obeyed, without being damned to eternal death; then it be madness to obey it, and the council of our Savior take place, (*Matt.* x. 28), *Fear not those who kill the body but cannot kill the soul*" (emphasis in original). Here Hobbes follows out the implications of Matthew 10:28; *do* fear those that can kill the soul by giving commands contrary to what is necessary for reception into heaven.

9. See Hobbes, *Leviathan*, Part I, Ch. 11, p. 85: "it is impossible to make any profound inquiry into natural causes, without being inclined thereby to believe there is one God eternal." Reason intimates but cannot prove the existence of the Christian god. See also ibid., Part III, Ch. 32, p. 271: "for though there be many things in God's word *above* reason; that is to say, which cannot by natural reason be either demonstrated, or confused; yet there is nothing contrary to it" (emphasis added). See also Augustine, *City of God*, Bk. XXI, Ch. 5, p. 971: "many things are to be believed though not susceptible to rational proof."

10. See Tocqueville, *Democracy in America*, vol. II, Part II, Ch. 9, p. 528: "if the doctrine of self-interest properly understood were concerned with this world only, that would not be nearly enough. For there are a great many sacrifices which can only be rewarded in the next. However hard one may try to prove that virtue is useful, it will always be difficult to make a man live well if he will not face death." See also ibid., Part I, Ch. 5, pp. 442–44.

11. This is not to say that reason alone is not a window to God, only that it does not let in enough light to clarify God's intentions for humankind. See William E. Connolly, *Political Theory and Modernity* (New York: Basil Blackwell, 1988), pp. 21–24. Hobbes's "method" (which Locke follows as well) is to establish the purview of reason's light *and then defer in matters which are beyond its purview*. In this respect he follows Augustine. See Augustine, *City of God*, Bk. XI, Ch. 3, p. 431: "now we ourselves are our own witness for the knowledge of things which are within the reach of our senses, whether interior or exterior. . . . And so we clearly need *other witnesses* for things which are out of reach of our senses, since we cannot base our knowledge on our own senses" (emphasis added). Here, each person *must* rely on their own evidence up to a point and then defer to Scripture. Also to be noted is that Hobbes's procedure of using reason first to clear away false religion and then turning to a discussion of true religion is one adopted earlier and most prominently by Augustine in the *City of God*.

12. Even Rousseau, whose eloquence about ancient virtue and modern impotence is unsurpassed (see "Has the Restoration of the Sciences and Arts Tended to Purify Morals?" in *The First and Second Discourses*, ed. Roger D. Masters and Judith R. Masters [New York: St. Martin's Press, 1964], pp. 35–74), conceded that Christianity "has won completely" (Rousseau, *The Social Contract*, Bk. IV, Ch. 8, p. 179). Nietzsche would say no less.

13. Pufendorf is reputed to have alluded to Hobbes's theology in this way. See Istvan Hont, "The Language of Sociability and Commerce: Samuel Pufendorf and the Theoretical Foundations of the 'Four-Stages Theory,'" in *The Languages of Political Theory in Early Modern Europe*, ed. Anthony Pagden (Cambridge: Cambridge University Press, 1987), for the argument that Pufendorf "attempted to reconstruct Grotius' jurisprudence by applying the intellectual method of Thomas Hobbes" (p. 253). While Pufendorf may have

attempted to do this, it is not the case that the "intellectual method of Hobbes" can be reduced to what is present in the first part of the *Leviathan*. This chapter, in fact, is an attempt to show another logic in Hobbes besides the one to which Pufendorf (and Hont) allude. This other logic is concerned with Hobbes's "perverse theology."

14. Matt. 5:17. Hobbes cites this passage in *Leviathan*, Part III, Ch. 42, p. 381, and also in *De Cive*, Ch. XVII, p. 337.

15. See Saint Augustine, *Confessions*, Bk. I, Ch. 1, p. 21: man "bears about him the mark of death, the sign of his own sin, to remind him that you *thwart the proud.*" For Augustine, only divine intersession by God the Son is able to atone for human pridefulness—a view to which Hobbes would never accede.

16. I mention again, here, the passages from Saint Paul to which I alluded in the Introduction. That Christ is purported to be a solution to the problem of loss of eternal life can be found in I Cor. 15:21, 22: "For since by man came death, by man came also the resurrection of the dead. For as in Adam all die, even so in Christ all shall be made alive." That Christ is purported to be a solution to the problem of pride can be found in Rom. 5:19: "For as by one man's disobedience many were made sinners, so by the obedience of one shall many be made righteous." To my knowledge Hobbes never cites this second passage.

17. Again, see Hobbes, *Leviathan*, Part III, Ch. 39, p. 340: "*temporal* and *spiritual* government, are but two words brought into the world, to make men see double, and mistake their *lawful* sovereign" (emphasis in original). See also Calvin, *Institutes*, Prefatory Address, p. 19: "our God is not the author of division, but of peace."

18. Hobbes, *Leviathan*, Part I, Ch. 3, p. 31, *passim*.

19. See J. W. N. Watkins, *Hobbes' System of Ideas* (London: Hutchinson, 1965). Watkins argues that Hobbes was writing in response to the Puritan revolution, which led to the 1642 Civil War and to the beheading of the king in 1649 (p. 13). Moreover, Watkins suggests that Hobbes believed that Puritan ideology was an inflated expression of individual avarice and pride (p. 165).

20. God's representative on earth is the Church, properly conceived. In Hobbes's words: "I define a Church to be, *a company of men professing Christian religion, united in the person of one sovereign, at whose command they ought to assemble, and without whose authority they ought not to assemble*" (*Leviathan*, p. 340, emphasis in original).

Hobbes complains in *Behemoth* (Dialogue 1, pp. 21–22) that the effect of the controversy between the pope and the reformed church was, in effect, to bring the word of God within the reach of the Israelites, which Moses, in receiving the word of God *on the mount*, had not done. The pope, in keeping Scripture out of the hands of the people, had acted (rightly!) as Moses had. While the Reformed Church may have been correct in denying authority to the pope, the effect of the controversy between them undermined the authority of both, for now the word of God was in the hands of the people. "After the Bible was translated into English," Hobbes says, "every man, nay, every boy and wench, that could read English, thought they spoke with God Almighty, and understood what He said" (ibid., p. 21).

21. Hobbes, *Leviathan*, Part IV, Ch. 47, pp. 500–501.

22. In Holmes's words, "the greatest source of anarchy is pride; and (as Pascal showed) there is no mythology more effective in attacking pride than the mythology of sin and

redemption. Society would certainly be more peaceful if both 'glory' and 'vengeance' could be reserved to God, as Scripture says they should be. It is no accident that Hobbes lifted his central metaphor, the state as the king of the children of pride, from the Bible" (*Behemoth*, Introductory Essay, p. xlvi).

Luther would, in his own way, agree: the *superbia* of pride must be vanquished, and this is why the Law, the Old Testament, is so necessary. It confirms the Christian's *inability* to act righteously, and this confirmation is the beginning of salvation. See Gerrish, *Grace and Reason*, p. 109: "the law *must* precede the Gospel [for Luther], else no man believe the Gospel. The law is given to humble man's pride, to make him receptive. The one thing which stands between God and man is man's arrogant assumption that he can *win* salvation" (emphasis in original).

23. Hobbes, *De Cive*, Ch. 1, p. 112.

24. Hobbes, *De Cive*, Ch. 1, p. 112. Kraynak's exposition of Hobbes's theory of civil history is quite good on this point. As civilization "advances" it comes to be dominated less by force and more by opinion, which is a more valuable currency in Hobbesian psychology than the conveniences of life. This situation "has produced a new type of warfare that primitive men were spared by their ignorance: in civilized societies, the wars among tribes for territory and plunder have been superseded by wars among intellectuals over opinions and doctrines" (Robert P. Kraynak, *History and Modernity in the Thought of Thomas Hobbes* [Ithaca: Cornell University Press, 1991], p. 16). Notwithstanding Kraynak's astute observations about the "age of doctrine," his study attributes to Hobbes an impulse to derogate authority which, while present in his science, is not at all present in matters of ultimate concern.

25. Hobbes, *Leviathan*, Part II, Ch. 17, p. 131; *De Cive*, Ch. V, pp. 168–69.

26. Hobbes, *De Cive*, Ch. 1, p. 113.

27. Hobbes, *De Cive*, Ch. 1, p. 117. See Hirschman, *The Passions and the Interests*, for the view that Hobbes wished to found "a state so constituted that the problems created by passionate men are solved once and for all" (p. 31), a thought Hobbes expresses, to be sure, in *Leviathan*, Part I, Ch. 13, p. 100. Hirschman's intent is to show that Hobbes was part of that tradition concerned with substituting interest (which was constructive) for passion (which was destructive). This view, however, disregards the entirety of Hobbes's thought about biblical history and its political import.

28. Hobbes, *Leviathan*, Part II, Ch. 17, p. 132 (emphasis in original). No other beings besides human beings have the "privilege of absurdity" that pride affords (ibid., Part I, Ch. 5, p. 43). The violent dissensions this privilege produces make an awful Leviathan necessary.

29. Hobbes, *De Cive*, Preface, p. 104.

30. Hobbes, *De Cive*, Ch. X, p. 224. Not only is pride produced by the higher passions, but it does not wish to have limits placed on it. It finds itself sufficient unto itself and wishes to extend its range, unimpeded, over the entire domain. Theologically, pride is the attempt by the finite to "absolutize" itself, whether wittingly or unwittingly. The desire to be free of God—or to be *as* God—is its most ambitious form. See also Augustine, *City of God*, Bk. XIV, Ch. 13: "pride is the start of every sin. [It is] a longing for a perverse kind of exaltation [which abandons] the basis on which the mind should be firmly fixed, [and wishes to become] as it were, based on oneself, and so remain."

Contrast this to Aristotle, *Ethics*, Bk. IX, Ch. 4, 1166a22: "everyone . . . wishes only what is good for himself as a man: . . . no one would choose to become a god."

31. Hobbes, *De Cive*, Ch. IX, p. 215.

32. Hobbes, *De Cive*, Ch. VI, p. 178.

33. Hobbes, *De Cive*, Preface, p. 103. Contrast this to Nietzsche, for whom "a legal order thought of as sovereign and universal, not as a means in a struggle between power-complexes but as a means of *preventing* all struggle in general . . . would be a principle *hostile to life*, an agent in the dissolution and destruction of man, an attempt to assassinate the future of man, a sign of weariness, a secret path to nothingness" (Nietzsche, *Genealogy*, Second Essay, §11, p. 76; emphasis in original).

34. Hobbes, *Leviathan*, Part II, Ch. 18, p. 141. Note the parallels between this and Luther's theological formulation of the relationship between Christ and all Christians.

35. Hobbes, *Leviathan*, Part I, Ch. 13, p. 98; *De Cive*, Ch. I, p. 114.

36. Hobbes, *De Cive*, Ch. III, p. 143 (emphasis in original). Hegel's observation in *The Spirit of Christianity* that "the Greeks were to be equal because all were free, self-subsistent; the Jews equal because they were incapable of self-subsistence" (§1, p. 198) is apropos here for the purpose of analytical clarity though not for descriptive accuracy. According to Hegel, the equality Hobbes would wish to institute would restrict freedom, not enlarge it. Rousseau's *Second Discourse* and Tocqueville's *Democracy in America*, of course, offer these two kinds of equality as well.

37. Hobbes, *De Cive*, Ch. X, p. 228.

38. Hobbes, *De Cive*, Ch. X, p. 227. See also Hobbes, *Behemoth*, Dialogue 1, p. 59: human beings enjoy liberty when they enjoy "an exemption from the constraint and insolence of their neighbors."
At times Tocqueville speaks of the dangers of democracy in Hobbesian terms. See, for example, *Democracy in America*, vol. I, Part II, Ch. 7, pp. 257–58. What is also striking about Tocqueville is that, like Hobbes, sovereignty can only be a unity. See p. 251: "there is in truth no such thing as mixed government . . . since in any society one finds in the end some principle of action that dominates all the others."

39. Hobbes, *De Cive*, Ch. X, p. 232. The temptation of voice, of speaking, of words appears throughout Hobbes's work—as it does later in Rousseau and earlier in Augustine. For Rousseau, the crucial matter was to listen to the voice of nature below the din of voices in civil society. Augustine worried greatly about his temptation to become a "vendor of words" (*Confessions*, Bk. IX, Ch. 5, p. 189), instead of listening to the voice of God. For both Hobbes and Augustine, hearing the voice to which one *ought* to listen is linked to obedience of the "sovereign."

40. Hobbes, *De Cive*, Ch. X, pp. 229–30. Compare this to Tocqueville, for whom it was precisely the participation of all citizens in politics that is necessary to combat the real enemy: a narrow egoism, an Augustinian self-enclosure of the psyche, that would diminish the motion of the polity to an unhealthy level. See Tocqueville, *Democracy in America*, vol. II, Part II, Ch. 4, pp. 509–13. Augustine, like Hobbes, thought that eloquence often concealed a desire for self-elevation. See Augustine, *Confessions*, Bk. III, Ch. 4, p. 58. For an earlier expression of Hobbes's insight into the power of words to

injure and affront, see ibid., Bk. X, Ch. 37, p. 245: "the human tongue is a furnace in which the temper of our souls is daily tried."

41. Hobbes, *De Cive*, Ch. I, p. 113.

42. Hobbes, *Leviathan*, Part II, Ch. 21, p. 163 (emphasis in original). While the terms of the debate are somewhat different in Rousseau, he, too, would agree. See Rousseau, *Emile*, Bk. V, p. 461: "each man who obeys the sovereign obeys only himself, and . . . one is more free under the social pact than in the state of nature."

43. Gen. 16:1.

44. Augustine, *City of God*, Bk. XIV, Ch. 12, p. 571 (emphasis added).

45. Calvin, *Institutes*, Bk. III, Ch. VII, p. 7.

46. See F. C. Hood, *The Divine Politics of Thomas Hobbes* (Oxford: Clarendon Press, 1964), pp. 174–75: "man's mistaken confidence in his own ability to judge between good and evil is that original sin of pride, in which all men participate. In disobeying his sovereign, the subject repeats the sin of Adam, for he disobeys God." My treatment here of Hobbes is consistent with Hood's; the difference is one of emphasis. My concern here is with how the pattern of the equality of all under the one is an antidote to the problem of pride, and how this theological insight plays itself out in Hobbes's thought. While I cannot consider the matter here, I suggest that the context into which Hobbes's thought must be placed is the Reformation preoccupation with the meaning of Christ's fulfillment of the Old Testament. Hobbes's politics *is* Divine, but the crucial question is what his understanding of the relationship between the two Testaments is. This matter is not made explicit by Hood.

Completely off the mark is Strauss, for whom "the whole scheme suggested by Hobbes [is made possible by] the disenchantment of the world, by the diffusion of scientific knowledge, or by popular enlightenment." Strauss continues, "Hobbes's is the first doctrine that necessarily and unmistakably points to a thoroughly 'enlightened,' i.e., a-religious or atheistic society as the solution of the social or political problem" (Leo Strauss, *Natural Right and History* [Chicago: University of Chicago Press, 1953], p. 198).

47. Hobbes, *Leviathan*, Part I, Ch. 4, p. 34; Ch. 5, p. 44; Ch. 8, p. 61, *passim*.

48. Hobbes, *De Cive*, Preface, p. 98.

49. Hobbes, *De Cive*, Preface, p. 98. Rousseau, too, was concerned with these "hermaphrodite opinions." Arguing that the movement from the state of nature to civil society enlarges human faculties—or, to use Hobbes's language, develops the higher passions—Rousseau claimed that the abuses of these faculties "lower him to something worse than" the state of nature (Rousseau, *The Social Contract*, Bk. I, Ch. 8, p. 65). Consider also Locke, who would write, "Religion which should distinguish us from Beasts, and ought most peculiarly to elevate us, as rational Creatures, above Brutes, is that wherein Men often appear most irrational, and more senseless than Beasts themselves" (Locke, *Essay*, Bk. IV, Ch. XVIII, §11, p. 696).

50. Hobbes, *De Cive*, Preface, p. 98.

51. Compare this to Aristotle, for whom political life is the highest form of human association. Rather than restraining human beings from considering justice Aristotle insists that the fully human being must do so. See Aristotle, *Politics*, Bk. I, Ch. 1, 1253a: "he who is without a polis . . . is either a poor sort of being, or a being higher than man."

In Aristotle the "man-beast" arises, not because he is allowed to participate in political life, but because he is *without* a political life. See also Augustine, *City of God*, Bk. XII, Ch. 22, p. 502: God "created man's nature as a kind of mean between angels and beasts, so that if he submitted to his Creator . . . he should pass over into the fellowship of the angels . . . but if he used his free will in arrogance and disbelief . . . he should live like the beasts . . . and be the slave of his [own] desires."

52. Hobbes, *De Cive*, Preface, p. 97.

53. Hobbes, *De Cive*, Ch. XIV, p. 310. Hobbes uses this passage to argue that God gave humankind a second chance, as it were, when He formed a covenant with Abraham (Gen. 17:7, 8). Consistent with Hobbes's argument that only the sovereign can deliberate on matters of good and evil, he suggests that humankind fell because it disobeyed the God who "did require a most simple obedience to his commands, without dispute whether [they] were *good* or *evil*" (ibid., p. 311; emphasis in original). Abraham's covenant, however, is not yet a political covenant. This would have to wait for Moses.

54. I Cor. 1:22,23.

55. Augustine, *City of God*, Bk. I, Ch. 31, p. 42.

56. See Ricoeur, *The Symbolism of Evil*, pp. 232–78.

57. See Plato, *Republic*, Bk. X, 611d–e: "we must look . . . to the soul's love of wisdom [to see what it really is]. We must mark what it knows. We must disclose the yearning that links it to the immortal and divine and so to eternal being." Also see Aristotle, *Ethics*, Bk. X, Ch. 7, 1177b35–1178a3: "we should try to become immortal as far as that is possible and do the utmost to live in accordance with what is highest in us. For though this is a small portion [of our nature], it far surpasses everything else in power and value. One might even regard it as each man's true self, since it is the controlling and better part." Augustine's argument against Plato was that the source of corruption was not only in the appetites, but in the mind as well. See Augustine, *City of God*, Bk. XIV, Ch. 2, p. 548.

58. Nietzsche, *Genealogy*, Second Essay, §23, p. 94.

59. Hobbes, *Leviathan*, Part II, Ch. 31, pp. 263–64. Hobbes's is a theology of *glory*, not of salvation!

60. Hobbes, *Leviathan*, Part III, Ch. 38, p. 325 (emphasis in original). So much for the thesis still possessing currency that Hobbes saw in human beings only the desire to flee from "natural death." Quite to the contrary, Hobbes understood that the desire to attain eternal life was even more consequential.

See also Baron de Montesquieu, *Spirit of the Laws*, trans. Thomas Nugent (New York: Hafner Press, 1949), vol. II, Bk. 24, Ch. 14, p. 36: "how shall the man be restrained by laws who believes that the greatest pain the magistrate can inflict will end in a moment to begin his happiness?"

61. The problem of pride is related to the spiritual corruption within the human soul in the way that the problem of loss of eternal life is not. Hobbes avoids imputing this spiritual corruption to humankind by suggesting that evil is a social construct; it is a name put on a (natural) fear, desire, etc. That is, evil is not constitutional. See *De Cive*, Preface, pp. 100–101.

This notion that evil is a social construct would later have appeal for Rousseau, for whom naming and the presence of evil were coterminous with the emergence of civil society. While Rousseau clearly believed that evil emerges in civil society, however, Hobbes's state of nature portrays humankind in a kind of fallen state for which the Leviathan—the king of the children of pride—is a solution. In spite of what Hobbes says, in other words, it is clear that a notion of the fallenness of humankind is central to his overall vision. Rousseau himself believed that Hobbes conceived of the natural human as evil, and he argued against this notion. See Jean-Jacques Rousseau, "Discourse on the Origin and Foundations of Inequality among Men" in *The First and Second Discourses*, ed. Roger D. Masters and Judith R. Masters (New York: St. Martin's Press, 1964), p. 128. Rousseau would later remark that for both Hobbes and Locke the state of nature was constructed out of the material at hand in their own civil period. This material was not only civil in character, however; it was Christian as well.

62. A theological analysis consistent with a portion of the argument presented here can be found in Pocock's "Time, History, and Eschatology in the Thought of Thomas Hobbes," in *Politics, Language, and Time*, pp. 148–201. Pocock argues that contrary to the conventional understanding of Hobbes which would have it that history is relatively unimportant in his thought—witness, for example, the nonhistorical character of the movement from the state of nature to the state of civil association—history, in fact, plays a crucial role. For Hobbes, the Christian God came in the past and promised to come again in the future. Humankind lives between these two infinitely significant moments, yet must be content to live without the presence of God in this moment of history. In certain respects this analysis is correct; because of the absence of the Divine in the interim of history, Hobbes posits an interim solution to the problem of pride: the Leviathan. But this is only half the story. The other half is the ongoing covenant between God and humankind in history that Hobbes traces back to Moses.

This point is of no small moment. In *The Machiavellian Moment*, Pocock argues that it was because of the political vacuum left by Christianity's affirmation of the supremacy of God's kingdom over the kingdom of this world that Roman republicanism flowed into the channels that it did. From the thought of Hobbes, however, one cannot draw the conclusion that there is a political vacuum left by Christianity, or that in the Christian commonwealth God is absent in history. Therefore it cannot be claimed that the Roman republican tradition enters with the vacuum left in Christianity's wake, not on theoretical grounds anyway. Christian thought, too, *is political*—or rather, on Hobbes's reading, *temporal.*

63. Christ will come again at the end of history; He is not, as Luther would have it, a figure who can be *for us*, who is transhistorical. See Hobbes, *Leviathan*, Part IV, Ch. 44, p. 451: the "kingdom of God by Christ begineth at the day of judgment." Hobbes would reject Luther's claim that there is an escape from the "unbearable burden of history." See ibid., Part IV, Ch. 46, p. 486, where Hobbes rejects the idea of *Nunc-stans*. While a *Nunc-stans* is not available, however, God's *trace* is present in history. This will become clear when Christ's renewal of the covenant is discussed.

64. See Luther, "Freedom" in *Works*, vol. 31, p. 357: "all sin is swallowed up by the righteousness of Christ." What Augustine says of God—by yielding to You, "my mind was free from the gnawing anxieties of ambition and gain" (*Confessions*, Bk. IX, Ch. 1, p. 181)—Hobbes would say of the Sovereign.

65. True, Hobbes does suggest that "there [should] be laws of honour, and a public rate of worth of such men as . . . deserve well of the commonwealth" (*Leviathan*, Part II,

Ch. 18, p. 139), yet those who hold such titles are, according to Hobbes, "annexed to the sovereignty" (ibid., p. 139). Not as citizens do they receive honors, but as adjuncts to the sovereign.

66. Hobbes does mention that "he that hath strength to protect all, wants not sufficiency to oppress all" (*De Cive*, Ch. VI, p. 181n), but he does not seem to see the Leviathan as much of a threat. For all his somber realism, Hobbes here would have it that the *oaths* the sovereign takes not to violate the laws of nature or God's positive laws would offer "some security for subjects" (ibid., p. 181n; emphasis added). Hobbes notes at the place just cited and in the *Leviathan*, Part II, Ch. 18, p. 141, that the inconveniences incumbent on a political order ruled by a Leviathan are exceeded when the pride of the many is left unchecked. But in the final analysis this Achilles heel of his entire project can only withstand assault if the Leviathan is *unlike* his subjects. See also Hobbes, *Behemoth*, Dialogue 1, pp. 44–45, where the virtues of the subject are contrasted with the virtues of the sovereign. Perhaps on this one point Hobbes would have agreed with Aristotle: the king can be king because "he is self-sufficient and superior to his subjects in all good things" (*Ethics*, Bk. VIII, Ch. 10, 1160b4). Judging from the virtues Hobbes attributes to the sovereign, Aristotle does not seem out of place.

67. Hobbes's picture of the sovereign is to be contrasted, for example, to that portrayed by Richelieu in his *Political Testament* (Madison: University of Wisconsin Press, 1961), compiled at about the same time as the *Leviathan* was written. The *Testament* speaks of a real flesh and blood sovereign, in contrast to what Hobbes offers. This curious lack of personification (as the contemporary mind would understand the term) of the Leviathan is not incidental; it is, in fact, an essential feature of who the sovereign is: a mediary of God—yet different from the Centaur offspring of the union of man and God in the myth of Ixion!

68. Hobbes, *Leviathan*, Part II, Ch. 17, p. 132.

69. Rousseau's admiration of Hobbes stems from Hobbes's efforts to unify sovereignty. Of all the Christian philosophers, Rousseau argues, Hobbes was the only one "who saw clearly both the evil and the remedy" to Christian dualism (*The Social Contract*, Bk. IV, Ch. 8, p. 180).

70. Hence, the ease with which Hobbes proclaims that "covenants exhorted by fear are valid" (*Leviathan*, Part I, Ch. 14, p. 110). Warrender is, I think, incorrect in suggesting that "the principle of keeping covenants has a moral status *because it is natural law*" (Howard Warrender, *The Political Philosophy of Thomas Hobbes* [Oxford: Clarendon Press, 1957], p. 233; emphasis added). His argument that "there is in Hobbes's philosophy a theory of an obligation of the same type, that runs through the whole of his account of man, both apart from and within civil society" (p. 7), and that this theory of obligation is based upon natural law, trivializes Hobbes's reading of Scripture (p. 229). True, "the prior instrument of obligation is natural law which does not fall under covenant" (p. 248), but without covenants based on fear, the legitimate foundation of which is the Mosaic covenant, natural law would not be obeyed. Theologically, the light of reason *dimly* grasps the laws of nature; but God, through his Word, *supplemented* that dim light with a biblical narrative that binds us, that offers a light which sets the conclusions of natural reason on a more secure foundation. Natural law is the purview of reason; the Mosaic covenant is the supplement that assures that the

conclusions of natural reason will be *enforced*. Warrender's theological position, in effect, is that the light of unassisted reason is sufficient unto itself (p. 322). Hobbes makes it quite clear that reason must be supplemented by fear. See Hobbes, *Leviathan*, Part II, Ch. 17, p. 129: there must be a "visible power to keep [men] in awe, and tie them by fear of punishment to the performance of their covenants." What Augustine said of the soul's relationship to God, Hobbes would say of the citizen's relationship to the Leviathan: "you have curbed my pride by teaching me to fear you and you have tamed my neck to your yoke. And now that I bear your yoke, I find its burden light" (*Confessions*, Bk. X, Ch. 36, p. 244).

71. See Hobbes, *Leviathan*, Part I, Ch. 12, p. 88: "the gods were first created by human fear." Luther's would say just the opposite, as his exegesis of Gen. 3:8 makes clear. Adam and Eve are fearful only *after* their errancy from God. "After their conscience had been convicted . . . Adam and Eve lose their confidence in God and are so filled with fear and terror that when they hear a breath or a wind, they immediately think God is approaching to punish them and they hide" ("Lectures on Genesis," in *Works*, vol. 1, p. 170). The effect of errancy *from* God is mistaken by Hobbes as the cause of the search *for* God. Machiavelli, in turn, would be unconcerned with the etiology; the important matter is that *there be* fear of God, for such fear helps to make a republic strong. See *Discourses*, Bk. I, Discourse XI, pp. 139–41.

72. See Hobbes, *Leviathan*, Part III, Ch. 35, pp. 299–300, where, when the people of Israel no longer obeyed their rightful king, they rejected not their king but God (I Samuel 8:7). For Hobbes, obedience to God is closely linked to obedience to the sovereign. See also ibid., Ch. 43, pp. 424–36, where Hobbes discusses obedience to God the Father and faith in God the Son.

73. Contrary to Macpherson, who argues that Hobbesian man is atomistic and unto himself, citizens of which Hobbes speaks must be understood to derive their sociality from the Sovereign, as in Luther. Macpherson's thesis that Hobbes's citizens are self-interested market actors is, I think, incorrect. Macpherson's further claim, consistent with the supposition with which he begins his entire inquiry, is that Hobbes is unable to deduce obligation from his psychology. See Macpherson, *The Political Theory of Possessive Individualism*, pp. 70–106. Hobbes theory of obligation comes from the Bible, not from psychology.

Sabine makes the same error Macpherson does. See George H. Sabine, *A History of Political Theory* (New York: Henry Holt & Co., 1937), p. 467: "since all human behavior is motivated by self-interest, society must be regarded as a means to an end. Hobbes was at once a complete utilitarian and a complete individualist."

Interestingly, the notion that the sovereign provides the ground for secure association among all who are equal under him can be found, in transmuted form, in John Rawls, *A Theory of Justice* (Cambridge: Harvard University Press, 1971), p. 346: "the role of promises is analogous to that which Hobbes attributed to the sovereign. Just as the sovereign maintains and stabilizes the system of social cooperation . . . so men in the absence of coercive arrangements establish and stabilize their private ventures by giving one another their word."

74. Hobbes, *Leviathan*, Part III, Ch. 38, p. 327.

75. Hobbes, *De Cive*, Ch. XVII, p. 334. Until the time of His return Christians must have faith, and by faith Hobbes means only that one believe *"that Jesus is the Christ"* (ibid., Ch. XVIII, p. 377; emphasis in the original). See also Hobbes, *Leviathan*, Part III, Ch. 43, p. 425.

76. See, for example, Hobbes, *Leviathan*, Part III, Ch. 41, p. 353: "the kingdom of Christ is not to begin until the general resurrection."

77. Hobbes, *De Cive*, Ch. XVII, p. 335 (emphasis in original).

78. Hobbes, *De Cive*, Ch. XVII, p. 333.

79. Hobbes, *De Cive*, Ch. XVII, p. 338.

80. Hobbes, *Leviathan*, Part III, Ch. 38, p. 329.

81. Hobbes, *Leviathan*, Part III, Ch. 38, p. 328. In Hobbes's work it is difficult to overlook his attempt to "despiritualize" Christianity. Consider, for example, his understanding of inspiration. According to Hobbes, inspiration is to be taken literally; that is, "God inspire[s] into man the breath of life" (*Leviathan*, Part III, Ch. 34, p. 295). In this regard see Augustine, *City of God*, Bk. XIII, Ch. 24, pp. 540–46, for an effort to clear up the meaning of God's inspiration into Adam. The Greek Scriptures, he notes, contain two words for inspiration: *pneuma*, inspiration in the metaphorical sense, and *pnoê*, inspiration in the literal sense. Cf. Nietzsche, *Genealogy*, First Essay, §7, pp. 31–32, on how unsymbolic, how unmetaphorical, the noble man is.

Of the rhetorical import of this emphasis upon the body see David Johnston, "Hobbes's Mortalism," *History of Political Thought* 10, no. 4 (1989), pp. 647–63. Johnston notes that Hobbes intended "to eliminate the threat posed to civil authority by divine sanctions by crippling the hopes and fears associated with these sanctions at their source" (p. 666). Johnston recognizes Hobbes's opposition to priestcraft, but would make him an Erastian.

82. John 5:46–47.

83. Hobbes, *Leviathan*, Part III, Ch. 41, p. 352. Hobbes speaks of redeemer, king, and teacher at this place and of renewer of the covenant elsewhere.

84. Hobbes, *Leviathan*, Part III, Ch. 41, p. 354.

85. Hobbes, *Leviathan*, Part III, Ch. 38, p. 338. Cf. Nietzsche, *Genealogy*, Second Essay, §§21–22, pp. 91–93.

86. Hobbes, *Leviathan*, Part III, Ch. 41, p. 357; Ch. 42, p. 368. In this second passage Hobbes cites Acts 2:38: "Then Peter said to them, Repent, and be baptized every one of you in the name of Jesus Christ for the remission of sins, and ye shall receive the gift of the Holy Ghost."

87. Hobbes, *Leviathan*, Part III, Ch. 42, p. 362. Cf. Hegel, *Philosophy of History*, Part III, Sec. III, Ch. II, p. 325: "considered only in respect to his talents character and morality—as a Teacher and so forth—we place him in the same category with Socrates and others, though his morality may be ranked higher." Hegel's Christ, unlike Hobbes's, was Spirit made flesh; despiritualizing Him betrays a failure to grasp the Spirit—which only Spirit can do (ibid., p. 326).

88. Hobbes, *Leviathan*, Part III, Ch. 42, pp. 361–62. Locke would later make a variant of this same argument about coercion and religious conviction, though he would also add that the right of interpretation belongs to each person, not to the sovereign.

89. Hobbes, *Leviathan*, Part III, Ch. 43, p. 429 (emphasis in original). The whole of Chapter 43, on obedience and faith, deserves careful study; it demonstrates Hobbes's facility with this Reformation question of the relationship between obedience and faith, between the claims of the Old Testament and the claims of the New.

90. See Hobbes, *De Cive*, Ch. XVII, p. 336: "that the discerning of right [and wrong] was not committed to Christ in this world, neither among the faithful nor among the infidels, is apparent in this; that that right without all controversy belongs to princes, as long as it is not by God himself derogated from their authority." See also ibid., Ch. XVII, pp. 344–45, where Hobbes says that Christ did not come "into the world to teach *logic*. It remains therefore that the judges of . . . controversies, be the same with those whom God by nature had instituted before, namely, those who in each city are constituted by the sovereign" (emphasis in original).

91. Hobbes, *Leviathan*, Part I, Ch. 13, p. 100.

92. Hobbes, *Leviathan*, Part I, Ch. 13, p. 100.

93. Hobbes, *Leviathan*, Part III, Ch. 35, p. 297.

94. Hobbes, *De Cive*, Ch. XVI, p. 315.

95. Hobbes, *Leviathan*, Part III, Ch. 35, p. 302.

96. The importance of God's speech cannot be underestimated in Hobbes. Speech from God, say, to Abraham (*Leviathan*, Part III, Ch. 35, p. 297; Genesis 27:7, 8) or to Moses (*Leviathan*, Part III, Ch. 35, p. 298; Exodus 19:5), is the necessary but not sufficient condition for the right of kingdom to be exercised. The additional factor needed is consent and obedience by a particular people (*Leviathan*, Part III, Ch. 35, p. 299), by which Hobbes means that the people agree to let one person mediate between them and God. He is perhaps thinking of Exodus 32:26, where the sons of Levi consent to obey Moses, God's mediary, and do not themselves deign to speak *for* or *of* God. The precedent for this demeanor is drawn from Exodus 20:19, where the people say to Moses, "*speak now to us, and we will hear thee, but let not God speak to us lest we die*" (*Leviathan*, Part III, Ch. 42, p. 378, emphasis in the original). In *De Cive*, Ch. XVI, p. 319, Hobbes cites Exodus 19:24, 25 for much the same thought. In his words, private men "were prohibited with most heavy threats, *to hear God speak*, otherwise than by means of Moses" (emphasis in original). It is not far from this thought to the idea that the individual cannot be judge for himself in matters of good and evil (*De Cive*, Ch. XII, p. 244, *passim*). A sovereign, an intermediary, is necessary. See, for example, Hobbes's statement that "the will of God is not known except through the state," in *On Man*, in *Man and Citizen*, trans. Bernard Gert (Gloucester, MA: Humanities Press, 1978), Ch. XV, p. 85. (Would Hegel have differed?) The myth of Ixion, invoked by Hobbes at the outset of *De Cive*, is also consonant with this idea. For Hobbes, it is by virtue of God's speech that humankind's "own weak reason" receives its corrective (*Leviathan*, Part III, Ch. 40, p. 349). While Locke would later make this same argument, his focus was on Christ's clarification of the truth of Adam, not Christ's renewal of the truth of Moses. These are two different dialectics.

97. Hobbes, *De Cive*, Ch. XVI, p. 310.

98. The kingdom is *there* with Abraham, but it is not yet *called* a kingdom until Moses. See Hobbes, *Leviathan*, Part III, Ch. 35, p. 298.

99. The sign of circumcision was, in Hobbes's view, a way by which "Abraham and his seed should *retain the memory* of [their] covenant" with God (*De Cive*, Ch. XVI, p. 311; emphasis added). Luther, on the other hand, saw it as a challenge to reason—which faith cannot but do. See Gerrish, *Grace and Reason*, p. 19: "circumcision made the Jews a laughing-stock, so utterly pointless did the practice seem. Luther replies that the point of circumcision is precisely to offend reason, to force it to surrender its vanity. If God had given a token which reason could approve, then man's arrogance would have remained." Hobbes is concerned with "retaining the memory" of the covenant because, in his view, the crucial problem is that subjects always seem to *forget* their obligation to obey their sovereign. Luther, in turn, thought that the crucial problem was that reason's effort to grasp the message of Christianity—and no doubt he had in mind here the Roman Church—could only corrupt that message.

100. Gen. 22:16–18.

101. Gen. 26:3–4.

102. Gen. 28:13–14.

103. Exodus 3:6 and 19:5–6. See Hobbes, *De Cive*, Ch. XVI, p. 314, and *Leviathan*, Part III, Ch. 40, p. 343, for his discussion of Abraham, Isaac, Jacob, and Moses.

104. Hobbes, *De Cive*, Ch. XVI, pp. 321–22.

105. Hobbes, *De Cive*, Ch. XVI, p. 323.

106. Hobbes, *Leviathan*, Part III, Ch. 40, p. 348. Hobbes's citation, quoted in part, is from 1 Samuel 3:5. The covenant ends with the election of Saul. See ibid., Ch. 41, p. 354. The difference between Hobbes and Augustine is nowhere made more clear than in their readings of Saul. See Augustine, *City of God*, Bk. XVII, Ch. 7, p. 731: the Greek version of 1 Samuel 15:23–29 reads: "'The Lord has torn the kingdom *from* Israel, out of your hand.' The purpose of this reading is to make it plain that 'out of your hand' means the same as 'from Israel.' Thus the man Saul figuratively personified Israel, the people which was to lose its kingdom when Christ Jesus our Lord should take the kingship under the new covenant, a spiritual instead of physical kingship." Hobbes insisted that the covenant lost with Saul was renewed through Christ; Augustine insisted that Christ brought about a *new*, spiritual, kingdom.

107. Hobbes, *Leviathan*, Part III, Ch. 40, p. 348. Hobbes accuses the subjects of Charles I of, in effect, being Israelites, of no longer knowing why they owed obedience to the king, in *Behemoth*, Dialogue 1, p. 4. This is the last of seven causes contributing to the English Civil War.

108. Hobbes, *Leviathan*, Part III, Ch. 40, p. 351.

109. In order for Christians to know the reason why they must obey the sovereign they must be convinced that Jesus did renew the covenant, that is, that He was the Son of God, and that what He said about the necessity of obeying the sovereign had divine authority. The sovereign, again, must have divine authority to rule. In Hobbes's words, "the king, and every other sovereign, executeth his office of supreme pastor by immediate authority from God, that is to say in *God's right* or *jure divino*" (Leviathan, Part III, Ch. 42, p. 395; emphasis in original). Locke would later argue that natural reason could

know the foundation of morality and duty without the need of a sovereign authority *after Christ first came.* Hobbes claims that Christ's authority merely convinces human beings of the necessity of obeying the sovereign, of submitting to his authority.

110. Hobbes, *Leviathan,* Part III, Ch. 41, p. 355 (emphasis in original).

111. Matt. 3:1.

112. Hobbes, *Leviathan,* Part III, Ch. 41, pp. 356–57 (emphasis in original).

113. See Hobbes, *De Cive,* Ch. XVII, p. 368: "for a *Church* and a *Christian city* is but one thing" (emphasis in original). Also see ibid., Ch. XVII, p. 352: "we must therefore grant to the definition of a Church . . . not only the possibility of assembling, but also of doing it lawfully."

114. Acts 2:38.

115. Hobbes, *Leviathan,* Part III, Ch. 42, pp. 374–75.

116. Hobbes, *Leviathan,* Part III, Ch. 42, p. 380 (emphasis in original).

117. See Hobbes, *Leviathan,* Part III, Ch. 42, pp. 359–61. Here Hobbes extends the relationship between Christ and Moses to include the apostles as well. Moses represents the Father, Christ represents the Son, and the apostles represent the Holy Ghost. See also Hobbes, *On Man,* Ch. XV, p. 85, where the trinity is understood in terms of the *personations* of God—a position consistent with Hobbes's view that God requires a mediator between Himself and humankind.

Locke, too, would subsequently argue that the Holy Ghost was necessary to carry forward the work of the apostles. For Locke, however, the reason is not that they lacked authority, but rather that they could not yet *bear the truth* of Christ's kingdom. Locke's understanding of Christ is that He unconcealed the foundation of reason to those who were initially unprepared to see it. The Holy Ghost *completes the unconcealment* begun with Christ. For Hobbes, the Holy Ghost convinces hearers of the Gospel of its *authoritativeness* prior to the time when there was an authoritative sovereign who could interpret for the commonwealth.

118. Cf. Augustine, *City of God,* Bk. V, Ch. 26, pp. 220–21.

119. Hobbes, *Leviathan,* Part IV, Ch. 47, pp. 498–99. Hobbes devotes considerable energy to refuting a particular work by Cardinal Bellarmine (*De Summo Pontifice*) which purports to show that the Roman Church is the wellspring of spiritual authority and that such authority is justified by virtue of the supersession of the New Testament over the Old. See ibid., Part III, Ch. 42, pp. 399–423.

120. Hobbes, *Leviathan,* Part IV, Ch. 47, p. 499.

121. In light of this culmination in the Anglican commonwealth, Voegelin's claim that Hobbes's "attempt at freezing history into an everlasting constitution is an instance of the general class of Gnostic attempts at freezing history into an everlasting final realm on this earth" (Voegelin, *The New Science of Politics,* pp. 160–61) must be considered. Hobbes is quite clear that the Redemption is the real and final act of fulfillment, which he does not anticipate shortly. God's *trace* is present in the person of the sovereign, to be sure; but the disposition of the entire scheme is one of a patient-waiting-for the everlasting final realm. More on the mark is Voegelin's observation that Hobbes "denied the existence of a tension between the truth of the soul and the truth of society" (ibid.,

pp. 159–60). If this is transposed to read that Hobbes denied the conflict between the "City of God" and the "City of Man," it would clearly be true.

122. Hobbes, *Leviathan*, Part III, Ch. 42, p. 376. We can only speculate as to whether Hobbes deliberately intended with this thought to remind us of Plato's famous formulation: "Unless either philosophers become kings . . . or those who are now called kings and rulers come to be sufficiently inspired with a genuine desire for wisdom . . . there can be no rest from troubles . . ." (*Republic*, Bk. V, 473d). Although Hobbes thought that Plato was "the best philosopher of the Greeks" (*Leviathan*, Part IV, Ch. 46, p. 481), in part, perhaps, because of Plato's insistence that sovereignty be unified, the differences are massive—not the least of which is the importance of biblical history to Reformation political theory.

123. A faction, for Hobbes, is defined as "a city within a city." See *De Cive*, Ch. XIII, p. 266. Rousseau, too, was deeply concerned with faction; for both, acting against the laws of society rendered the offender an alien to the city. In Rousseau's case, this was punishable by death. See Rousseau, *The Social Contract*, Bk. II, Ch. 5, p. 79: "by violating [a country's] laws, he ceases to be a member of it; indeed he makes war against it." The right of the community to "throw [the offender] back again into the savage and outlaw state against which he has hitherto been protected" (*Genealogy*, Second Essay, §9, p. 71) takes on a different meaning for Nietzsche: the lesson here is the origin of debt and guilty conscience. Tocqueville's assessment is perhaps the most chilling of all. Modern tyranny "leaves the body alone and goes straight for the soul. The master no longer says: 'Think like me or you will die.' He does say: 'You are free not to think as I do; you can keep your life and property and all; but from this day you are a stranger among us'" (Tocqueville, *Democracy in America*, vol. I, Part II, Ch. 7, p. 255).

124. Hobbes, *De Cive*, Ch. XII, p. 250.

125. Hobbes, *De Cive*, Ch. XIII, p. 259.

126. Hobbes, *De Cive*, Ch. VI, p. 175. This is also Hobbes's fifth Law of Nature. See Hobbes, *Leviathan*, Part I, Ch. 15, p. 118.

127. Hobbes, *De Cive*, Ch. XI, p. 240.

128. Hobbes, *De Cive*, Ch. XVII, p. 343.

129. Hobbes, *De Cive*, Ch. XVII, p. 349.

130. Hobbes, *De Cive*, Ch. XVII, pp. 349–50. Michael Polanyi has claimed, like Hobbes, that interpretation is dependent on authority, though the authority with which Polanyi is concerned is the scientist's, not the sovereign's. According to Hobbes, the interpretation of scientific truth derives from the proposition itself—which the unaided individual can judge. Religious truth, in turn, derives from the authority of the person propounding it (*De Cive*, Ch. XVIII, pp. 373–75). This, in conjunction with his idea that "the want of science disposes men to rely on the authority of others" (*Leviathan*, Part I, Ch. 12, p. 93), led Hobbes to the belief that science was wholly beneficent and could not serve sinister ambitions (*Behemoth*, Dialogue 2, p. 96). Polanyi's position is that this tidy distinction breaks down, for as scientific truth becomes ever more sophisticated, individuals must undergo an extended period of training in which they must trust in the authority of the person teaching them before they can learn to interpret scientific findings correctly. In Polanyi's view, scientific truth comes increasingly to resemble religious truth, not in terms of its content, but in terms of the relationship between interpretation

and authority. See Michael Polanyi and Harry Prosch, *Meaning* (Chicago: University of Chicago Press, 1975), pp. 182–97.

Musing about the future of revolutions, Tocqueville thought they would become increasingly rare precisely because of this relationship between authority and interpretation. "As men grow more like each other . . . it becomes harder for any innovator whosoever to gain and maintain great influence over the mind of a nation. . . . For, taking a general view of world history, one finds that it is less the force of the argument than the authority of a name which has brought about great and rapid changes in accepted ideas" (*Democracy in America*, vol. II, Part III, Ch. 21, p. 641).

131. Hobbes, *Leviathan*, Part III, Ch. 40, p. 346. For Hobbes, representation must be understood to extend in two different directions: on the one hand the sovereign represents God to the people and on the other the sovereign represents the people. Hobbes makes mention of both of these kinds of representation in the *Leviathan*, Part I, Ch. 18, pp. 134–35. To be sure, this twofold scheme in which the citizen is represented yet must accede to the sovereign's laws and interpretation does not accord with contemporary and commonsense view of representation. See, for example, Hanna Fenichel Pitkin, *The Concept of Representation* (Berkeley: University of California Press, 1972), p. 37: "when we see the final result of the definition [of representation] embodied in a Hobbesian political system with an absolute sovereign, we feel that something has gone wrong, that representation has somehow disappeared while our backs were turned." The difficulty of Hobbes's concept of representation for the contemporary mind is that it is biblical and, for that reason, somewhat strange. Citizens are represented by the Leviathan in the way God's chosen people were represented by Moses.

132. Hobbes, *Leviathan*, Part III, Ch. 38, pp. 335–36; see also ibid., Ch. 41, p. 353.

133. Hobbes, *Leviathan*, Part III, Ch. 32, p. 275. For a different interpretation see David Johnston, *The Rhetoric of the Leviathan* (Princeton: Princeton University Press, 1986), p. 184, for the argument that Hobbes's subordination of prophecy was intended "to transform men and women into the rational and predictable beings they would have to be before [Hobbes's] vision of political society could ever be realized." Hobbes subordinates prophecy, however, because this is not the age of the prophet. In this age, God "speaks" through the Leviathan.

134. See Hobbes, *Leviathan*, Part I, Ch. 16, p. 127: "the king of any country is the *public* person, or representative of all his subjects" (emphasis in original). And at the same place, "a multitude of men, are made *one* person, when they are by one man, or one person represented . . . for it is the *unity* of the representer, not the *unity* of the represented, that maketh the person *one*" (emphasis in original).

Oakeshott is, I think, incorrect in finding in Hobbes's political thought a citizen whose identity is sacrosanct. See Oakeshott, *Rationalism in Politics*, p. 251: "Hobbes's starting point . . . was with unique *human* individuality; and, as he understood it, his first business was to rationalize *this* individuality by displaying its 'cause', its components and its structure." The only identity that matters for Hobbes, however, is the sovereign's, not the individual's. Oakeshott's attempt to find a theory of obligation in the "morality of the individual" (p. 250) is flawed, therefore, from the outset.

135. The full force of this point is shown in Hobbes's treatment of the Scriptural claim that we must obey God above other men. If Christ or His prophets were here, he

claims, we could simply listen to them speak; but since we have only Scripture—which does not speak of its own accord—we must listen to it speak through the sovereign. It is God who speaks through such interpretation; hence, in obeying the sovereign we obey God. See Hobbes, *De Cive*, Ch. XVIII, p. 370.

136. Hobbes, *Leviathan*, Part III, Ch. 42, p. 365.

137. Hobbes, *De Cive*, Ch. XII, p. 244 (emphasis in original). See also ibid., Ch. XII, p. 249; and Hobbes, *Behemoth*, Dialogue 3, p. 144: "common people know nothing of right and wrong by their own meditation; they must therefore be taught the grounds of their duty, and the reasons why calamities ever follow disobedience to their lawful sovereign."

138. Matt. 5:17.

139. Hobbes, *Leviathan*, Part III, Ch. 43, p. 427.

140. See Luther, "Temporal Authority," in *Works*, vol. 45, p. 108.

141. Cf. Tocqueville, *Democracy in America*, vol. II, Part III, Ch. 19, p. 632, where pride may be the necessary palliative in ages when the spirit of equality has finally won! Pride and ambition are dangers, Tocqueville suggests, only in moments of transition from an aristocratic age to a democratic age. See ibid., p. 628.

142. Gen. 32:22: "thou knowest the people [Moses], they *are set* on mischief." This is the theological equivalent of Hobbes's assertion that our natural passions carry us "to partiality, pride, revenge and the like" (*Leviathan*, Part II, Ch. 17, p. 129). Without a sovereign human beings become self-enclosed and worship themselves; without "Moses" the natural passions do not receive their corrective.

143. Gen. 32:26: "Then Moses stood in the gate of the camp, and said, Who *is* on the LORD'S side? *Let him come* unto me. And all the sons of Levi gathered themselves together unto him."

144. See Joel Schwartz, "Hobbes and the Two Kingdoms of God," *Polity* 18, no. 1 (1985), pp. 7–24, for the claim that Hobbes recognized only two kingdoms, the Jewish kingdom in the distant past and the Christian kingdom to come in the distant future (upon Christ's second coming). This view fails to account for the *renewed* Mosaic covenant made possible by Christ's first coming.

145. For Hobbes, the ground of unity and of the equality of all is to be found in the *will of one*; for Locke the ground is to be found in the *reason of all*. See Locke, *Second Treatise*, Ch. II, §7, p. 271.

146. Luther, "Freedom," in *Works*, vol. 31, p. 363.

147. What Luther said of Moses he might well have said about the Leviathan: "we need quite another Mediator than Moses or the Law" in order to be justified ("Lectures on Galatians," in *Works*, vol. 26, p. 139).

148. John 6:32.

149. Hobbes, *Behemoth*, Dialogue I, p. 46. See also ibid., pp. 51–52.

CHAPTER THREE

1. A significant theoretical difference between Luther and Locke lies in the latter's insistence that morality and virtue fall within the spiritual realm. Luther, recall, insisted

that Christian righteousness was not to be confused with morality and virtue. The thrust of Locke's theological position is that moral and virtuous acts are not performed merely to escape the "terrors of conscience," as Luther would have it. Because virtue and morality are known by reason—itself granted by God and further illuminated by Christ—they fall within the spiritual realm.

2. Locke's *First Treatise* is devoted to refuting Filmer's claim that God did, in fact, establish a legitimate chain of rulers which began with Adam. Filmer's task is to establish continuity from the time of Adam to the present day. (Hobbes, recall, attempts something of the same project, though his point of departure is the covenant established between God and Moses *to which the people acceded*. Hobbes's chain of rulership, then, is based more obviously upon human agency and less obviously upon passive obedience to hereditary kings.) Locke, like Filmer, returns to God's original grant to Adam to find the foundation of government. Locke's claim, however (*contra* Filmer), is that *difference develops out of* the initial grant, but is not established there at the outset.

3. Locke, *Reasonableness*, §212, p. 149, *passim*.

4. John Locke, "A Letter Concerning Toleration" (Indianapolis: Bobbs-Merrill, 1955), p. 18.

5. Locke's call for toleration is based on the belief that reason must not be constrained by external power and that with the light of reason the foundation of Christian morality and duty can come to be known. For a contrary argument see Jeremy Waldron, "Locke: Toleration and the Rationality of Persecution," in *Justifying Toleration*, ed. Susan Mendus (Cambridge: Cambridge University Press, 1988), pp. 61–86. Toleration *is* a matter of self-interest, in Locke, but in the broadest possible sense of the word: because the self is interested in salvation, the truth of Christianity (which countenances toleration) ought to be heeded. Toleration cannot be justified by *political* means alone! Later, in Mill's "On Liberty," where toleration is defended on the basis of a dialogical theory of truth (which requires *difference* for society to progress) there is a movement away from biblical justifications of toleration; yet even here—where the horizon of history is unequivocally not constituted by the events of errancy, concealment, and atonement—the Christian notion of *conscience* is the sacred foundation upon which his entire edifice rests. Toleration *is* based on self-interest in Mill, but selves are not merely prudent calculators or rational optimizers; they are beings with conscience who are perpetually *called* beyond the native disposition of human beings to be herd animals!

6. For Luther, however, the power found in the carnal realm must be distinguished from the *powerlessness* of the spiritual realm. Powerlessness (as a theological concept) is not found in Locke's thought.

7. Locke, "Letter," p. 19.

8. Locke, "Letter," p. 42. See also Hobbes's argument against the Papists in *Behemoth*, Dialogue 1, p. 5.

9. This, in effect, is the position Hobbes takes also, though Hobbes claims that this is the case *after* Christ's first coming as well. The Leviathan, like Moses before him, is granted the right to interpret because reason remains unilluminated by God; it tends to go astray, to get caught up in itself. See Hobbes, *Leviathan*, Part I, Ch. 12, pp. 87–97, where, because reason cannot know first principles (God), it often falls into superstition. See also Hobbes's reference to the myth of Ixion in *De Cive*, Preface, pp. 97–98. Here

Ixion is not allowed to sit at Jupiter's table because the result is always "contention and bloodshed."

10. Locke, "Letter," p. 43.

11. Locke, "Letter," p. 13.

12. See Locke, *Reasonableness*, §240, p. 168: yet the revelation of the Old Testament "was shut up in a little corner of the world. . . . But our Savior, when he came, *threw down this wall of partition*" (emphasis in original).

Compare this to Hegel, for whom "to the [obedience to the moral law] alone, [and] not to the descent from Abraham, did Jesus ascribe value in the views of God" (Hegel, *Positivity of Christian Religion*, Part I, §3, p. 70). Both Locke and Hegel are here attempting to specify the way in which the particular gives way to the universal—or from another vantage point, how the universal *fulfills* the particular.

Luther, too, was concerned about the particularity of Moses and his bearing upon the Christ event which supersedes it. See Martin Luther, "How Christians Should Regard Moses," *Luther's Works*, vol. 35, pp. 164–65: "Moses was an intermediary solely for the Jewish people. It was to them that he gave the law. . . . Moses is dead. His rule ended when Christ came."

13. Contrast this to Luther, for whom not freedom *from* power but rather powerlessness gives rise to Christian righteousness: a power over all things. For Locke, the withdrawal of political power from the spiritual realm is the occasion for a movement toward universality; power over the spiritual realm serves to maintain religious heterodoxy, which is politically disruptive.

14. Note that *The Reasonableness of Christianity* was written six years *after* the "Letter" (in 1695), and that while this conviction is there in the *Reasonableness*, it is merely consistent with the sentiment expressed in the "Letter." In the "Letter," however, the justification for tolerance is not expressed in terms of the unconcealment of reason. Perhaps Locke was working toward that notion in the "Letter" and fully articulated it later, in the *Reasonableness*.

But see J. W. Gough, *John Locke's Political Philosophy* (Oxford: Clarendon Press, 1950), p. 175, for the claim that Locke's thoughts on toleration had already coalesced in 1659. Regarding Gough's more general claim that "the essential question [of Locke's toleration] is a political one" (p. 176), I argue that Locke's doctrine of toleration is essentially theological.

15. Hobbes, of course, argues that the task of the sovereign is precisely that: to exercise political power in matters of doctrinal interpretation (though not, he claims, in matters of faith).

This view accords more or less with that of Spinoza, who claims that the frequent disputes in Christian states stem from the separation of ecclesiastical and political orders. See Benedict de Spinoza, *Theologico-Political Treatise* (New York: Dover Publications, 1951), Ch. XIX, pp. 254–55: "the Christian religion was not taught at first by kings, but by private persons, who, against the wishes of those in power . . . were for a long time accustomed to hold meetings in secret churches. . . . [A separation between ecclesiastical and political power was later further effected by the] multiplication of dogmas of religion to such an extent . . . that their chief interpreter was bound . . . to have leisure for a host of idle speculations: conditions which could only be fulfilled by a private individual with much time on his hands." Locke would have agreed with Spinoza (and with Hobbes) on the matter of the unity of ecclesiastical and political power, *had not Christ come into the world and separated the two realms.* Christ has no significant place in Spinoza's *Treatise;* in his view, the New Dispensation and Old teach the same lesson: the necessity of *obeying* God. See, for example, Spinoza, ibid., Ch. XIV, p. 183, where both Moses and the New Testament enjoin obedience.

16. Locke, "Letter," p. 54.

17. Locke, "Letter," p. 57. Cf. John Locke, *The First Tract on Government,* in *Two Tracts of Government,* ed. Philip Abrams (Cambridge: Cambridge University Press, 1967), p. 160: "there hath been no design so wicked which hath worn the vizor of religion, nor rebellion which hath not been so kind to itself as to assure the specious name of reformation, proclaiming a design either to supply the defects or correct the errors of religion, that none ever went about to ruin the *state* but with pretense to build the *temple*" (emphasis in original). An abiding concern in the *First Tract* is the way in which religion may be used to subvert politics; the abiding concern of the "Letter" is the way in which politics may be used to subvert religion. While Locke's thinking did change between the two works with respect to how the two may be separated, these different ways of addressing the problem all suppose that only a certain *kind* of Christian can see a clear distinction between external modes of worship and saving faith. The *understanding* of this distinction is logically prior to changing institutional arrangements meant to comport with it.

18. Recall Luther's observation that when the two worlds, spiritual and carnal, are confused "the door is opened for every kind of rascality, for the world as a whole cannot receive or comprehend it" (Luther, "Temporal Authority," *Works,* vol. 45, p. 92). Locke echoes this view: It is "out of a fond conceit of themselves" that human beings wish to intercede in the spiritual affairs of others. Doing so dishonors God because it supposes that His ways are easily discernible by beings whose judgment is corrupted by the flesh. It is these who believe that "they ought to vindicate the cause of God with swords in their hands" (Locke, *First Tract,* p. 160). Here, the state is given the right to intercede in matters of indifference. This offers a check upon the human *tendency* to confuse what is essential and what is accidental in matters of faith.

19. Locke, "Letter," p. 59.

20. Locke is really concerned with two kinds of difference that make a difference: (1) heterodoxy and (2) differences among different religions. Regarding this second type, Locke argues that persons of different religious orientation cannot be heterodox to each other. Heterodoxy only occurs within a religious community where "the rule of faith and worship are of the same religion" ("Letter," p. 59). This latter type of difference is so foreign as to be no threat to civil peace at all. Difference of this sort, Locke seems to suggest, does not occur within one state and therefore is not problematic, though it can be a source of contention between states. See I Cor. 5:12: "For what have I to do to judge them also that are without? Do not ye judge them that are within?"

21. As already pointed out, toleration, for Locke, is necessary because of the truth of Christianity. It should not be surprising, therefore, for him to say: "those are not to be tolerated who deny the being of God. Promises, covenants, and oaths, which are the bonds of human society, can have no hold on the atheist. The taking away of God, though but even in thought, dissolves all" ("Letter," p. 52).

22. See Hobbes, *Behemoth*, Dialogue 1, p. 3. In his view, not having an authorized interpreter produced a heteronomy that contributed to the English Civil War.

23. John Locke, *An Essay Concerning Human Understanding*, Bk. I, Ch. 1, §5, p. 45: human beings "have light enough to lead them to the knowledge of their Maker, and the sight of their duties"; and ibid., Bk. I, Ch. XIX, §21, p. 698: "*Revelation* is natural *Reason* enlarged by a new set of Discoveries communicated by GOD immediately" (emphasis in original).

24. Only the last four of the fifty pages of the "Letter" are concerned with internally generated difference. In Revelation 22:18, 19 John enjoins everyone "that heareth the words of the prophecy of this book" neither to add to nor subtract from it.

25. Locke, "Letter," p. 62. In Locke's definition, a heretic or schismatic is a person who separates from or adds to that content.

26. For Luther, the content of the Scripture is revealed in the abyss of powerlessness where the Gospel is grasped "with eyes other than those reason uses, that is, with spiritual eyes" (Luther, "Lectures on Galatians," *Works*, vol. 27, p. 86). In the abyss of powerlessness the light of the Gospel is revealed, to borrow Locke's language. For Locke, because Christ supplied the light, human beings can with their reason discover the content "manifestly contained" in the Gospel. The abyss of powerlessness (and the will necessary to encounter it) do not occasion the light that illuminates. It is simply there to be seen. There is an understandable content; though some may "separate from" or "add on to" it, the content remains there to be seen by all who possess the faculty of reason. Luther, in other words, finds the *will* the key to the meaning of the Gospel, while Locke finds the key in the faculty of *reason*.

27. Where, for Locke, Christ brought into the world the light and foundation of Christian duty, for Hobbes, Christ renewed the covenant with God, which renewal grants the sovereign the authority to interpret the Gospel. In Locke's case, the light of revelation shines brightly enough (now) for all to interpret (along the same lines because Christ revealed the necessary foundation). In Hobbes's case, Christ was not the revealer, but the renewer; reason *remains* in the dark, as it were, after Christ as well as before His first coming.

28. Locke, "Letter," p. 34.

29. Locke, "Letter," p. 35.

30. For this reason church affiliation must be completely voluntary; see "Letter," pp. 20–26. All must be free to choose the church in which they worship, according to their own conviction.

Much has been made of Locke's voluntarism. Indeed, it seems consistent with the supposed atomism of the liberal soul. Locke's voluntarism, however, must be seen in terms of his argument about the dialectic of biblical history and not in terms of the analytical distinction between atomistic and socially constituted human beings, a distinction that plagues efforts to understand both Locke and Hobbes.

31. Locke's *political* vision, then, rests first and foremost on Adam and not on Christ. Notably, he derives the equality of all human beings from the truth about Adam not Christ, unlike Luther. In Luther's view, Christ levels all differences by virtue of the interiority of faith that is accessible to all. Luther's equality derives from this. Hobbes, in turn, wishes to establish the equality of all under the sovereign, though he concedes that

this would be something of a noble lie. For Hobbes, Adam is significant only with respect to the religious problem of loss of eternal life, to which Christ offers a solution. No positive "political" conclusions follow from the truth of Adam, for Hobbes.

Regarding the centrality of Adam in Locke's thought, I am in substantial agreement with James Tully, A Discourse on Property (Cambridge: Cambridge University Press, 1980). Tully is, I think, correct in seeing in Adam the basis of Locke's epistemological theory, doctrine of property, and notion of the responsibility of government. In this chapter I extend the analysis further and consider Locke's understanding of Christ's fulfillment of Adam. Saint Paul's writings, in which is found the Adamic myth, receive a considerable treatment by Locke. See John Locke, A Paraphrase and Notes on the Epistles of St. Paul, ed. Arthur Wainwright (Oxford: Oxford University Press, 1988), 2 vols. Political theorists have ignored this substantial work.

It should not be forgotten that Luther, too, devoted considerable exegetical effort to the works of Saint Paul. See Luther, "Lectures on Galatians," Works, vol. 26, p. 232: "let us make the effort to read Paul often and with great diligence."

32. In the editor's introduction to the "Letter," Romanell erroneously claims that "Filmer is a blind for Hobbes in the First Treatise" (see "Letter," p. 10). Sabine makes the same claim. See Sabine, A History of Political Theory, p. 524, passim.

33. John Locke, First Treatise of Government, in Two Treatises of Government, ed. Peter Laslett (Cambridge: Cambridge University Press, 1988), Ch. IV, §29, p. 161 (emphasis in original).

34. Locke, First Treatise, Ch. IX, §92, p. 209. Augustine has a different view. See Confessions, Bk. XIII, Ch. 23, p. 332: "it is man's power to judge all things that is symbolized by his rule over the fishes in the sea, and all that flies through the air, and the cattle, and the whole earth and all creeping things that move on earth." Dominion means the possession of spiritual gifts which differentiate human beings from the created world. There is no theory of property deriving from Augustine's reading of Genesis; his intention, like Luther's, was to show how the Old already prefigured the New, how even in the creation of the world the spiritual domain which supersedes it is already there.

35. Locke, Second Treatise, Ch. I, §1, p. 267 (emphasis in original).

36. See Sir Robert Filmer, Patriarcha, in Patriarcha and Other Writings, ed. Johann P. Sommerville (Cambridge: Cambridge University Press, 1991), Ch. 1 §§3–4, pp. 6–7. Filmer's argument there is with Bellarmine. They disagree not about whether Adam was one human being, but rather about the implications of that fact. Locke, as I have said, argues that Adam is humankind and so supersedes the terms of Bellarmine and Filmer's argument.

37. The fence metaphor is not to be overlooked in Locke; it is a border around a self that should not be violated because the self enclosed has a sanctity about it.

The fence metaphor appears in Montesquieu as well. See, for example, Montesquieu, Spirit of the Laws, Bk. XII, Ch. 2, p. 184, where, with respect to false witness, "when the subject has no fence to secure his innocence, he has none for his liberty"; Bk. XV, Ch. 12, p. 243, where the danger of having too many slaves within one political community is that they "see the security of others fenced by laws," but are themselves "without any protection"; and his disquieting fascination with the unfenced peoples of the North (notably the Tartars) who possess the kind of virtuous frugality and self-renunciation which enables them to conquer the fenced peoples—the more servile, voluptuous, cultivators—of the southern regions below them (Bks. XVII, XVIII, *passim*). For Montesquieu, fences enclose space, order it, and render it possible to establish the speed and direction of the motions most felicitous to the preservation of that space. With Locke, however, the fence around man was established *ab origine*, by God; and it is government's duty to protect against incursions.

It is ironic that Tocqueville would later worry that America, a land so imbued with the spirit of Locke, would "enclose thought within a formidable fence" (*Democracy in America*, vol. I, Part II, Ch. 8, p. 255), and so make free thinking impossible here.

38. Locke, *Second Treatise*, Ch. V, §35, p. 292 (emphasis in original). Quentin Skinner sees in Locke's claim that the right of property derives from God an answer to the dilemma that emerged in the post-Lutheran Thomistic tradition. Briefly, there was a confusion within that tradition over the relationship between the laws of nature, the laws of nations, and positive human laws. The clarifications tended to identify the law of nations as positive human laws. This, of course, undermined the justification for property—a thought not lost on the Levelers. Locke, Skinner claims, rejustifies property by claiming that it is a right of nature rather than by virtue of a mere positive human law. See Skinner, *The Foundations of Modern Political Thought*, vol. 2, pp. 148–54. Locke's position, Skinner argues, was the "best line of escape" from the dilemma (ibid., p. 153).

This explanation, however, does not take full measure of Locke's political project. Locke's politics is a politics of reason. His intention is to show that reason and the right of dominion survived Adam's fall and that natural reason was given authoritative illumination with the first coming of Christ. (This latter claim is the basis of Locke's call for toleration). The significance of Adam, therefore, is closely linked with Christ, and his doctrine of property and of toleration are aspects of his overall project: to defend a politics of reason. Skinner does speak of toleration (ibid., pp. 244–49, *passim*), but not as it occurs in Locke's thought. Skinner cites neither the "Letter" nor the *Reasonableness*, both of which are concerned with the role Christ plays in the unconcealment of reason. What is at issue in these texts is the soul's right relationship to God, in and out of political life. Given Skinner's substantive supposition—that politics can be dissevered from theology (ibid., p. 349)—it is not surprising that he would disregard Locke's theology.

39. There are those, however, who *would* impinge upon the claims of another. The "quarrelsome and contentious" (Locke, *Second Treatise*, Ch. V, §34, p. 291) would clearly wish to take from others. But they are not significant within the theoretical schema Locke advances to account for the emergence of private property. What makes this schema move forward is the presence of those who *do* adhere to God's ordinance: the "industrious and rational" (ibid., p. 291). The quarrelsome and contentious are, in effect, accidents in the dialectic of property—as are the idle. Understood as political rhetoric, as Ashcraft's fine study notes, Locke's thinking on property provides "a defense of the 'industrious' and trading part of the nation—the constituency to whom the Whigs addressed their appeals—against the idle, unproductive, and Court-dominated property owners" (Richard Ashcraft, *Revolutionary Politics and Locke's Two Treatises of Government* [Princeton: Princeton University Press, 1986], p. 264).

40. Locke, *Second Treatise*, Ch. V, §28, p. 288. See also ibid., Ch. V, §43, p. 298: "Nature and the Earth furnish only almost worthless materials" and that labor "*puts the greatest part of Value upon the Land*" (emphasis in original). *Mother* nature must be supple-

mented by industrious labor (which derives, ultimately, from God the *Father*) for nature to be bountiful. Mother is passive; father is active. One of the things that fascinated Tocqueville about America was that the English possessed the kind of restless activity proportionate to the land they inhabited, whereas the French of Canada did not. Father industriousness is received by mother nature, and indeed does not overwhelm her. See Tocqueville, *Democracy in America*, vol. I, Part II, Ch. 9, pp. 282–84. Indeed, for Tocqueville, the Americans had worked out the relationship between the sexes quite well: man had dominion over woman, yet he esteemed her. See ibid., vol. II, Part II. Ch. 12, pp. 600–603.

41. Locke, *Second Treatise*, Ch. V, §29, p. 289 (emphasis in original).

42. Locke, *Second Treatise*, Ch. V, §38, p. 295.

43. Locke, *Second Treatise*, Ch. V, §§42–44, pp. 297–99.

44. Locke, *Second Treatise*, Ch. V, §46, p. 300 (emphasis in original).

45. But see Locke, *Second Treatise*, Ch. V, §28, p. 289, where he makes a passing allusion to the master-servant relationship. The servant, however, is not another property holder. He or she is involved in the production of another's property.

46. Locke, *Second Treatise*, Ch. V, §46, p. 300.

47. Locke, *Second Treatise*, p. 343 (emphasis in original).

48. Locke, *Second Treatise*, p. 344. Although I will not discuss this matter in chapter 4, Rousseau's theory of property is not derived from sacred text. The extent of legitimate differentiation of property, therefore, is not determined by the criterion of "useless perishing," as it is for Locke. For Rousseau, the finitude of real goods was reached when inheritances increased until there was no land left. At that point property "could no longer be enlarged except at the expense of another" (*Second Discourse*, p. 156).

49. Gough sees this ending point in the development of property as evidence that Locke "brought the economic structure of his own age within the bounds of natural law" (Gough, *The Social Contract*, p. 141). See also Macpherson, *Theory of Possessive Individualism*, pp. 220–21: "Locke's doctrine of property . . . provides the moral foundation for bourgeois appropriation. . . . [Locke] erased the moral disability with which unlimited capitalist appropriation had hitherto been handicapped [and provided] a positive moral basis for capitalist society." Macpherson is, I think, half-right. Property no longer has any natural limits, to be sure, but Locke's property must be understood as *stewardship*. It is God's world, and human beings have an obligation to live within the conditions of His grant—which means being rational, not avaricious. See Tully, *Discourse*, pp. 131–54.

50. Locke, *Second Treatise*, Ch. VI, §54, p. 304 (emphasis in original).

51. Locke, *Second Treatise*, Ch. VI, §56, p. 305. Cf. Luther, "Lectures on Genesis," in *Works*, vol. 1, p. 61: "I am afraid that since the loss of this image (of God in Adam) we cannot understand it to any extent. Memory, will, and mind we have indeed; but they are most depraved and seriously weakened, yes to put it more clearly they are utterly leprous and unclean." See also ibid., pp. 141– 42.

52. Only "Lunaticks and Ideots" never become self-sufficient. See Locke, *Second Treatise*, Ch. VI, §60, p. 308 (emphasis in original). Also note that family has a kind of priority over economy; family is the precondition for the development of that rationality which economy allows and encourages to operate.

53. See Locke, *First Treatise*, Ch. I, §4, pp. 142–43: "[Filmer tells] us, we are all born Slaves, and must continue so; there is no remedy for it: Life and Thraldom we enter'd into together, and can never be quit of the one, till we part with the other." Locke's position, however, was not that the unfree child is a slave. See *Second Treatise*, Ch. XV, §170, p. 381: "the Affections and Tenderness, which God hath planted in the Breasts of Parents, toward their Children, makes it evident, that this is not intended to be a severe Arbitrary Government, but only for the Help, Instruction, and Preservation of their Offspring."

54. Locke, *Second Treatise*, Ch. VI, §57, p. 305 (emphasis in original).

55. See Locke, *Second Treatise*, Ch. VI, §58, pp. 306–7: While still a child "wherein he has not *Understanding* of his own to direct his *Will*, he is not to have any Will of his own to follow: He that understands for him, must *will* for him too; he must prescribe to his Will, and regulate his Actions; but when he comes to the Estate that made his *Father a Freeman, the Son is a Freeman* too" (emphasis in original).

56. See Locke, *Second Treatise*, Ch. VI, §71, p. 314: "these two *Powers, Political and Paternal, are . . . perfectly distinct and separate*" (emphasis in original). Contrast this to Aristotle, for whom, "*resemblances* to [the three forms of government and their corruptions] can be found in the household" (*Ethics*, Bk. VIII, Ch. 10, 1160b22, emphasis added). Locke, like Luther, insists that the key to linking political and paternal power is historical, not analogical. While there is no likeness, paternal power becomes political power as history moves forward; indeed, even when paternal power has been superseded, in true dialectical fashion a residual of it remains.

Tocqueville, on the other hand, is less concerned with the logical relationship between these domains than with might be called the "spill-over effects." See Tocqueville, *Democracy in America*, vol. I, Part II, Ch. 9, p. 291: "in Europe almost all the disorders of society are born around the domestic hearth and not far from the nuptial bed. It is there that men come to feel a scorn for natural ties and legitimate pleasures and develop a taste for disorder, restlessness of spirit, and instability of desires. Shaken by the tumultuous passions which have often troubled his own house, the European finds it hard to submit to the authority of the state's legislators." See also Rousseau, *Emile*, Bk. V, p. 363: it is "by means of the small fatherland which is the family that the heart attaches itself to the large one."

57. See Augustine, *City of God*, Bk. X, Ch. 14, p. 392. See also Neal Wood, *The Politics of Locke's Philosophy* (Berkeley: University of California Press, 1983), pp. 109–20. The project of Locke's *Essay*, Wood argues, is to cleanse the human mind of its irrationalities, that both individuals and the species may approach the rule of reason.

58. Locke, *Second Treatise*, Ch. VIII, §107, p. 338.

59. Locke, *Second Treatise*, Ch. VIII, §107, p. 339.

60. Locke, *Second Treatise*, Ch. VII, §109, pp. 340–41. There are echoes here of portions of Luther and of the early Hegel: the Jews under the Old Dispensation are the "children," while the Christians under the New Dispensation are the "adults." Having said this, however, there is a dialectical prefiguration of the New *already there* in the Old Dispensation in the form of the *consent* of the governed. See Exodus 32:26.

61. Locke, *Second Treatise*, Ch. VIII, §111, p. 343.

62. Locke, *Second Treatise*, Ch. VIII, §107, p. 338. See also Locke, *First Treatise*, Ch. II, §10, p. 148: "the Natural Vanity and Ambition of Men [is] too apt of itself to grow and increase with the Possession of any Power." Tully notes, in Locke's view "money disrupts [the] natural order, and government is required to constitute a new order of social relations which will bring the actions of men once again in line with God's intentions"; *Discourse*, p. 154.

63. See Ricoeur, *The Symbolism of Evil*, p. 313: "the serpent [in the Garden of Eden] is . . . the Other, it is the Adversary . . . about which one can say nothing except that the evil act [of Eve], in positing itself, *lets itself be seduced* by the Evil One, by the Diabolical" (emphasis in original). Here evil is present *before the fall*.

64. Locke, *Second Treatise*, Ch. VIII, §111, p. 342.

65. Like Hobbes, Locke attributes to Adam the loss of eternal life. Both go out of their way to avoid treating the problem of pride in Christian terms. Both, moreover, recur to Greek themes at crucial points when it becomes necessary to give some account of pride. While Locke does speak of "the baseness of human nature" (*Second Treatise*, Ch. VII, §92, p. 327), his presumption is that human nature becomes base when humans "quit their reason, which places [them] almost equal to Angels" (*First Treatise*, Ch. V, §58, p. 182). Human corruption is accidental, while industriousness and rationality are essential. Hobbes, recall, deliberately skirts the predominant Reformation interpretation of pride by recurring to the myth of Ixion. While both Hobbes and Locke avoid the conventional Reformation interpretation of pride, Hobbes's Leviathan is Christ-like, as I have said, and so Hobbes is more able to think within the confines of the stark Augustinian view of pride—having, as it were, a way out of the dilemma it poses. See John Dunn, *The Political Thought of John Locke* (Cambridge: Cambridge University Press, 1969), p. 193, for comments on Locke's psychological inability to confront the problem of pride.

Tarcov, on the other hand, argues that Locke acknowledged the existence of "natural pride" (Locke's term) which expresses itself as a "native propensity [to be] merely insensitive to the suffering of others," and that this "natural pride" could develop (without proper education) to such an extent that the result would be an "actual pleasure in the pain of others" (Nathan Tarcov, *Locke's Education for Liberty* [Chicago: University of Chicago Press, 1984], p. 163). For the relevant original passages, see John Locke, *Some Thoughts Concerning Education*, in *The Educational Writings of John Locke*, ed. James L. Axtell (Cambridge: Cambridge University Press, 1968), §§102–16, pp. 206–27. Locke argues in *Some Thoughts* that pride is not original sin; right education can impede pride from manifesting itself—a thought not lost to Rousseau in *Emile*. See ibid., §§103–7, pp. 207–11.

66. Locke, *Second Treatise*, Ch. VIII, §111, p. 343 (emphasis in original).

67. Hobbes, *Leviathan*, Part IV, Ch. 47, p. 499.

68. There will, however, be residuals of rule by the father even in a government ruled by reason. Chapter XIV, "Of Prerogative," in the *Second Treatise* (§§159–68, pp. 374–80), addresses the question of how the *willfulness* of the ruler may stand in respect to the *reason* of the adult society. The father is not completely done away with in adult society! As in Luther's view of the relationship between Law and Gospel and Freud's view of ontogenetic and phylogenetic history, earlier stages may be superseded, but cannot be wholly vanquished.

69. Locke, *Second Treatise*, Ch. IX, §124, pp. 350–51 (emphasis in original). See also ibid., Ch. VII, §94, p. 329.

70. See Ricoeur, *The Symbolism of Evil*, p. 244: "in Adam we are one and all; the mythical figure of the first man provides a focal point at the beginning of history for man's unity-in-multiplicity."

71. Locke, *Second Treatise*, Ch. VII, §93, p. 328. See also ibid., Ch. XVIII, §199, pp. 398–99, where the tyrant is characterized as one whose will would supervene over the law established by reason. Reason's law is something to which *all* can assent because all are one through Adam's reason. The tyrant who would stand outside of the community in Adam, who would violate the law of reason, has transgressed against the very foundation of community; in Locke's words, *"Where-ever Law ends, Tyranny begins"* (ibid. Ch. XVIII, §202, p. 400, emphasis in original).

72. Locke, *Second Treatise*, Ch. VII, §93, p. 328 (emphasis in original). Rousseau later expressed the same view in a criticism of Hobbes. See Rousseau, *The Social Contract*, Bk. I, Ch. 2, p. 51: Hobbes believed that "the human race [is] divided into herds of cattle, each with a master who preserves it only in order to devour its members."

Luther, too, used this predator-prey metaphor; in his writing however, the "wolves" are not government but rather *works*—these are the deceivers! See Luther, "Freedom," in *Works*, vol. 31, p. 363. The original biblical allusion comes from Matt. 7:15: "Beware of false prophets, which come to you in sheep's clothing, but inwardly they are ravening wolves."

73. Tocqueville, in his own way would argue this same point later in *Democracy in America*. The success of the commercial spirit in America, the spirit of rationality, is *achieved* with the aid of the family, political participation, and religion. Without these institutional supports human beings simply withdraw into themselves; in good Catholic fashion he argues that the human *tendency* toward irrationality can and must be corrected by certain institutional arrangements.

74. Locke, *Second Treatise*, Ch. XI, §136, p. 359.

75. Hirschman asserts that this is the core of Locke's teaching. Identifying passion with uncertainty and interest with certainty, Hirschman claims that "although Locke does not appeal to interest to keep inconstancy at bay, there is clearly an affinity between the commonwealth he is attempting to construct and the 17th Century image of a world ruled by interest" (*The Passions and the Interests*, pp. 53–54). This reading fails to account for Locke's theological justification of property and his thoughts about the biblical foundation of reason.

76. Locke, *Second Treatise*, Ch. XIV, §168, p. 379–80. This is not to say, however, that the appeal to a judge on earth is without divine sanction. Dunn is quite right in saying of Locke's position that, "when men judge the offenses of their fellows and execute sentences upon them for these offenses, they judge them in their capacity as agents of God" (*The Political Thought of John Locke*, p. 127).

77. For Hobbes, of course, Christ solves the problem of loss of eternal life at the end of history. With His first coming, however, He renews the covenant. Locke, like Hobbes, did not wish to see in Christ a malefactor against government. See Locke, *Reasonableness*, §120, pp. 82–84.

78. Adam is the foundation; the political edifice erected stands firm on him; Christ is the flying buttress that reinforces the entire conformation. Contrast this to Thomas Pangle, who in *The Spirit of Modern Republicanism* (Chicago: University of Chicago Press, 1988) argues that the Founders, drawing on Locke, "attempted to exploit and transform Christianity in the direction of Liberal rationalism" (p. 21). Pangle assumes that Locke emancipates reason from Christianity. But this is not the case. The focus on reason in Locke should not be understood as a counter-Christian impulse.

79. Locke, *Reasonableness*, §16, p. 10.

80. Locke, *Reasonableness*, §I, pp. 1–2.

81. Locke, *Reasonableness*, §I, p. 1.

82. Locke does speak of the propensity to disobey God's commands, but only by attributing to human beings a "frailty and weakness" (*Reasonableness*, §181, p. 136). In speaking of the death brought into the world by Adam, Locke rejects the idea that death in the Testaments is symbolic of "spiritual death." See, for example, Locke, *Reasonableness*, §4, p. 4, where death means only "ceasing to be."

83. Locke, *Reasonableness*, §22, p. 13. See Gal. 3:10: "Cursed *is* every one that continueth not in all things which are written in the book of the law to do them."

84. Locke, *Reasonableness*, §180, p. 136.

85. Rom. 4:19–24, paraphrased in Locke, *Reasonableness*, §24, p. 15 (emphasis in original).

86. Locke, *Reasonableness*, §25, p. 16 (emphasis in original). With this Hobbes would have agreed; though for him the sovereign would have had the right to interpret to the subject what the word of God *meant*—and to this interpretation the subject would have had to assent.

87. Locke, *Reasonableness*, §15, p. 10.

88. See Mircea Eliade, *A History of Religious Ideas*, trans. Willard R. Trask (Chicago: University of Chicago Press, 1984), vol. 2, §224, pp. 359–61, for a synopsis of the three theological explanations possible for the delay of the Parousia: either a more fervent apocalyptic hope, a deferment of the kingdom until some future date, or a new life possible now because of Christ. Locke takes this third alternative in certain respects, but, like Hobbes, insists that the real kingdom of God is to come at the end of history.

In *Paradise Lost*, Milton takes the third alternative. Comforting Adam with an account of what will come to pass in the future, the Angel Michael leads Adam down the hill (to Eve) with the promise that they will "leave this Paradise, but shall possess a Paradise within thee, happier far" (John Milton, *Paradise Lost* [New York: Viking Press, 1949], Bk. XII, p. 546).

89. Locke, *Reasonableness*, §238, p. 165 (emphasis in original).

90. Locke, *Reasonableness*, §241, p. 170.

91. For Locke, the society ruled by reason is the free society. See, for example, Locke, *Second Treatise*, Ch. VI, §57, p. 306: "*the end of* [the] *Law* [of Reason] is not to abolish or restrain, but *to preserve and enlarge Freedom*" (emphasis in original). Adam's reason is the basis of human freedom.

Locke, like Luther before him, did believe Christianity provided the "bonds of union"—Rousseau's term—necessary to hold society together. It was Rousseau's subsequent claim that Christianity did not provide such bonds. See Rousseau, *The Social Contract*, Bk. IV, Ch. 8, p. 186.

92. Locke, *Reasonableness*, §241, p. 170. Augustine, much earlier, expressed the same thought in his *City of God*. The heading of Bk. II, Ch. 7 reads: "The conclusions of the philosophers are ineffective as they lack divine authority. Man is easily corrupted and God's examples influence him more than the argument of man" (p. 54). Montesquieu gives an interesting twist to this view. "The Christian religion," he says, "coming after this philosophy fixed, if I might use the expression, the ideas which [philosophy] had prepared" (*The Spirit of the Laws*, vol. 2, Bk. 1, Ch. 21, p. 19). That is, Christianity does not more fully authorize what philosophy had discovered, but rather *ossifies* its pattern of worldly renunciation. See also Tocqueville, *Democracy in America*, vol. II, Part I, Ch. 5, p. 443.

93. Locke, *Reasonableness*, §241, p. 171.

94. Locke, *Reasonableness*, §243, p. 179. Macpherson's argument on this point is quite unsatisfactory. He claims that Locke's intention is to show that "the laboring class, beyond all others, is incapable of living a rational life" (*The Theory of Possessive Individualism*, p. 226) and that this served as a justification for the political disenfranchisement of all wage earners. Locke, however, is not concerned with wage earners in the passage cited; he is concerned to show that Christ's revelation is the Divine supplement to the natural reason of the philosophers.

Hobbes notes, as well, that "it is impossible that the multitude should ever learn their duty, but from the pulpit and upon holidays" (*Behemoth*, Dialogue 1, p. 39). He goes on to say that what they learned was disobedience and that the reason they learned this was that those who preached were themselves taught at the universities set up by the pope. Hence, his claim (*Leviathan*, Review and Conclusion, pp. 510–11) that his work is the antidote that ought to be taught in the universities. "I despair," he says, "of any lasting peace amongst ourselves, till the Universities here shall bend and direct their studies to the settling of it, that is, to the teaching of absolute obedience to the laws of the King" (*Behemoth*, Dialogue 1, p. 56). Locke's education unto reason begins with the child (hence, his *Thoughts*); Hobbes's education unto obedience begins with those attending the universities who will teach the multitude what it can and must believe. See also Luther, "Christian Nobility," in *Works*, vol. 44, pp. 200–207, where the biggest problem in the universities is the teaching of Aristotle and the turning away from Scripture.

95. In this instance both Locke and Hobbes agree: authority is essential for belief. See Locke, *Reasonableness*, §238, pp. 165–66, where, rational men did worship the one true God "in their own minds," but reason could not "prevail upon the multitude." For Locke, Christ provides the authority; for Hobbes the Christ-like Leviathan *is* the authority. See Matt. 7:29.

96. Locke, *Reasonableness*, §243, p. 177.

97. Locke, *Reasonableness*, §243, p. 176.

98. Luther's notion of the equality of all human beings is a not-too-distant cousin of this formulation of Locke's. For both, Christ levels all heretofore-considered-significant differences. See Luther, "Temporal Authority," in *Works*, vol. 45, p. 117: "there is no superior among Christians, but Christ Himself and Christ alone."

99. Locke, *Reasonableness*, §§58–61, pp. 35–39.

100. Locke, *Reasonableness*, §29, p. 18.

101. John Locke, *A Discourse of Miracles*, in *John Locke*, ed. I. T. Ramsey (Stanford: Stanford University Press, 1958), p. 86. It was Locke's position that "the holy Men of Old . . . had outward Signs to convince them of the Author of [the] Revelations" they received (Locke, *Essay*, Book IV, Ch. XIX, §15, p. 705) and that these signs have now ceased. What, then, is to be made of the claims by enthusiasts that they had received revelations from God? Locke argues that reason must be the judge of such claims. That enthusiasts *believe without reasons* disqualifies their claims. Reason is the standard by which claims of the receipt of revelation must be judged. In matters where even reason cannot be certain, however, revelation—which was accompanied by outward signs—is the guide. Thus, reason where possible; revelation where not. That reason should be the criterion of knowledge rather than *belief*, then, does not mean that philosophy is higher than religion; rather it means that if the claims of religious enthusiasts are not evaluated by reason (which was granted to Adam in the beginning and assisted by Christ upon His first coming), they cannot be considered true.

Compare this to Rousseau for whom the very notion of miracles and of revelation is problematic. "Apostle of truth, what have you to tell me of which I do not remain the judge? 'God himself has spoken. Hear His revelation.' That is something else. God has spoken! That is surely a great statement. To whom has He spoken? 'He has spoken to men.' Why, then, did I hear nothing about it? 'He has directed other men to give you His word.' I understand: it is men who are going to tell me what God has said. I should have preferred to have heard God Himself" (Rousseau, *Emile*, Bk. IV, p. 297). Here the only *authority* is the self that experiences the miracle. Hegel's approach further develops Rousseau's position. He concludes that the ascription of miracles to Christ has led Christians to think that Christ's positive commands are authoritative rather than his call to faith. In Hegel's words, "nothing has contributed so much as these miracles to making the religion of Jesus positive, to basing the whole of it . . . on authority" (*The Positivity of the Christian Religion*, Part I, §9, p. 78). The authority of miracles is a kind of external proof. What Hegel sought was the inner truth of Christianity, the moral teachings of Christ which could be known to the subject. Here, as in Rousseau, human subjectivity is crucial; miracles become fundamentally unimportant.

102. Locke, *Reasonableness*, §§61–72, pp. 38–46, and §108, p. 70. Strauss saw in Locke's exposition of Christ's gradual unconcealment an explication more of Locke's view of the necessity of caution when speaking or writing for the public than of the truth of Christ (see Strauss, *Natural Right and History*, p. 207, *passim*).

Strauss's method of close textual analysis cannot be disregarded in favor of a view that would place authors in their immediate historical context. These authors cannot be fully understood in terms of their *immediate* context, for that is but an occasion for a consideration of the meaning of those events as disclosed by that context of history not fully graspable by reason alone. The immanent events are drawn up beyond themselves and become instances of a universal narrative which must be heeded. Only a close reading of the text discloses the meaning of the events at hand, for it is the text which draws attention to the connection between immanent events and their transhistorical meaning. In a word, I accept Strauss's method, but not his substantive conclusion that Christianity is not germane to the development of modern political thought except perhaps as something which had to be responded to, countered, deflected, etc. Strauss's insight into the importance of esoteric teaching was his great contribution to the discipline. His error was to take an insight that must be relied upon in studying *some* political philosophers and applying it as his master hermeneutic principle to *all* political philosophers. In the case of Luther, Hobbes, and Locke, it is not the philosophers who are esoteric, but rather the Book which is their referent! Theologically, Strauss's error is to locate the universal *in the world*: here, it is purported, there is a *universal* accord among philosophers that truth is esoteric.

103. Locke, *Reasonableness*, §74, p. 47.

104. Locke, *Reasonableness*. §140, p. 98.

105. Locke, *Reasonableness*, §140, p. 99. See also ibid., §156, p. 115, where, in a reference to John 16:12, Christ spoke obscurely because his hearers *could not bear it.* See John 16:25. The Book of John alludes to unconcealment throughout.

106. Locke, *Reasonableness*, §124, p. 85. Perhaps the most notable instance of the use of parables—notable because of what it reveals about Locke's understanding of the relationship between open declaration and intimation—is the Sermon on the Mount and the Sermon on the Plain; see Locke, *Reasonableness*, §93, pp. 58–59, *passim.* While the Sermon on the Plain speaks of the kingdom in parables, the Sermon on the Mount speaks, not of the kingdom, but of moral duty. This, Christ discusses in clear language. What His kingdom was could not be revealed expressly on the Plain (to the person who expected an earthly kingdom). Moral duty, however, could be revealed clearly on the Mount (to the person accustomed to the use of reason and not under the sway of the priests on the Plain). But the truth of Christ's kingdom revealed after His death substantiates what was only intimated on the Plain and provides the authority to bring down from the Mount—to disseminate broadly, as if by gravity—the moral teachings that could only be grasped there by the few.

107. This dialectic of death and revelation is found, in philosophical form, in Hegel's thought as well. There, in its starkest formulation, *Geist* reveals itself to itself "on the slaughter bench of history." See G. W. F. Hegel, *Reason in History* (Indianapolis: Bobbs-Merrill, 1953), p. 27. See also Hegel, *Phenomenology of Spirit*, Preface, p. 19: the life of spirit "wins its truth only when, in utter dismemberment, it finds itself."

108. Locke, *Reasonableness*, §156, pp. 115. See also ibid, p. 116: "my death and resurrection, and the coming of the Holy Ghost, will speedily enlighten you; and *then* I shall make you know the will of the father" (emphasis in original). On this reading the Enlightenment *is* the Age of the Holy Ghost.

In Hegel's view, similarly, the Holy Ghost was also necessary for the apostles to be imbued with the divine. Speaking of the time when Christ openly declares His kingdom, Hegel says, "now for the first time Jesus ventures to speak to his disciples of his impending fate; but Peter's consciousness of the divinity of his teacher at once assumes the character of faith only; the faith which senses the divine but which is not yet a filling of his whole being with the divine, not yet a reception of the Holy Ghost" (*The Spirit of Christianity*, §4, p. 267). For Hobbes, too, the Holy Ghost was the agent of the acceptance of the truth of Christianity. But for Hobbes the Holy Ghost acted only when there was no authority present to interpret Scripture (see Hobbes, *Leviathan*, Part III, Ch. 42, p. 380). When an authority emerges the unauthorized hearer of the Gospel no longer has the right of interpretation. In Hobbes's view, in other words, Christ does not provide the light by which the reason possessed by every human being may know the truth of Scripture once it has been unconcealed—as Locke would have it.

Contrast Hobbes's position with that found in II Cor. 3:13–14: "And not as Moses, *which* put a veil over his face, that the children of Israel could not steadfastly look to the end of that which is abolished: But their minds were blinded: for until this day remaineth the same veil untaken away in the reading of the old testament; which *veil* is done away in Christ.")

109. Locke, *Reasonableness*, §188, p. 140.

110. Locke, *Reasonableness*, §§238–41, pp. 165–72. One piece of evidence Locke cites for the universalization of what once was a particular claim is the fact that the apostles went out "among the nations" (ibid., §240, p. 168).

But see Hegel, *Positivity of Christian Religion*, Part I, §13, p. 80: "in the short time which they could devote on these journeys to the education and betterment of men, it was possible to achieve much. . . . As a method of extirpating Jewish superstition and disseminating morality, it could have no proceeds, because Jesus himself did not carry his most trusted friends very far in this direction even after years of effort and association with them." This, however, is not the opposition it appears at first blush to be; for both Locke and Hegel, the universal message of Christ could not be disseminated by the apostles alone: they stood in need of the Holy Ghost to fulfill their mission. Even Hobbes alleges this much.

111. Strauss's two cities, Athens (reason) and Jerusalem (revelation), are in Locke's view, united by the New Dispensation. See, for example, Locke, *Reasonableness*, §245, p. 185: "[upon a view of heaven], and upon this foundation alone does morality [discovered but undisseminated by philosophers] stand firm." See Leo Strauss, "Athens and Jerusalem," in *Studies in Platonic Political Philosophy* (Chicago: University of Chicago Press, 1988), pp. 147–73. Strauss notes certain convergences between Athens and Jerusalem, but intimates that the prophetic tradition, which anticipates *universal* peace, and the philosophic tradition, which cannot but speak to a few, cannot be unified. Strauss honors Jerusalem but loves Athens.

112. Hegel notes that "faith in the divine is only possible if in the believer himself there is a divine element which rediscovers itself, its own nature, in that on which it believes, even if it be unconscious that what it has found *is* its own nature" (*The Spirit of Christianity*, §4, p. 266, emphasis in original). Faith discovers its own authority, the authority it *had* but did not *know* it had. See also Augustine, *City of God*, Bk. XI, Ch. 26, p. 459, where the second moment of the Trinity, Christ, corresponds to *knowledge* in the soul.

113. See James Tully, "Governing Conduct," in *Conscience and Casuistry in Early Modern Europe*, ed. Edmund Leites (Cambridge: Cambridge University Press, 1988), p. 59, where, "[in Locke's view] God spreads Christianity by the same mode of governance as other opinions are spread." Christianity is the true religion, ascertainable by the light of reason, to be sure; yet the light of reason acquires its brightness by being guided by the *practices* in a Christian commonwealth. "Christian philosophers have come closer to demonstrating ethics than the pre-Christians, but this is not because, as they assume, they have an independent rule of reason to test moral principles. It is rather because their first principles are derived from Revelation. We grow up with the Gospel from the cradle. It seems 'natural' to us and we take it for 'unquestionable truths.' Rationalists think they

have discovered the foundations of morality, but they only 'confirm' Revelation. We would be lost without it. Revelation is the foundation of reason, of what we take to be 'self-evident'" (ibid., p. 59).

114. Locke's ideas about voluntary association should not be thought of as affirming the primacy of "the individual" over "the social" (an all-too-common criticism of his thought), but as the precondition for the emergence of the light of reason. See *Second Treatise*, Ch. VI, §73, p. 315.

115. John Dunn points out this tacit worry in Locke in the context of his *Essay* as well. In Dunn's words, "if Locke had begun by believing the demonstration of their duties to all mankind . . . either impossible or unnecessary, it is difficult to see why he should have troubled to compose at all the *Essay* with its persisting concern with the nature and accessibility of moral knowledge" (*The Political Thought of John Locke*, p. 190).

116. Luther, "Lectures on Genesis," in *Works*, vol. 1, p. 110 (emphasis added).

117. Luther's self, recall, had to negate itself and fall into the abyss of powerlessness in order to find the Divine Ground in Christ—in order for it to be sanctified. Luther's connecting link between the human and the Divine was through the Christ who appeared to the self in the moment of its negation and utter powerlessness; that is, in the utter interiority of faith.

118. Hobbes saw the (public) person of the Leviathan as the only person with a "link" to the Divine; and this because the Leviathan, as receiver of the covenant, is in some sense contiguous with Moses (with whom the original covenant with God was instituted). Hobbes's human being does not negate itself, as Luther's does; like Luther's self it, too, required an intermediary. And this intermediary, though also a Christ-like figure, is not the locus for the interiority of faith which in Luther's formulations Christ Himself provided.

119. I agree with Wolin that with Locke "the political order lost its quality of dramatic achievement" (*Politics and Vision*, p. 306), although the *reason* why it lost this quality is other than Wolin suggests. Politics need not be an achievement for Locke because its foundation is in Adam.

120. Locke, *Reasonableness*, §244, p. 181.

121. See John Dunn, "From Applied Theology to Social Analysis," in *Wealth and Virtue*, ed. Istvan Hont and Michael Ignatieff (Cambridge: Cambridge University Press, 1983), pp. 119–35, for a discussion of the differences between Locke's theocentrism and the subsequent thought of Smith and Hume. In Dunn's words, "Locke presumed that there were strict theoretical implications between the abandonment of theocentrism, the acceptance of a purely internal conception of human rational agency and the resting of all human rights and duties upon the contingencies of human opinion [Smith and Hume's position]. . . . The development of a purely internal conception of rational agency has left human individuals impressively disenchanted and undeceived. But it has also left them increasingly on their own and devoid of rational direction in social and political action, prisoners in a game of self-destruction to which, on these terms, there may be no rational solution" (ibid., p. 134). Elsewhere, and along the same lines, Dunn remarks, as Locke saw it, "once we have lost the religious guarantee that reason, 'the candle of the Lord,' shines brightly enough for all our purposes, we have no conclusive

reason to expect it to shine brightly enough for any. And once we can no longer see our purposes as authoritatively assigned to us from outside ourselves, it becomes very hard to judge just which purposes we have good reason to consider as (or to make) our own." See John Dunn, *Locke* (Oxford: Oxford University Press, 1984), p. 88.

122. Hobbes insists upon this point as well, and therefore urges patience. See Hobbes, *Behemoth*, Dialogue 1, p. 58: there should "be a quiet waiting for the coming again of our blessed Savior." In the following clause he adds, we must resolve "in the meantime to obey the King's laws (which also are God's laws)."

CHAPTER FOUR

1. Augustine, *Confessions*, Bk. I, Ch. 4, p. 23.

2. Hobbes, *Leviathan*, Part III, Ch. 43, pp. 429–30; Locke, *Reasonableness*, §28, p. 17: the great proposition concerned whether Jesus "was the Messiah . . . and the assent to that, was that which distinguished believers from non-believers." To this Rousseau rejoins: "doubtless there is not a moment to lose in order to merit salvation. But if in order to obtain it, it is enough to repeat certain words, I do not see what prevents us from peopling heaven with starlings and magpies just as well as with [human beings]" (*Emile*, Bk. IV, p. 257). See Matt. 10:32. Rousseau misses the biblical significance of assent here; it is not simply a *saying*, but rather a proclamation made upon the *real life* occasion of errancy and *admission* of the insufficiency of human effort in certain crucial matters. This voice, for Rousseau, conveys no content; only the prelinguistic voice of nature *truly* speaks.

3. "We are deceived by the appearance of right." Rousseau invokes this expression at the opening of the *First Discourse*, p. 34.

4. See James, *Religious Experience*, Lecture VIII, pp. 166–67.

5. See Rousseau, *Second Discourse*, p. 178: "the human race in one age [is not] the human race of another." See also Rousseau, *The Social Contract*, Bk. I, Ch. 8, p. 64, where the movement to civil society from a state of nature "produces a remarkable change in man."

6. See Patrick Riley, *Will and Political Legitimacy: A Critical Exposition of Social Contract Theory in Hobbes, Locke, Rousseau, Kant, and Hegel* (Cambridge: Harvard University Press, 1982), pp. 98–124. Riley understands modern contract theory to be an attempt to reconcile psychological theories with moral theories of political obligation, a difficulty most pronounced, in his estimation, in the thought of Hobbes. The histories that Hobbes, Locke, and Rousseau invoke, however, serve to specify a psychological theory (a notion of the identity of the psyche), and intimate as well what would constitute an appropriate political obligation for a being so constituted and living in the epoch of the history specified. Neither the psychological theory nor the political obligation can be derived from or reconciled by reason alone.

7. Luther, "Lectures on Genesis," in *Works*, vol. 1, p. 168. Rousseau, of course, would not have attributed the "fall" to sin.

8. In Luther, Hobbes, and Locke, atonement is possible through Christ, even though it may require *waiting beyond death*, until the second coming. Their temporal horizon extends from the Creation to the Redemption. This patience is absent in Rousseau, whose temporal horizon may go back *further* (about which more shortly), but ends at *this*

moment when both the full extent of errancy *and* its counterpoint, nature, the silent measure, is grasped. The future is all too easily a precipice over which the *continually* errant soul may fall without restitution by the *gift*. Hence the restive quality of his work. There can be no waiting *beyond* death for atonement here—though there is the possibility of "redemption" through attunement to the *Voice* that "cannot come in or through history but only in opposition to history's destructiveness" (Jean Starobinski, *Jean-Jacques Rousseau: Transparency and Obstruction,* trans. Arthur Goldhammer [Chicago: University of Chicago Press, 1988], p. 302).

9. See I Cor. 15:21–22; Rom. 5:18–19—passages I have referred to elsewhere. In the relation of Adam to Christ the pattern is clear: what Adam is the occasion for, Christ is the solution to; Adam is initiative, Christ is transformative. Whether the issue is death, man's relationship to God, or sin, the pattern is the same. The figure of Adam finds its answer in the figure of Christ. The one (Adam) provides the pattern for the life of all. The one (Christ), in turn, provides a solution for the all who inherit from the first one (Adam). Adam stands for human beings in the sense that they inherit from him. Christ, in turn, stands in for humans in the sense that through Him (Christ) the true meaning of the figure of Adam is disclosed. The reality of Christ standing in for human beings is what gives substance to the idea that Adam stands for the human. See Ricoeur, *The Symbolism of Evil,* pp. 232–78.

10. Rousseau, *Second Discourse,* pp. 102–3.

11. See Rousseau, *Emile,* Bk. IV, pp. 288–89: "the holy voice of nature [is] stronger than that of the gods." In context, he is arguing that the voice of nature is uniform and has established similar ideas of justice throughout the world that cannot be obliterated by the multiplicity of morals that religions impose. Unity is masked but not vanquished by multiplicity; religion, which comes after nature, is but a veneer over it.

A crucial passage for the Protestant understanding of Christianity is Rom. 7:23 ("But I see another law in my members, warring against the law of my mind, and bringing me into captivity to the law of sin which is in my members"), which I considered in the course of chap. 1. Rousseau intimates in *Emile,* Bk. IV, p. 293, that this sensing of a contrary law does indeed occur, but only *after* one has willed not to live in accordance with nature: "By willing to yield to their temptations, they finally yield to them in spite of themselves and make them irresistible. It is doubtless no longer in their power not to be wicked and weak; but not becoming so was in their power." Here the essential Protestant problem is *antedated* by a dereliction of duty to nature. The experience of (Christian) dualism is preceded by an errancy from nature—which suggests that the state of nature (in which the human being is unitary, not dual) is before the God of the Bible.

12. See Jean-Jacques Rousseau, "On the Origin of Languages," in *On the Origin of Language,* trans. John H. Moran and Alexander Gode (Chicago: University of Chicago Press, 1966), Ch. 5, p. 17, for the claim that the alphabet is to be found only amongst civilized peoples. See also Rousseau, *Second Discourse,* pp. 119–24, *passim.*

13. In the *Second Discourse,* Rousseau makes reference to the human being in the state of nature as being "nearly unrecognizable" (p. 91); to education as "corrupting" but not "destroying" natural man (p. 104); and to the "immense space that separates" the state of nature from the civil state (p. 178). Rousseau claims to have discovered and followed "the lost routes that must have led man from the natural state to the civil state."

(p. 178). Humankind is on the verge of being alienated from its true self, on the brink of becoming concealed to itself. Mythologically, the human soul is like the statue of Glaucus, "which time, sea, and storms had so disfigured that it looks less like a god than a wild beast" (p. 91). In Plato's *Republic* (Bk. X, 611d), of course, the statue of Glaucus is the real self, the immortal self, that emerges into view when the philosopher is engaged in the dialectic. See also Rousseau, *Emile*, Bk. II, p. 151: "habit gives us a second nature that we substitute for the first to such an extent that none of us knows the first anymore." See also ibid., Bk. IV, p. 292.

14. Rousseau, *Second Discourse*, p. 103 (emphasis added). See also *Emile*, Bk. II, p. 156 (note): "critical erudition absorbs everything, as if it were important whether a fact were true, provided that a useful teaching can be drawn from it. Sensible men ought to regard history as *a tissue of fables* whose moral is very appropriate to the human heart" (emphasis added). The truth can be found in the heart, not in the realm of historical facts. "It is in man's heart that the life of nature exists. To see it one must *feel* it" (ibid., Bk. III, p. 169; emphasis added). See also Matt. 6:21; and Hegel, *Philosophy of History*, Part III, Sec. III, Ch. 2, p. 326: "the pure heart is the domain in which God is present to man."

15. Rousseau, *Second Discourse*, p. 93. Might not this state of nature be analogous to the nonhistorical "clearing" of faith in which Luther's soul finds its sustenance and home ground, that place beneath the everyday world which reveals its insubstantiality and corruption, that place of respite for the twice-born? For Rousseau, the "clearing" is prior to the *word*—which raises the question of how he would have responded to Augustine's assertion that God's Truth is not to be found in the "libraries of huge books" (*Confessions*, Bk. III, Ch. 6, p. 60).

16. See Rousseau, *Emile*, Bk. III, p. 185: "it is on the basis of this very state that he ought to appraise all others." See also ibid., p. 487, n. 9. Previous expositions of the state of nature receive harsh treatment by Rousseau. The content of the state of nature in those expositions has been little more than a projection of the content of civil society back into nature (*Second Discourse*, pp. 94–95). The *otherness* of the state of nature is thereby concealed, as is the diremptive movement from a primitive unity in which human beings are wholly self-related to a civil state in which they are other-related (ibid., p. 179). See also Montesquieu, *Spirit of the Laws*, Bk. I, Ch. 2, p. 4.

17. Instead to identifying the preeminently real with *a* Testament, as Luther had done, Rousseau relegates *both* Testaments to the realm of the inauthentic, to the realm of exteriority, to borrow Luther's term. In effect, Rousseau adopts the *form* of Protestant thought—that history discloses the antinomies of human existence and experience—but not the *content*. This annulment and preservation, as it were, of Protestant thought in Rousseau makes it problematic to say simply that he breaks free of it, this in spite of the case being made here that for Rousseau the content of politically authoritative history is not biblical.

18. Rousseau, *Second Discourse*, pp. 103–4 (emphasis added). This *hearing* of another world is reminiscent of John 18:36–37. See also Rousseau, *Emile*, Bk. IV, p. 291: "if [nature] speaks to all hearts, then why are there so few of them who hear it? Well, this is because it speaks to us in nature's language, which everything has made us forget."

19. Rousseau, *Second Discourse*, pp. 103–4 (emphasis added). The words of the Bible, no doubt, are implicated as an aspect of the education which has corrupted human beings in civil society. Thus, in Rousseau's estimation, that Hobbes finds human beings evil in the state of nature and Locke thought them rational merely confirms that both of their respective states of nature have not escaped the sway of Christianity, and so do not plumb the depths of the problem.

20. Rousseau, *Emile*, Bk. II, p. 126 (emphasis added).

21. Plato, *Republic*, Bk. VI, 508e.

22. Rousseau, *Emile*, Bk. V, p. 360. The quote is a description of the relationship between the sexes. Man *appears* stronger than woman, but is actually weaker. The one who does not write (in the history of Western political thought, say) is the silent measure which no writing can comprehend. Writing betrays impotence not potency. Nietzsche correctly posed the question that most terrifies the philosopher: "supposing truth is a woman—what then?" (*Beyond Good and Evil*, Preface, p. 2).

23. I agree with Arthur Melzer (*The Natural Goodness of Man* [Chicago: University of Chicago Press, 1990]) that, for Rousseau, the human being is *essentially* a unity, and not a duality. (See Rousseau, *Emile*, Bk. IV, pp. 278–79, 292–93, *passim*.) Nevertheless, the antinomies of human *experience* which are, as it were, projected onto history in his *First* and *Second Discourses* are not to be overlooked. Dualism clearly offended Rousseau as much as it did Hobbes, but his extraordinary efforts to countervail it, to find that *hidden* unity that alone can give respite, betrays an unhappy soul that *experiences* division, that longs for a peace it only dimly intimates, and yet is allured by the transitory fortunes of society life which can never satisfy, as his *Confessions* attests. See Jean-Jacques Rousseau, *Confessions*, trans. J. M. Cohen (New York: Penguin Books, 1953). Essential unity, yes, but that is only for Emile, the one who has *not yet been* corrupted. All the rest must live in exile. See *Emile*, Bk. V, p. 474: "there are circumstances in which a man can be more useful to his fellow citizens outside of his fatherland than if he were living in its bosom. Then he ought to . . . endure his exile without grumbling. . . . But you, good Emile, on whom nothing imposes these painful sacrifices, you who have not taken on the sad job of telling the truth to men, go and live in their midst." Cf. John 7:7.

24. Rousseau, *First Discourse*, p. 38. Cf. Luther, "Lectures on Genesis," in *Works*, vol. 1, p. 169, where concealment is a consequence of knowledge of sin, *not* the development of society. "When sin has been brought to light it appears to carry with it such great disgrace that the mind cannot bear having it looked at. Therefore it tries to cover it. *No one wants to appear as what he is,* even though he is a thief, an adulterer, or murderer" (emphasis added). Luther's problematic, consequently, is how to atone for sin through Christ, while Rousseau's is how to remain uncorrupted by and in society. For Luther, this would be a delusion which sets its sights on the false hope of finding "salvation" through a right relationship to society. The community of salvation is not, however, to be found in the City of Man.

25. Rousseau, *First Discourse*, p. 37. Marx found Rousseau's analysis of the opacity of one human being to another in civil life quite compelling, though instead of attributing this opacity to the very nature of civil life he attributed it to the alienation caused by the power of money under capitalism; one form of civil association among others. See Karl

Marx, "Economic and Philosophical Manuscripts," in *Marx's Concept of Man*, ed. Erich Fromm (New York: Frederick Ungar Publishing, 1978), pp. 165–66: "that which exists for me through the medium of *money*, that which I can pay for, that *I am*, the possessor of money. My own power is as great as the power of money. . . . I am a detestable, dishonorable, unscrupulous and stupid man but money is honored and so also is its possessor" (emphasis in original). Not civil society but money masks vice. (Rousseau anticipates Marx's thought in *Emile*, Bk. III, p. 202: "if [a man] has the misfortune of being raised in Paris and of being rich, he is lost. So long as there are skillful artists there, he will have all their talents; but far away from them he will no longer have any.")

Rousseau does speak of money as being the occasion of the emergence of vice (*First Discourse*, p. 51), but sees it as coterminous with the emergence of civil society per se, not a particular form of it, as Marx thought. But see *Second Discourse*, p. 174, where society ruled by wealth is "the extreme limit of corruption."

26. Rousseau, *Second Discourse*, p. 180. See also ibid., p. 178, where society offers only "artificial man."

27. See Plato, *Republic*, Bk. II, 357a–367e. Throughout Rousseau's writings Glaucon's unjust man, who appears to be just without really being so, is revealed to be without happiness or substance. Things that appear to be substantial are revealed to be vacuous. The lost soul is drawn to things which glitter and glow; yet these things are only the residual *trace* of former greatness—which does not gaudily announce itself with ceremony and pretense. What he says of states—"every state which *shines* is in decline" (*Emile*, Bk. III, p. 194n., emphasis added)—is merely the application of a more general principle. See also Augustine, *Confessions*, Bk. II, Ch. 6, p. 50: "extravagance masquerades as fullness and abundance, but [God alone is] the full, unfailing store of never-ending sweetness."

28. Rousseau, *Second Discourse*, p. 155.

29. Rousseau, *First Discourse*, p. 39.

30. Friedrich Nietzsche, *Thus Spoke Zarathustra*, trans. Walter Kaufman (New York: Penguin Books, 1978), Prologue, pp. 16–19.

31. Rousseau, *Second Discourse*, p. 179.

32. Against Pufendorf, who argues in *The Law of Nature and of Nations* that external goods are like one's freedom in that both can be alienated, Rousseau points out that human freedom is qualitatively different and cannot be alienated. Freedom is located in the inner realm, and is the source of true worth. Goods are external things which can be transferred and contracted for, but not freedom. See *Second Discourse*, pp. 167–68. This kind of thinking, which would find freedom in an entirely interior realm is one of the characteristics of philosophers and theologians who must be twice-born to come unto themselves.

33. See Rousseau, *First Discourse*, p. 51: "two famous republics competed for World Empire: one of them was very rich, the other had nothing, and it was the latter which destroyed the former."

34. Jean-Jacques Rousseau, *Reveries of the Solitary Walker*, trans. Peter France (New York: Penguin Books, 1979), First Walk, p. 29.

35. Rousseau, *Reveries*, First Walk, p. 28. In George Orwell's *1984* (New York: Harcourt Brace Jovanovich, 1949), there is an even bleaker view of power. When O'Brien

and Winston meet prior to Winston's betrayal of Julia, O'Brien says to him, "Every day, at every moment [heresies] will be defeated, discredited, ridiculed, spat upon—and yet they will always survive. This drama . . . will be played out over and over again, generation after generation, always in subtler forms" (p. 221). For Orwell, the power of the oppressor grows stronger when it strips the opposer of everything; the disempowerment of the heretic does weaken the oppressor, for the oppressor (the state) merely turns to another victim once the first one is destroyed.

36. Rousseau, *Reveries*, First Walk, p. 29.

37. Rousseau, *Reveries*, Second Walk, p. 36.

38. Rousseau, *Reveries*, First Walk, p. 31 (emphasis added). Here is an antecedent of Nietzsche's Zarathustra. Zarathustra, the *Übermensch*, overcomes by going under, by entering into the abyss. Good and evil, moral concepts of the "last man," are left behind in this going under.

39. Rousseau, *Reveries*, First Walk, p. 33. While Rousseau's claim is not to be confused with Luther's, there is, nevertheless, this important similarity: the adversities of the exterior realm open up the avenue to an utterly interior realm where an essential truth comes to presence.

40. Rousseau, *Emile*, Bk. III, p. 205.

41. Rousseau, *First Discourse*, p. 37.

42. Rousseau, *First Discourse*, pp. 37–38.

43. Rousseau, *First Discourse*, p. 38.

44. Rousseau, *First Discourse*, p. 38.

45. Rousseau, *Second Discourse*, p. 139.

46. Rousseau, *Second Discourse*, p. 140. See ibid., p. 151 for the same thought. See also ibid., p. 173: "it is . . . difficult to reduce to obedience one who does not seek to command."

47. Rousseau, *Second Discourse*, p. 135.

48. Plato's distinction between the unmediated object of the appetites and the specific object it desires when reason comes into play is apropos here. See *Republic*, Bk. IV, 437d: "just in itself, thirst or hunger is a desire for nothing more than its natural object, drink or food, pure or simple." When reason comes into play the person then desires a particular object—cold drink when hot, warm drink when cold, etc. Reason chooses a specific object, not the natural object of the appetite. Rousseau's argument is similar, except that in his estimation the natural object of the appetites is lost from view when society refines the tastes of its members. Not reason, but the civil state is implicated in the loss of the natural object of the appetites.
See Rousseau, *Second Discourse*, p. 110; *Emile*, Bk. II, pp. 128, 151; Bk. IV, p. 214, *passim*.

49. Rousseau, *Second Discourse*, p. 156.

50. See Rousseau, *Second Discourse*, p. 114: "it is above all in the consciousness of his freedom the spirituality of his soul is shown . . . [for] in the power of willing, or rather of choosing, and in the sentiment of this power are found only purely spiritual acts about which the laws of mechanics explain nothing."

51. See, for example, Rousseau, *Second Discourse*, p. 80: the revolutions of the enslaved "almost always deliver them to seducers who only make their chains heavier."

52. Rousseau, *Second Discourse*, p. 174.

53. Rousseau, *The Social Contract*, Bk. I, Ch. 1, p. 49; also *Emile*, Bk. IV, p. 244. Augustine, much earlier, voiced a similar sentiment with this thought: "I cannot refrain from speaking about the city of the world, a city which aims at domination, which holds nations in enslavement, but is itself dominated by that very lust of domination" (Augustine, *City of God*, Bk. I, Preface, p. 5). In the *Republic*, Bk. IX, 575e–576a, Plato, too, writes of the *real* servitude of the master/tyrant. For all three, the master-slave relationship reveals the master to be a greater slave than the slave. Think, too, of Pharoah-Moses.

54. Rousseau, *Second Discourse*, p. 92. See Aristotle, *Ethics*, Bk. X, Ch. 9, 1179b: "in matters of action the end is not to study and attain knowledge of a particular thing to be done, but rather to do them." See also Mill, "On Genius," in *Collected Works*, vol. I, pp. 329–39; Ralph Waldo Emerson, "Experience," in *Emerson's Essays* (New York: Harper & Row, 1951), pp. 302–3.

55. Rousseau, *First Discourse*, p. 45. Adam Smith, on the other hand, argues that the Romans were a virtuous people because students could demand of their teachers that they teach virtue. "The demand for instruction produced," he says, "what it always produces, the talent for giving it; and the emulation which an unrestrained competition never fails to excite, appears to have brought that talent to a very high degree of perfection" (Adam Smith, *The Wealth of Nations* [Chicago: University of Chicago Press, 1976], vol. II, Bk. V, Ch. 1, p. 300). All was lost, not when they began to study it, but when teachers were no longer accountable to the student's demands, as they would have been if education, like other commodities, had been subject to the market.

Hegel would later see in the Romans and Greeks peoples who "neither learned nor taught [a moral system] but evinced by their actions the moral maxims which they would call their own" ("The Positivity of the Christian Religion," in *Early Theological Writings*, Part II, §2, p. 154). The significance of the ancients was that they exemplified in the past what Kant had only recently called for: a freedom given to humankind by itself, and not taught to it by others.

56. This is an argument of ancient pedigree, traceable to Plato's claim that an early education in music and gymnastics is necessary for the subsequent development of the soul (*Republic*, Bk. III, 404e, *passim*) and that the dialectician's art requires that the character be well formed by early and very physical training. The analog in Luther is that the Old Law must be *passed through* in order to go beyond it and rest with the New. (Recall, for example, his argument about the second use of the Law.) Rousseau's argument in *Emile* (Bk. II, pp. 77–163) is that although civil life supersedes natural life, the faculty of reason that is so highly developed in civil life is established only by an initial education of the body. The biblical analog is I Cor. 15:46.

57. Rousseau, *Second Discourse*, p. 115 (emphasis in original).

58. Rousseau's point speaks prophetically to his own later life. The *Reveries*, written in Rousseau's last, declining, years, bespeak an aging and less astute mind without the natural vitality it had long before abandoned when it learned to speak with a vigor all its own.

59. Rousseau, *Second Discourse*, pp. 115–16. Nietzsche would later offer a provocative version of this argument and use it against philosophers. See Nietzsche, *Beyond Good and Evil*, Part I, §9, p. 16: philosophy "always creates the world in its own image; it cannot do otherwise. Philosophy is this tyrannical drive itself, the most spiritual will to power, to the 'creation of the world,' to the *causa prima.*" Philosophy seeks to validate the will which animates its search. The search for truth is preceded by the will that wishes to articulate itself in the truth it purports to grasp.

60. Rousseau, *Second Discourse*, p. 95. The other principle anterior to reason is self-preservation. See also ibid., p. 96, where Rousseau wishes to avoid the mistake of making human beings philosophers before they are human.

61. Rousseau, *Second Discourse*, pp. 132–33. But see ibid., p. 157 where not reason but *unbridled* passion extinguishes natural pity. In both cases, however, the result is the same: pity, which in *Emile* is the only antidote to pride, is silenced.

62. Insofar as the object of Rousseau's contempt here is the bourgeois soul, it suggests that liberal regimes, constituted as they are by tamed souls, will not have the strength or stamina to resist an incursion by a more virile neighbor. In Schmitt's more contemporary words, "if a people no longer possesses the energy or the will to maintain itself in the sphere of politics, the latter will not thereby vanish from the world. Only a weak people will vanish" (Carl Schmitt, *The Concept of the Political* [New Brunswick, NJ: Rutgers University Press, 1976]). One need only peruse the pages of J. Glenn Gray's *Warriors* (New York: Harper & Row, 1970) to see that "liberal man," like any other, is more than willing to fall in battle. See also Freud, *Civilization and Its Discontents*, Ch. V, pp. 72–74, *passim*. The error may be in assuming that warfare is an extension of political *will* rather than being based on an aggressive *instinct* that would *more* wish to express itself upon another (society) as civilization becomes ever tamer.

63. Rousseau, *First Discourse*, p. 54.

64. Rousseau, *First Discourse*, p. 55. See also Plato *Phaedrus*, in *Collected Dialogues*, ed. Edith Hamilton and Huntington Cairns, trans. R. Hackforth (New York: Bollingen Foundation, 1961), 275a–b: writing offers only a "semblance, for by telling [human beings] of many things without teaching them you will make them seem to know much, while for the most part they know nothing, and as men filled, not with wisdom, but with the conceit of wisdom, they will be a burden to their fellows."

65. See Rousseau, *Second Discourse*, p. 149, where the natural human being becomes tame, begins to congregate, compares him or herself with others, rewards those who are the best at dancing, speaking, etc. This was "the first step toward inequality and, at the same time, toward vice." See also ibid., p. 133, where prior to civil society humans "knew neither vanity, nor consideration, nor esteem, nor contempt," and ibid., p. 144, where reflection became necessary for survival. Out of this developing sense of superiority over the beast came "the first stirrings of pride."

66. Rousseau, *Second Discourse*, p. 110.

67. See Rousseau, *Emile*, Bk. III, p. 177: "the happiness of the natural man is as simple as his life. It consists in not suffering; health, freedom, and the necessities of life constitute it. The happiness of the moral man is something else."

68. See Rousseau, *First Discourse*, p. 48: "astronomy was born of superstition; eloquence from ambition, hate, flattery, and falsehood; geometry from avarice; physics from vain curiosity; all, even moral philosophy, from human pride."

69. Rousseau, *First Discourse*, p. 47. The implication here is that humans should not have tasted of the tree of knowledge if they had wanted to retain the natural goodness attendant to their original condition. (See Gen. 3:3, 16–19.) See also ibid., p. 46: "luxury, licentiousness, and slavery . . . have been punishment for arrogant attempts to emerge from the happy ignorance." This quasi-Christian theme of the pre-fall state of nature (wherein knowledge was not possessed by humankind) is paralleled in the *Second Discourse*, p. 109 and p. 116, where Rousseau claims that the natural human being barely perceives his or her own death. Before the fall, so to speak, consciousness of death was almost nonexistent.

70. Rousseau, *First Discourse*, p. 39.

71. Rousseau, *First Discourse*, p. 49.

72. In the *Republic*, Bk. X, 601c, Socrates argues that only the horseman who *uses* the bit and bridle understands them. The craftsman who makes them is one step removed from understanding them, because he does not ride. The artist who paints them is two steps removed. Here, use is necessary that truth may be known rather than merely represented. Without use there is only the appearance of truth. Rousseau emphasizes this connection between truth and usefulness in *Emile*, notably in Bk. III.

73. See Rousseau, *First Discourse*, p. 63, where, "the soul gradually adapts itself to the objects that occupy it." This is a variant of the "great man" theory of history—but also a not too veiled allusion to Plato's *Republic*, Bk. VII, 517c–518b.

74. Rousseau, *First Discourse*, p. 36.

75. Rousseau, *First Discourse*, p. 45.

76. See Rousseau, *First Discourse*, pp. 62–63: "those whom nature destined to be her disciples needed no teachers." See also Plato, *Republic*, Bk. V, 455b. The rarity of nature's disciples and the danger that civil society will corrupt them corresponds with Plato's claim that the true philosopher is often used, and consequently corrupted, by others for their own purposes. See ibid., Bk. VI, 490e–497a.

77. Rousseau, *First Discourse*, p. 64.

78. Rousseau, *First Discourse*, p. 50.

79. Rousseau, *First Discourse*, p. 64.

80. See Rousseau, *Second Discourse*, p. 165: "it does not behoove slaves to reason about freedom." How can the other-related soul produced in civil society know what self-mastery means, or what it would cost?

81. Consider, for counterpoint, Max Weber, who, in his "Politics as a Vocation," sets forth an understanding of political life in which discontent and nonreconciliation *must* reign. Weber's is the political expression of the Nietzschean sentiment: "how much can you bear" in the absence (not hiddenness) of God?

82. Gen. 3:7–10.

83. Rousseau, *Emile*, Bk. III, p. 205 (emphasis added). Like Christ in John 8:23, who is "not of this world" and yet who dwells in it, Emile is to live in civil society but not be of it. Cf. John 17:11–16.

84. Rousseau, *First Discourse*, p. 59.

85. Rousseau, *First Discourse*, p. 59. This is consistent with the opening passage of *Emile*. There Rousseau claims, were human beings not to be "trained like a school horse . . . everything would go even worse" (Bk. I, p. 37). The degeneration incumbent to civil society would be even more monstrous were it not for education.

86. Rousseau, *First Discourse*, pp. 59–60.

87. Rousseau, *First Discourse*, p. 63.

88. Hobbes, *De Cive*, Ch. X, pp. 229–30, *passim*.

89. See Luther, "Lectures on Galatians," in *Works*, vol. 26, pp. 231–32.

90. Rousseau, *First Discourse*, p. 64. See Plato, *Republic*, Bk. V, 473c–d.

91. Rousseau, *Second Discourse*, p. 169.

92. Rousseau, *The Social Contract*, Bk. I, Ch. 6, p. 60. See also *Emile*, Bk. V, p. 460.

93. See Luther, "Freedom," in *Works*, vol. 31, p. 344: the Christian is "a perfectly free lord of all . . . and perfectly dutiful subject to all."

94. For Hobbes civil freedom can only arise when "the power and honour of the subjects vanisheth in the presence of the powerful sovereign" (*Leviathan*, Part II, Ch. 18, p. 140). The subjects' strength consists in their weakness before the sovereign.

95. For the view that the general will is at its root a theological concept, see Patrick Riley, *The General Will before Rousseau* (Princeton: Princeton University Press, 1986). Riley's argument, different from the one provided here, is that the notion of the general will originates from the question of whether God's will is a general will (according to which all are saved) or a particular will (according to which only a few are saved). This question, Riley argues, informs a long line of French speculation, from Pascal to Rousseau. In the case of Rousseau, he argues, this notion is philosophical, not theological (ibid., pp. 181–82). Here I emphasize the argument's theological overtones, not to suggest that Rousseau is first and foremost a "religious" thinker, but to intimate that Rousseau's general will is perhaps opaque without considering its overtones. Riley focuses on God's will; here I focus on the paradox that surrounds Christ's relations to all Christians. Riley writes of God the Father; I consider God the Son.

96. Rousseau, *The Social Contract*, Bk. I, Ch. 6, p. 60.

97. Rousseau, *The Social Contract*, Bk. I, Ch. 6, p. 60 (emphasis added).

98. See Maurice Cranston's Introduction to *The Social Contract*, pp. 41–42, for something of a psychological explanation of Rousseau's wish that citizens be "excessively" dependent on the state but not at all upon other citizens. For whatever reason, however, the pattern is still the same one found in Luther: diminished *lateral* relations between human beings and increased *vertical* relations between humans and the sovereign—the effect of which is that authentic and secure lateral relations become possible at all.

99. Rousseau, *The Social Contract*, Bk. I, Ch. 6, p. 61.

100. Rousseau, *The Social Contract*, Bk. I, Ch. 8, p. 64.

101. A massive difference, of course, is that Luther's "One" who stands above the law is not the collective; the collective still stands under the law for him. This view attenuates the prospect for collective injustice of the sort evinced in "the Terror" of post-Revolutionary France.

102. Rousseau, *The Social Contract*, Bk. I, Ch. 7, p. 62

103. See Emile Durkheim, "Le problème religieux et la dualité de la nature humaine," in *Bulletin de la Société française de Philosophie* 13 (February 1913), p. 69: "les dieux ne sont que les idéaux collectifs personifiés" (the gods are nothing but collective ideals personified), and further along, "la divinité n'est autre chose que la société transfigurée" (divinity is nothing else but society transfigured). One would have to turn to Calvin rather than to Luther in order to develop this argument further. There the analog to Durkheim's social body is the *Body* of Christ rather than the *Spirit* of Christ.

104. This is Hobbes's version of the noble lie. See Thomas Hobbes, *De Cive*, Ch. III, p. 143: "whether therefore men be equal by nature, the equality is to be acknowledged; or whether unequal, because they are like to contest for dominion, it is necessary for the obtaining of peace, *that they be esteemed as equal* . . . [and] that every man be accounted by nature equal to another; *the contrary to which law is pride* (emphasis in original).

105. For Hobbes's assertions to this effect see *Leviathan*, Part I, Ch. 16, p. 127. For Rousseau's argument that the general will is a public person see *The Social Contract*, Bk. I, Ch. 6, p. 61: "this act of association creates an artificial and collective body . . . and by this same act that body acquires its unity, its common *ego*, its life and its will. This public person thus formed . . ." (emphasis in the original). See also ibid., Bk. II, Ch. 1, p. 69, where the sovereign is referred to as the "collective being." Rousseau's public person is clearly more enigmatic than is Hobbes's, perhaps because the more explicitly *political* the pattern of thought I have been investigating becomes, its comprehensibility diminishes—if only because the referent of the pattern of thought is essentially *religious*.

106. See Hobbes, *Leviathan*, Part II, Ch. 21, p. 163: "for in the act of submission, consisteth both our obligation, and our liberty."

107. Rousseau, *Second Discourse*, p. 177.

108. Connolly is correct, I think, in suggesting that "the general will redeems the purity lost through the original fall from the innocence of nature. It is a condition where reason, sociality and complex emotions develop in harmony with virtue, where we are finally at one with ourselves and at home in the civil society in which we reside" (*Political Theory and Modernity*, p. 62).

109. Rousseau, *The Social Contract*, Bk. IV, Ch. 8, p. 181.

110. Rousseau, *The Social Contract*, Bk. IV, Ch. 4, p. 157.

111. Rousseau, *The Social Contract*, Bk. IV, Ch. 8, pp. 176–77.

112. Rousseau, *The Social Contract*, Bk. IV, Ch. 8, p. 177.

113. Rousseau, *The Social Contract*, Bk. IV, Ch. 8, p. 178.

114. Rousseau, *The Social Contract*, Bk. IV, Ch. 8, p. 179.

115. Rousseau, *The Social Contract*, Bk. IV, Ch. 8, p. 180. See also ibid., p. 184: "Christianity preaches only servitude and submission. . . . True Christians are made to

be slaves; they know it and they hardly care; this short life has too little value in their eyes."

116. Rousseau, *The Social Contract*, Bk. IV, Ch. 8, p. 185.

117. These are "the existence of an omnipotent, intelligent, benevolent divinity that foresees and provides; the life to come; the happiness of the just; the punishment of sinners; the sanctity of the social contract and law. . . . As for negative dogmas, I would limit them to a single one: no intolerance" (*The Social Contract*, Bk. IV, Ch. 8, p. 186).

118. Rousseau, *The Social Contract*, Bk. IV, Ch. 8, p. 186. Rousseau's assessment of Christianity was that it produces no "bonds of union" between human beings (ibid., p. 183). Hence the need for a civil religion.

Montesquieu argues that the real problem of Christianity was that it weakened paternal authority (*Spirit of the Laws*, vol. 2, Bk. XXIII, Ch. 21, p. 19). Paternal authority is the wellspring of a republic. Without the guidance of the father, the children's reason would not develop, and they would be ruled by their passions. Subvert the authority of the father and the *motion* of the children is quickened. Cf. Matt. 10:37.

119. He considered this to be his best work. See Rousseau, *Confessions*, Bk. XI, pp. 529–30.

120. See Rousseau, *Second Discourse*, p. 179: "the savage lives within himself; the sociable man, always outside himself."

121. The only book ever given to Emile is, of course, *Robinson Crusoe*. See Rousseau, *Emile*, Bk. III, p. 184.

122. In *The Education of the Human Race*, Lessing suggests that because individual human beings could not conceive of God without the thought slipping away, He educated a whole race (§§6–8, p. 35); and that the advancement of the race eventually imparts the wisdom achieved *back* to the individual (§93, p. 56). Phylogenetic development here assists ontogenetic development, though the two remain logically distinct. Kant also exhibited this dichotomy in his thought. See his *Critique of Practical Reason*, Part II, Conclusion, p. 166, where he distinguishes the utter interiority of the "moral law within" and the exteriority of the "starry heavens above." By this disjunction he intended to provide the soul with a means by which it could be free of the proceedings in the exterior world. Yet Kant also speaks of a dialectic of history, one according to which the unintended consequences of human actions would lead to a cosmopolitan world. His "Idea for a World History with a Cosmopolitan Purpose" in *Kant's Political Writings*, ed. Hans Reiss (Cambridge: Cambridge University Press, 1970), pp. 41–53, is a defense of this proposition. Here nature is providential; the perfection of the faculties is accomplished in history through social antagonisms. For both Kant and Rousseau these *twin* truths do not derive from biblical sources, though the pattern of thinking that informs the project as a whole is decisively Christian. See, for example, Michel Despland, *Kant on History and Religion* (Montreal: McGill-Queen's University Press, 1973).

123. The issue of the relationship between the ontogenetic development of the child and the phylogenetic development of the species (to borrow from biology) can be raised in the context of Rousseau's discussion of the language of infants. "Whether there was a language natural and common to all men has long been a subject of research. Doubtless there is such a language, and it is the one children speak before they know how to speak. . . . The habit of our languages has made us neglect that language to the point of

forgetting it completely. Let us study children, and we shall soon relearn it with them";
Emile, Bk. I, p. 65. Here the child recapitulates the natural human being, a view further
confirmed by comparing Rousseau's characterization of the first richly accented human
language ("On the Origin of Languages," Ch. 5, p. 16) to the kind of language to which
Emile is first to be exposed (*Emile*, Bk. II, pp. 148–49).

124. Rousseau, *Emile*, Bk. I, p. 66. See Augustine, *Confessions*, Bk. I, Ch. 6, pp. 25–
26: as an infant I wanted "to make my wishes known to others, who might satisfy them.
But this I could not do, because my wishes were inside me, while other people were outside, and they had no faculty which could penetrate my mind. So I tossed my arms and
legs about and made noises. . . . And if my wishes were not carried out, either because
they had not been understand or because I wanted what would have harmed me, I would
get cross with my elders, who were not at my beck and call, and with people who were
not my servants, simply because they did not attend to my wishes; and I would take my
revenge by bursting into tears." Cf. Freud, *Civilization and Its Discontents*, Ch. 1, p. 14.
There, the cry gives birth only to the separation of the ego and the external world.

125. Rousseau, *Emile*, Bk. I, p. 66. Cf. Augustine, *City of God*, Bk. XIV, Ch. 13: "it
was *in secret* that the first humans began to be evil; and the result was that they slipped
into open disobedience" (emphasis added). Rousseau's view was that this secret intention could be thwarted by making sure that the child experiences the necessity of things
rather than the indeterminacy of wills. The secret intention, in other words, can be put
to sleep until reason is awakened, at which time reason would have the strength to constrain it. Human beings can be evil, but need not be, contra Augustine. Locke, too,
recognizes that the child's will-to-dominion can be silenced. See Locke, *Some Thoughts*,
§103, *passim*.

126. Understood phylogenetically, this development recalls Marx's dialectic of history, and refutes it. For Marx, the original opposition between humankind and nature
occurs because nature provided the wherewithal for human life only reluctantly. The
dialectic of history is the means by which that initial scarcity is overcome, though not
without considerable suffering (especially in the penultimate, capitalist, stage of history). Rousseau argues that while the desire to secure the necessities of life is prior to the
desire for power after power, this latter desire superimposes itself upon natural *amour de
soi*. In Marx's terms, while scarcity may have been present from the beginning (thus making it *appear* to be the original problem), the present and predominant problem is the
desire for power after power. The dialectic of history may, in other words, proceed up to
the point where scarcity is almost solved, only to reveal the predominant motive behind
even the struggle to overcome scarcity: the desire for power. We end, then, not with
communism, but rather with Orwell's *1984*. Errancy from nature leads to the tyranny of
power: the master theme of the *Second Discourse*.

127. Rousseau, *Emile*, Bk. II, pp. 92–93. See also *The Social Contract*, Bk. I, Ch. 2,
p. 50: "as soon as [a person] reaches the age of reason . . . he becomes his own master."
Reason liberates the child from the binding power of *amour-propre*. The general will spoken of in *The Social Contract* can be understood as a mechanism by which the secret
intention that corrupts is constrained and freedom and servitude are reconciled. See
Emile, Bk. II, p. 85: what is necessary is to "substitute law for man and to arm the general
wills with a real strength superior to the action of every particular will. If the laws of
nations could, like those of nature, have an inflexibility that no human force could ever

conquer, dependence on men would become dependence on *things* again" (emphasis in original). See Madeleine B. Ellis, *Rousseau's Socratic Aemilian Myths* (Columbus: Ohio State University Press, 1977), for a provocative consideration of the relationship between *The Social Contract* and *Emile.*

128. Cf. Augustine, *Confessions,* Bk. II, Ch. 2, pp. 43–44, where the antidote for pride is neither political nor educational: pride can only be amended by returning to God.

129. See Tocqueville, *Democracy in America,* vol. I, Part II, Ch. 9, pp. 301–5.

130. Rousseau, *Emile,* Bk. II, p. 119.

131. See Nietzsche, *Thus Spoke Zarathustra,* Part IV, §20, p. 324.

132. Rousseau, *Emile,* Bk. IV, p. 296.

133. Rousseau, *Emile,* Bk. IV, p. 295. Compare this to Locke, for whom the miracles related *through words* in the New Testament are the foundation of faith. The massive difference between Rousseau and Locke on this point cannot be overemphasized. Locke's entire political, epistemological, and theological edifice rests on the claim that reason is supplemented by Revelation, and that reason assents to Revelation, the *witness* of which is the *Word,* because miracles are the proof (again, attested to, by, and in words) of its veracity. See Locke, *Essay,* Bk. IV, Ch. XVI, §14, p. 667; Ch. XIX, §15, p. 705.

134. See Luther, "Bondage," in *Works,* vol. 33, p. 28: "all men have a darkened heart, so that even if they can recite everything in Scripture, they yet apprehend and truly understand nothing of it. . . . The Spirit [alone] is required for the understanding of Scripture."

135. Rousseau, *Emile,* Bk. IV, p. 295 (emphasis added). Cf. Matt. 5:8; 6:21.

136. In this regard, see Paul Tillich, *Systematic Theology* (Chicago: University of Chicago Press, 1951), vol. III, p. 125: "the liberation of the Christian conscience from the church's authority by the reformers also produced the desire for liberation from the new authorities, i.e., from the letter of the Bible and the creedal statements of its theological interpreters. It was an attack, in the name of the Spirit, both on the pope of Rome and on the new pope—the Bible and its scholarly guardians. Since the Spirit means "God present," no human form of life or thought can be shut off from the Spirit. God is not bound to any of his manifestations. The spiritual Presence breaks through the established Word and the established sacraments."

137. Emerson would later take this insight in a different direction. "All religious error," he says, consists "in making the symbol too stark and solid, and, at last, nothing but an excess of the organ of language" (Ralph Waldo Emerson, "The Poet," in *Emerson's Essays,* pp. 285–86). The poet is capable of renewing the once vital and now ossified language of religion. Language is forever in the process of dying to its living referents, and so must be renewed by the poet. More recently, Rorty makes the same move. See Richard Rorty, *Contingency, Irony, and Solidarity* (New York: Cambridge University Press, 1989), p. 20: "the poet, in the generic sense of the maker of new words, the shaper of new languages, [is] the vanguard of the species." The present moves forward into a *living* future out of the mouth of the poet. Finally, Tocqueville, too, seems to have grasped this relationship. Those who would be satisfied with the world use prose, while those who would change the world use poetry, he says (*Democracy in America,* vol. II, Part III, Ch. 21, p. 634).

138. Rousseau, *Emile*, Bk. V, pp. 397–98. Merit here is the *withstanding* of the propensity toward errancy. Cf. Luther, "Lectures on Genesis," in *Works*, vol. 1, p. 145, where, in answering why God should have allowed Eve to be tempted by Satan, he replies: "it pleased the Lord that Adam should be tempted and should test his powers." (See also ibid., p. 111.) For Augustine's view of merit, life, and eternal life, see *City of God*, Bk. XIII, Ch. 23, pp. 536–37. Nietzsche's contempt for the idea of Christian merit is conveyed in the *Genealogy*, First Essay, §13, p. 46.

139. Rousseau, *Emile*, Bk. V. p. 417.

140. Rousseau, *Emile*, Bk. V, p. 397. See also Plato, *Republic*, Bk. VII, 535c. Cf. Locke, *Reasonableness*, §245, p. 184: "the philosophers indeed showed the beauty of virtue; they set her off so, and drew man's eyes and approbations to her; but leaving her unendowed, very few were willing to espouse her." For Locke, the problem is not quite as Plato and Rousseau imagined; the light of natural reason is forever dim; human beings cannot be the consorts of wisdom at all without the spiritual light of Christ which supplements the light of reason. Wisdom remains a spinster without God's revelation.

141. Gen. 4:15–17. Cain was *marked* as a murderer so that no one might kill him. The "city" is to endure; corruption is to endure. The "city" is the necessary counterpoint to the purity of the "desert." In Rousseau's language, only in the silence of the desert/countryside can the voice of God/Nature be heard; the overbearing noise of the city obliterates all but the *trace* of Nature—and yet *both* are constitutive elements of human experience. See Augustine, *City of God*, Bk. XV, Chs. 1–2, pp. 595–98, where Cain and Abel prefigure the City of Man and the City of God.

142. Rousseau, *Emile*, Bk. V, p. 404.

143. Rousseau, *Emile*, Bk. V, p. 441.

144. Rousseau, *Second Discourse*, Preface, p. 95. See Judith N. Shklar, *Men and Citizens* (Cambridge: Cambridge University Press, 1969), p. 54: "suffering is, in any case, the most universal human experience and Rousseau's identification of active consciousness with suffering was the very essence of his egalitarian vision."

Cf. Ludwig Feuerbach, *The Essence of Christianity* (New York: Harper & Row, 1957), Ch. V, p. 60: "out of the heart, out of the divine instinct of benevolence . . . which excludes none, not even the most abandoned and abject, out of a moral duty of benevolence in the highest sense, as having become an inward necessity, i.e., a movement of the heart,—out of the human nature, therefore, as it reveals itself through the heart, has sprung what is best, what is true in Christianity—its essence purified from theological dogmas and contradictions." On this reading Rousseau would have been one of the first to discover the nonalienated truth of Christianity.

145. Rousseau, *Emile*, Bk. V, p. 444. See John. 12:25.

146. Rousseau, *Emile*, Bk. V, 450.

147. See Plato, *Phaedo*, in *Collected Dialogues*, trans. Hugh Tredennick, p. 46, 64a: "those who really apply themselves in the right way to philosophy are directly and of their own accord preparing themselves for dying and death."

148. Plato, *Republic*, Bk. IX, 592b.

149. Plato, *Republic*, Bk. V, 473d.

150. Bloom's translation (*Emile*, Bk. V, p. 474) does not convey the thought as powerfully as does the Foxley translation, which I have cited here. See Jean-Jacques Rousseau, *Emile*, trans. Barbara Foxley (New York: E. P. Dutton & Co., 1928), Bk. V, p. 438.

151. See Matt. 24:36.

152. See Nietzsche, *Genealogy*, Third Essay, §28, pp. 162–63.

153. See Augustine, *City of God*, Bk. XI, Ch. 22: in regard to the apparent evil in the world, "Divine providence thus warns us not to indulge in silly complaints about the state of affairs, but to take pains to inquire what useful purposes are served by things."

154. Rousseau, *The Social Contract*, Bk. I, Ch. 1, p. 49. See also *Emile*, Bk. I, p. 43: "the first gifts [children] receive from you are chains."

155. Rousseau, *Emile*, Bk. IV, p. 236. The note at the bottom of the page reads: "the universal spirit of the laws of every country is always to favor the strong against the weak and those who have against those who have not. This difficulty is inevitable, and it is without exception." See *Second Discourse*, pp. 158–60.

156. Plato, *Republic*, Bk. I, 352d.

157. Plato, *Republic*, Bk. X, 614b–621d.

158. Rousseau, *Confessions*, Bk. I, p. 30; *Emile*, Bk. IV, p. 282, *passim*.

159. See Starobinski, *Jean-Jacques Rousseau*, p. 11: "Rousseau is one of the first writers (perhaps one should say poets) to cast the Platonic myth of exile and return in a form pertaining not to some heavenly homeland but to the condition of childhood." This is not something original to Rousseau, however. Starobinski remarks that with Rousseau, "historical distance is reduced to mere interior distance" (ibid., p. 19). The first prominent appearance of this reduction appears, however, in Saint Paul's Adamic myth. There, in the Epistles, the historical distance back to the origin recorded by the Old Testament is reduced to the distance within every soul between Adam and Christ. The birthmark of Adam (who is the source of phylogenetic *and* ontogenetic history) is borne by every soul. *Emile* is the functional equivalent of the Adamic myth, while *The Second Discourse* is the functional equivalent of the history of the Jews who, while sprung fully formed in Adam (natural man), stand in need of rebirth by the end of the Old Testament.

160. Augustine, *City of God*, Bk. X, Ch. 14, p. 392 (emphasis added). Augustine's *City of God*, comments O'Meara in his Introductory Essay, is "the application of the *Confessions* to the history of humankind" (p. xvii). History has a spiritual significance that mirrors the spiritual journey *each individual* Christian may take. See also Freud, *Civilization and Its Discontents*, Ch. III, pp. 43–44.

161. See Bernard Yack, *The Longing for Total Revolutions* (Princeton: Princeton University Press, 1986).

162. See Blaise Pascal, *Pensées*, trans. A. J. Krailsheimer (New York: Penguin Books, 1966), Part 1, §5, 110, p. 58: "it is through [the heart] that we know first principles, and reason, which has nothing to do with it, tries in vain to refute them. . . . It is on

[the knowledge coming from the heart] that reason has to depend and base all its argument."

CONCLUSION

1. Reason, while deferring, of course, must also be strengthened. See Connolly, *Political Theory and Modernity*, p. 24: "the retreat of God to the heavens requires that reason be improved as an instrument through which his light is transmitted. God, after withdrawing from the mundane world of words and events, leaves the telescope of reason to enable human beings to discern his will for them from a distance." See Locke, *First Treatise*, Ch. IX, §86, p. 205, where reason is characterized as '*the Voice of God*' (emphasis in original); and Hobbes, *Leviathan*, Part I, Ch. 8, p. 67: "the Scripture was written to show unto men the kingdom of God, and to prepare their minds to become obedient subjects; leaving the world, and the philosophy thereof, to the disputation of men, for the exercising of their natural reason." Augustine notes: "we are too weak to discover the truth by reason alone and for this reason [we] need the authority of sacred books" (*Confessions*, Bk. VI, Ch. 5, p. 117).

2. Nietzsche, *Genealogy*, Third Essay, §27, p. 160 (emphasis in original).

3. Hobbes, *Leviathan*, Part I, Ch. 12, p. 94. See Tocqueville, *Democracy in America*, vol. I, Part II, Ch. 9, p. 295: "eighteenth-century philosophers had a very simple explanation for the gradual weakening of beliefs. Religious zeal, they said, would die down as enlightenment and freedom spread. It is tiresome that the facts do not fit the theory at all." See also ibid., p. 297: "faith is the only permanent state of mankind." The so-called secularization of the world, about which Tocqueville was not unaware, is the result of the massive historical shift from aristocracy to democracy—subject to abandonment when, by Providential hand, equality comes to prevail!

In more biological terms, following Hans Blumenberg (*Work on Myth*, trans. Robert M. Wallace [Cambridge, MA: MIT Press, 1985]), the achievement of upright posture so extended the horizon from which reality can "come at one" (p. 5) that it became necessary for the imagination to arrest the "existential anxiety" (p. 6) that ensued when the human being nakedly faced the unoccupied, unnamed, horizon. Myth fills that horizon and arrests anxiety. On this reading myth is a permanent need of human beings, diminished perhaps, but never overcome, by the machinations of logos which would tame "the world." Tocqueville, too, seems to have recognized this need of "the human spirit never [to see] an unlimited field before itself" (*Democracy in America*, vol. I, Part II, Ch. 2, p. 292).

4. Alfred North Whitehead, *Science and the Modern World* (New York: Macmillan Publishing Co., 1925), Ch. XII, pp. 192–93. In this work, Whitehead, like Hobbes and Locke, carves out the domain graspable by reason and then speaks of what reason cannot grasp and what can only be "known" through *worship*.

5. Spinoza, *A Theologico-Political Treatise*, Preface, p. 3 (emphasis added).

6. Hobbes seems to recognize that these are the two alternatives in *Leviathan*, Part IV, Ch. 45, pp. 460–77. Relics of prebiblical religion (aspects of which are to be found in the Catholic Church [ibid., pp. 475–77]) he treats under the heading of the "Kingdom of Darkness." The alternatives are either a "Christian Commonwealth" (Part III) or a "Kingdom of Darkness" (Part IV). A secularized world is not a genuine possibility; the

attempt to deny religion its due leads not to a world enlightened by autonomous reason, but rather, ironically, one dominated by superstition and steeped in the kingdom of darkness!

7. Tocqueville, *Democracy in America*, vol. I, Part II, Ch. 9, p. 286. Prosperity alone cannot account for this enigma, as Tocqueville himself recognizes. The conditions of equality discredit the idea that knowledge must often be predicated upon the authority of another. Hence his observation: "equality give[s] men . . . a very high and often thoroughly exaggerated conception of human reason" (ibid., vol. II, Part I, Ch. 2, p. 434).

8. Nietzsche, *Genealogy*, Third Essay, §27, p. 161 (emphasis in original). So, too, would a self-confident age blink at Plato's suggestion that the most important truths are ones which are "hard to accept, but also hard to reject" (*Republic*, Bk. VII, 532d).

9. Ludwig Wittgenstein, *Tractatus Logico-Philosophicus* (London: Routledge & Kegan Paul, 1981), p. 189.

10. Heidegger, "The Essence of Truth," in *Martin Heidegger: Basic Writings*, p. 134 (emphasis added).

11. Again, Augustine, *Confessions*, Bk. I, Ch. 4, p. 23. I have cited this passage in several places; it may be taken to be the most succinct formulation of the way in which God exists for human beings prior to the Redemption for Protestants.

12. Luther, "Lectures on Galatians," in *Works*, vol. 26, p. 5.

13. Heidegger, *Being and Time*, Division II, Ch. 5, §38, pp. 219–24, *passim*.

14. William E. Connolly's letter to Augustine in *Identity/Difference* (Ithaca: Cornell University Press, 1991), pp. 123–57, is much too brittle. It fails to grasp the dialectical aspect of identity in Augustine and sees in piety only a strategy of power (p. 142). Piety must wage war against the impiety of carnality (the *other*); yet the impious one is less other than prefigurement, the one who is on the way through Rome. See Augustine, *Confessions*, Bk. XIII, Ch. 23, p. 333: "no man, even though he has the gifts of the Spirit, can pass judgment on the peoples of this world who struggle on without your grace." He *must* say this because grace is a battle with the carnal world which both is and is not self. See Rom. 7:23. The easy opposition between self and other, between us and them, between saved and damned is only one (necessary) aspect of a Christian—and also early modern—notion of self. This aspect is taken *for the whole* once authoritative history is jettisoned. Gone, then, is the notion of prefigurement, concealment, etc. Here we have the contemporary view, which would make identity wholly self-enclosed, without an historical horizon which specifies a *then* which it *now* both is and is not. Connolly's Augustine, in short, suffers the failing of most liberal constructions of identity.

15. Luther, "Temporal Authority," in *Works*, vol. 45, p. 108.

16. Exodus 19:12.

17. Because Moses is not eloquent, his brother Aaron speaks to the people. Hobbes does not remark about this. See Exodus 4:10–16, 30.

18. See Gen. 18:13–15.

19. Hobbes, *Leviathan*, Part II, Ch. 18, p. 135.

20. Locke, "Letter," p. 52. See also Hobbes, *Leviathan*, Part II, Ch. 26, pp. 205–6.

21. Exodus 5:2.

22. Luther, "Bondage," in *Works*, vol. 33, p. 179, *passim*. See also Luther, "Lectures on Genesis," in *Works*, vol. I, p. 173: "thus it happens—and this is the nature of sin—that the farther man withdraws from God, the farther he still desires to withdraw."

23. Nietzsche, *Genealogy*, Second Essay, §23, p. 94.

24. See Luther, "Lectures on Galatians," in *Works*, vol. 26, pp. 231–32.

25. See Rousseau, *Emile*, Bk. IV, p. 284: "what need is there to look for hell in the other life? It begins in this one in the hearts of the wicked." Rousseau does note, however, that the *idea* of an afterlife can give human beings *hope* while they live. See ibid., Bk. II, p. 82.

26. See Laslett's Introduction to the *Two Treatises*, p. 90: "it is of importance to see in Locke, the recognized point of departure for liberalism, the liberal dilemma already present, the dilemma of maintaining a political faith without subscribing to a total, holistic view of the world."

27. See MacIntyre, *After Virtue*, p. 53, where, on the Protestant view there is "*no genuine comprehension of man's true end*" (emphasis in original). See ibid., pp. 250–51, where Hobbes and Locke, among others, are purveyors of the "individualist view" in which society is "nothing but a collection of strangers, each pursuing his or her own interest under minimal constraints." MacIntyre fails to understand that the Protestant dialectic of history is an answer to the Thomistic analogical vision. In the former there is no telos of the sort MacIntyre envisions, to be sure, but this does not mean there is no vision of a whole. The liberal thought against which MacIntyre writes is an alternative to the theoretical framework out of which the notion of telos arises, not a lapse from it.

28. Plato, *Republic*, Bk. VI, 505b.

29. Nietzsche, *Thus Spoke Zarathustra*, First Part, "On the Thousand and One Goals," p. 59.

30. Carl Schmitt, *The Crisis of Parliamentary Democracy* (Cambridge, Mass.: MIT Press, 1985). Commenting on Marxism's response to bourgeois rationalism Schmitt notes, "as Trotsky justly reminded the democrat Kautsky, the awareness of relative truths never gives one the courage to use force and to spill blood" (p. 64). See also Rousseau, *Emile*, Bk. III, p. 183: "in vain does tranquil reason make us approve or criticize; it is only passion which makes us act." Rousseau's comment, of course, only pertains to the stage in the development of the soul where reason begins to be awakened by the right exercise of the body, after which we become adults. Schmitt's opposition to the so-called liberal soul, for whom there is no transcendent truth, is less a criticism of early modern thought than of the caricature it becomes in the hands of those who would divest the self of its link to the Source through an authoritative history. The self disencumbered of its authoritative history, it would seem, has before it two prominent alternatives: a kind of formalism without grounding (the so-called liberal soul) or passion-driven action which accomplishes much but which amounts to little more than romantic excursions into "bad infinity" (Schmitt et al.)—the alternatives Hegel sought to surmount with his historical dialectic.

31. See Tocqueville, *Democracy in America,* vol. II, Part II, Ch. 4, pp. 509–13. The political problem is how, in the light of the absence of permanent links forged between human beings in the now superseded age of aristocracy, to draw the ego outside of itself that a vital polity with the right amount of motion (following Montesquieu) may be maintained. His answer is political participation at the local level. Having said this, however, there is a complementary problem: how to slow down the *excess* motion of the democratic soul. For this religion is needed. See ibid., vol. I, Part II, Ch. 9, p. 294, where Tocqueville asks, "what can be done with a people master of itself if it is not subject to God?" Also see Augustine, *Confessions,* Bk. VII, Ch. 11, p. 128.

32. Gen. 3:10.

33. Gen. 3:9.

34. Gen. 1:26.

35. Hegel, *Philosophy of History,* Part III, Sec. III, Ch. II, p. 324 (emphasis added). For Augustine, of course, this elevation from the natural and participation in the Divine is possible only through the intercession of a Mediator. See Augustine, *City of God,* Bk. XIV, Ch. 11, p. 569—hence the profoundly important question: *Who* was Christ, and what does it mean to be *Christian?* For both Augustine and Luther, unlike Hegel, "remnants of sin" forever make it impossible for humankind to divest itself of its natural being: the Word made Flesh was a *one time event,* not recapitulated over and over again in history (as Hegel would have it)!

36. Hobbes, *Leviathan,* Part I, Ch. 14, p. 110.

37. Gen. 22:18, *passim.*

38. Exodus 16:2, 17:3. Cf. John 6:41, where the Jews murmur against Christ in their dis-ease about what He would ask of them.

39. Exodus 32:1–7. When Moses is on the Mount speaking to God, the Israelites, thinking he will not return, fashion a golden calf to worship, thus violating the charge God had placed upon them in Exodus 20:3–4. Hobbes cites this passage in *Leviathan,* Part I, Ch. 12, p. 96.

40. Hobbes, *Leviathan,* Part II, Ch. 17, p. 129. On Hardin's reading, "Hobbes is perhaps the original discoverer of the fact that ordinary exchange relations are, in other words, a Prisoner's Dilemma problem unless there is some coercive power to back them up" (Russell Hardin, "Hobbesian Political Order," in *Political Theory* 19, no. 2 [1991], p. 174). On the reading I have offered, that problem appears first in the Mosaic covenant.

41. Lord Acton, "The History of Freedom in Christianity," in *Essays in the History of Liberty,* ed. J. Rufus Fears (Indianapolis: Liberty Press, 1985), vol. I, p. 47 (emphasis added).

42. Rawls, who disregards the politics of biblical history, notes this linkage, though for him recurrence to the Creator of Adam merely serves to provide a general principle to which all may accede in the original position of ignorance. See Rawls, *A Theory of Justice,* p. 132. This is a "move," for Rawls, which solves a problem of contract, not, as it was for Locke, part of an answer to the Reformation question about the meaning of Christ's fulfillment.

43. Locke, *Second Treatise*, Ch. V, §31, p. 290. See I Cor. 4:1–2: "Let a man so consider us, as servants of Christ and stewards of the mysteries of God. Moreover it is required in stewards that one be found faithful."

44. Rousseau, *Emile*, Bk. IV, p. 293.

45. The Latin, *Decipimur specie recti,* appears at the opening of Rousseau's *First Discourse,* p. 34.

46. Rousseau, *Emile*, Bk. II, p. 151.

47. Rousseau, *Second Discourse*, pp. 109–10.

48. See Robin W. Lovin and Frank E. Reynolds, "In the Beginning," in *Cosmogony and Ethical Order* (Chicago: University of Chicago Press, 1985), pp. 1–35. In their words, "the study of cosmogonies and cosmogonic myths themselves are attempts to find a pattern for human choice and action that stands outside the flux of change and yet within the bounds of human knowing. What unites the cosmogonies is this underlying function of bestowing on certain actions a significance that is not proportional to their empirical effects or to the individual goals of their agents, but derives from their relation to an order of the world that begins with the beginning of the world as we know it" (pp. 5–6).

49. Dunn also agrees. See *The Political Philosophy of John Locke,* p. 125: "the structure of political obligation is logically dependent on the structure of religious duty."

Not incidentally, John Rawls and Robert Nozick, for whom there is no politically authoritative history, each presume that action is wholly self-assumed. Rawls I have mentioned earlier. See Robert Nozick, *Anarchy, State, and Utopia* (New York: Basic Books, 1974), for an attempt to justify the minimal state based on the Lockean state of nature. Adam, who figures centrally in Locke, makes no appearance in Nozick.

50. Augustine, *City of God,* Bk. I, Ch. 3, p. 9. This, too, is Tocqueville's veiled charge against the Catholics of Europe: they had sought to unify, not harmonize, the City of Man and the City of God. See Tocqueville, *Democracy in America,* vol. I, Part II, Ch. 9, pp. 297–301.

51. Gal. 4:4.

52. Hegel, *Philosophy of History,* Part III, p. 279.

53. Hegel, *Philosophy of History,* Part III, Sec. III, Ch. II, p. 320.

54. Hegel, *Philosophy of History,* Part III, p. 279; Augustine, *City of God,* Bk. I, Preface, p. 5. Augustine's thesis is that Rome had abandoned the True God. See also Hegel, ibid., Part III, Sec. III, Ch. II, p. 318.

55. Hegel, *Philosophy of History,* Part III, Sec. III, Ch. II, pp. 321–23.

56. Hegel, *Philosophy of History,* Part III, Sec. III, Ch. II, p. 324.

57. Hegel, *Philosophy of History,* Part III, Sec. III, Ch. II, p. 328.

58. Hegel, *Philosophy of History,* Part IV, Sec. III, Ch. I, p. 417.

59. Rousseau, *First Discourse*, p. 42n.

60. See Tocqueville, *Democracy in America,* Author's Introduction, p. 12: "the Christian nations of our present day present an alarming spectacle; the movement which carries them along is already too strong to be halted, but it is not yet so swift that we must despair of *directing* it; our fate is in our hands, but it may soon pass beyond control" (em-

phasis added). Directing it requires *ideas*, of course, and the Americans who have suc-cessfully directed it came to the New World, he says, "in obedience to a purely intellec-tual craving" (ibid., vol. I, Ch. 3, p. 36). The Americans of the south, in contrast, were "gold-seekers" (ibid., p. 34). The American identity is therefore rooted in New England and emanates outward from there (ibid., p. 35).

61. Tocqueville, *Democracy in America*, vol. II, Part IV, Ch. 8, p. 705.

62. The stage is set for the drama of *Democracy in America* early on, in vol. I, Ch. 3, pp. 56–57, when Tocqueville offers these alternatives; thereafter he concludes now this way, now that, about whether America has or can indeed escape from the threat of servitude.

63. See Karl Marx, "German Ideology," in *Marx's Concept of Man*, ed. Erich Fromm (New York: Frederick Ungar Publishing, 1978), p. 198.

64. Tocqueville, *Democracy in America*, vol. II, Part I, Ch. 5, pp. 443–44 (emphasis added).

65. Tocqueville, *Democracy in America*, vol. II, Part I, Ch. 5, p. 446 (emphasis added). See also Alexis de Tocqueville, *The Old Régime and the French Revolution*, trans. Stuart Gilbert (Garden City, NY: Doubleday & Co., 1955), Part I, Ch. 3, p. 13, where the *idea* of equality could not take hold of Europe prior to the eighteenth century because the *real life* conditions did not yet accord with it.

66. See Tocqueville, *Democracy in America*, vol. I, Part II, Ch. 9, pp. 286–87: "every religion has some political opinion linked to it by affinity. The spirit of man, left to follow its bent, will regulate political society and the City of God in uniform fashion; it will, if I dare put it so, seek to *harmonize* earth with heaven. Most English America was peopled by men who, having shaken off the pope's authority, acknowledged no other religious supremacy; they therefore brought to the New World a Christianity which I can only describe as democratic and republican; this fact singularly favored the establishment of a temporal republic and democracy. From the start politics and religion agreed, and they have not since ceased to do so" (emphasis in original).

67. The Jews do not figure prominently in Tocqueville, it can be argued, because the fulfillment that occurs does not involve the movement from natural consciousness (Rome, for Hegel) to spiritual consciousness (the Jews, for Hegel).

68. See Locke, *Reasonableness of Christianity*, §§57–161, pp. 35–121.

69. Luther, "Freedom," in *Works*, vol. 31, p. 347. Cf. John 6:14–15; 28–29, *passim*.

70. Mark 15:39.

71. The Gospel of Mark originally ended with 16:8 ("And they went out quickly, and fled from the sepulcher; for they trembled and were amazed: neither said they any thing to any *man*; for they were afraid"), not with 16:20 ("And they went forth, and preached everywhere, the Lord working with *them*, and confirming the word and signs following. Amen"), as it is in King James. In the original version those who awaited the Messiah *never* understood Him when He came. *They* ended in isolation and fearfulness.

72. See Marx, "German Ideology," in *Marx's Concept of Man*, p. 210: "we call com-munism the *real* movement which abolishes the present state of things" (emphasis in original).

73. Marx, "The Eighteenth Brumaire of Louis Bonaparte," in *The Marx-Engels Reader*, p. 595.

74. I Cor. 1:23. See also Niebuhr, *Nature and Destiny*, vol. II, pp. 6–34. Nietzsche, of course, suggested that the Pharisees emerged victorious precisely by *denying* Christ! See Nietzsche, *Genealogy*, First Essay, §8, pp. 34–35.

75. Weber, "Politics as a Vocation," in *From Max Weber*, p. 78 (emphasis added).

76. Hobbes, *Leviathan*, Part I, Ch. 13, p. 100 (emphasis added).

77. Hobbes, *De Cive*, Ch. VI, p. 179 (emphasis added).

78. Rousseau, *Second Discourse*, pp. 176–78. These two alternatives, the equality of all and the equality of all under the one, are precisely the ones Tocqueville sees for future democracies. See Tocqueville, *Democracy in America*, vol. I, Part I, Ch. 3, pp. 56–57.

79. Rousseau, *Emile*, Bk. I, p. 53.

80. Rousseau, *Emile*, Bk. V, p. 473.

81. Augustine, *City of God*, Bk. I, Preface, p. 5.

82. Heidegger, *Being and Time*, Division I, Ch. 5, §35, pp. 211–14.

83. Huxley intimates that no totalitarian system can be created or sustained without denaturing the terror of death. See Huxley, *Brave New World*, p. 110, where the Savage receives an account of how death is handled in the brave new world: "Death conditioning begins at eighteen months. Every tot spends two mornings a week in a Hospital for the Dying. All the best toys are kept there, and they get chocolate cream on death days. They learn to take dying as a matter of course . . . like any other physiological process."

84. Heidegger, *Being and Time*, Division II, Ch. 1, §52, pp. 299–304, *passim*.

85. Rousseau, *Emile*, Bk. II, p. 82, and Bloom's Introduction, p. 9.

86. Nietzsche, *Genealogy*, First Essay, §11, p. 43. See also, Nietzsche, "On Free Death," *Thus Spoke Zarathustra*, Part 1, §21, pp. 71–74.

87. The insight can be found already in Augustine's *City of God*, Bk. XIX, Ch. 4, p. 852: "eternal life is the Supreme Good, and eternal death the Supreme Evil . . . to achieve the one and escape the other, we must live rightly." The political forms adduced by Luther, Hobbes, and Locke purport to make such "right living" possible.

88. Aristotle, *Ethics*, Bk. VIII, Ch. 9, 1159b29–32.

89. Aristotle, *Ethics*, Bk. VIII, Ch. 3, 1156b6.

90. Smith, *Wealth of Nations*, Bk. I, Ch. 2, p. 18.

91. Aristotle, *Ethics*, Bk. IX, Ch. 9, 1169a9.

92. Aristotle, *Ethics*, Bk. IX, Ch. 8, 1168b6.

93. Friendship between brothers is, for Aristotle, the paradigmatic instance of having things in common. In his words, "brothers are, therefore, in a sense identical, though the identity resides in separate persons" (*Ethics*, Bk. VIII, Ch. 12, 1161b32–33).

94. Not Christ but rather Adam establishes the equality of all for Locke. See Locke, *First Treatise*, Ch. IV, §29, p. 196. Reason, granted to Adam, is the sovereign under whom all are equal—hence, his claim that every person in the commonwealth, including the sovereign, must accede to the law.

95. See Tocqueville, *Democracy in America*, vol. I, Part I, Ch. 3, p. 57, *passim;* Aristotle, *Ethics*, Bk. VIII, Ch. 10, 1160b10–23; *Politics*, Bk. III, Ch. VII, 1279a20–1279b10.

96. See Tocqueville, *Democracy in America*, vol. II, Part I, Ch. 5, p. 444: "I doubt whether man can support complete religious independence and entire political freedom at the same time. I am led to think that *if he has no faith he must obey, and if he is free he must believe*" (emphasis added). There will always be obedience, Tocqueville seems to say; the only question is whether obedience will be toward God or toward the (human) tyrant.

97. Consider South Africa, where Christianity's influence conduced to an equality of all *white Christians* under God to the exclusion and derogation of all others. See Leonard Thompson, *The Political Mythology of Apartheid* (New Haven: Yale University Press, 1985), p. 29, *passim.* Freud suggests that the attempt by Christians to bind a community together through an injunction to love one another necessitates the construction of an *other* on whom the community may vent its aggression. See Freud, *Civilization and Its Discontents*, Ch. V, p. 72: "the Jewish people, scattered everywhere, have rendered *most useful services*" to their host countries by being their *other* (emphasis added). So, too, does Ishmael, the *natural* child of Abraham and Hagar (Gen. 16:15), serve as the *other* for Isaac, the child of the *promise* of Abraham and Sarah (Gen. 21:3).

98. Tocqueville, Author's Introduction, *Democracy in America*, p. 16. Cf. Ralph Waldo Emerson, "Politics," in *Emerson's Essays* (New York: Harper & Row, 1951), p. 409: "democracy is better for us, because the religious sentiment of the present time accords better with it."

99. Cf. Nietzsche, *Beyond Good and Evil*, Part V, §202, p. 116: "the *democratic* movement is the heir of the Christian movement" (emphasis in original). The theoretical relationship between Christianity and Judaism, and hence democracy and Judaism, is a question which demands attention. For Nietzsche, Christianity and democracy are the fruits of the tree of Judaism—all have as their root the ethic of resentment. Yet this too easily glosses over the tension between the *particular* claim to be God's chosen people and the *universal* claim of Reformation Christianity, which looks upon the Jews, dialectically, as the *already* and the *yet not*. Historically, Weber notes, it was in Puritan America (where this dialectical view held sway) that the (Reformed) Jews were well received. "These groups of Jews were at first welcomed without any ado whatsoever and are even now welcomed fairly readily, so that they have been absorbed to the point of the absolute loss of any trace of difference. This situation in Puritan countries contrasts with the situation in Germany, where the Jews remain—even after long generations—'assimilated Jews.' These phenomenon clearly manifest the actual kinship of Puritanism to Judaism"; (Max Weber, *Economy and Society*, ed. Guenther Roth and Claus Wittich [Berkeley: University of California Press, 1978], vol. I, Ch. VI, §xv, p. 623).

100. See Samuel P. Huntington, "Religion and the Third Wave," in *National Interest*, Summer 1991, pp. 29–42; and George Frost Kennan, *The Cloud of Danger: Current Realities of American Foreign Policy* (Boston: Little, Brown & Co., 1977), pp. 41–46. Kennan notes: "those Americans who profess to know with such certainty what other people want and what is good for them in the way of political institutions would do well to ask themselves whether they are not actually attempting to impose their own values, tradi-

tions, and habits of thought on peoples for whom these things have no validity and no usefulness" (ibid., p. 43).

101. Tocqueville, *Democracy in America,* vol. I, Part II, Ch. 9, p. 287. To institute democracy around the world, on this reading, would be but a kinder and gentler imperialism.

102. See, for example, MacIntyre, *After Virtue,* pp. 250–51, where Hobbes and Locke, among others, are purveyors of the "individualist view" in which society is "nothing but a collection of strangers, each pursuing his or her own interest under minimal constraint."

103. Augustine, *Confessions,* Bk. IV, Ch. 4, p. 75.

104. See Robert Bellah, *Habits of the Heart* (New York: Harper & Row, 1985), especially pp. 142–63.

105. Gal. 3:28.

106. Ralph Waldo Emerson, "History," in *Emerson's Essays* (New York: Harper & Row, 1951), p. 6.

107. See Rousseau, *Emile,* Bk. II, p. 110: "can anyone believe that . . . the historical is so little connected with the moral that the one can be known without the other."

108. Emerson, "History," in *Essays,* p. 28.

109. Emerson, "History," in *Essays,* p. 7 (emphasis in original).

110. Emerson, "History," in *Essays,* p. 29.

111. Emerson, "History," in *Essays,* p. 29. Locke (*Reasonableness,* §242, p. 172) responds: "suppose [that moral percepts] may be picked up here and there—some from Solon and Bias in Greece, others from Tully in Italy, and to complete the work, let Confucius, as far as China, be consulted, and Anacharis, the Scythian, contribute his share. What will all this do to give the world a complete morality that may be to mankind the unquestionable rule of life and manners?"

112. That the apostles went out "among the nations" is proof of the universality of Christianity for Locke. See Locke, *Reasonableness,* §240, p. 168. Cf. Matt. 28:19–20; Mark 16:15.

113. Heidegger, *Being and Time,* Ch. VI, §§78–83, pp. 456–88.

114. Emerson, "History," in *Essays,* p. 29.

115. See Ralph Waldo Emerson, "Nominalist and Realist," in *Essays,* pp. 431–32, where, noting the tendency to relegate all innovation to a place "in our old army files," he asks, "why have only two or three ways of life, and not thousands?"

116. Cf. Michael Oakeshott, *Experience and Its Modes* (Cambridge: Cambridge University Press, 1985), p. 127: "'God in history' is, then, a contradiction, a meaningless phrase. Wherever else God is, he is not in history. . . . And this, among other reasons, is why we must deny to the ancient Hebrews any proper historical consciousness. 'God in history' indicates an incursion of the practical past into the historical past, an incursion which only brings chaos." Oakeshott would describe the entire (early modern) project I have outlined here as one that is not properly historical. Emerson's retort to Oakeshott is to be found in the early pages of his "History" essay. "Time," he says, "dissipates into shining ether, the solid angularity of facts" (Emerson, "History," in *Essays,* p. 6).

Tocqueville may be most on the mark with his intimation that the construction of historical *systems* is evidence of the victory of equality (*Democracy in America*, vol. II, Part I, Part I, Ch. 20, p. 495).

117. Ricoeur, *The Symbolism of Evil*, p. 74.

118. See Reinhold Niebuhr, *The Nature and Destiny of Man* (New York: Charles Scribner's Sons, 1964), vol. I, Ch. VII, pp. 178–207; Ricoeur, *The Symbolism of Evil*, Ch. II, pp. 47–99.

119. Hegel, *Philosophy of History*, Part III, Sec. III, Ch. II, p. 321.

120. Niebuhr, *Nature and Destiny*, vol. II, p. 6.

121. Rousseau, *The Social Contract*, Bk. IV, Ch. 8, p. 186.

122. Tocqueville, *Democracy in America*, vol. I, Part II, Ch. 7, pp. 254–56.

123. Augustine, *City of God*, Bk. XII, Ch. 28, p. 508 (emphasis added).

124. Connolly, *Identity/Difference*, p. x. Connolly's efforts I take to be on the forefront of the ecumenical movement in political theory. What *may* make his version more pernicious than Emerson's view is that he would wish to *politicize* difference, while Emerson would not. Emerson accords with Plato that politics too often fills a void rather than a need. See Plato, *Republic*, Bk. VII, 521a; and Emerson, "Politics," in *Essays*, p. 415: "the antidote to [the] abuse of formal Government, is, the influence of private character, the growth of the Individual; the reappearance of the principle to supersede the proxy; the appearance of the wise man, of whom the existing government, is, it must be owned, but a shabby imitation."

125. Locke, *Reasonableness*, §241, p. 170.

126. Friedrich Nietzsche, *The Birth of Tragedy*, trans. Francis Golffing (Garden City, NY: Doubleday & Co., 1956), §XXIII, pp. 136–37 (emphasis added).

127. Gen. 3:5. See also Ralph Waldo Emerson, "Character," in *Essays*, p. 331: "we boast of our emancipation from many superstitions; but if we have broken with idols, it is through a transfer of idolatry."

128. Nietzsche, *Genealogy*, First Essay, §9, p. 36. Tocqueville echoes: the French Revolution was (Christian) religion in disguise; it sought to supplant a "particularist" social structure with a "universal" one, something unprecedented in political history—yet something still being played out in the ecumenical movement of today. See Tocqueville, *The Old Régime*, Part I, Ch. 3, pp. 10–13; Nietzsche, *Genealogy*, First Essay, §16, p. 54.

BIBLIOGRAPHY

Acton, Lord John Emerich. "The History of Freedom in Christianty." In J. Rufus Fears, ed., *Essays in the History of Liberty*, vol. 1. Indianapolis: Liberty Press, 1985.

Aquinas, Thomas. *Summa Theologiae*. Garden City, NY: Image Books, 1969.

Ashcraft, Richard. *Revolutionary Politics and Locke's "Two Treatises of Government."* Princeton: Princeton University Press, 1986.

Aristotle. *The Politics*. Translated by Ernst Baker. Oxford: Oxford University Press, 1958.

———. *Nicomachean Ethics*. Translated by Martin Ostwald. New York: Macmillan, 1986.

St. Augustine. *City of God*. Translated by Henry Bettenson. New York: Penguin, 1984.

———. *The Confessions of St. Augustine*. Translated by R. S. Pine-Coffin. New York: Penguin Books, 1961.

Beard, Charles. *An Economic Interpretation of the Constitution*. New York: Macmillan, 1913.

Bellah, Robert. *Habits of the Heart*. New York: Harper & Row, 1985.

Bercovitch, Sacvan. *The Puritan Origins of the American Self.* New Haven: Yale University Press, 1975.

Blumenberg, Hans. *The Legitimacy of the Modern Age*. Translated by Robert M. Wallace. Cambridge: MIT Press, 1983.

———. *Work on Myth*. Translated by Robert M. Wallace. Cambridge: MIT Press, 1985.

Boniface VIII. *Unam Sanctum*. Cited in R. H. Tawney. *Religion and the Rise of Capitalism*. London: John Murray, 1936.

Bork, Robert. "Neutral Principles and Some First Amendment Problems." *Indiana Law Journal* 47, no. 1 (1971), pp. 1–35.

Calvin, John. *Institutes of Christian Religion*. Translated by Henry Beveridge. Grand Rapids, MI: Wm. B. Eerdmans Publishing Co., 1989.

Clebsch, William A. "The Elizabethans on Luther." In Jaroslav Pelikan, ed., *Interpreters of Luther: Essays in Honor of Wilhelm Pauck*, pp. 97–120. Philadelphia: Fortress Press, 1968.

Collingwood, R. G. *The Idea of History*. Oxford: Oxford University Press, 1956.

Connolly, William E. *Political Theory and Modernity*. New York: Basil Blackwell, 1988.

———. *Identity/Difference*. Ithaca: Cornell University Press, 1991.

Derrida, Jacques. *Of Grammatology*. Baltimore: Johns Hopkins University Press, 1976.

―――. "Plato's Pharmacy." In *Dissemination*, pp. 63–171. Translated by Barbara Johnson. Chicago: University of Chicago Press, 1981.

Despland, Michel. *Kant on History and Religion*. Montreal: McGill-Queen's University Press, 1973.

Diamond, Martin. "Democracy and *The Federalist:* A Reconsideration of the Framers Intent." *American Political Science Review* 53, no. 1 (1959): 52–68.

Dunn, John. *The Political Thought of John Locke*. Cambridge: Cambridge University Press, 1969.

―――. "From Applied Theology to Social Analysis." In Istvan Hont and Michael Ignatieff, eds., *Wealth and Virtue*, pp. 119–35. Cambridge: Cambridge University Press, 1983.

―――. *Locke*. Oxford: Oxford University Press, 1984.

Dunne, John S. *A Search for God in Time and Memory*. Notre Dame: University of Notre Dame Press, 1977.

―――. *The City of the Gods*. Notre Dame: University of Notre Dame Press, 1978.

Durkheim, Emile. "Le problème religieux et la dualité de la nature humaine." *Bulletin de la Société française de Philosophie* 13 (February 1913): 63–113.

Eisenach, Eldon J. *Two Worlds of Liberalism: Religion and Politics in Hobbes, Locke, and Mill*. Chicago: University of Chicago Press, 1981.

―――. "John Stuart Mill and the Origins of 'A History of Political Thought.'" In Manueal J. Peláez and Miguel Martínez López, eds., *Essays in the History of Political Thought: Studies in Honor of Ferran Valls I Taberner*, 8:2347–62. Barcelona: Promociones Publicaciones Universitarias, 1988.

―――. "Hobbes on Church, State, and Religion." In *History of Political Thought* 3, no. 2 (1982): 215–43.

Eliade, Mircea. *A History of Religious Ideas*, vol. 2. Translated by Willard R. Trask. Chicago: University of Chicago Press, 1984.

Ellis, Madeleine B. *Rousseau's Socratic Aemilian Myths*. Columbus: Ohio State University Press, 1977.

Elster, Jon. *Making Sense of Marx*. Cambridge: Cambridge University Press, 1985.

Emerson, Ralph Waldo. *Emerson's Essays*. New York: Harper & Row, 1951.

Feuerbach, Ludwig. *The Essence of Christianity*. New York: Harper & Row, 1957.

Filmer, Sir Robert. *Patriarcha*. In *Patriarcha and Other Writings*. Edited by Johann P. Sommerville. Cambridge: Cambridge University Press, 1991.

Freud, Sigmund. *Civilization and Its Discontents*. Edited by James Strachey. New York: W. W. Norton & Co., 1989.

Gerrish, B. A. *Grace and Reason: A Study in the Theology of Luther*. Oxford: Clarendon Press, 1962.

Gough, J. W. *John Locke's Political Philosophy*. Oxford: Clarendon Press, 1950.

―――. *The Social Contract*. Oxford: Oxford University Press, 1957.

Gray, J. Glenn. *The Warriors*. New York: Harper & Row, 1970.

Hancock, Ralph C. *Calvin and the Foundations of Modern Politics*. Ithaca: Cornell University Press, 1989.

Hardin, Russell. "Hobbesian Political Order." *Political Theory* 52, no. 2 (1991): 156–80.

Hegel, G. W. F. *Early Theological Writings*. Edited by Richard Kroner. Philadelphia: University of Pennsylvania Press, 1971.

———. *The Phenomenology of Spirit*. Translated by A. V. Miller. Oxford: Oxford University Press, 1977.

———. *The Philosophy of History*. New York: Dover, 1956.

———. *Philosophy of Right*. Translated by T. M. Knox. Oxford: Oxford University Press, 1967.

———. *Reason in History*. Indianapolis: Bobbs-Merrill, 1953.

Heidegger, Martin. *Being and Time*. Translated by John Macquarrie and Edward Robinson. New York: Harper & Row, 1962.

———. "The Essence of Truth." In *Martin Heidegger: Basic Writings*. New York: Harper & Row, 1977.

Hirschman, Albert O. *The Passions and the Interests*. Princeton: Princeton University Press, 1977.

Hobbes, Thomas. *De Cive*. In *Man and Citizen*. Translated by Bernard Gert. Gloucester, MA: Humanities Press, 1978.

———. *On Man*. In *Man and Citizen*. Translated by Bernard Gert. Gloucester, MA: Humanities Press, 1978.

———. *Leviathan*. Edited by Michael Oakeshott. New York: Macmillan Publishing Co., 1962.

———. *Behemoth*. Edited by Ferdinand Tönnies. Chicago: University of Chicago Press, 1990.

Hofstadter, Richard. *The American Political Tradition*. New York: Vintage Books, 1948.

Hont, Istvan. "The Language of Sociability and Commerce: Samuel Pufendorf and the Theoretical Foundations of the 'Four-Stages Theory.'" In Anthony Pagden, ed., *The Languages of Political Theory in Early Modern Europe*. Cambridge: Cambridge University Press, 1987.

Hood, F. C. *The Divine Politics of Thomas Hobbes*. Oxford: Clarendon Press, 1964.

Hume, David. *The History of England*, vol. 1. Indianapolis: Liberty Press, 1983.

———. "Of National Characters." In Eugene Miller, ed., *Essays, Moral, Political, and Literary*, pp. 197–215. Indianapolis: Liberty Press, 1985.

———. *A Treatise on Human Nature*. Oxford: Clarendon Press, 1978.

Huntington, Samuel P. "Religion and the Third Wave." *National Interest*, Summer 1991, pp. 29–42.

Huxley, Aldous. *Brave New World*. New York: Harper & Row, 1946.

James, William. *The Varieties of Religious Experience*. New York: Penguin Books, 1982.

Johnston, David. *The Rhetoric of the Leviathan*. Princeton: Princeton University Press, 1986.

―――. "Hobbes's Mortalism." *History of Political Thought* 10, no. 4 (1983): 647–63.

Kant, Immanuel. *Critique of Practical Reason*. Translated by Lewis Beck. Indianapolis: Bobbs-Merrill, 1956.

―――. *Kant's Political Writings*. Edited by Hans Reiss. Cambridge: Cambridge University Press, 1970.

Katz, David S. *Philo-Semitism and the Readmission of the Jews to England, 1603–1655*. Oxford: Clarendon Press, 1982.

Kennan, George Frost. *The Cloud of Danger: Current Realities of American Foreign Policy*. Boston: Little, Brown & Co., 1977.

Koselleck, Reinhart. *Critique and Crisis: Enlightenment and the Pathogenesis of Modern Society*. Cambridge: MIT Press, 1988.

Kraynak, Robert P. *History and Modernity in the Thought of Thomas Hobbes*. Ithaca: Cornell University Press, 1991.

Lessing, Gotthold. *The Education of the Human Race*. New York: Columbia University Press, 1908.

Locke, John. *First Treatise of Government*. In *Two Treatises of Government*. Edited by Peter Laslett. Cambridge: Cambridge University Press, 1988.

―――. *Second Treatise of Government*. In *Two Treatises of Government*. Edited by Peter Laslett. Cambridge: Cambridge University Press, 1988.

―――. "A Discourse of Miracles." In I. T. Ramsey, ed., *John Locke*. Stanford: Stanford University Press, 1958.

―――. "A Letter Concerning Toleration." Indianapolis: Bobbs-Merrill, 1955.

―――. *The Reasonableness of Christianity*. Edited by George W. Ewing. Washington, DC: Regnery Gateway, 1965.

―――. *An Essay Concerning Human Understanding*. Oxford: Oxford University Press, 1975.

―――. *A Paraphrase and Notes on the Epistles of St. Paul*. Edited by Arthur Wainwright. Oxford: Oxford University Press, 1988.

―――. *Some Thoughts Concerning Education*. In James L. Axtell, ed., *The Educational Writings of John Locke*. Cambridge: Cambridge University Press, 1968.

―――. "Can Anyone by Nature Be Happy in This Life? No." In W. von Leydon, ed., *Essays on the Law of Nature*, pp. 221–42. Oxford: Clarendon Press, 1954.

―――. *The First Tract on Government*. In *Two Tracts of Government*. Edited by Philip Abrams. Cambridge: Cambridge University Press, 1967.

Lovin, Robin W., and Frank E. Reynolds, eds. *Cosmogony and Ethical Order*. Chicago: University of Chicago Press, 1986.

Löwith, Karl. *Meaning in History*. Chicago: University of Chicago Press, 1949.

―――. *From Hegel to Nietzsche*. Translated by David E. Green. New York: Columbia University Press, 1964.

Luther, Martin. *Luther's Works.* Edited by Helmut T. Lehmann. Philadelphia: Fortress Press, 1967.

Machiavelli, Niccolò. *The Discourses.* Edited by Bernard Crick. New York: Penguin Books, 1970.

MacIntyre, Alasdair. *After Virtue.* Notre Dame: University of Notre Dame Press, 1984.

Macpherson, C. B. *The Political Theory of Possessive Individualism: Hobbes to Locke.* Oxford: Clarendon Press, 1962.

Mansfield, Jr., Harvey C. *The Spirit of Liberalism.* Cambridge: Harvard University Press, 1978.

Marcuse, Herbert. *One-Dimensional Man.* Boston: Beacon Press, 1964.

Marx, Karl. *The Marx-Engels Reader.* Edited by Robert C. Tucker. New York: W. W. Norton & Co., 1978.

———. *Marx's Concept of Man.* Edited by Erich Fromm. New York: Frederick Ungar Publishing, 1978.

McDonough, Thomas M. *The Law and the Gospel in Luther.* Oxford: Oxford University Press, 1963.

Melzer, Arthur. *The Natural Goodness of Man.* Chicago: University of Chicago Press, 1990.

Mill, John Stuart. *Collected Works of John Stuart Mill.* Edited by John M. Robson and Jack Stillenger. Toronto: Toronto University Press, 1981.

———. *Three Essays.* Oxford: Oxford University Press, 1975.

Milton, John. *Paradise Lost.* New York: Viking Press, 1949.

Mitchell, Joshua. "John Locke and the Theological Foundation of Liberal Toleration: A Christian Dialectic of History." *Review of Politics* 52, no. 1 (1990): 64–83.

Monaghan, Henry. "Our Perfect Constitution." *New York University Law Review* 56, nos. 2–3 (1981): 353–96.

Montesquieu, Baron de. *The Spirit of the Laws.* Translated by Thomas Nugent. New York: Hafner Press, 1949.

Niebuhr, Reinhold. *The Nature and Destiny of Man.* 2 vols. New York: Charles Scribner's Sons, 1964.

Nietzsche, Friedrich. *Thus Spoke Zarathustra.* Translated by Walter Kaufman. New York: Penguin Books, 1978.

———. *Beyond Good and Evil.* Translated by Walter Kaufman. New York: Vintage Books, 1966.

———. *On the Genealogy of Morals.* Translated by Walter Kaufman. New York: Vintage Books, 1967.

———. *The Birth of Tragedy.* Translated by Francis Golffing. Garden City, NY: Doubleday & Co., 1956.

Nozick, Robert. *Anarchy, State, and Utopia.* New York: Basic Books, 1974.

Oakeshott, Michael. "The Moral Life in the Writings of Thomas Hobbes." *Rationalism in Politics*, pp. 248–300. New York: Basic Books, 1962.

————. *Experience and Its Modes.* Cambridge: Cambridge University Press, 1985.

Orwell, George. *1984.* New York: Harcourt Brace Jovanovich, 1949.

Pangle, Thomas. *The Spirit of Modern Republicanism.* Chicago: University of Chicago Press, 1988.

Pascal, Blaise. *Pensées.* Translated by A. J. Krailsheimer. New York: Penguin Books, 1966.

Pitkin, Hanna Fenichel. *The Concept of Representation.* Berkeley: University of California Press, 1972.

Plato. *Republic.* Translated by Richard Sterling and William C. Scott. New York: W. W. Norton & Co., 1985.

————. *Collected Dialogues.* Edited by Edith Hamilton and Huntington Cairns. Translated by R. Hackforth. New York: Bollingen Foundation, 1961.

Pocock, J. G. A. "Time, History, and Eschatology in the Thought of Thomas Hobbes." *Politics, Language, and Time,* pp. 148–201. New York: Atheneum, 1973.

————. *The Machiavellian Moment.* Princeton: Princeton University Press, 1975.

Polanyi, Michael, and Harry Prosch. *Meaning.* Chicago: University of Chicago Press, 1975.

Preus, James Samuel. *From Shadow to Promise.* Cambridge: Harvard University Press, 1969.

Rawls, John. *A Theory of Justice.* Cambridge: Harvard University Press, 1971.

————. "Justice as Fairness: Political not Metaphysical." *Philosophy and Public Affairs* 14, no. 3 (1985): 223–51.

Reventlow, Henning Graf. *The Authority of the Bible and the Rise of the Modern World.* Philadelphia: Fortress Press, 1985.

Richelieu. *Political Testament.* Madison: University of Wisconsin Press, 1961.

Ricoeur, Paul. *The Symbolism of Evil.* Boston: Beacon Press, 1967.

————. *Time and Narrative,* vol. 1. Translated by Kathleen McLaughlin and David Pellauer. Chicago: University of Chicago Press, 1984.

Riley, Patrick. *Will and Political Legitimacy: A Critical Exposition of Social Contract Theory in Hobbes, Locke, Rousseau, Kant, and Hegel.* Cambridge: Harvard University Press, 1982.

————. *The General Will before Rousseau.* Princeton: Princeton University Press, 1986.

Rorty, Richard. *Contingency, Irony, and Solidarity.* New York: Cambridge University Press, 1989.

Rousseau, Jean-Jacques. *The First and Second Discourses.* Translated by Roger D. Masters and Judith R. Masters. New York: St. Martin's Press, 1964.

————. *Emile.* Translated by Allan Bloom. New York: Basic Books, 1979.

————. *Emile.* Translated by Barbara Foxley. New York: E. P. Dutton & Co., 1928.

————. *The Social Contract.* Translated by Maurice Cranston. New York: Penguin Books, 1984.

————. "On the Origin of Languages." In *On the Origin of Language.* Translated by John H. Moran and Alexander Gode. Chicago: University of Chicago Press, 1966.

————. *Reveries of a Solitary Walker.* Translated by Peter France. New York: Penguin Books, 1979.

————. *Confessions.* Translated by J. M. Cohen. New York: Penguin Books, 1953.

Sabine, George H. *A History of Political Theory.* New York: Henry Holt & Co., 1937.

Sandel, Michael. *Liberalism and the Limits of Justice.* Cambridge: Cambridge University Press, 1982.

Schmitt, Carl. *The Crisis of Parliamentary Democracy.* Cambridge: MIT Press, 1985.

————. *The Concept of the Political.* New Brunswick, NJ: Rutgers University Press, 1976.

Schwartz, Joel. "Hobbes and the Two Kingdoms of God." *Polity* 18, no. 1 (1985): 7–24.

Shklar, Judith N. *Men and Citizens.* Cambridge: Cambridge University Press, 1969.

Skinner, Quentin. *The Foundations of Modern Political Thought.* 2 vols. Cambridge: Cambridge University Press, 1980.

Smith, Adam. *The Theory of Moral Sentiments.* Indianapolis: Liberty Press, 1982.

————. *The Wealth of Nations.* Chicago: University of Chicago Press, 1976.

Spinoza, Benedict de. *A Theologico-Political Treatise.* New York: Dover Publications, 1951.

Starobinski, Jean. *Jean-Jacques Rousseau: Transparency and Obstruction.* Translated by Arthur Goldhammer. Chicago: University of Chicago Press, 1988.

Strauss, Leo. *The Political Philosophy of Thomas Hobbes.* Chicago: University of Chicago Press, 1963.

————. *Natural Right and History.* Chicago: University of Chicago Press, 1971.

————. "Athens or Jerusalem." *Studies in Platonic Political Philosophy,* pp. 147–73. Chicago: University of Chicago Press, 1988.

Tarcov, Nathan. *Locke's Education for Liberty.* Chicago: University of Chicago Press, 1984.

Tawney, R. H. *Religion and the Rise of Capitalism.* London: John Murray, 1936.

Taylor, Charles. *Hegel and Modern Society.* Cambridge: Cambridge University Press, 1979.

Tillich, Paul. *The Courage To Be.* New Haven: Yale University Press, 1951.

————. *Systematic Theology.* Chicago: University of Chicago Press, 1951.

Tocqueville, Alexis de. *Democracy in America.* Edited by J. P. Mayer. New York: Harper & Row, 1969.

————. *The Old Régime and the French Revolution.* Translated by Stuart Gilbert. Garden City, NY: Doubleday & Co., 1955.

Thompson, Leonard. *The Political Mythology of Apartheid.* New Haven: Yale University Press, 1985.

Troeltsch, Ernst. *Protestantism and Progress.* Philadelphia: Fortress Press, 1986.

Tully, James. *A Discourse on Property*. Cambridge: Cambridge University Press, 1980.

―――. "Governing Conduct." In Edmund Leites, ed., *Conscience and Casuistry in Early Modern Europe*, pp. 12–71. Cambridge: Cambridge University Press, 1988.

Voegelin, Eric. *The New Science of Politics*. Chicago: University of Chicago Press, 1952.

Waldron, Jeremy. "Locke: Toleration and the Rationality of Persecution." In Susan Mendus, ed., *Justifying Toleration*. Cambridge: Cambridge University Press, 1988.

Walzer, Michael. *Exodus and Revolution*. New York: Basic Books, 1985.

Waring, Luther H. *The Political Theories of Martin Luther*. New York: G. P. Putnam's Sons, 1910.

Warren, Scott. *The Emergence of Dialectical Theory*. Chicago: University of Chicago Press, 1984.

Warrender, Howard. *The Political Philosophy of Thomas Hobbes*. Oxford: Clarendon Press, 1957.

Watkins, J. W. N. *Hobbes's System of Ideas*. London: Hutchinson, 1965.

Weber, Max. *The Protestant Ethic and the Spirit of Capitalism*. New York: Charles Scribner's Sons, 1958.

―――. "Politics as a Vocation." In H. H. Gerth and C. Wright Mills, eds., *From Max Weber*, pp. 77–128. New York: Oxford University Press, 1946.

―――. *Economy and Society*. Edited by Guenther Roth and Claus Wittich. Berkeley: University of California Press, 1978.

White, Hayden. *Tropics of Discourse*. Baltimore: Johns Hopkins University Press, 1978.

Whitehead, Alfred North. *Science and the Modern World*. New York: Macmillan Publishing Co., 1925.

Wittgenstein, Ludwig. *Tractatus Logico-Philosophicus*. London: Routledge & Kegan Paul, 1981.

Wolff, Otto. *Die Haupttypen der neueren Lutherdeutung*. Stuttgart: W. Kohlhammer, 1938.

Wolin, Sheldon. *Politics as Vision*. Boston: Little, Brown & Co., 1961.

Wood, Neal. *The Politics of Locke's Philosophy*. Berkeley: University of California Press, 1983.

Yack, Bernard. *The Longing for Total Revolutions*. Princeton: Princeton University Press, 1986.